Walking
His Way

Book Review by Dr. Monroe Brewer
Training and Partnership Facilitator for East-West Ministries, Plano, TX, and
Adjunct Missions Professor of Dallas Theological Seminary

Don Fanning has his D.Min. from Dallas Theological Seminary. He served
as a missionary for 30 years in Colombia, Argentina, and Paraguay.. He has
been the Director of the Global Studies Department at Liberty University
School of Divinity in Lynchburg, VA for 16 years. He and his wife, Jan, have
four adult children, 10 grandchildren, and live in Pensacola, Florida. Don
continues to serve as a missionary with East West Ministries in Cuba as
Associate Director of Church Planting Movements.

REVIEW OF THE BOOK, WALKING HIS WAY

In the most famous Great Commission passage, Matthew says, "Therefore
go and make disciples of all nations, baptizing them in the name of the
Father and of the Son and of the Holy Spirit, and **teaching them to obey
everything I have commanded you**" (NIV, Matt. 28:19-20a). In the first
half of this Great Commission, making disciples by planting churches
is emphasized. In the second half of this Great Commission, making
disciples by teaching them to obey all Jesus' commands is emphasized.
Isn't it interesting that the one thing Jesus asked us to do in finishing the
Great Commission—teaching them to obey all His commands—is the one
thing most of us never do? And, in fact, there is no book in print that I'm
aware of that has ever made available to us in a systematic, user-friendly
fashion all the commands of Jesus. Until now.

Don Fanning has done the Christian Church a great service through
his work, Walking His Way. Don's book is a study of all New Testament
commands, including all those given by Jesus. Every day of the year
focuses on a different command and includes a pastoral, non-judgmental,
and thoroughly biblical exegetical commentary and warm devotional
reading on each text. The daily devotionals include great illustrations and
biographical glimpses of famous missionaries. All include a prayer at the
end of each day to guide the reader in focusing on the "command of the
day," as well as a prompt in how to apply the command in one's daily life.

This book is ideal for personal Bible study, small groups, discipleship
cohorts, mentoring, ministry enrichment, and meditations in how to
improve your walk with God. The commands are cataloged into 13
different categories to help us better understand the mind of Christ. An
index of Scripture references at the back of the book makes it easy to
look up any text. Along with the book is an eighty-three page, eight-
lesson workbook which organizes the commands in a six-step learning
process to help the learning community to master the commands—in a
participatory, self-discovering, fun way to learn and grow.

Walking His Way

A Discipleship Tool:
An Analysis of New Testament Commands
to Be Taught to Every Believer

Don Fanning

Branches
PUBLICATIONS

Pensacola, Florida

First Edition 2011,

Second Edition 2017

Published by
Branches Publications
2040 Downing Dr.
Pensacola, Florida 32505

Branches Publications was started to publish missions and discipleship training tools to equip leaders and teachers to be strategic with their lives by making disciples and fulfilling the Great Commission. More materials are available at www.tgcresources.com and a daily discipleship Bible study at www.WalkingHisWay.com.

© 2011, 2017 Copyright: Branches Publications
Don Fanning
Layout and Cover Design: Krista Freeman
All rights reserved
ISBN: 978-0-9855812-3-7

All Scripture quotations, unless otherwise indicated, are taken from the New King James Version, Copyright © 1986, Thomas Nelson. Other versions cited include NET Bible, Biblical Studies Press, L.L.C., 1996-2006; ESV, (English Standard Version, 2016); NIV (New International Version, 2011) and the NLT (New Living Translation, 2007)

Contents

FOREWORD

Who is da boss of you?

Kids everywhere have a defense against others who give them commands. They say, "You aren't da boss of me." Adults don't say that but we may think it a lot.

The people who speared my dad and four of his friends to death when I was a boy have a culture in which there are no bosses; no police, no chiefs, and no employers. Everyone just does whatever they want to do, whenever they want to do it. In the 60 some years that I have known them I have never heard anyone over the age of about 12 tell another person what to do.

That is probably why they were the most violent society in the world. They had a homicide rate of over 60%. The oldest man in the tribe was in his early thirties when they speared my dad. Now, three of the warriors who killed dad and his friends are still living. So, they must be about 90.

You know what stopped most of the killing? It stopped when my Aunt Rachel and a young Waodani refugee, Dayuma, (along with the widow of one of dad's martyred friends) told them that Wangongi didn't see it well that they should kill each other. Even people living in the stone age know that the Creator of the world needs to be obeyed. The Waodani just didn't know what Wangongi's commandments were.

Being a Christ follower means accepting Jesus as "da Boss of us." Surprisingly, God hasn't given us many commands not to do things. Most of His commands tell us things that God does want us to do.

My very good friend Don Fanning has compiled 365 of God's commands from the New Testament in this book, "Walking His Way." There is one command for each day of the year. And, because Don is a brainiac, he not only gives us the command and the verse where it is found, but then he explains each command and suggests the happy result of keeping that particular command.

If you are a typical Christian you can probably only remember about 10 or 12 of Christ's commands. Now you can spend a few minutes every day remembering some you have forgotten and discovering others you haven't ever heard about.

Best of all, as you remember and discover New Testament commandments, you can pass them on to your children, friends and co-workers.

Steve Saint - enjoy!

Preface

Jesus said, "Go therefore and make disciples of all the nations, baptizing them in the name of the Father and of the Son and of the Holy Spirit, teaching them to observe all things that I have commanded you" (Matt 28:20[NKJ]). Yet one is hard-pressed to find any study on the practical application of the New Testament commands Jesus wants all believers to consciously obey. Yet that is what He asked us to do.

Whenever the word *commands* is mentioned, it seems that people immediately put up their defenses and begin to argue why certain commands are unnecessary. Some say they do not want to be controlled by any "commandment"; rather, they want to be led by the Spirit. But it was the Spirit that gave us all the New Testament commandments by inspiration, since they were all written down twenty to sixty years after Jesus ascended. We are expected to learn what He said and trust Him to give us the power to obey it.

Some argue that focusing on the commandments is a step toward legalism. Many perceive any rule or regulation as legalism to be avoided at all costs. The antinomian spirit is prevalent today, as believers prefer the mystical voice of the Spirit to the conscious decision to submit and obey.

True legalism has many negative effects on a believer's spiritual development. First, legalism can be dangerously understood as the means for gaining acceptance before God, and it can provide a false sense of the security of salvation. No amount of obedience or moral perfection can ever make any person acceptable to God, because one sin in a lifetime can condemn a person (James 2:10)—just think of the garden of Eden. Salvation and acceptance by God are only possible through His grace who offers to completely pay for all our sins by His death and His blood, shed on the cross of Calvary. When we trust in His payment for our sin's results, we are rewarded with the gift of Christ's righteousness—that alone is what can make us acceptable (2 Cor 5:21).

Second, legalism can lead believers to think obedience to their own strict, made-up standards will make them more spiritual. Men set the standards of modesty (e.g., length of dress, body coverings) to make sure believers are obeying this command. But many of the biblical commands are generic: the command to be modest does not describe what modesty means in different cultures or historical periods. When people comply with these man-made definitions, they feel spiritual and righteous. No longer do they need to think about the issue and make appropriate decisions. If they follow the rules, then they are accepted by their peers in the faith.

Then approval by their peers becomes their primary concern, and they equate it with God's approval. God wants every individual to meditate before Him for guidance on how to apply a command to his or her own situation. These personal decisions that follow such meditations are the steps to genuine maturity.

There are no legalistic behavioral standards defined in the New Testament, rather the commands are designed to fit any culture. What does it mean to love your neighbor? Who decides? What should I do?

The nature of these commands requires thought and purpose. They force us to decide how we will personally express our obedience to His commands as we apply them in our daily lives. Believers are to follow His commands in their lives just to please Him (not to please men).

In this book, I seek to explain the nature of each of the imperative commands in the New Testament in their context, giving its use in the context, then suggestions for personal applications.

In the New Testament Greek, there are four basic types of imperatives, and I will indicate these types with a code after each verb:

~~   Indicates a *present progressive imperative*, which means to "be continually or habitually doing it"
~| Indicates a *negative present imperative*, which generally means "stop doing it," which can imply they had been doing this action.
*~   Indicates a *present aorist imperative*, which means "immediately start doing it"
*| Indicates a *negative aorist imperative*, which means "don't ever do it"

Knowledge of the meaning supplied by these imperative types can lead us toward a deeper and more mature understanding of His commands. Spiritual maturity is a result of the decisions we make to acquire the mind of Christ through understanding His commands and the conscious decision to change our attitudes, priorities, values, and personal convictions with the objective to better express our love of God to others around us and around the globe.

Let's commit ourselves to helping each other practice these principles as we grow together in His likeness. May we learn to say with David, "I will delight myself in Your commandments, which I love" (Psa 119:47).

Don Fanning

Introducción

OBEDIENCE:
THE FINAL TEST OF LOVE FOR CHRIST

"The person who has my commandments and obeys them is the one who loves me. The one who loves me will be loved by my Father, and I will love him and will reveal myself to him." (Jn. 14:21 NET)

The final test of love is obedience, not sweet emotions, not willingness to sacrifice, not zeal, but obedience to the commandments of Christ!

Our Lord drew a line plain and tight for everyone to see. On one side He placed those who keep His commandments and said, "These love Me." On the other side He put those who keep not His sayings, and said, "These love Me not."

The commandments of Christ occupy in the New Testament a place of importance that they do not have in current evangelical thought. The idea that our relation to Christ is revealed by our attitude to His commandments is now considered legalistic by many influential Bible teachers, and the plain words of our Lord are rejected outright or interpreted in a manner to make them conform to religious theories ostensibly based upon the epistles of Paul.

The Christian cannot be certain of the reality and depth of his love until he comes face to face with the commandments of Christ and is forced to decide what to do about them. Then he will know!

I think we should turn for a while from fine-spun theological speculations about grace and faith and humbly read the New Testament with a mind to obey what we see there. Love for Christ is a love of willing, as well as a love of feeling, and it is psychologically impossible to love Him adequately unless we will to obey His words!

W. A. Tozer

JANUARY 1
Believe in the Gospel

Mark 1:15—*"And saying, 'The time is fulfilled, and the kingdom of God is at hand. Repent and* **believe**~~ *in the gospel.'"*

There is a difference between *believing* a person (i.e., knowing he tells the truth) and *believing in* a person (i.e., deciding to trust him with your life). Nothing expresses our loyalty to and trust in our Savior more than obeying the command to "believe in" the good news of our Lord Jesus. The word *believe* means to "think or count on something to be true or to place one's confidence in." It is used 124 times in the New Testament; it is used 10 times as a present imperative command, which means to "be continually believing."

This act of believing is not merely an intellectual exercise or a superficial acknowledgment of the facts of Christ's death and resurrection; rather, Paul clarified that we must *"believe in [our] heart[s] that God raised Him from the dead"* (Rom 10:9–10).

The idea of "believing in your heart" is best captured in Proverbs 3:5: *"Trust in the Lord with all your heart, and do not rely on your own understanding"*—that is, we must get wisdom outside of ourselves, especially from God's revealed word. When you depend exclusively and constantly on a truth or an object that is believed in, then you trust (and believe) with all your "heart," or life. Are you willing to risk your eternity on the promises of the words of Christ?

Jesus wanted us to believe enough in His promised good news that we would decide to continually trust in the offering of His sacrificial death as full payment for all our personal sins. As in Proverbs 3, if someone trusts with all his heart in the Lord, then whatever Jesus says is likewise accepted as true and trustworthy and can be counted on as the best way to live.

Paul said, *"Just as you have received Christ Jesus as Lord [by trusting in His word], continue to live your lives in him"* (Col 2:6). Our trust in Christ is never *just* for the benefit of salvation. We are to believe in Him as a whole person and to trust Him completely—at all times, in every circumstance, and in everything He says. Can you trust Him with your life *now*—not just for eternity—and continuously trust His instructions? Tell Him so now.

"Lord, as I learned to trust You for my salvation through Your word, so teach me to trust You for how to live every day."

JANUARY 2
Repent

Mark 1:15—*"He said, 'The time is fulfilled and the kingdom of God is near. Repent~~ and believe the gospel!'"*

Jesus began His earthly ministry with these two commands: *"Repent and believe the gospel!"* He knew that in order to believe the gospel, we must change our minds about false beliefs and accept the truth.

God calls out to us to change our views about ourselves. Everyone tends to thinks he or she can be good enough for God, but that is false. Most of people think their "good" must be greater on a scale than their "bad," so they convince themselves that they aren't all that bad.

He also calls us to change our views about God: many doubt if He even exists. He demands that we change our views about His Son: many accept that He was a good example to follow, but God expects us to believe that He personally came into the world to receive the just punishment for all our sins. And He expects us to change our views about God's word: it is trustworthy and means what it says about us.

Unconverted people must change their views (*repent*) about their own goodness and recognize their personal sinfulness (*"for all have sinned"*; Rom 3:23). Then they are commanded in the present tense to be continually *believing* in Jesus. He expects us to always trust His word. We face a continual decision to discard popular opinions and accept God's perspective.

The gospel (lit. "good news") gives the sinner the option to trust that God's plan is perfect and true. God declared the only way for us to find forgiveness is to accept that God's wrath against sin is only satisfied by Christ's death on the cross. *"God made Christ, who never sinned, to be the offering for our sins, so that we could be made right with God through Christ"*; 2 Cor 5:21^NLT). A completed act of payment cannot be repeated or repaid—only accepted thankfully.

The sinner is totally in debt to Christ for His offer of forgiveness and full acceptance. We are called to change from trusting our own goodness to totally trusting in God's gracious forgiveness through Christ. Such acceptance is offered to anyone who repents and believes.

"Thank You, Lord. I do not have to be perfect or even good enough for Your acceptance, because I fail so miserably. I trust You with all my heart."

JANUARY 3

Don't be too Ambitious

James 3:1—*"**Not** many of you should **become**~~ **teachers**, my brothers and sisters, because you know that we will be judged more strictly."*

According to Scripture, the first requirement to become a bishop, elder, or pastor is a strong desire to do the work of a "bishoping," or overseeing others (1 Tim 3:1). Why would anyone desire this ministry?

James considered himself a teacher (notice how James changes from "you" to "we"). The highest honor is to be in this class of service, but the risks are great. He has several reasons for cautioning us to think twice about wanting to become a teacher.

First, you will be subject to a more severe scrutiny of your personal appearance before the judgment seat of Christ. Second, it is also implied that the church will strictly review your every teaching and doctrine.

The primary means of communication during that time was oral, so it was vital for teachers to control what they said. From such a position, they could easily introduce false concepts, mistaken ideas, divisive issues, or exaggerations, all of which would discredit the church ministry.

The churches tended to have *"itching ears"*—they wanted to hear what made them feel good (2 Tim 4:3). There was no shortage of deceptive teachers who sought to please their audiences.

The idea that those who teach will be judged more severely is derived from Luke 12:48: *"To whom much is given from him much is required."* Paul commented on how he would discipline his *"body and bring it into subjection, lest when I have preached to others, I myself should become disqualified"* (1 Cor 9:27)—that is, God would remove him from the ministry.

James's warning is meant to limit those whose motives may be influenced by the desire for the spotlight; it is not meant to discourage those who seek to help others mature in unity, obedience, and love for one another.

Beware the lust for position and prestige. The singular motive should be to help others understand the word of God and to delight in helping them live out its truths like you do. Is this your motivation?

"Lord, my secret ambition to feel important too often overshadows Your plan for my life. Teach me to be useful to You."

JANUARY 4
Be Humble

James 4:10—*"Humble yourselves*~ before the Lord and he will exalt you."*

Jesus began His discourse with the first beatitude: *"Blessed are the poor in spirit [i.e., "the humble"], for theirs is the kingdom of heaven"* (Matt 5:3). James wrote, *"God is opposed to the proud, but gives grace to the humble"* (4:6).

The aorist command, *"immediately humble yourselves,"* means you must urgently decide to "make yourself a low priority in comparison to others." There are several aspects of this command if we are going to think God's way.

First, humility comes from the sense of our unworthiness because of our sinful nature and actions. When Isaiah saw the holiness of God on the throne in Isaiah 6, he cried out, *"Woe is me, for I am ruined! Because I am a man of unclean lips, and I live among a people of unclean lips; for my eyes have seen the King, the Lord of hosts"* (Isaiah 6:5).

Second, God tends to hear the prayers of the humble. The psalmist said, *"You have heard the desire of the humble; You will strengthen their heart, You will incline Your ear"* (Psa 10:17). The Lord promised Solomon, *"If My people . . . humble themselves and pray and seek My face and turn from their wicked ways, then I will hear from heaven, will forgive their sin and will heal their land"* (2 Chron 7:14).

Third, the promise is sure that *"whoever exalts himself shall be humbled; and whoever humbles himself shall be exalted"* (Matt 23:12).

Fourth, the core principle of the Christian life is a demonstrated love for each other, as in Philippians 2:3: *"Do nothing from rivalry or conceit, but in humility count others more significant than yourselves."* The best definition of practical humility is when we consider other people a higher priority than ourselves.

Just as we would quickly respond to a need requested by a president or a general, the humble person always responds to the needs of others around him. This is the opposite of competing with others to see who is the most important or acting out of selfish ambition.

Paul describes a humble person as one who *"look[s] not only to his own interests, but also to the interests of others"* (Phil 2:4). Focusing on yourself, your needs and importance, therefore, is sin.

This is probably the most beautiful characteristic of our Savior: *"Learn of me for I am gentle and lowly of heart"* (Matt 21:5). How much can we learn from Jesus's attitude toward others today?

"My Lord, Your word is so convicting to my pride. May my thoughts and prayers prioritize the needs and biblical maturity in others."

JANUARY 5

Speak and Act Responsibly

James 2:12—*"**Speak**~~ and **act** ~~ as those who will be judged by a law that gives freedom."*

Accountability can be an uncomfortable experience. While in college, my classmate Bob and I met early and headed to the dining hall, where we worked as waiters. Each morning, Bob would greet me with "Don, are you rejoicing in the Lord?" At first I hesitantly responded, "Yeah, more or less." He challenged me: "That's not good enough. God's word says, *'Rejoice in the Lord always!'"* (Phil 4:4). Days later, his persistence motivated me to go to the prayer room in our hall to refresh my thanksgiving to Christ for His gracious sacrifice. That morning, I remember giving Bob an affirmative answer, to which he responded, "Isn't it great? Now walk throughout the day rejoicing." He never asked me again, but I have never forgotten the lesson.

We are to "continually speak" and "continually act" as those who are freed from sin's condemnation, but we still face the judgment seat of Christ—for how we have lived in obedience. This judgment does not determine our salvation, but rather our rewards. We are rewarded for how we choose to be obedient. These commands give freedom: not freedom to sin freely but freedom from guilt and the choice of following His wisdom.

The gospel is the law of liberty because it liberates the believer in Jesus Christ from the addiction, condemnation, and punishment of sin (Rom 8:1), freeing him to choose to make the kingdom of God his top priority, since it will be his eternal home. This law of liberty frees us to follow the Lord willingly out of love and gratitude, rather than out of fear or obligation.

The Christian is to live daily in the light of a coming judgment. This is the divine sense of accountability. Do we know the commands about how we are to speak? Can we identify the commands about how we are to act? We will be evaluated by His word, but we can trust the Spirit to enable us to follow His word. This is what the power of the filling of the Spirit means: the power to enable us to be obedient.

Peter warns us about the abuse of the freedom experienced in the Christian life: *"Live as free men but do not use your freedom as a cover-up for evil; live as servants of God"* (1 Pet 2:16). Do you want to be free to choose how to practice His principles? Does it seem too burdensome to take the commands as your personal guideposts?

"What a frightful thought that nothing escapes Your oversight. May this motivate me to take seriously Your every command and to learn to love them."

JANUARY 6

Be Generous in Secret

Matt 6:3—*"But when you do your giving, **do not let** your left hand **know***/ what your right hand is doing."*

Jesus taught that when giving "alms" or a mercy gift to the poor or needy *"do not sound a trumpet before you as the hypocrites do in the synagogues and in the streets, they may have glory from men"* (Matt 6:2). Perhaps this is an exaggeration, but the end goal is the same: self-recognition and self-glory.

It is ridiculously easy to get anyone to converse at length about himself or herself by asking a few personal questions. It is as if they are dying to tell you all about themselves or their accomplishments, but seldom do they return the interest in you.

Matthew 6:3 begins with the connective *"but"* (Gk.,"on the contrary") to mean that the application of verse 2 in spiritual acts is not to be done for personal benefits. Because it is impossible for you to do anything with your left hand without the right hand knowing, then this is a hyperbole—an exaggeration to prove a point. The idea is that the closest person should not know what you gave in your offering. The focus is on *secretly* performing spiritual acts to benefit others (6:4).

We must beware that generous actions on our part could be motivated from wanting to be appreciated or recognized. The solution is to be secretive or spontaneous about doing things to benefit others. Could you give someone a gift in cash with no name on the envelope? Can you imagine doing an unsolicited favor for someone without letting him or her know who did it?

If God promises a reward for deeds done in secret, is that sufficient motivation to sacrifice for others without letting them know your sacrifice for them? Do you believe God sees your secret actions? Do you believe His reward is worth more than receiving a person's gratitude?

Why would anyone trade the divine recognition and reward for the transient praise you might receive from a benefactor? Practice secret acts of benefit to others and see what it does to your heart. Do you trust Him to reward you? Whom can you help secretly today?

"Lord, why do I want people to think I am something special or spiritual when I know I am not? Teach me to love to do things that only You will ever know about."

Be Careful with Pride

Matt 6:1—*"**Be careful**~~ not to display your righteousness merely to be seen by people. Otherwise you have no reward with your Father in heaven."*

The desire to be famous or renowned for spiritual activities is a deceptive trap. The present command, *"be continually being careful,"* comes from a word meaning "to hold the mind on something or to pay attention." In other words, we are to take great care not to be faking a walk with God.

This brings us to the meaning of love: doing things to benefit others without concern for personal benefit. When we do things for personal benefit, it is not motivated by love.

This command suggests that we should prepare our hearts before engaging in spiritual actions such as tithing (Matt 6:2), praying (6:5), and fasting (6:16), etc. We should meditate on our heartfelt purpose or motive before doing any spiritual activity.

Never do any spiritual service *"to be seen by people."* The word for "to be seen" means "to be noticed." It is a term related to the word *theater* or *acting*. Don't just play the part of a spiritually motivated person. The word *hypocrite* is the word for actors in a play. Live as though God is your only audience.

This is not a restriction from doing public ministry, but a warning to be careful about your motives. God rewards us beyond our imaginations for sincere service for His honor (Matt 5:12), but when we seek the glory or benefit for ourselves, the reward disappears from heaven's balance sheet: *"they have their glory from men,"* but that is all they will receive (5:2).

Testifying to what God has done through our lives that seek to honor His name and exalt His power should always point to the Savior, not to the speaker. None of this should inhibit us from daring service for our King, but it should keep us monitoring our motives and confessing and repenting of our pride.

Paul wrote, *"if I give over my body in order to boast, but do not have love, I receive no benefit"* (1 Cor 13:3). That is, even martyrdom means nothing to God if we hope for personal glory with no benefit to others. Take care to focus on serving others for their benefit and the honor of our Lord's name.

"Lord, I need Your wisdom to know how to talk about what You do through my life without desiring any credit or recognition. You alone are worthy."

JANUARY 8

Do Not Be Deceived

Gal 6:7—*"Do not be deceived~]. God will not be made a fool. For a person will reap what he sows."*

What a person believes about being accountable to God is how he will live. In Galatians 5:13–26, Paul had just concluded a description of Christian freedom acting in the opposite direction from the works of the flesh. He concluded, *"If we live by the Spirit [i.e., as Spirit-indwelt persons], let us also walk by the Spirit [i.e., empowered by the Spirit, thereby enabled to conquer the works of the flesh]"* (5:25).

Paul warns the readers, *"Stop deceiving yourselves,"* implying they had been thinking incorrectly. When we think, "Nothing happened when I sinned, so I guess God will let me get away with this secret sin," we are deceiving ourselves. God is slow to anger, so He may not bring chastisement immediately, but He never fails to do so. We should refuse to listen to any thought that justifies or makes it easier to be disobedient.

There are two reasons it is not good to let such wrong thoughts deceive you: First, *"God will not be made a fool"* or *"God is not mocked."* When we show contempt for God's commands, we make Him look like a liar for not doing what he said or a fool for not punishing us immediately. Such arrogance will be addressed eventually. Are you conscious of sins you think you have gotten away with?

Second, there is a payday someday; in other words, "a person will reap what he sows." No one can deceive God; whatever seeds you plant in the early spring will sprout and bear the same fruit by harvest time. Seeds of secret sins, when they sprout, may destroy your reputation, damage the people in a ministry, destroy relationships, or bring you to the point of death. God is committed to keeping you from sin, but if you insist, He will let sin destroy you so that others may fear.

"Lord, keep me from thinking You do not care about whether I sin or not, and give me a sensitive heart to know when I am justifying my sin or presuming I can get away with it. Why do I want to be the exception to the rule? You give me time to be honest with You, but I deceive myself into thinking no one will ever know. Keep me honest before You."

JANUARY 9

Live Out What God Has Put in You

1 Pet 1:17—*"And if you address as Father the one who impartially judges according to each one's work, **live out***~ the time of your temporary residence here in reverence."*

Whatever a person is like in his thought life will be reflected in his behavior. A sincere follower of Christ who addresses God as his Father must know that He is the impartial judge of everyone's individual works.

The notion of calling God your Father recalls Jesus' teaching of how to pray—*"Our Father"* (Matt 6:9). This is continued in Peter's metaphor of us as "born again to a living hope" (1 Pet 1:3). He then presents the image of us as "obedient children" (1:14) born of an imperishable seed (1:23). The conditional clause "if you address" could also be translated as "since you address," indicating a relationship between the reader and God.

However, we should not presume upon the grace of God's mercy, treating it as a license to sin with impunity just because we are His children. God judges His children "impartially"—he has no special exceptions for believers. God is a Father-Judge, not a Santa Claus–type person who gives "goodies" and closes His eyes to our evildoings. Don't be deceived. If we are His children, then we must expect His chastisement when we are disobedient (Heb 12:4–6).

The phrase *"in reverence"* (or *"in fear,"*[NKJ] "reverent fear"[NIV.]) is in the emphatic position to indicate that Someone is watching, and He has no favoritism to blink at our sins without teaching us a lesson to despise sin as He does. If He promises to do this, then we had better "fear" He will discipline us; thus we should live to avoid such punishment.

Salvation is primarily an inward work of the Spirit (*"believe with all your heart,"* Acts 8:37,[NAS,] compare Rom 10:9). Paul is calling us to "immediately decide to live out from now on" what the Spirit has worked into the believer. If we trust Him inwardly, then we must trust Him outwardly in how we obey Him. The transformed mind (Rom 12:2) motivates a transformed life.

"Lord, help me show how much You mean to me. I am so thankful for what You have done for me and for the joy of Your peace in my life. Help me make Your presence in my life evident to others."

Be Firm in Your Commitment

1 Cor 15:58—*"So then, dear brothers and sisters, **be firm**~~. Do not be moved! [adjective] Always be outstanding [participle] in the work of the Lord, knowing that your labor is not in vain in the Lord."*

Paul's conclusion after establishing the great truth of the resurrection and our life with Christ is thus to be steadfast by being immovable, increasingly active in serving others and knowing no effort for Him is wasted.

The present imperative—to be *"continually being firm"*—refers to someone who is "settled or resolved" about the reality of the resurrection and eternal rewards from Christ as the greatest value.

"Immoveable" means "not [able to be] moved from side to side." The "unstable" person in James 1 doubted God's purpose in suffering and thus became as one standing in the waves of the ocean. What we believe either stabilizes us or makes us unstable.

"Abounding" means to "exceed the number expected or required." Because of our gratitude for His grace we should determine to outdo ourselves in service to our King, ignoring the often-repeated advice to "take it easy." One of the models of this perspective was Epaphroditus, who "came close to death for the work of Christ, risking his life" (Phil 2:25, 30).

The great personal motivation for the believer is to be *"knowing"* the value of the rewards that Christ has planned for His servants. The word *knowing* means "to turn your attention to this theme, to focus on it, and to keep it in your thoughts and values that are important to you."

Though we may not know the particulars, we can trust Him that our *"labor [for His kingdom] is not in vain."* Jesus said, *"I am coming quickly, and My reward is with Me, to render to every man according to what he has done"* (Rev 22:12).

This is not about how good we are or how many times we went to church, but what we personally helped accomplish for the kingdom. If He can trust us to finish His task now, He will reward us with even greater responsibility in eternity (Luke 19:17).

"Lord, keep me from discouragement in serving You. Teach me to trust You to reward my every act of faithfulness, even when others do not see it."

JANUARY 11
Do Not Judge Others

1 Cor 4:5—*"So then, **do not judge~| anything before the time. Wait until the Lord comes. He will bring to light the hidden things of darkness and reveal the motives of hearts. Then each will receive recognition from God."*

How easy it is to be critical, even cynical, of people and to destroy their credibility and acceptance before others. Such attitudes presume to judge the motives and intents of someone else's heart and mind.

Playing God's role has dangerous consequences both because one usurps the place of God in judging His own servants and because there is a high probability that such critical judgments are mistaken, exaggerated, or out of context, resulting in cruel injustices.

God told Samuel, *"Do not look at his appearance or at his physical stature . . . For the Lord does not see as man sees, for man looks at the outward appearance, but the Lord looks at the heart"* (1 Sam 16:7).

Why is it so hard to let God be the judge of His people? Could it be a selfish motive for vengeance, or do we not trust Him to do what we think is needed to teach someone a lesson? God is so different from us.

Paul writes that God *"will bring to light the hidden things of darkness and reveal the motives of hearts."* This could be a scary experience, except for one factor: God promised to never remember our sins. In Isaiah 43:25, He says, *"I, even I, am He who blots out your transgressions for My own sake. And I will not remember your sins."* In Hebrews 10:17, he adds, *"Their sins and their lawless deeds I will remember no more."*

God's purpose is revealed in the summation: *"Then each will receive recognition from God."* He is not judgmental or critical of us seeking to destroy who we are; rather, His inspection seeks to find every last thought, dream, or motive that sought His honor and His glory— anything He can use to justify what He wants more than anything: to give us His "recognition" or "praise" before all the saints of heaven.

God only wants to praise us for our faithfulness. That is all He is about . . . so this is how we must think about others as well.

"Forgive me, Lord, for being so critical of others and especially for feeling more spiritual. Teach me to value only Your recognition and praise."

JANUARY 12

Follow Jesus as a Servant

John 12:26—*"If anyone wants to serve me,* **he must follow**~~ *me, and where I am, my servant will be too. If anyone serves me, the Father will honor him."*

As long as following Jesus meant the possibility of fame, power, and fortune the disciples were willing and able. In Mark 10:37, the disciples James and John asked, *"Let one of us sit at your right and the other at your left in your glory."* Jesus asked them, *"Are you able to drink the cup [bitter cup of suffering*[NIV]*] that I drink and be baptized with the baptism [of suffering*[NIV]*] that I am baptized with? They said to Him, 'We are able"* (10:38–39).

A few minutes later, the other disciples caught on that these two were trying to get the best and most powerful positions in Christ's kingdom. They were mad with jealousy. Evidently, they too were following Jesus for their own personal benefit. However, Jesus was not going to a glorious earthly kingdom, but to a cross . . . and they were to follow Him there.

Jesus taught how He thought and lived: *"Those who love their life lose it, and those who hate their life in this world will keep it for eternal life"* (Jn 12:25). Jesus did not cling to His life in glory; He left it behind to be sent to earth to give his life for the redemption of others. After the resurrection, Jesus told His disciples, *"As the Father has sent me, so I am sending you"* (20:21). He expects us to live for the same purpose. This is not an option for a select few.

How does a person serve Christ? In a negative sense, it is evident that Jesus directly perceived anything done to the believers as being done to Him. He said, *"Saul, Saul, why are you persecuting Me?"* (Acts 9:4), but Saul had never even seen Jesus. Persecuting believers was the same as persecuting Jesus. Positively, Jesus taught, *"Assuredly, I say to you, inasmuch as you did it to one of the least of these My brethren, you did it to Me"* (Matt 25:40). We serve Jesus by serving His followers and completing His mission in the world.

Will it be worth it? Jesus said, *"The Father will honor him."* The thrill of God in eternity will be to honor all who voluntarily gave up their lives to follow Christ in reaching and serving others for His honor and glory. Would you prefer earthly honor or the Father's honor? It is your choice. Follow your dreams or dream to follow your King.

"Lord, I want to live for the honor You promised Your servants and cease seeking the honor from others."

JANUARY 13

Watch Out Not to Lose Rewards

2 Jn 8—*"Watch out~~, so that you do not lose the things we have worked for, but receive a full reward."*

False teachers had invaded the churches by the end of the first century with their winsome and persuasive personalities, and their ability to do phenomenal wonders and miracles (Matt 7:21–23) deceived many followers of Christ. The key to not being deceived by false teachers is to know the clear teachings of the written word of God.

The warning in this present command is to make a continual practice of discerning and examining all teachings, philosophies, ideas, and stories that supposedly are Spirit led. John commanded, *"Do not believe every spirit, but test the spirits, whether they are of God, because many false prophets have gone out into the world"* (1 Jn 4:1[NKJ]). Paul wrote, *"If anyone considers himself a prophet or spiritual person, he should acknowledge that what I write to you is the Lord's command"* (1 Cor 14:37). Error is always based on logic, deductions, or mental impressions, which tend to add to or twist the Scripture.

All our works for the kingdom of Christ are equated to *"gold, silver, precious stones, wood, hay, straw"* (1 Cor 3:12). These will be tested by fire to reveal what is genuine and of acceptable "quality" (3:13). We are not told what these symbols represent, but gold, silver, and precious stones can withstand the test of fire.

The other elements are consumed and disappear. If I could speculate a moment, it sounds as if for the wrong motives or for our self-centered actions, which nullify our rewards (Matt 6:1-18).

John revealed that believers could diminish their potential rewards if they allowed themselves to be deceived by false teachers. He wrote that true *"love [means] that we walk according to his commandments"* (2 Jn 6), but *"many deceivers have gone out into the world"* (2 Jn 7). Rather than being cautious, *"everyone who goes on ahead and does not abide in the teaching of Christ, does not have God"* (2 Jn 9). The standard that everyone must be measured against is the apostolic "teaching" (2 Jn 10), which along with Jesus's teaching, laid the foundation of the church (Eph 2:20). We must know it and live by it faithfully.

"My heart's desire is to show You how much You mean to me for all You have done. May any reward I receive only prove to all how great it is to serve the King of kings."

JANUARY 14

Do Not Be Afraid: He Will Take Care of You

Luke 12:32—*"Do not be afraid~|, little flock, for your Father is well pleased to give you the kingdom."*

Whatever we fear, there is a tendency to give in to it or give up. In this context, Jesus warns us not to fear the loss of material security. Those who pursue the advancement of the kingdom of God in the world are promised sufficient material provisions from God.

Jesus had just given the command not to fear in verse 4 (not to fear persecution) and verse 7 (not to fear being unnoticed), and now we are told not to fear being abandoned or left without sufficient provisions. In verse 15, He warns about covetousness, which is the root cause of this fear.

In verse 22, Jesus tells us not to be anxious about what we will eat or wear. Then He gives a series of illustrations of how God takes care of less important creatures to demonstrate how much more He would take care of His servants.

The *fear* in this context is the doubt that your personal needs will be met if you were to give your whole life to fulfill God's will in the world. He does not show us how He will take care of us; he only tells us that He will.

For many, the thought of giving up a potentially lucrative position in order to play a significant role in completing the Great Commission is so difficult to consider that only a few ever take it seriously. Many are scared they will not have the support to survive, so they give up the idea before they even start. Jesus is commanding us not to doubt His ability to take care of us and commit to a key role in God's mission in the world.

Are you afraid of the will of God? What if God burdened your heart with an unreached group of people in India? Would you be willing to trust God for your provisions? What if God wanted you to be more generous in your involvement to advance the boundaries of the gospel?

God has a tendency to lead His children toward a cross as He did His Son, toward something that will cost them everything. A cross is never cheap. However, there is a kingdom on the other side, and *"it is the Father's good pleasure to give you the kingdom."* Never be afraid to pour out your life and resources for His kingdom. You will never be overlooked.

"Lord, teach me to see how selfish 'fear' is and how to value Your rewards above earthly gains."

JANUARY 15

Listen to God's Word

Luke 16:29—*"But Abraham said, 'They have Moses and the prophets; they must respond*~ to them.'"*

In the story of the rich man and Lazarus, the rich man is suffering the pains of hell while pleading with Abraham to send someone to tell his five brothers about the reality of hell. He was convinced that if his brothers talked to someone sent back from the dead, they would believe.

But Abraham responded, "They have the Old Testament prophets, *obey* them." This is the message of Abraham through Christ's message to the world. If you want to know the reality of eternity, then learn well the revealed word of God and obey what you find there. If the rich man's brothers would not respond to the major message of God in His word, then they would not listen to a messenger, even if he came from the grave.

God is amazingly gracious with His creatures, but they have to choose. If they choose to live life without God, paying no attention to His word, then God will let them do so in this life and then forever live without Him forever.

God's primary means of communicating His will and hope for mankind is through His written word. It seems men want any other means to hear from God except a revealed written word. Jesus came to declare God's will and then inspired His chosen disciples to record His will for all time. Now the only way we will ever know His will is to search it out in His written word.

Second, He reveals the principle that it is not miraculous messengers or signs that will convert a soul. The brothers would be shocked or awestruck by the appearance of such resurrected souls with a message directly from hell, but this would have no life-changing power. They might be so awestruck that they would superficially worship God even more, but they would ultimately fail to yield to His commands.

A follower must believe *from the heart*—that is, he must want Jesus to be constant companion and his authority in this life. Miracles are only effective in convincing people that God is real, but they do not make a person want Jesus as a permanent part his life.

Abraham in essence told the rich man, "No! This is not how God works with men." The only way to know the truth that will free the sinner from his sins is through the written word of God. Once you know what He says, can you trust it?

"Forgive me, Lord, for not being satisfied with Your word alone for my guidance in life. Give me Your wisdom to apply all that I learn from Your commands."

Work and Serve

Col 3:23–24—*"Whatever you are doing,* **work~~ at it with enthusiasm,** *as to the Lord and not for people, because you know that you will receive your inheritance from the Lord as the reward.* **Serve ~~ the Lord Christ.***"*

The motivations behind our actions are important in Scripture. One of the chief defects of the first-century slave was the lack of motivation to behave with zeal unless threatened with punishment. The temptation for the slave was to do as little as he could get away with.

The priority of the New Testament was to spread the gospel and not be clouded with social reconstruction. If the first-century slave could follow these principles to honor Christ, then any employee today can as well.

A Christian slave owed complete obedience to his master as though his service was *"as to the Lord."* The word *"whatever"* extends beyond what is normally expected. The present tense means to *"continually be working at it with enthusiasm"* (lit. "with all your soul"), seeking to benefit everyone around you.

We are not to serve men—that is, we are not to be men-pleasers. Jesus warned in Matthew 6:1 that anything done to be seen or approved by men would receive no reward from Him. We are always to do excellent work whether anyone is looking or not, just to honor our Savior who sees us.

Two aspects of the motivation are to be kept in the servant's mind: First, whatever one does, it is *"as to the Lord and not for people."* The Lord, who sees all and knows all, looks for what He can reward. Second, one must be continually knowing or thinking of his *"inheritance from the Lord as the reward"* for faithful service, which would make life's efforts worthwhile. Paul gave dignity and hope even to the servant by describing the reward that would be personally given by the Lord.

Even while remaining as slaves (or employees), believers are continually or habitually to be serving the Lord Jesus through their workplace. The triple repetition of the focus toward the Lord suggests that the slave/employee should constantly repeat in his mind that his loyalty is focused on Christ, which transcends his devotion to his human master/boss. This makes it easier to bear the harsher and more unpleasant features of his enslavement or job. Whatever your task, do it is as if for the Lord Himself.

"Teach me Your perspective for how to live for You through serving others around me. I trust You, Lord, to remember every detail, because it is all for You."

Love, Do Good, and Lend

Luke 6:35—*"But **love~~ your enemies**, and **do good~~, and lend~~**, expecting nothing back. Then your reward will be great, and you will be sons of the Most High, because he is kind to ungrateful and evil people."*

Some commands have immediate benefits, while others have eternal consequences. If we are obedient to these three commands, we are promised a *"great"* reward from God Himself. We will be rewarded because we have chosen to behave like God Himself, who "is kind to ungrateful and evil people."

The three commands are present imperatives: they are meant to be continual or habitual actions of Jesus's followers. Christians are unique because they are to *"love [their] enemies."* Because "love" in this case is not an emotional affection but a commitment to care enough to benefit another, thus this command is an action to be done, not a feeling to be felt.

If the Bible meant love to be an emotion, the opposite would be hate. However, if *love* is an action verb, then the opposite of love is *selfishness*. Defining who is the beneficiary of one's actions draws the line: in selfish actions, I am the beneficiary, and in loving actions, others always benefit.

Since the Spirit indwells us this is a possible command to obey through the empowerment or filling of the Spirit. We cannot feel warmly toward those we despise, but we can decide to benefit the *"ungrateful and evil people"* in our lives. If it is the *"goodness of God that leads to repentance"* (Rom 2:4), why can't we add that "the goodness of believers" can help lead sinners to trust in the Savior?

If the command to *"love your enemies"* is somewhat generic, the command to *"do good"* is a more specific clarification of what love does, which is followed by a more specific illustration: *"lend, expecting nothing back."*

If you ever give money to someone whom you care about, forget all hope or expectation of ever recuperating those funds. In your mind, think of it as a gift and let it go. People matter more than your money.

The killer of relationships is selfishness, such as demanding your rights, seeking personal gratification, or getting even. Do we really want to be like God, or do we prefer His selfish, self-centered, and self-serving enemy, Satan?

"Lord, teach me to be like You in caring more about winning the hearts of other undeserving people to Your gracious and generous love."

JANUARY 18
Listen to Him

Matt 17:5—*"While he was still speaking, a bright cloud overshadowed them, and a voice from the cloud said, 'This is my one dear Son, in whom I take great delight. **Listen~~to him!**'"*

Peter, James, and John had just witnessed the miraculous transformation of Jesus's normal human appearance into His heavenly, glorified splendor as the bright Shekinah of Jehovah. This extraordinary Man was revealing Himself to them as divine. Paul wrote, *"But [He] made Himself of no reputation, taking the form of a bondservant, and coming in the likeness of men. And being found in appearance as a man, He humbled Himself and became obedient to the point of death, even the death of the cross"* (Phil 2:7–8).

This scene the only audible message from God the Father to us: *"This is my one dear Son, in whom I take great delight. Listen to him!"* The purpose was to make sure His disciples took seriously everything He said and later would say through the Spirit's inspiration to the apostles and prophets.

Peter later described this moment as secondary to possessing the record of the words of God: *"And we ourselves heard this utterance made from heaven when we were with Him on the holy mountain. And so we have the prophetic Word made more sure [i.e., more certain than witnessing Jesus transformed in His glory], to which you do well to pay attention as to a lamp shining in a dark place"* (2 Pet 1:18–19). To Peter, it was more important for him to have the record of God's message to man in the written Scripture than it was to have seen Jesus transformed.

Everyone becomes like the one(s) to whom he listens! The most repeated command in the book of Revelation is this: *"He who has an ear, let him hear what the Spirit says to the churches"* (Rev 2:7). Nine times "hear" is a command in the Revelation (2:7, 11, 17, 29; 3:6, 13, 20, 22; 13:9). The aorist form of these verbs demands an immediate response to what is commanded. Are we searching, as we read, for a command to obey today?

When a cohort asks for something, we can debate it or ignore it with few consequences. When a policeman asks us to do something, we had better do it, especially when we think he is watching! When a president or a king asks us to do something, men will die to do it without hesitation. When the King of kings asks us to do anything, which of these three responses do you practice?

"When I read Your Words, I want to understand the same delight You had to hear from the Father. I want to take everything You have sent to us in Your word as my guide."

JANUARY 19
Produce Fruit

Luke 3:8—*"Therefore **produce fruit***~ that proves your repentance, and don't begin to say to yourselves, 'We have Abraham as our father.' For I tell you that God can raise up children for Abraham from these stones!"*

John the Baptist was insistent that those who "changed their minds" or repented about their own sinfulness and wanted forgiveness from God must understand that an inward change results in an outward change.

One of the main ways to "prove your repentance" is to demonstrate that God lives within you by the evidence of the *"fruit of the Spirit"*—that is, *"love, joy, peace, long-suffering, kindness, goodness, faithfulness, gentleness, self-control"* (Gal 5:22–23).

In Galatians, Paul describes specifically how this works in practical ways. If *"we are Christ's,"* then we *"have crucified the flesh with its passions and desires"* (5:24); therefore, he tells *"us not [to] become conceited, provoking one another, envying one another"* (5:25).

We should not compete with each other to see who is the most spiritual; rather, we should always demonstrate His love by how we care for others.

The Jews tended to wrongly presume they automatically had God's blessings—no matter how they behaved—because they were descendants of Abraham. Gentile believers might presume that God has forgiven them because they were baptized, go to church, or have Christian parents while continuing to live a carnal, self-centered, egotistical lifestyle. We must beware of a shallow or fake Christianity.

God is not impressed with a superficial, mechanical, or ritual religion that does not change a person's heart; rather, God seeks people who have a heartfelt commitment to Christ and who genuinely want to be like Him (as demonstrated by the fruit of the Spirit). Do you sense the conviction of the Spirit when you sin? Do you have an inward desire to change?

Fruit is the result of the life source of the vine flowing into the branches. If we are bonded to the Vine of Christ by the Spirit, His word will bear fruit that will be inevitable in our lives.

"Lord, my heart's desire is to show the fruit of Christ living in my life to all who know me. As people get closer to me, may Your presence be increasingly evident."

JANUARY 20
Don't Stop the Children

Matt 19:14—*"But Jesus said, '**Let** the little children **come*~** to me and **do not try to stop~/ them**, for the kingdom of heaven belongs to such as these.'"*

How Jesus loved little children! The disciples were rebuking the parents for bringing their children to Jesus to talk with them and pray for them. Perhaps the disciples thought Jesus was too important or too busy to be bothered with children. But Jesus gave orders to "immediately let the little children come to me" and *"cease trying to stop them."*

Apparently, the disciples had missed the recent lesson (Matt 18:2) on children, when He called a child next to Him saying, *"Unless you turn and become like children, you will never enter the kingdom of heaven."* He then added that the characteristic of a child that He admires is humility (18:4): a willingness to trust Jesus's word without question.

Young children can understand the gospel perfectly. It is not a mystery reserved for the intellectuals. Rather, the gospel is designed for anyone who wants to know God and live with Him forever.

When children, or anyone, first recognize that they have broken His law (e.g., *"Do not bear false witness or tell a lie"* [ninth commandment], then they begin to understand their sinfulness. Now they can see their need for forgiveness. Jesus came to save sinners (1 Tim 1:15), not those who think they were good people. Jesus welcomes anyone seeking His forgiveness and acceptance, regardless of age.

These children wanted to know Jesus personally. Jesus knew that the future of His church was in the hands of these little children. He also knew that the humble, open receptivity of these children was in stark contrast to the stubborn pride of the religious and intellectual people who let their education, pride, or sophistication overcome the simple faith needed to believe in Jesus. Anyone of any age who comes to Christ in faith with a willingness to trust whatever Jesus says has a warm welcome from Jesus now and later in His kingdom.

"Lord, as a child trusts his father, may my heart and mind always trust whatever You say in Your word. Teach me to obey You as a submissive child."

JANUARY 21

Save Yourself from This Generation

Acts 2:40—"*With many other words he testified and exhorted them saying, '**Save yourselves***~ from this perverse generation!'*"

Peter knew that men must be told the truth about themselves, about God, and especially about the love of Christ; otherwise, they would destroy their lives and forever be separated from God because of their sins. Peter could not remain silent.

He "*testified and exhorted*" his audience. The word *exhorted* means to "call upon, admonish, beg, instruct, encourage, or teach." He was compelled to every oral expression possible to persuade his audience to turn to Jesus.

Paul wrote of his compelling urgency to speak: "*Since we have such hope, we use great boldness of speech*" (2 Cor 3:12). Do we really believe the gospel is the only hope for the lost?

Peter challenged his audience to "urgently decide to save yourself," not in the sense that they could effect their own salvation, but that individually each one must decide whose side they are on: the side of their perverse generation, with all its customs, vices, and self-seeking sensualities, or the side of God in Jesus Christ.

Paul wrote to all who would follow Christ, "*Be blameless and innocent, children of God without blemish in the midst of a crooked [the same Greek word as our text] and twisted generation, among whom you shine as lights in the world, holding fast to the word of life*" (Phil 2:15–16a).

Being saved from a "*perverse generation*" does not mean we must be isolated. It means we should be strengthened internally so that the generation in which we live does not affect us; rather, we should affect it, pointing it to the Savior.

"*My heart aches for the disinterest in and rebellion against Your word in my generation. Keep me faithful to You today.*"

JANUARY 22

Keep the Commandments

Matt 19:17—*"He said to him, 'Why do you ask me about what is good? There is only one who is good. But if you want to enter into life, **keep*~ the commandments.'"***

The rich young ruler had just asked Jesus, *"Good Teacher, what good deed must I do to have eternal life?"* (Matt 19:16).

Jesus's response to his inquiry might seem harsh, but Jesus knew what was in his heart. His opening remark corrects the ruler's incorrect view of Jesus's deity and eliminates all human hope of ever being good enough to become acceptable. He says, *"There is only one who is good,"* referring to God. Should he have responded, "You are truly God in human form and I am not worthy"? But there was no such response.

So Jesus gave him a second test: *"If you want to enter into life, [immediately decide to] keep [or obey] the commandments."* If he were honest he would have admitted his failure to obey them and his need for mercy.

When the young ruler proudly asked, *"Which one?"* he revealed his desire to brag about his self-righteousness. Jesus quoted five commandments, concluding with *"You shall love your neighbor as yourself"* (Matt 19:19). Blinded by his own ego, pride, and self-delusion, the ruler boasted that he had always obeyed these commandments. Again, he refused to recognize he was a sinner.

With one final attempt to break through his pride, Jesus asked him to go and sell all that he had and give it to the poor, then *"Come and follow me."* The ruler's unwillingness to sell his possessions should have revealed to him his own covetousness (violating the tenth commandment), and then he should have confessed, "Lord, I see how selfish and covetous I am. I'm a sinner by every one of the commandments. Can there be any forgiveness for such a sinner as I?"

Instead, he went away sorrowful, but not with the sorrow that leads to repentance; rather, he left with the sorrow of unwillingness to be broken, which leads to self-centered remorse and self-pity. His love for money and possessions revealed his disobedience to the first and tenth commandments (Ex 20:3, 17). If he had confessed as a child, openly admitting his sin, he would have been forgiven and freed.

"Lord, I'm thankful that my failure to be good in Your sight has not alienated me from Your love. Your grace is astounding to me. Thank You Jesus"

JANUARY 23

Walk in the Light

Jn 12:35—*"Jesus replied, 'The light is with you for a little while longer.* **Walk**~~ *while you have the light, so that the darkness may not overtake you. The one who walks in the darkness does not know where he is going.'"*

Jesus had just described the *"death he was going to die"* (Jn 12:32–33), as being *"lifted up from the earth,"* but the crowd thought the Old Testament had said the *"Christ remains forever"* (12:34), so if He was going to die, they began to doubt He was the promised One.

Rather than directly answer their question, He gave them a principle to follow even when they do not experience what they were expecting. He told them to *keep on continually walking* in the "light," or the truths of Jesus' teachings, no matter what happens.

When He was gone, the darkness from the lack of His personal guidance and His teachings would overtake them, leaving them with a sense of being lost as one who *"does not know where he is going."*

Doubt, frustration, and disillusionment are the results of having been deceived by evil powers or simply by selfish expectations, leading one to believe he deserves better in life. The crowd wanted a Messiah who was important, powerful, and permanent, but Jesus was poor, unknown, not politically connected, and, by His own declaration, temporary. Why should they put their trust in Him and risk their lives for someone who appeared to be a weak failure?

When doubts arise, keep on walking in the light that you know in the word. James said that *"the testing of your faith produces patience"* (James 1:3), which is the sign of being made *"perfect and complete, lacking nothing"* (1:4); thus one becomes the character of Christ. Our testings are part of His plan to bring us to maturity.

The command was needed because, in spite of the miracles He did, *"they still did not believe in him"* (Jn 12:37). Many might be following Jesus to see what happens but they have not stepped into the light with all their hearts to trust Him fully for everything in life. Can anything discourage you from trusting Christ in today's problems?

"Lord, I want to be committed to all the principles and commands that You have given to us as an expression of my trust in You. "

JANUARY 24

Come to the Water of Life

Rev 22:17—*"And the Spirit and the bride say, "Come*~!" And let the one who hears* **say***~: *"Come!"**~ *And* **let** *the one who is thirsty* **come***~; **let** *the one who wants it* **take***~ *the water of life free of charge."*

The Holy Spirit through the bride, that is the church, extends a threefold invitation. Anyone who hears this incredibly gracious offer is commanded to urgently and immediately extend the invitation to the thirsty and whoever wants to taste of the water of life. The Spirit says through the bride—that is, the church—*"Come!"* not as an optional invitation to consider but as a decisive invitation/command to obey immediately, knowing that time is short and the end is going to come suddenly, at which time the offer will end.

The aorist command means to *"urgently decide to say,"* "advise or affirm." Everyone who hears of this invitation is commanded to share it. To *hear* means more than just to listen, but to obey it personally.

God's great concern is that everyone would hear of His grace, yet only a few are telling it to others. Those who know the truth are silent. Are they ashamed to be identified with Christ?

Through the Scriptures, the Spirit speaks through the church members to the thirsty of the world and to those who want to know the truth, if only someone would tell them. The power of the gospel (Rom 1:16) begins to work when His people begin to obey the command to say, "Come to Christ now."

The power of the gospel is evident in illuminating the darkened mind, convicting the sinner of his lostness, and drawing the spirit of the unbeliever to want to know Christ. We can trust in the power of the gospel.

The thirsty and the seekers of truth will be drawn to His gracious offer. Jesus promised the *"water of life"* to the Samaritan woman (Jn 4:10–15). He told the Pharisees, *"Whoever believes in me, as the Scriptures has said, streams of living water will flow from within him"* (7:37), but they were neither thirsty nor willing.

Is it a coincidence that the first command Jesus gave after the resurrection—*"Go quickly and tell"* (Matt 28:7)—is similar to His last command for the church: *"Say [urgently], 'Come'"*?

"Oh, how You have satisfied my soul. Thank You for filling my deepest needs and accepting me without conditions even though I am so unworthy."

JANUARY 25

Do Not Wrongly Suppose Things

Jn 5:45—*"**Do not suppose***~ that I will accuse you before the Father. The one who accuses you is Moses, in whom you have placed your hope."*

Whatever a person "supposes" about the world is how he sees life and reality. Jesus was constantly correcting the beliefs of His generation so they could understand Him and reality. They thought Jesus was accusing them, and they supposed Moses was their defender and intercessor, just as he had been on earth when they sinned by worshiping the golden calf (Ex 32:30–32).

Jesus's clarification was an offense against their pride of attempting to be faithful followers of Moses's law, even adding more rules of their own just to make sure. The truth was that Moses' writings would be their accuser, not their defender. Moses taught the depth of their guilt, which Jesus promised to forgive.

John the Baptist pointed to Jesus as the *"Lamb of God who takes away the sins of the world."* Their worldview did not need another sacrifice for their sins; they thought they were good enough. They had missed three great truths about the law.

First, they exaggerated the commands and twisted the meanings so they could feel like they were obeying them. Their pride in their legalistic strictness and man-made rules gave them a false sense of approval.

Second, they failed to understand that one act of disobedience to a command cannot be offset by a hundred acts of obedience. Naïvely, many today also believe that their "good" can outweigh their "bad" thus gaining their acceptance before God.

James wrote, *"For the person who keeps all of the laws except one is as guilty as a person who has broken all of God's laws"* (James 2:10). If you lie once, you are a liar (ninth commandment) forever. No amount of truth-telling can undo a lie.

Third, they missed the entire purpose of the law, which was to reveal their failure as sinful people to live up to God's standard and to point to their desperate need for a means of forgiveness outside of themselves. Paul wrote, *"The law was our tutor to bring us to Christ, that we might be justified by faith"* (Gal 3:24). The law (Moses) accuses us of our transgressions so that we will flee to the Lamb of God, Jesus, for our forgiveness. Can you say, "Thank you, Jesus"?

"Lord, it is so easy to believe misconceptions or false notions about You, but teach me to understand all You have revealed about who You are and how we are to live in Your presence."

JANUARY 26

Do Not Be Deceived about Who Is Saved

Ephesians 5:5–6, *"For you can be confident of this one thing: that no person who is immoral, impure, or greedy (such a person is an idolater) has any inheritance in the kingdom of Christ and God.* **Let nobody deceive~| you** *with empty words, for because of these things God's wrath comes on the sons of disobedience."*

Some have the notion that God's grace is so forgiving that they can treat sin as though it doesn't make any difference. They say to themselves, "God loves me, so He will not harm me if I keep sinning."

Paul wanted to be very clear that anyone who was *"[sexually] immoral, impure [or promiscuous], or greedy [lustful or covetous]"* was *"an idolater"* who had no place with Christ in heaven.

If the *"fear of the Lord"* means that God will do exactly as He says in His word, then we must *"flee youthful lusts"* (2 Tim 2:22), and *"flee sexual immorality"* (1 Cor 6:18). Even flippantly joking about such sins in conversations can encourage participation Paul had just said (Eph 5:4).

If we know God, our attitude toward sin has changed: *"For the grace of God has appeared, bringing salvation to all men, instructing us to deny ungodliness and worldly desires and to live sensibly, righteously and godly in the present age"* (Titus 2:11–12).

We are commanded to stop letting anybody *"deceive [us] with empty words"* (Eph 5:6). Some attempted to persuade the believers that there were no consequences to delving into sinful practices, since everything would be forgiven. *"Empty words"* are those without any biblical proof.

Why should anyone who knows God's attitude toward sin ever want to join in the sinful, pornographic, and lustful practices of the *"sons of disobedience"*? These self-destructive and filthy practices attract God's displeasure. The *"sons of disobedience"* are the *"children of wrath"* (Eph 2:2). Previously, believers may have practiced such *"darkness,"* but now they *"are light in the Lord [and are to] Walk as children of the light"* (5:8).

Evidence of God's Spirit in a believer is that sin is not the same; it brings a sense of shame and guilt, but before it was a pleasure. The Spirit comes to *"convict the world of sin"* (Jn 16:8). Do not quench the Spirit's conviction, but repent and take steps to avoid any behavior that dishonors our Savior

"Sin is so prevalent around me that sometimes it loses its awfulness and offensiveness to me. Teach me to despise sin as You do."

JANUARY 27

Do Not Continue in Unbelief

John 20:27—*"Then he said to Thomas, '***Put***~~ your finger here, and* ***examine*****~ my hands.* ***Extend****~~ your hand and* ***put*****~ it into my side.* ***Do not continue****~/ in your unbelief, but believe.'"*

It is hard to understand how Jesus's disciples still did not "believe" in Him after three years. Thomas remained skeptical until given irrefutable proofs that Jesus had arisen from the dead. He saw Him die. It had been eight days, and he had heard the testimonies. But Thomas had not been there when Jesus appeared. This moment was planned specifically for Thomas. Jesus wanted to teach a visual lesson.

When Thomas saw Jesus, he recognized that He was very different from Lazarus, whom Jesus had restored to life. His was not a physical body subject to physical limitation, nor was he an apparition of a spirit, because he could be touched. Jesus also ate with them.

Here was a person with an entirely different form: a resurrected form that Jesus promised to all who believe in Him. Thomas became convinced by seeing and touching Him, and Jesus accepted his firm belief. Then Jesus said, "*Blessed are those who have not seen and yet have believed*" (Jn 20:29).

Thomas could have taken the word of his cohorts, but he wanted concrete evidence. In mercy, Jesus gave Thomas all that he needed and more. "*Put your finger here . . . Extend your hand and put it into my side.*" How foolish were his doubts that Jesus was truly alive, which could only mean one thing: Jesus was and had been God incarnate in human form those past three years. How foolish he must have felt for his doubts. He was standing in the presence of God.

In humble submission and conviction, Thomas declared, "*My Lord and my God!*" He thought, "You really are who You said You were!" As far as we know, his life was never the same. Tradition says that Thomas would carry the news of Jesus's life and resurrection to the shores of India.

Jesus said, "*Do not [be continuing] in your unbelief, but believe.*" We can trust the record of Scripture that He is real and alive today. "*Faith comes from what is heard, and what is heard comes through the word of Christ*" (Rom 10:17). Sufficient evidence has been recorded for all time in God's word. We must decide to trust it—all of it—without doubting.

"Lord, from my heart I want to demonstrate my trust in Your word. Give me courage to act on what I know from it without needing any special signs or confirmations to practice all Your commands."

Fear the Right Person

Luke 12:4–5—*"And I say to you, My friends, do not fear those who kill the body, and after that have nothing more that they can do. But I will warn you whom you should fear:* **Fear*~ the one** *who, after the killing, has authority to throw you into hell. Yes, I tell you,* **fear*~him***!"*

Jesus commanded his disciples to be fearless even when threatened with physical death for proclaiming the good news. At worst, the opposition can only bring about physical death, which is meaningless in comparison to eternity in hell. Jesus was advising the disciples that faithfulness to Him would likely result in a death sentence from the state, but it was not to be feared—it was to be welcomed!

God commands us to fear Him. Whomever you fear, you will obey. When people fear the authorities are watching or will find out about their actions, they tend to obey to the laws.

Likewise, Christians can become presumptuous because of God's patience, deceiving themselves into believing that God will do nothing. They think He is too loving and forgiving to punish them. Satan deceived Eve into believing that God would do nothing if she disobeyed. When she believed the lie, she became vulnerable to disobedience.

Proverbs 1:7 says, *"The fear of the Lord is the beginning of knowledge, but fools despise wisdom and discipline."* The first lesson a believer should learn—the beginning of wisdom—is that it is a painful experience to disobey our Lord. The author of Hebrews wrote, *"My son, do not despise the chastening of the Lord. Nor be discouraged when you are rebuked by Him. For whom the Lord loves He chastens. And scourges every son whom He receives . . . But if you are without chastening, of which all have become partakers, then you are illegitimate and not sons"* (Heb 12:5–6). Christians are forgiven their sins, but God will teach us not to be disobedient by certain chastisement.

If we do not fear God's promise of chastisement, then we tend to be morally loose. If we fear that He will do what He says in His word, then we begin to take His commands seriously. This is a healthy motivation to learn what God expects of us as His children—this is where wisdom begins.

"The fear of criticism or what others will say is so debilitating that I am more interested in preserving my ego and aggrandizing my reputation than in following You. Give me an opportunity today to demonstrate to You my courage to be unashamed."

See or Examine Our Sonship

1 John 3:1—*"See*~ **what sort of love** the Father has given to us: that we should be called God's children—and indeed we are! For this reason the world does not know us: because it did not know him."*

It may seem strange that a command would be necessary for us to "see" the manifestations of the Father's love, but we cannot forget it.

The imperative form means to "urgently decide to stare at," or to "become acquainted with by experience." Our Father's love for us must be ever present in our minds. It must become sufficient for us. It must fill our souls.

John had just told the readers how to see the reality of the new birth as it transforms into godly behavior, and now he commands the reader to meditate on the greatness of God's love.

The specific focus of God's love is that He has graciously decided to call us His "children" (lit. "genuine descendants"). The privilege of being earthly royalty pales in comparison to being part of the family of God. According to John 1:12 God graciously gave us the right to be His "children."

The expression *"what sort of love"* is a translation of a word meaning "how great, or something beyond what has previously been experienced." How could the holy and majestic God of all creation welcome into His family the vilest of sinners (us) who have done everything that He abhors? We can never imagine how much God afflicted His Son on the cross so that He could be just in forgiving us. We can only marvel that He was willing to allow Jesus to suffer cruelly in order to accept us as His children and be just in doing so, that is, Jesus' agony was how much God hates sin.

John warns that we should not draw the wrong conclusion. This privilege does not mean that we will be treated like royalty in *this* life. We should not expect any different treatment than His Son, Jesus, received in this world, because "it did not know him."

Our self-worth does not come from the world's acceptance; it comes from the assurance that God has taken us into His family as His beloved children. This is a far greater value than being the son of an earthly king. Is this enough to satisfy your heart's needs now?

"Lord, nothing in this life compares to knowing that in Your sight I am considered Your child and forever accepted in Your family. Thank You."

JANUARY 30

Reside in Him or His Teachings

1 John 2:27—*"Now as for you, the anointing that you received from him resides in you, and you have no need for anyone to teach you. But as his anointing teaches you about all things, it is true and is not a lie. Just as it has taught you, you* **reside~~ in him**.*"*

Since the beginning of time, and especially in the age of the church, the evil one has sought to lead God's people astray. Jesus warned the disciples that *"many will come in my name, claiming, 'I am the Christ,' and deceive man"* (Matt 24:4–5). John's readers were not deceived yet, but deceivers were active.

The readers were assured that the *"anointing that [they] received from him resides in [them]."* All believers have received the "anointing"—that is, the Holy Spirit—at the time of their conversion. Paul clarified this in Romans 8:9: *"If anyone does not have the Spirit of Christ, he does not belong to Christ."*

In 1 John 4:1, John wrote to *"test the spirits"* in order to discern the true from the false teachings. All believers have the same capability. A key test is to recognize whether the new teaching contradicts the inspired word of God as already revealed in the Bible.

The power of the gospel (Rom 1:16) is the ability of the Holy Spirit to "convict" or "convince" the world of sin (Jn 16:8). The Spirit can teach even the unsaved of their need of a Savior.

False teachers will become more prevalent in the end times according to 1 Timothy 4:1–2: *"Now, the Spirit speaks expressly, that in the latter times some shall depart from the faith, giving heed to seducing spirits, and doctrines of devils, speaking lies in hypocrisy; having their conscience seared with a hot iron."* Demons can whisper into a receptive mind ideas that appear to be new insights or revelations.

Following the declaration that the *"anointing . . . resides in you"* comes the command to *"continually always be residing in him [or it]."* The latter pronoun could be rendered "it"—that is, as the Spirit convinces you of what is true, abide in it. Do you consciously decide to live by what you learn in His word each day?

"My life has been given to You. By day and by night Your presence is my joy and satisfaction. Your word teaches me all about You, and I want to live in its light today."

JANUARY 31

Have Faith in God

Mark 11:22—*"Jesus said to them, '**Have**~~ **faith** in God."*

Teaching moments are spontaneous opportunities to illustrate an important principle or truth. During a Jewish holiday, Jesus and His disciples had been walking back and forth from Bethany to Jerusalem. The previous morning, they walked past a fig tree that was barren of fruit. Strangely, He declared, *"Let no one eat fruit from you ever again"* (Mark 11:14). He was setting up a future teaching moment.

The next morning, walking back into Jerusalem, they passed this same fig tree, only now *"the fig tree dried up from the roots"* (Mark 11:20). Shocked, Peter exclaimed, *"Rabbi, look! The fig tree which You cursed has withered away"* (11:21), to which Jesus replied, *"Have faith in God."*

The disciples were to have an unwavering trust in the omnipotent God who can do anything that He wills to do for His own purposes. The key to an unconditional faith is to have a "no-matter-what" trust and an "anything-is-possible" kind of confidence in the God who cares; though He may seem silent at time, He is always present and can change things any time He wants.

If you fully give your life over to God (Rom 12:1–2), then whatever God allows to happen in your life is OK. It belongs to Him. He can do with it whatever He wants, even if that means tragedies or miraculous interventions. Either one is OK, since now your life belongs to Jesus. He makes no mistakes.

The one who learns to trust God fully knows He can be trusted with however He may decide to answer to his prayers. Jesus continues in the next verse, *"For assuredly, I say to you, whoever says to this mountain, 'Be removed and be cast into the sea,' and does not doubt in his heart, but believes that those things he says will be done, he will have whatever he says"* (Mark 11:23).

Jesus, by using hyperbole, illustrated the virtually limitless possibilities for the believer with faith who *"does not doubt in his heart."*

Earlier Jesus had said, *"With men it is impossible, but not with God; for with God all things are possible"* (Mark 10:27). As committed as you are to His word and purpose in life, you can count on His power to assist you to accomplish His will and purpose for your life. "Have faith..."

"Father, Thank you for the lesson of the fig tree. My heart's desire is to bear fruit for you. Give me wisdom to show You how much I love You by how I care for all those that are Your family."

Accept Your Share of the Suffering

2 Tim 1:8—*"So do not be ashamed of the testimony about our Lord or of me, a prisoner for his sake, but by God's power **accept your share of suffering***~ for the gospel."*

How could we ever be ashamed of Christ, the King of kings and Lord of lords, especially in front of strangers we will never see again? To be caught with gospel tracts in our possession or a Bible in hand would signal to everyone that we are followers of Jesus. Then we must be fanatics! By the way, the word *fanatic* means being a "fan" of someone. Why should we be ashamed to be fans of Jesus?

In 2 Timothy 1:8, Paul commands Timothy to not be ashamed of being identified with him as a prisoner or with the gospel of Christ. In AD 66, to be identified as a Christian brought persecution, yet Paul commanded Timothy to accept his "share of suffering for the gospel." We share in the suffering now, then the glory later.

Paul never saw his imprisonment as a bad thing. He only saw it as an opportunity to spread the gospel. Could you have thought of a better way to spread the gospel throughout the Praetorian Guard?

Paul considered himself a "prisoner for His sake." He wrote to the believers at Philippi, *"Now I want you to know, brethren, that my circumstances have turned out for the greater progress of the gospel, so that my imprisonment in the cause of Christ has become well known throughout the whole Praetorian Guard and to everyone else, and that most of the brethren, trusting in the Lord because of my imprisonment, have far more courage to speak the word of God without fear"* (Phil 1:12–14). This made it worthwhile.

The command of the passage is for Timothy to share in Paul's highest purpose in life: to *"know [Christ] and the power of His resurrection and the fellowship of His sufferings, being conformed to His death"* (Phil 3:10).

Any time a sinner is confronted with his sin, he may respond negatively, but this is a risk we have to take. *"God's power"* gives us grace to endure anything. However, the grace only flows when needed. We can count on it.

"Lord, my self-protective interests have kept me silent too often, especially when I knew I would be criticized for openly identifying with You. I feel so ashamed. Please give me strength today to point someone to You."

Accumulate Treasure in Heaven

Matt 6:20—*"But **accumulate**~~ **for yourselves** treasures in heaven, where moth and rust do not destroy, and thieves do not break in and steal."*

The greatest financial strategy is heavenly savings. Christ commands us to accumulate treasures in heaven. How do we do it?

Paul was grateful to the Philippian church for their support of his ministry: *"Now you Philippians know also that in the beginning of the gospel, when I departed from Macedonia, no church shared with me concerning giving and receiving but you only. For even in Thessalonica you sent aid once and again for my necessities"* (Phil 4:15–16).

To put this in perspective, Thessalonica was about sixty miles (100 km) from Philippi, and Paul was there approximately four to six weeks. Someone had to walk the distance round trip twice with their financial support ("once and again," Phil 4:16). No wonder Paul described their generosity as "a sweet-smelling aroma, an acceptable sacrifice, well pleasing to God" (Phil 4:18).

Paul expresses the eternal perspective of this transaction of generosity in Philippians 4:17: *"Not that I seek the gift, but I seek the fruit that abounds to your account."* Paul encouraged them to share in the ministry because there is a record kept in heaven that registers all such generosity.

Giving to the poor to assist in their needs will *"provide yourselves money bags ... a treasure in the heavens that does not fail"* (Luke 12:33). Sacrificing your goods to benefit others is another means for transferring treasures to heaven, especially if it facilitates the spread of the gospel.

When such sacrifices are measured, God will probably outlandishly exaggerate our rewards according to however He may wish to express His appreciation for our sacrifice in His kingdom (Luke 6:23; 1 Cor 4:5). We are His voice, hands, feet, and wallet to bless and aid the needy and the lost in the compassion of Christ.

God weighs our motives and the benefits of all our actions to His kingdom to determine how we are to be rewarded. We must guard our hearts from selfish interests. The only long-term, significant investment with high returns is to be a resource and an instrument for the kingdom of our Lord Jesus.

"Lord, teach me Your priorities and give me grace to make them mine. Help me see the opportunities to advance Your kingdom."

Rejoice in the Degree of Your Suffering

1 Pet 4:13—*"But **rejoice**~~ in the degree that you have shared in the sufferings of Christ, so that when his glory is revealed you may also rejoice and be glad."*

There is a camaraderie experienced when people suffer together, even for a short time. What will we discuss throughout eternity? Business deals? Fun we had? Or sacrifices we made for our Savior?

If we are on the same team as our suffering Savior, then perhaps we should not expect to be popular when He was not. The reason for rejoicing now is twofold: first, because we share a similar experience with Jesus, and second, because something special awaits the unashamed believer when Jesus returns.

Paul wrote to the Romans, *"We are children of God, and if children, then heirs, heirs of God and joint heirs with Christ—if, in fact, we suffer with him so that we many also be glorified with Him"* (Rom 8:16–17). If we identify with Christ in His reproach of this world, then it shows our identification with Him and demonstrates that our faith is genuine. The depth of our joy in Christ's return or in meeting Him in glory is directly proportional to our disposition to suffer with Christ now.

This is not a reference to suffering from sickness, mistakes, accidents, or foolish decisions that have nothing to do with the ministry or identifying with Christ in the public marketplace.

The next verse specifies the issue: *"If you are insulted for the name of Christ, you are blessed, because the Spirit of glory and of God rests upon you"* (1 Pet 4:14). Peter could not forget the words of Jesus: *"Blessed are you when people insult you, persecute you and falsely say all kinds of evil against you because of Me"* (Matt 5:11[NIV]).

A special grace comes on a person under this kind of attack to remain true to Christ with a special bond to Him. It is a deep joy to know the Lord observes our bitter experiences and is with us, sharing in our hurt. Furthermore, He will make it more than worthwhile in His glory. Be encouraged today to be unashamed of belonging to Jesus.

"Today may I experience the camaraderie of the ranks of the unashamed and bold who wear the banner of Christ across their chests with pride."

FEBRUARY 4

Do Not Suffer as an Evildoer

1 Pet 4:15—*"But **let none of you suffer**~~ **as a murderer** or thief or criminal or as a troublemaker."*

There are many types of suffering. Not all suffering has the promise of the Holy Spirit's relief. Violation of the law can result in penalty or prison. Criminals just have to take their punishment and learn from it.

The command in 1 Peter is understandable, yet the addition of the word *troublemaker* in the list might seem surprising. The term means a "troublesome meddler," and it is only used here in the New Testament. The comparatively minor term in this list means an "agitator" or "one who meddles in things alien to his calling."

Paul corrected similar unchristian conduct Thessalonica: *"We hear that some among you are leading an undisciplined life, doing no work at all, but acting like busybodies. Now such persons we command and exhort in the Lord Jesus Christ to work in quiet fashion and eat their own bread"* (2 Thes 3:11–12).

Christians are not to be troublemakers or agitators in work or society. We are to be obedient, speak evil of no one, avoid quarreling, and show perfect courtesy toward all people (Titus 3:1–2).

This appears to restrict political activism and civil agitation or illegal activity against a government. Punishment for this type of activity is not considered biblical persecution, though it may be considered political persecution. Ours is a concern for the gospel awareness, not a perfect government!

In the mind of unbelievers, discrediting a Christian discredits the gospel, and Christianity becomes merely another religion of hypocrites. On the other hand, when Christians are persecuted merely for being faithful to the word, confronting sinners with their sins (even though done in love), or quietly sharing their faith in a respectful and conversational manner, the result is the opposite.

If a Christian is willing to endure ridicule and persecution for his or her faith, then there must be something genuine to consider. May our lives always provoke the thought in others that our God is real and alive and that He is the cause for our motivation and lifestyle.

"May Your grace in my life keep me from foolish acts or reactions that would bring disgrace to Your name."

FEBRUARY 5

Beware, God Will Do What He Says

Acts 13:40—*"Watch out~~, then, that what is spoken about by the prophets does not happen to you."*

God's word is to be taken seriously. Satan's initial attack to Eve was to deny that God would do what He said He would (Gen 3:4). Once Eve was not afraid that God would punish her, she was open to further temptation and disobedience.

In Acts 13:40 Paul was on his first evangelistic missionary journey into the interior of modern-day Turkey in a small Jewish synagogue in Pisidian Antioch after a dangerous hundred-mile trek across the Taurus mountain range.

At the conclusion of his sermon (13:16–41), Paul quoted Habakkuk 1:5, which warned Israel that if they did not repent, God would raise up Babylon to destroy Israel. It probably did not seem a likely threat at the time, so the prophet's warnings were ignored. They had no fear that God would do what He said, so why pay attention to His prophet?

Now Paul's warning was for Israel to repent of their self-righteous pride then to confess their sins, accepting Christ's forgiveness (Acts 13:38), and trust in His justification *"from all things from which [they] could not be justified by the law of Moses"* (13:39). The law was given to reveal our need for a Savior (Gal 3:24), not as a means to save us.

No matter how "good" you might be, it cannot erase your sins; in fact, Isaiah wrote, *"All our righteousnesses are like filthy rags"* (Isa 64:6) because they are so tainted with our sins. Our only hope is for God to provide the gift of forgiveness through a substitutionary payment for our sins, which is why Jesus shed His blood on the cross.

Paul quoted Habakkuk: *"I work a work in your days, a work which you will by no means believe, though one were to declare it to you"* (Acts 13:41). Now Paul warned Israel again, but they could not believe God would do anything to Israel.

Yet in twenty years Israel would be destroyed as a nation. They had no fear that God meant what He said through His apostle, so they ignored his message. If God judged Israel, He will do it to anyone who ignores Him. Are you afraid of being disobedient to His word?

"Lord, help me respect the commands in Your word above all things."

FEBRUARY 6

Do Not Be Surprised by Suffering

1 Pet 4:12—*"Dear friends, **do not be astonished**~/ that a trial by fire is occurring among you, as though something strange were happening to you."*

Jesus warned us, *"If the world hates you, you know that it has hated Me before it hated you"* (Jn 15:18). The horror of a "trial by fire" must have been terrifying during the time of the Neronian persecution, when Christians were used as living torches in the imperial gardens at night.

Persecution and suffering are part of God's plan to perfect Christians. Peter wrote, *"In this you rejoice, though now for a little while, if necessary, you have been grieved by various trials, so that the tested genuineness of your faith—more precious than gold that perishes though it is tested by fire—may be found to result in praise and glory and honor at the revelation of Jesus Christ"* (1 Pet 1:6–7). The phrase *"if necessary"* means some may avoid this experience, at least in its severity, but not everyone. Peter has these instructions for us about persecution:

False accusations. *"Keep your conduct among the [unbelieving] Gentiles honorable, so that when they speak against you as evildoers, they may see your good deeds and glorify God on the day of visitation"* (1 Pet 2:12).

Ridicule. *"Do not repay evil for evil or reviling for reviling, but on the contrary, bless, for to this you were called, that you may obtain a blessing"* (1 Pet 1:9).

Maligning. *"With respect to this they are surprised when you do not join them in the same flood of debauchery, and they malign you"* (1 Pet 4:4).

Godly men and women who stand for the gospel have universally been ridiculed, tortured, and killed. Millions have gone through far more than we will ever have to suffer, not to mention what our Savior suffered on our behalf. Dare we ever shrink back from the little that God allows us to suffer for His name's sake? How will we stand before our Savior with rejoicing if we were ashamed of Him in our little world and brief time on earth?

Paul put it this way: *"I consider that the sufferings of this present time are not worth comparing with the glory that is to be revealed to us"* (Rom 8:18). Meditate on how much you are willing to suffer for Christ and why.

"Help me anticipate the denunciation of unbelievers and accept their rejections with Your grace and patience toward them."

Be Sober and Alert against the Devil

1 Peter 5:8—*"**Be sober***~ **and alert***~. Your enemy the devil, like a roaring lion, is on the prowl looking for someone to devour."*

In the Christian life, we are called to *"urgently decide to be sober and alert"* because an enemy *"is on the prowl."* To be *sober* means to be "calm and collected in spirit, [or] temperate and dispassionate."

This attitude allows us to look at reality with a clear mind, in full control of our disposition. In the fullness of the Spirit this attribute becomes one of the characteristics that marks a Spirit-filled person ("self-control", Gal 5:22).

To be *alert* means to "watch, give attention to [especially to God's revelation], or be watchful for opportunities and dangers, both internal and external forces seeking to harm or destroy." Jesus warned Peter just before his betrayal, *"Simon, Simon, Satan has asked to sift you as wheat. But I have prayed for you, Simon, that your faith not fail"* (Luke 22:31–32). A few hours later, Peter was careless to watch and pray (Matt 26:41), which led to his denial of the Lord Jesus.

Satan accuses the Christian in the presence of God (Rev 12:10) as he did in the Old Testament times (Zech 3:1–5; Job 1:6). Furthermore, the world is under the power of this "evil one." Peter described Satan as a *"roaring lion . . . looking for someone to devour."* Humans are no match for this most powerful enemy.

Jesus taught His disciples to pray, *"Deliver us from the evil one"* (Matt 6:31). John declared that believers *"have conquered him by the blood of the Lamb and by the word of their testimony, for they loved not their lives even unto death"* (Rev 12:11); nevertheless, believers must always be alert *"against the devil's schemes"* (Eph 6:11) and protect themselves with spiritual armor (6:11–18).

Martin Luther wrote in his hymn "A Might Fortress Is Our God," "The prince of darkness grim, we tremble not for him; His rage we can endure, for lo! His doom is sure, one little Word shall fell him."

"Lord, keep me from being deceived by the evil one. May I avoid emotional reactions to circumstances today and instead see every encounter as a divine opportunity to share Your wisdom."

FEBRUARY 8

Resist the Devil

1 Peter 5:9—*"Resist him*~, strong in your faith, because you know that your brothers and sisters throughout the world are enduring the same kinds of suffering."*

The believer must know the tactics of the enemy and how to resist him. The word *resist* means to "stand against or oppose." In James 4:7, we are told to *"submit to God. Resist the devil and he will flee from you."* We have the authority to resist Satan, and the promise that he will flee.

First, Satan uses the alluring temptation of sensuality, fame, or greed and relies on our curiosity as long as we believe the lie that the world can satisfy our needs: *"Love not the world nor the things in the world . . . For all that is in the world, the lust of the flesh and the lust of the eyes and the boastful pride of life, is not from the Father, but is from the world."* (1 Jn 2:15–16).

Second, Satan attacks our marriage and family relations. God's design is that man's sensual satisfactions and soul-mate companionship are met in a healthy marriage relationship for life: *"The husband must fulfill his duty to his wife [sexually], and likewise also the wife to her husband . . . Stop depriving one another, except by agreement for a time, so that you may devote yourselves to prayer, and come together again **so that** Satan will not tempt you because of your lack of self-control"* (1 Cor 7:3,5).

Third, Satan attacks us through the false ideas, arguments, or teachings that occur to our minds. Satan can induce ideas or concepts that appear to be reasonable, correct, or novel. Paul wrote in 1 Timothy 4:1, *"Now the Spirit expressly says that in latter times some will depart from the faith, giving heed to deceiving spirits and doctrines of demons."* These attacks seem reasonable enough that we begin to believe these errors.

In every realm of attack, Satan seeks to justify selfishness, self-exaltation, and self-will in our lives. So we must bring *"every thought into captivity to the obedience of Christ"* (2 Cor 10:5). Recognize Satan's lies and resist them.

"When discouragement and depression dominate my spirit, may I recognize the influence of demons and resist them by Your authority. "

FEBRUARY 9

Arm Yourself with Realistic Thinking

1 Pet 4:1—*"So, since Christ suffered in the flesh, you also **arm***~ **yourselves** with the same attitude, because the one who has suffered in the flesh has finished with sin."*

In 1 Peter 4:1, Peter is calling the churches to "urgently decide to arm" themselves—that is, to "furnish themselves with arms" or metaphorically "to take on the same mind-set" with a positive attitude toward dying for our Lord.

In the early church, many eagerly anticipated when it would be their turn to die for Christ, considering it their highest honor. Jesus spoke about this attitude: *"If anyone wishes to come after Me, he must deny himself, and take up his cross daily and follow Me"* (Luke 9:23).

We like to spiritualize the "cross" to mean anything from physical hardships to difficulties. However, Jesus was serious when He said, *"He who does not take his cross and follow after Me is not worthy of Me. He who has found his life [guarding it for himself] will lose it, and he who has lost his life for My sake will find it"* (Matt 10:38–39).

The willingness to suffer results in one who *"has finished with sin."* This is a perfect tense verb, meaning a completed action that has present effects. As a result of this mental preparation, fleshly sins or clinging to this life now have no attraction or meaning.

Jesus came to earth intentionally to die for others by bearing their sins; we can't do this, but we *can* arm ourselves with His attitude: *"for the joy that was set before Him [, He] endured the cross"* (Heb 12:2).

The worst that can happen to us as believers is that we suffer death, which is truly the best thing that could happen because it means that our battle with sin is finally over.

Most believers die from accidents or diseases, but the glorious possibility of dying for Christ gives these verses richer meaning and deeper encouragement: *"But when . . . this mortal will have put on immortality, then will come about the saying that is written, 'Death is swallowed up in victory. O death, where is your victory? O death, where is your sting?'"* (1 Cor 15:54–56). Can you meditate on these concepts until death, especially if it is for Christ's testimony, is welcomed?

"Lord, help me prize the negative reactions of those who make fun of Your name. The honor to be identified with You is worth more than popularity."

Do Not Lose God's Perspective of Time

2 Pet 3:8—*"Now, dear friends,* **do not let this one thing escape your notice~/, that** *a single day is like a thousand years with the Lord and a thousand years are like a single day."*

In 2 Peter 3:8, Peter has been discussing the return of Christ. Some doubted He would ever return. The Lord Jesus will return to earth, as promised, but in God's timetable. His word promises that He will return (Acts 1:11), but He has delayed that return *"not willing that any should perish, but that all should come to repentance"* (3:9). There is a plan to His delay, and it has to do with the offering of salvation worldwide.

Jesus was asked, *"Tell us, when will all this happen? What sign will signal your return and the end of the world?"* (Matt 24:3). After giving a number of catastrophic signs, Jesus concluded with a categorical statement: *"This gospel of the kingdom will be preached in all the world as a witness to all the nations* [Gk. *ethnos*, or ethnic people groups], *then the end will come"* (24:14). Mat 24:15-36 deals with the horrible seven years of *"great tribulation"* (24:21), which will begin after Jesus returns to rapture all the believers living on earth (1 Thes 4:15–17).

The fulfillment of the Great Commission (Matt 28:19–20), which mandates the approximate 1,600 unreached people groups with no gospel message in their language must become the priority of the global church. This must be why Jesus is delaying His return. Jesus waits for the church to complete the one thing He told them to do: *"Make disciples of all nations."*

Why does Christ not return? He is committed to letting every language group on earth hear of His sacrificial death on the cross before He returns. Peter literally writes, *"Stop letting this one thing escape your notice,"* because he wants us all to recognize that there is a purpose to Jesus's delay.

We are getting close. At the beginning of the opening of the seven-sealed book in heaven or at the beginning of the tribulation, there are already some from *"every tribe, language, people and nation [ethnos]"* (Rev 5:9). Someone accomplishes the mission! Pioneers and translators are still needed. Will you pray for this mission?

"Father, I want every day to be as important to me as a thousand years. Help me see every encounter as part of Your divine purpose, and give me courage to make them count for eternity."

FEBRUARY 11

Do Not Be Surprised if the World Hates You

1 Jn 3:13—*"Therefore **do not be surprised~**/, brothers and sisters, if the world hates you."*

Jesus warned His disciples that they would be hated (Jn 15:18–19) just as He had been. Today there is a strong undercurrent of disdain for Christians everywhere.

The implication of the negative present tense verb is to "stop being surprised," implying that these believers were astonished by how much the world hated them. John is telling them to cease being surprised. Just as Cain unreasonably hated Abel and sought to kill him, so the world will be delighted to eliminate all true Christians.

A core part of Christianity is its willingness to be rejected by the majority. Attempting to be popular and acceptable leads to compromise, syncretism, or excessive temptations. Being dispised is understood as a part of the Christian life. It is the cross we are commanded to bear.

The attempts of believers to minimize this hatred against Christians by seeking *"friendship with the world"* James declares as *"enmity with God . . . Therefore whoever wishes to be a friend of the world makes himself an enemy of God"* (James 4:4). This is distinct from loving the world as God does. This passage means to seek or desire what the world offers for selfish satisfaction and pleasure.

Since true believers do not need worldly things or pleasures for meaning and fulfillment in life, they seem strange and different. When the believers decided not to participate in the world's excesses, they were considered an unsociable group, a counterculture, or an anomaly; they were seen as rejecting the traditions of the nation. They suddenly were viewed as aliens, enemies, and virtual traitors.

The writer of Hebrews put it this way: *"Therefore Jesus also, that He might sanctify the people with His own blood, suffered outside the gate. Therefore, let us go forth to Him, outside the camp, bearing His reproach. For here we have no continuing city, but we seek the one to come"* (Heb 13:12–14). Don't be surprised by the world's "reproach"; rather, anticipate it—yea, welcome it!

"Forgive me, Lord Jesus, for wanting to be more a friend of the world than part of the unashamed friends that follow You so closely. Teach me to be content to be faithful to You regardless of how I am treated."

FEBRUARY 12

Do Not Make an Offering without Reconciling

Matt 5:23–24—*"So if you are offering your gift at the altar and there remember that your brother has something against you,* **leave***~ **your gift** *there in front of the altar. First* **go**~~ **and be reconciled***~ *to your brother and then* **come***~ **and present** *~~ your gift."*

So many of us believe that we can perform a valid spiritual act regardless of the condition of our hearts. Even more deceptive is the belief we can separate our relationship with God from our relationship with our fellow believers.

In the first case, there is no ceremony or sacrificial spiritual act of worship that can change your spiritual relationship with God. Jesus is saying God will not accept an act of worship that does not include the mending of any broken or offended relationship with a fellow believer.

In the second case, we are only pretending—that is, faking—in any act of worship if we have offended a brother. Any brother, whether we like him or not, is part of the body of Christ. Just as when Paul was persecuting Christians and Jesus asked him, *"Saul, Saul, why are you persecuting Me?"* (Acts 9), so anything done (good or bad) to a Christian brother is equally done directly to Jesus.

The over-arching principle is this: A believer's relationship with the Lord is no better than his relationship with his brothers in Christ. If we have gossiped about, criticized, or verbally abused a brother, hurting him or his reputation, then we have done the same hurt to Jesus, with the result that He is grieved just as the brother is grieved by our actions. Anyone who thinks he has the right to hurt, crush, or humiliate a subordinate brother is inflicting the same hurt to the Savior. If grieving Jesus means anything, then repentance is in order.

The tense of the aorist command is to *"urgently decide to be reconciled"* to your brother. Decide now to make amends. The verb *reconcile* means to "change the mind of anyone," or to "renew friendship with someone." Do not wait around until the other person changes or comes and asks forgiveness. Do not believe that it will pass, be forgotten, or get better with time. Just as you would humble yourself before the Lord for having offended Him, so you should go and reconcile with whomever you have offended, persuading him of your sorrow for hurting him (with no attempt to justify your action or words). The objective is to restore the relationship and the sense of oneness in Christ. Only then can we worship our Lord with sincerity.

"Why do I continue to think I can have an intimate relationship with You while I hurt others with my tongue or refuse to humble myself to ask forgiveness? Lord, keep me from living in denial so I can please You."

FEBRUARY 13

Submit Yourselves to God

James 4:7a—"*So submit**~ *to God.*"

James begins a series of ten commands with the command to "*immediately decide to submit yourself*" to God. The word used for *submit* literally means "to submit to someone's control, to yield to admonition or advice, to surrender voluntarily, or to obey."

It is a Greek military term meaning "to arrange [troop divisions] in a military fashion under the command of a leader." In a nonmilitary usage, it means "a voluntary attitude of giving in, cooperating, assuming responsibility, and carrying a burden."

Just as the army teaches a soldier that he must submit to orders regardless of the risk to his life because of his duty and love of country, so the believer is to submit to God's directives. Submission is measured by obedience to expressed commands.

Submission is a key characteristic of the Christian community: children are to be submissive to their parents; wives to husbands; slaves to masters; and everyone to governing authorities and to the rules of society.

All believers are to be submissive to their elders and pastors and to the biblical rules within their congregation, and they are to be mutually submissive to one another, just like a married couple. Rebellion to authority in your sphere of life is contrary to God's intended order.

Submission to God is the expression of humility, which has great promise: "*God opposes the proud, but gives grace to the humble. Submit yourselves therefore to God*" (James 4:6–7). Humility is the evident manifestation of your submissive spirit to God. Later, James wrote, "*Humble yourselves before the Lord, and He will exalt you*" (4:10).

Submission to God means to have resigned your self-will in this life and to be subject to His Word, ready to listen to Him and obey Him. If we are to submit to God, then we must learn all that He expects of us, yield our will to him, and practice His directives. Can we say to God, "Your wish is my command"?

"Lord, in my mind I want to give You my life, but my selfish heart wants to hold back to make sure I get all I want out of life. Teach me to desire all that You want out of my life."

Draw Near to God

James 4:8a—*"**Draw near*~ to God** and he will draw near to you."*

There is no possibility of faking this commitment. Matthew warned of seeking God for selfish motives when he wrote, *"These people draw near with their mouth and honor Me with their lips, but their hearts are far from Me, and in vain they worship Me, teaching as doctrines the commandments of men"* (Matt 15:8–9). Do you really want to get closer to God?

David counseled his son Solomon with similar words: *"Know the God of your father, and serve Him with a whole heart and a willing mind; for the Lord searches all hearts, and understands every intent of the thoughts. If you seek Him, He will let you find Him"* (1 Chron 28:9).

There is nothing that God delights in as much as intimate fellowship with His creatures. John wrote, *"And I, if I am lifted up from the earth [referring to the cross], will draw all people to Myself"* (12:32). There is no question that God wants us to walk closely with Him, agreeing with everything He says and trusting that His way is best.

In Hebrews we read, *"Let us draw near with confidence to the throne of grace, so that we may receive mercy and find grace to help in time of need . . . Let us draw near with a sincere heart in full assurance of faith, having our hearts sprinkled clean from an evil conscience and our bodies washed with pure water"* (Heb 4:16; 10:22).

The heart cry of the redeemed is for deeper communion with God. The psalmist describes this passion for God: *"My heart says of you, 'Seek His face!' Your face, Lord, I will seek"* (Psa 27:8). Then he wrote, *"O God, you are my God, earnestly I seek you; my soul thirsts for you. My body longs for you, in a dry and weary land where there is no water. I have seen you in the sanctuary and beheld your power and your glory. Because your love is better than life, my lips will glorify you. I will praise you as long as I live"* (63:1–4).

The more we are assured of His complete forgiveness of all our sins, and the more we understand the horrible price our Savior paid to be able to forgive us, the more we will want to trust Him and know Him intimately.

"Jesus, when I worship You in our gatherings, it is so easy to sing the songs and feel Your presence in the phrases we sing to You, but I wonder if I truly love the lost as You do. I don't want to be near You just to feel good; I want to be near You to be like You."

FEBRUARY 15
Take the Lord's Supper

1 Cor 11:24—*"And when He had given thanks, He broke it and said, 'Take*~, eat*~; this is My body which is broken for you; do~~ this in remembrance of Me."*

There are only two observances Jesus told His disciples to practice in obedience and honor to Him: baptism and the Lord's Supper. Paul received instruction of the Lord's Supper directly from Jesus during His post-resurrection appearances. Paul wrote, *"I received from the Lord what I also delivered to you"* (1 Cor 11:23).

As His last meal with His disciples began, Jesus *"took bread and gave thanks"* for the meal to come; then He made a statement: *"This is my body which is for you."* At the conclusion of this meal (1 Cor. 11:25), He took a cup of wine and said, *"This cup is the new covenant in my blood. Do this as often as you drink it, in remembrance of Me."*

The Bible does not teach a mystical view (that Christ is somehow mystically present in the elements) or a magical view (that Christ is physically present in the elements).

The command is the key to this passage: the churches are to *"be continually doing this [action] in remembrance of Me"* (i.e., to regularly or habitually remember the body and blood of Jesus given for the redemption of all sinful people). Could we forget what He did for us on the cross? The answer apparently is yes. We need to be reminded.

The Lord promised a new covenant to Israel in Jeremiah 31:33: *"I will put my law within them and write it on their hearts and minds. I will be their God and they will be my people."* Jesus now opens this covenant to all who put their trust in His death and the shedding of His blood for the cleansing of their sin. Jesus's sacrifice of a once-and-for-all payment for our sins demands a perpetual refreshing in our minds (Heb 9:23–28).

The purpose of the Lord's Supper is not a focus on the elements, or us, but a continual focus on Christ's death for us on the cross of Calvary. Does meditation on the cross still break your heart that God had to go to such extremes just so He could forgive your sins?

"As I focus on Your cross and what it took for You to pay for my sins, I feel so unworthy and increasingly committed to not hurt You or Your precious church body that You love.".

FEBRUARY 16

Examine Yourself, Then Eat and Drink Communion

1 Cor 11:28—*"A person **should examine himself**~~ **first**, and in this way let him eat~~ the bread and drink~~ of the cup."*

When believers gathered in the early church, they shared a meal with the Lord's Supper. How they practiced this meal became an issue.

The King James Version warns that *"whoever, therefore, eats the bread or drinks the cup of the Lord **unworthily** will be guilty of the body and blood of the Lord"* (1 Cor 11:27); other versions have translated *unworthily* correctly *"in an unworthy manner."* Many miss the fact that *unworthily* is an adverb, which modifies the action of the verb. The question is not whether we are worthy but whether the Lord's Supper is being shared in a manner that communicates the oneness of the body of Christ.

The context in 1 Corinthians 11:17–22 describes how the Lord's Supper had allowed social distinctions or other divisions to be evident in the church, especially at the Lord's Supper (11:18–19). Those who could bring food ate their food without sharing or waiting on others who might have needs (11:21–22), thus making some feel unwanted. Paul scolded them, *"Do you despise the church of God and humiliate those who have nothing?"* (11:22).

The exhortation to *"examine himself"* uses a word that means to habitually "scrutinize, or test" yourself to see if your actions, words, or life are building up the unity of the body of Christ or being divisive or hurtful to members of the body. It is all about the church.

The context can be extended to convey the principle of the passage: do all our actions convey to every member of our body that he or she is an important part of the body of Christ—the church—or do our attitudes isolate or reject others? This is the meaning of 1 Corinthians 11:29: *"Anyone who eats and drinks without discerning the body eats and drinks judgment on himself."* It is not the "body" of Christ in the elements but the body of Christ as the unity of the church that is the issue. Ignorance of this command can bring serious chastisement (11:29–30).

The church is to be a haven of acceptance and caring for one another. Let us constantly watch our attitudes and relationships toward our brothers and sisters in Christ. Remember, it is His body, or the church.

"Lord, help me be honest with myself to admit when I have offended one of Your children, and give me the courage to reconcile every relationship I may have hurt."

Be Glad and Rejoice Together

Phil 2:17—*"Yes, and if I am being poured out as a drink offering on the sacrifice and service of your faith, I am glad and rejoice with you all. For the same reason you also **be glad~~ and rejoice~~ with me.**"*

In Philippians 2:17, Paul is calling for the Philippian church to be as joyous as he was in his imprisonment and service for them. Paul referred to his potential death as being "poured out as a libation" (a Jewish drink offering) as an *"offering . . . of your faith"*—that is, he would stand firm for the clarity of the gospel regardless of criticism, ostracism, ridicule, torture, and possible martyrdom.

This was not expressed in a morbid, self-pitying sense but in the sense of privilege, honor, and glory for being a part of the salvation of the Philippians. Regardless of what it would cost Paul, he found great delight in helping others come to Christ and learn to walk with Him in the midst of their problems of life.

Ironically, the offering of one's life for the Lord and others brings a deep joy that external circumstances cannot quench. These believers live in the presence of the Lord all the time and find it wonderful. Peter had this attitude when he and the other apostles were flogged and ordered *"not to speak in the name of Jesus"*; nevertheless, they *"went on their way from the presence of the Council, rejoicing that they had been considered worthy to suffer shame for His name"* (Acts 5:40–41). Oh, to be counted worthy!

Selfless service for Christ and others is not a loss but an offering to God. Anything given up for Christ is replaced with something infinitely more valuable and gratifying. As Paul wrote, *"This light momentary affliction is preparing for us an eternal weight of glory beyond all comparison"* (2 Cor 4:17).

Peter challenged his readers, *"To the degree that you share the sufferings of Christ, keep on rejoicing, so that also at the revelation of His glory you may rejoice with exultation"* (1 Pet 4:13).

Can you look up from your circumstances and rejoice in Christ and then continue to pour out your life for others with joy today?

"Lord, give me friends that are willing to stand up for You in the public arena, and may we encourage each other."

FEBRUARY 18

Flee from Idolatry

1 Cor 10:14—*"Therefore, my beloved, **flee~~ from idolatry**."*

In 1 Corinthians 10:14, Paul uses the present progressive command to tell us to *"be constantly fleeing"* from idolatry, greed (1 Tim 4:10–11), *"youthful lusts"* (2 Tim 2:22), and *"sexual immorality"* (1 Cor 6:18). They have no part in a Christian's life.

Paul begins his exhortation with an assurance of intimate friendship: *"my beloved."* There are some things we warn children about without having to explain every detail ("Don't touch the hot stove!").

Those who submit to an idol are saying that someone or something is more valuable, more powerful, and more trustworthy than God By this act, they declare that the only true God is weak, self-seeking, and insufficient for meeting their needs; thus they cannot fully trust God. This opens them up to many temptations.

Since the fall of humanity, man has sought to make God in his own image. Since man's god is too weak to create all things, man must therefore speculate how things must have come to be by chance.

When we develop a theory that answers our questions, we become vain and proud, believing our theory to be fact. When we feel we have "figured it out," *reason* then becomes the god we choose to serve.

Whatever becomes the source of fulfillment, the resource for dependency, the focus for happiness, and the answer to all your questions about life has become your god.

However, there is no other God. God cannot be reduced to an image, nor can He be visualized by human minds. Supreme loyalty to personal ambitions, desires, possessions, fame, and so on can also become idolatry (Matt 6:21).

Covetousness is idolatry, as evidenced by greedy materialism (Eph 5:5). Lust or inordinate desires are idolatry; Paul described the *"enemies of the cross of Christ, whose end is destruction, whose god is their appetite, and whose glory is in their shame, who set their minds on earthly things"* (Phil 3:18–19). Have you substituted your loyalty to God with something else? Tell Him so.

"Lord, if only I could hate sin as You do. Teach me to never love anything that takes my heart from being true to You. Remind me today when choices arise that challenge my loyalty to You."

FEBRUARY 19

Treat Others as They Should Treat You

Luke 6:31—*"Treat~~ others in the same way that you would want them to treat you."*

The "Golden Rule" is not the gospel—that is, no one will go to heaven by following the Golden Rule or the Sermon on the Mount. These sermons are policies for living out the Christ life today. The teachings in this context focus on our attitudes. These are Christlike dispositions, not legal duties.

Luke showed us how to demonstrate God's unconditional love in our attitudes toward others: (1) love your enemies (6:27a); (2) do good to those who hate you (6:27b); (3) bless those who curse you (6:28a); (4) pray for those who mistreat you (6:28b); (5) do not retaliate (6:29a); (6) give freely (6:29b–30); and (7) treat others the way you want to be treated (6:31). The disciples were exhorted to have the same merciful attitude toward others that God had toward them.

Relationships are built on trust—that is, each party will protect the interests and needs of the other.

The secular tendency toward reciprocity as the basis of social relationships is motivated by the need for selfish personal benefit in return—that is, one acts in a generous way in order to make friends so the favor to them can be returned in the future. This social interaction is shallow, self-serving, and corrupting. It is merely another form of manipulation, which builds resentment instead of a relationship.

Our command is similar to saying, *"Love your neighbor."* The present-tense imperative means "to be continuously producing, [or] causing something to happen," especially for the benefit of another person in this context. The Golden Rule has no restrictions, because love is not dependent on the response of the other person.

Our actions toward others should not be determined by their reaction to us. Our objective is to reflect the attitude of God toward others. His patience, love, forgiveness, commitment, and care for sinners become our attitude at all times toward all people.

"My Savior, thank You for Your unconditional love for me, especially when I do not deserve it. Your example from Your word is ever before me. Keep me remembering how You cared for others."

FEBRUARY 20
Receive One Another

Rom 15:7—*"Receive one another~~, then, just as Christ also received you, to God's glory."*

Ideally, the church, a fellowship of the followers of Christ, should be the greatest haven for people with problems, yet some churches are just the opposite, as Paul wrote in 1 Corinthians 11:17[NIV]: *"Your meetings do more harm than good."*

We all need to have someone or a special group of people who fully and unconditionally accept us for who we are now. In such an environment, we do not have to change or pretend to be someone else; we are genuinely secure with this group of folks or this special person. We all crave this experience from the depths of our souls.

Furthermore, this deepest need of all people is *free*. It does not cost a penny, yet most Christians are stingy and make acceptance of others very expensive to acquire. This attitude is learned from childhood and secular social clubs, where the right clothing, the right physique, the right financial status or success, the right family heritage, and the right acquaintances are all essential to acceptance.

The church in Rome at this time was a mixture of Jews and Gentiles who naturally despised each other and socially ridiculed each other. In the church, this attitude was prohibited. All divisiveness, quarreling, contentiousness, and criticism were considered unacceptable, carnal behavior. Jesus warned in a parable that if one had received grace and forgiveness, he was obligated to demonstrate it to others or risk severe chastisement (Matt 18:23–33).

The present imperative *"to be constantly accepting"* means to continually "take to oneself, take along with oneself, or take as one's companion." We are commanded to act in this way *"as Christ also received [us],"* which, thankfully, was unconditional; now we must demonstrate the same. This is how to glorify God.

Singing praises means nothing without a Christlike attitude toward others. We must be as accepting, loving, and caring, just as He is, in order to give glory to God.

"Lord, You raise the bar so high for us to imitate. Some people are hard to accept, even those who claim to follow You. Teach me to give the gift of total acceptance to someone today, especially to someone I would normally avoid."

Do Not Be Conceited

Rom 12:16—*"Live in harmony with one another; do not be haughty but associate with the lowly. **Do not be conceited~/**."*

How can sinful people who have built-in self-interest and superior opinions about themselves ever get along with each other? If our Creator tells us how to build relationships, we should listen.

The context of this passage begins in Romans 12:9–16 with a series of participles describing conditions that will result in harmony and unity; thus the passage is given imperative force in translations. Here is my paraphrased translation:

"When we love or care for each other, it should be without pretense or self-interest; we should hate pornographic or sensual evil, and we should adhere to things that are good and wholesome. Relationships should be developed with family affection by showing honor and giving priority to each other. Everyone should diligently and eagerly apply these principles and always be passionately motivated to serve each other as in peak season—continually rejoicing in hope, corporately or individually bearing up under pressure or distress, sharing necessities with other believers, and especially continuing the pursuit of hospitality toward their brethren. Be a help or blessing (the only imperative) *to those who persecute* (same word as *pursue* in previous phrase) *you; remember to always bless others and never wish someone ruin or bad luck. Empathy should be shared with those who are glad and rejoicing, but we are also to weep with those who weep. Everyone should have this same mind-set—not seeking or minding lofty or prestigious things but rather going along with or beside the humble or those of lower social classes and making them feel like equal partners in Christ."*

The second imperative in this concluding statement is *"do not be continually conceited, or wise in yourselves."* Proverbs warns of such conceited people: *"Do you see a man wise in his own conceit? There is more hope for a fool than for him"* (Prov 26:12). This kind of "fool" (Heb. *kesil*) is someone who is so full of himself that he hates any correction or knowledge that was not his idea (Prov 18:2). He is immature, always wanting his way. He uses "friends" and destroys them (13:20). He believes everything revolves around him.

"Lord Jesus, I despise conceit in others, but do I demonstrate conceit in my own life? Teach me to value humility more than being right all the time or being the best at anything. Please, Lord, do not let me become a 'fool' in Your sight."

FEBRUARY 22

Please Your Neighbor

Rom 15:2—*"Let each of us please~~ his neighbor for his good to build him up."*

A major area of conflict between peoples of any culture is in the arena of personal rights. Should restrictions be placed on my liberties just because someone else is offended or tempted?

Romans 15:2 deals with the issue of the weaker brother and the stronger brother. Who is supposed to yield to the conviction of the other when there is a disagreement as to right and wrong? The principles guiding the decision of whether to eat meat offered to idols are applicable to many other convictions.

Romans 15:1 states, *"We then who are strong ought to bear with the scruples of the weak, and not to please ourselves."* The "weak," those who are "lacking capability in functioning adequately, powerless," are noted for their "extra strict rules or scruples." The "weak" in this case are converts who have recently repented of their besetting sins, whose flesh still has a strong grip on them.

If they want to be effective in evangelizing the lost, especially the addicted, eventually they will have to be strong enough to mix with people addicted to all kinds of vices without being tempted. The mark of a strong believer is that he can be around people with such vices and, instead of being influenced to sin, influence them to turn to Christ and find forgiveness and liberation from their sins.

In the meantime, the strong believer must *"please his neighbor for his good to build him up."* If working with young believers susceptible to too much drink, then the strong must decide to never drink alcohol again.

Paul wrote, *"Do not destroy the work of God for the sake of food [that you are free to eat biblically]. For although all things are pure, it is evil for the man who eats with offense [or who causes another to stumble]. It is good [or better] neither to eat meat [i.e., pork] or drink wine nor to do anything by which your brother stumbles or is offended or is made weak [to temptation]"* (Rom 14:20–21). Are you willing to give up your right to food and habits to help a weaker brother to mature?

"Why do I struggle so much to give up my rights to please those around me? Forgive me for not caring enough to do things for others without seeking some benefit in return."

FEBRUARY 23

Constantly Tweak Your Life

2 Cor 13:11a—*"Finally, brethren, farewell. **Become complete**~~"*

Parents often want to tell their children, "Grow up!" Some things just take time and patient instruction. The command with the nuance of the present progressive tense is to *"be continually becoming complete,"* which is a translation of a word meaning to "adjust, fit, mend, finish or arrange in its appropriate condition." It is used metaphorically of restoring a person in error (Gal 6:1).

Paul is calling on the church (the verb is plural) to fit or conform to the word of God. Spiritual wholeness comes when the church as a whole, as well as its individual members, commits to learning and living out complete conformity to God's word and His commands.

Paul ended his letters with a list of commands or exhortations that God's Spirit directed him to give to the churches, such as Colossians 4:2–6 (*"be continuously in prayer, boldly speak the gospel, be wise toward the unsaved, redeem the time, speak graciously with salt in your answers"*) or 1 Thessalonians 5:12–22 (*"respect your leaders, be at peace, warn the undisciplined, comfort the discouraged, help the weak, be patient, refuse vengeance, pursue kindness with each other, rejoice always, pray without stopping, be thankful, do not quench the Spirit, do not scoff at prophecies, test everything, and avoid every kind of evil"*).

It is hard to remember all these things, so we must continually remind ourselves of each one of them. In the Epistles, we are commanded twenty-three times to commit these instructions to memory. Peter wrote, *"Always be able to remember these things"* (2 Pet 1:15).

The church and its members are to take the commands seriously. This is called *integrity*. As individuals grow in grace, they are to constantly check their values and priorities, make sure they are thinking biblically, and mend any area that deviates from His commands to restore spiritual wholeness. Paul wrote to the Thessalonians that he could help them *"complete what [was] lacking in [their] faith"* (1 Thes 3:10)—namely, a more complete obedience.

One author writes, "Powerful evangelism is a by-product of spiritual integrity; it is the natural outflow of a church that is in holy harmony with God's will." Ask God to give you the grace today to conform your life to everything you know of His commands. Don't make Him tell you twice!

"Lord, there are so many things to remember to be mature and full of Your wisdom in my daily life. Teach me to value the results of living by Your principles."

FEBRUARY 24

Perpetually Be Encouraged

2 Cor 13:11b—*"Be encouraged~~."*

As the old joke goes, "Cheer up, things could get worse." So I cheered up, and sure enough, things got worse! Believers could leave the world's problems outside the gathering and together celebrate the unchangeable wonder of personally knowing the God of creation and the redemption of the One who cares for them.

In 2 Corinthians 13:11, Paul uses the passive command form of the verb: *"be comforted, or take our appeal to heart."* The verb form is used 105 times in the New Testament. It is an important element of our walk with Christ.

Paul was not exempt from suffering and discouragement. Nothing went the way he had planned. Bearing the greatest news since the dawn of creation, he was still met with hostility and rejection. After being beaten and left for dead by the road, imprisoned, and thrown out of towns with only a handful of precious converts for all his effort, he arrived in Corinth extremely discouraged. He wrote, *"We were crushed and overwhelmed beyond our ability to endure, and we thought we would never live through it"* (2 Cor 1:8NLT).

Paul's discouragement seemed to reach a peak by the time he got to Corinth. He did not know if he could go on. Then, at the end of his strength and determination, Paul learned in the midst of failure that a deeper consolation is waiting to be claimed: Jesus is with us through it all. *"Lo, I am with you"* (Matt 28:20) is our comfort.

In 2 Corinthians 1:3b–4, Paul wrote, *"The God of all comfort, who comforts us in all our troubles so that we may be able to comfort those experiencing any trouble with the comfort with which we ourselves are comforted by God."*

The word *comfort* is the same verb as in 2 Corinthians 13:11. Paul tells us, *"I learned in whatever state I am to be content. I know how to be abased [in need], and I know how to abound. Everywhere and in all things I have learned both to be full and to be hungry, both to abound and to suffer need. I can do all things through Christ who strengthens me"* (Phil 4:11–13). If Paul could be comforted by walking close to Jesus, so can I, and so can you.

"Keep my heart satisfied in Your presence and my mind filled with Your purposes for my life. Grant me enough encouragement each day to stay positive for others who might become discouraged."

FEBRUARY 25

Agree with One Another

2 Cor 13:11c—*"Agree with one another ~~."*

The appeal for unity is frequent in Paul's writings, especially with such diverse congregations of slaves and the poor and Gentiles and Jews: *"Be of the same mind toward one another. Do not set your mind on high things, but associate with the humble. Do not be wise in your own opinion"* (Rom 12:15). The verb in 2 Corinthians 13:11 means to "think about this, develop this attitude of mind." This is not a superficial legalistic conformity but an inward attitude toward how we think about each other and how we treat each other.

Paul's prayer for such harmony is evident in Romans 15:5: *"Now may the God of patience and comfort grant you to be like-minded toward one another, according to Christ Jesus, that you may with one mind and one mouth glorify the God and Father of our Lord Jesus Christ."*

In Philippians, Paul explained the meaning of this oneness of mind: *"Fulfill my joy by being like-minded, having the same love, being of one accord, of one mind"* (Phil 2:2). The next verses describe this oneness: *"Let nothing be done through selfish ambition or conceit, but in lowliness of mind let each esteem others better [more important] than himself. Let each of you look out not only for his own interests, but also for the interests of others"* (2:3–4).

This commitment to the attitude of Christ is not just an individual obligation but a responsibility of the church to team together to practice the same unity that is experienced within the Godhead itself. John 17:21 is not just a euphemism but a genuine goal for the churches: *"[I pray] that they all may be one, as You, Father, are in Me, and I in You, that they also may be one in Us, that the world may believe that You sent Me."* Paul explains in part how this works out in practice: *"Now I plead with you, brethren, by the name of our Lord Jesus Christ, that you all speak the same thing, and that there be no divisions among you, but that you be perfectly joined together in the same mind and in the same judgment"* (1 Cor 1:10). This corporate testimony of unity is a powerful evangelistic testimony.

Instead of arguing over minor issues, let us unite over the main practice of the commands and agree to encourage and help each other obey them for His honor.

"Forgive me, Lord, for wanting to avoid others who disagree with me and especially for not wanting to help them or care for them. I have so much to learn from You."

Live in Peace

2 Cor 13:11d—*"Live in peace~~ and the God of love and peace will be with you."*

Whenever a group of sinners gather together, arguments and disharmony are a natural result. However, when the group is empowered by the Spirit and mutually committed to obeying the word, a different atmosphere is created like no other place on earth.

The present command in 2 Corinthians 13:11 to *"be continually living in peace"* is not a reference to an individual's peace with God through redemption, but a practical, corporate peace that is to be maintained by individual commitments to obey this command for His reputation's sake.

The New Testament was written for the church, for corporate obedience. It is how we are to live together, not just privately, with the Lord.

Paul wrote, *"Let us pursue the things which make for peace and the things by which one may edify another"* (Rom 14:19). Even in the most contentious relationship between the early Christian Jews and the Gentile believers, the objective in the church body was to practice peace: *"He Himself is our peace, who has made both one, and has broken down the middle wall of separation, having abolished in His flesh the enmity, that is, the law of commandments contained in ordinances, so as to create in Himself one new man from the two, thus making peace"* (Eph 2:16). The *"new man"* is not an individual believer but a new body of believers who are at peace with each other as they are at peace with Christ. If Jews and Gentiles can live at peace, any group can.

The command is reiterated in Colossians 3:15: *"Let the peace of God rule in your hearts, to which also you were called in one body and be thankful."* This is also a plural command for a group to obey together. The rule of peace must govern all gatherings of believers. Anything that would break this peace should be discouraged. Disagreements must be discussed under the umbrella of the rule of peace. When peace is broken, Christ is not honored, His church is disgraced, and His Spirit is destroyed.

"Live in peace" might mean giving up selfishness, pride, self-exaltation, conceit, and independence in order to keep peace. It requires a trust in God's word that this command is of high value to Christ. Plus, it comes with a special promise: *"The God of love and peace **with be with you."***

"Lord, You have given me such amazing peace in my spirit, and now You ask me to be just as much at peace with my brothers and sisters in Christ. "

FEBRUARY 27

Greet One Another

1 Cor 16:20—*"All the brothers and sisters send greetings. **Greet one another***~ with a holy kiss."*

As Paul concluded his Letter to the Corinthians, he mentions several individuals in Ephesus who had ties to those in Corinth. Paul is writing from Ephesus.

These were mostly house churches, as is evident from the preceding verse: *"Aquila and Priscilla greet you heartily in the Lord, with the church that is in their house"* (16:19). They had been with Paul in Corinth establishing house churches and now are in Ephesus continuing the same work.

The aorist command is to *"greet one another with a holy kiss."* This command is repeated verbatim in Romans 16:16, and it is slightly varied in 2 Corinthians 13:12 and 1 Thessalonians 5:26. In 1 Peter 5:14, this greeting is called a "kiss of love." Believers were expected to show their affection and respect to each other in the form of a holy kiss.

In most of the world, a kiss in the air as the right cheeks touch is a common greeting for family and close friends. Some cultures greet with one, two, or three kisses on opposite cheeks. Handshakes are reserved for formal occasions and new acquaintances. In more reserved cultures, cheek kissing between men is uncomfortable and is seen as inappropriate, even though it was practiced in Acts 20:37 when the elders of Ephesus said good-bye to Paul.

Its basic function is a sign demonstrating oneness, and mutual acceptance for all believers, regardless of class, gender, or race in the body of Christ. It is to show that the family of God is as important as one's immediate blood family, regardless of any superficial differences.

It is called a *"holy"* kiss because its purpose is not sensual but spiritual—that is, to communicate that we are family. Whatever the cultural application of this principle, it is a command. People need to be constantly assured that they are accepted in the family or the body of Christ. This is, in effect, a ministry of encouragement and care of the feelings and needs of each other. How do you communicate your affectionate acceptance of others?

"We can only imagine how You are going to greet us in heaven, but may we practice our eternal family greetings every time we meet on earth to show our bond."

FEBRUARY 28

Do Not Abuse Your Freedom

Gal 5:13a—"*For you were called to freedom, brothers and sisters; only* **do not use~/** *your freedom as an opportunity to indulge your flesh.*"

If man is fully forgiven of all his sins, how then should he live?

Mankind lives under the lure of addictions to alcohol, drugs, sexual passions, violence, greed, and other forms of bondage that enslave people. Jesus said, "*Truly, truly, everyone who commits sin is the slave of sin*" (Jn 8:34). The more we indulge in self-centered liberty, the more we become enslaved to sins.

There is only one escape: "*If therefore the Son shall make you free, you shall be free indeed*" (Jn 8:36) from guilt and enslavement to sins. This is the theme of Galatians and the hallmark of Christianity: there is freedom in Christ because of the gift of His righteousness and empowerment to live in the freedom of obedience.

Paul declares that we are "*called to freedom.*" The Christian life is neither legalistic bondage nor libertinism. The purpose of the Old Testament law was to reveal sin in its awfulness and lead a person to seek forgiveness in Christ: "*Therefore the law was our tutor to bring us to Christ, that we might be justified by faith*" (Gal 3:24).

On the other hand, the New Testament gives the promise of perfect righteousness being credited to the believer, once and for all eternity, making him fully acceptable to God. The commands of the New Testament are given to teach us how to think as the forgiven family of God and how to live responsibly and unselfishly for others. They are not for earning righteousness, but how the Spirit can empower believers to live devoutly and free from an enslaving world. The commands of the New Testament yield freedom, not bondage.

We are commanded, literally, "*Stop using your freedom as an opportunity to indulge your flesh.*" The "flesh" here refers not to the physical body but to the sinful enslaving appetites. In this way, we show our grateful love for Him Peter wrote, "*Act as free men, and do not use your freedom as a covering for evil, but use it as bond-slaves of God*" (1 Pet 2:16).

"Your salvation is so free and unconditional; we are eternally grateful, yet sometimes we can deceive ourselves into thinking it is okay to sin just this once. Forgive me, Lord, for desiring what You despise and gave Your life to forgive."

Serve One Another

Gal 5:13b—*"But through love **serve one another**~~."*

There is always an argument that supports selfish and self-centered action: "I deserve it," "Everyone else is doing it," or "I need it or I will be frustrated." Such excuses to gratify fleshly desires always destroy relationships, credibility, and one's character. Out of gratefulness to Christ, Paul wrote that we should *"be continually serving one another."*

Christian freedom is not the freedom to sin, but the freedom to love, which means the liberty to serve others. Paul wrote, *"If you must live under the law, live under the law of love—that is, the law of Christ"* (Gal 6:2).

The New Testament commands are motivated and empowered by the Spirit within, not imposed by an external authority. They are a new way of thinking about life and others. The Spirit leads us how to implement the commands of the New Testament in hundreds of ways. The commands are not legalistic, because they are not dictated by man, nor can they be performed superficially. The New Testament concepts are internally attitudinal and outwardly unselfish; that is, they are designed to benefit others, not ourselves.

If we have been bonded to Christ by salvation, then His love for others becomes our love for others: *"The love of God has been poured out in our hearts by the Holy Spirit who was given to us"* (Rom 5:5). If we have the Holy Spirit, then the love of God for others and the world is now a part of our new nature. If we want to be Spirit led, then we must be willing to *"serve one another."* *Love* means to seek to benefit others without self-interest, regardless of possible negative feelings toward the one in need.

The word *serve* is a strong verb, which comes from the common Greek noun for *bondslave* (see Gal 1:10 and 2 Cor 4:5). A servant can be paid to serve, but a slave is owned by another to do his will. Jesus cannot demonstrate His love toward people today except through us.

The passion of Christ as described in Galatians 2:20 (*"the Son of God, who loved me and gave Himself for me"*) becomes the theme of the Christian life: In Christ's place, we love others and give ourselves for them especially those who do not know Him. Are you willing to be His vessel? It might cost you everything.

"Thank You, Father, for giving me the wisdom to follow Your example of serving others through Your love."

MARCH 2
Open Wide Your Hearts

2 Cor 6:13—*"Now as a fair exchange—I speak as to my children—**open wide your hearts***~ to us also."*
2 Cor 7:2—*"**Make room for us in your hearts***~; we have wronged no one, we have ruined no one, we have exploited no one."*

Paul had been deeply hurt by the Corinthians, yet he continued to pour out himself for them. He described his sacrificial and dangerous ministry for them in 2 Corinthians 6:4–10. When Paul discusses his attitude toward the Corinthians, he says, *"Our heart is wide open"* (2 Cor 6:11), meaning in context that he loved them no matter how they responded to him.

Paul expands this thought in verse 12: *"You are not restricted by us,"* or better, *"We do not withhold affection for you"* (2 Cor 6:11^{NIV}). Paul did not allow the Corinthians "to be squeezed out" of his affections by their lack of response to him.

Naturally, Paul's heart was expecting a reciprocating response, *"Now as a fair exchange"* (2 Cor 6:13). It seems apparent that they showed little appreciation for his sacrifices for them. The principle for the church is to love their leadership in the same manner as they love the church. Have you ever been disappointed by the lack of response from others for your service to them?

Paul again demonstrates his love for the Corinthians by not making them feel bad or rebuking them; rather, he lays down a principle that as a leader, or anyone who sacrifices for his congregation, he should receive their appreciation as well. The aorist command means to *"immediately decide to open wide your hearts."* Although directed at the Corinthians in their relationship to their pastor, Paul, the principle transcends the centuries to apply to churches today.

So important is this command that he repeats it in 2 Corinthians 7:2: *"Make room for us in your hearts."* This is the model for churches everywhere. There must always be a reciprocal expression of appreciation and affection. However, regardless of their response, Paul's affection for the people of God would not change. This is the love of God in Paul's life.

We must learn to love regardless of the response we receive, but ideally, the response should be reciprocal. God's grace and closeness can make up the difference.

"Dear Lord, since You have commanded us to love one another, we surely are able to do it. Help me understand how to 'open wide' my heart to my Christian family."

MARCH 3

Cleanse Your Hands and Purify Your Hearts

James 4:8b—"*Cleanse*~ your hands, you sinners ... **Make your hearts pure*~**, you double-minded.*"

James, the brother of our Lord, had just delivered a series of exhortations to submit to God, resist the devil, and draw near to God. Now James gives two urgent aorist commands for the believer-priest as he draws near to God: "*cleanse your hands*" and "*make your hearts pure.*" As the believer goes to prayer, it is with the expectation of desiring the will of God by practicing His word and showing God's care for people.

Let us beware lest we abuse the grace and forgiveness of God to the point that we are no longer conscious of our sins and lose interest in His word and in the needs others to satisfy our own desires and lusts.

Although James is confident God has already planted His word in these readers, who were "*brought forth by the Word of truth*" (James 1:18), he is addressing this command to "sinners." It is sin that separates man from God. David wrote, "*The wicked will not stand in the judgment, nor sinners in the assembly of the righteous*" (Psa 1:5).

Even believers lose sight of the awfulness of their sins and their desperate need for constant cleansing. Thankfully, "*if we [are continually confessing] our sins* [Gk. "*missing the mark, wandering from the commands*"], *He is faithful and just to forgive us our sins and to cleanse us from all unrighteousness*" (1 Jn 1:9). May we never lose our sense of need for constant cleansing for our acceptance in His presence!

This Hebraic parallelism between "cleanse your hands" and "make pure your hearts" reminds us of Psalm 24:3–4: "*Who may ascend into the hill of the Lord? And who may stand in His holy place? He who has clean hands and a pure heart.*" Repentance is not just from outward offenses but also from inward corruptions. Jesus said, "*Out of the heart come evil thoughts, murders, adulteries, fornications, thefts, false witness [lies], slanders*" (Matt 15:19). The "*double-minded*" are those who pretend to be spiritual outwardly yet still love the flesh inwardly. They are living a lie.

We need to continually be cleansed from our actions of selfishness and disobedience and to purify our motives from self-centered desires so that we are being transformed into the image of the most wonderful person in the universe, the Lord Jesus.

"*Dear Lord, since I am only a sinner saved by Your wonderful grace, give me understanding and a willingness to be continually confessing my sins as Your Spirit points them out in me.*"

MARCH 4

Beware Not to Consume One Another

Gal 5:15—*"However, if you continually bite and devour one another,* **beware~~ that you are not consumed** *["ruined, burnt up"] by one another."*

There is nothing more helpful, and potentially destructive, than the tongue. It can encourage or destroy. It can build up or crush into a heap. How we speak is always an issue of the heart, *"for out of the abundance of the heart the mouth speaks"* (Matt 12:34).

In Galatians 5:15, Paul is commanding the church (sense of plural command) to be alert to how they talk about each other. The terms *bite* and *devour* are used to refer to wild animals battling in a death struggle, biting each other. Power struggles occur when we feel someone is threatening our ambitions or pride.

Interpersonal problems are primarily personality conflicts or differing opinions. Soon the campaign begins to discredit and ostracize the "troublemaker." Of course, the "troublemaker" is often never confronted or helped to bring harmony. Once the case against that person is strong enough or sufficient, people tend to be embittered toward the problem person; he is eliminated, run off, fired, or crushed emotionally. Who cares? No one! The problem is gone . . . until the next troublemaker emerges.

Continual discord and contention in the churches in Galatia provoked this command. This is what Paul meant when he warned the Corinthians concerning the Lord's Supper: they were not *"discerning the Lord's body"*—that is, the church body. People were hurt, and no one cared. "Factions" or cliques form in any organization, and they tend to unite against newcomers, criticizing and judging them as inferior, problematic, or useless failures. It can get pretty cruel. Who cares if someone is destroyed? Only Jesus cares!

The ruling principle is love, which helps us build each other up or look for the best in others. When thinking of others, we are commanded to *"fix [our] thoughts on what is true, and honorable, and right, and pure, and lovely, and admirable"* (Phil 4:8). You can never hurt someone by thinking these things about him. This is how Christ thinks of us, and now He commands us to think of each other in the same way.

"Heavenly Father, as I observe other believers, help me think only good thoughts about them. Then help me look for ways to encourage and build them up for Your honor and glory."

MARCH 5

Carry One Another's Burdens

Gal 6:2—*"Carry one another's burdens*~~, *and in this way you will fulfill the law of Christ."*

Some folks drain our emotions, while others recharge them. In Galatians 6:2, Paul commands us to be bonded together as believers regardless of each other's needs, backgrounds, or problems.

The continuous sense of the present tense imperative means to "be habitually be carrying one another's burdens." The word *carry* means "to take up with the hands, to put on one's self," or to "bear what is burdensome." The root word refers to heavy loads that are difficult to carry and is used here metaphorically to represent difficult circumstances or problems with which a person cannot cope. This burden could be psychological, relational, social, financial, or moral.

Most people attempt to cover character flaws with a mask of calm. God permits personal vulnerability to temptation in order to prevent self-righteousness, and He gives us the need for counsel and encouragement from other believers. The travesty occurs when no one is there because no one has decided to care in obedience to this command.

By helping a family member in Christ bear his excessive burden in a tangible way, we *"fulfill the law of Christ,"* who said the night before His crucifixion, *"A new commandment I give to you, that you love one another"* (Jn 13:34). The law of Christ is our commitment to help others.

God's plan is never that we become independent of each other. Pride makes a person want to "go it alone." On the contrary, He makes us dependent on each other so we can live out the life of Christ as we help each other through life's maze of conflicts, temptations, and discouragements. The bond of Christ compels us to accept the task of helping others. Each of us has a spiritual gift to empower us to serve the needs of others: *"A spiritual gift is given to each of us so we can help each other"* (1 Cor 12:7[NLT]). If you are not committed to helping others, then your spiritual gift is wasted.

The bond of the church is made deeper by our commitment to restore and assist a brother or sister in Christ. Are we close enough to our fellow believers to see through their masks and come to their aid? Do we even care?

"Dear God, You command believers to bear one another's burdens. I want to be emotionally ready and wise enough to help my fellow Christians as You make me aware of the burdens they carry."

MARCH 6

Lay Aside Falsehood, and Speak the Truth

Eph 4:25—*"Therefore, having laid aside falsehood, each one of you* **speak~~ the truth** *with his neighbor, for we are members of one another."*

Paul had just described the *"new man, which was created according to God"* (Eph 4:24). The new man must *"put off"* the *"old man, which grows corrupt according* to the deceitful lusts." In Ephesians 4:25, Paul now begins to describe what it looks like to *"put on the new man."*

The *"therefore"* introduces the first command of the new life in Christ. Since the reader has been regenerated into a new life, the lies and falsehoods of the devil (*"there is no truth in him,"* Jn 8:44) of a false hope in begin good enough have been laid aside by the acceptance of the truth of the gospel.

To the Colossians, Paul made it even clearer: *"Do not lie to one another, since you have put off the old man and his deeds"* (Col 3:9). This is written as though lying is the chief characteristic of the unsaved *"old man."* One of the first sins to go must be the old tendency to lie, deceive, cheat, exaggerate, "stretch the truth," and tell half-truths for deceitful motives.

Obviously, wisdom is required. Truthfulness does not mean revealing everything you know to everyone—this can become destructive gossip. Confidence shared is confidence protected especially among family. However, truth withheld or manipulated to deceive or mislead is lying.

Why would anyone want to lie? They may want to exchange their circumstances, their perceived behavior, or their feelings for a fantasy world in which they are better than they actually are. Satan has seduced them to believe that the only way to make these changes or accomplish their goals is to lie. They see no alternative. They have been blinded.

The reason for this imperative is that we are *"members one of another."*

Once lying starts, then every statement becomes suspect. No one is trusted. Everyone becomes cynical. Trust vanishes, sides are taken, and the wars begin. The church cannot function under these conditions. A loving honesty must undergird every relationship if we are to minister to one another. We must learn to speak *"the truth in love"* (Eph 4:15). Will you be honest today, no matter how much it hurts?

"Give me wisdom, Lord, to communicate truth in every way as I relate to other believers each day. May You be honored and may others be blessed as a result of my interactions with them."

MARCH 7

Be Kind, Compassionate, and Forgiving of One Another

Eph 4:32—*"Instead, **be~~ kind to one another**, be compassionate, be forgiving one another, just as God in Christ also forgave you."*

Biblical love is not an emotional, sensual response to another person, but an unselfish commitment to help, benefit, or build up another person without consideration of deriving potential personal benefits for your actions.

This is an unconditional action modeled by our Lord. As Luke wrote, we are to *"love [our] enemies [helping, benefiting them, not necessarily liking them], and do good, and lend, expecting nothing in return; and [our] reward will be great, and [we] will be sons of the Most High, for He Himself is kind to ungrateful and evil men"* (Luke 6:35b). The concepts of this verse describe what it means to love others practically.

The present imperative verb in Ephesians 4:32 is to *"be continually or habitually acting"* in three descriptive manners: kindness, compassion, and forgiveness. To be *kind* means to act in a "gracious, mild, or pleasant" manner in stead of being cruel, harsh, hard, or sharp. This is the **physical** response to the needs of others.

To be *compassionate*, means to "be tenderhearted," which comes from a word for *bowels*, or "gut feeling"—a kind of gnawing of empathy that allows us to feel the pain of a person in need. Peter wrote that we should be *"of one mind [the same priority] having compassion for one another, love as brothers, be tenderhearted, be courteous"* (1 Pet 3:8). This is the **emotional** response to the needs of others.

Lastly, we are to be habitually and continually *"forgiving one another just as [in the same manner as] God in Christ forgave you."* The word *forgiving* is from the root word for *grace*, thus meaning "to grant a favorable status or give acceptance without conditions, as a gift," just because the other person needs to know he or she is forgiven by you. This is the **relational** response to the needs of others. We can harbor no resentment or bitterness against anyone.

This is the new paradigm of the Christian life: we are to live as Jesus did and forgive as He continues to forgive us daily. To be a part of a community like this would be like heaven on earth.

"Loving Father, as You have forgiven me, I ask that You give me the understanding and the will to forgive and care for those who may hurt me. May I surrender my own feelings and needs to You, the true and just judge."

MARCH 8

Have the Same Attitude toward One Another

Phil 2:5—*"You should have the same attitude*~~ *toward one another* that Christ Jesus had."*

Our verse today falls between two majestic passages, making it difficult to decide whether *"the same attitude"* refers to the previous passage, which deals with our humble service to one another, or to the following passage, which describes Christ's incarnation. More likely, it refers to both. The passages describe the objective of the transformation of our minds to be like His.

The goal of the new life in Christ is to *"Be not conformed to this world: but be transformed by the **renewing of your mind**, that you may prove what is that good, and acceptable, and perfect, will of God"* (Rom 12:2). The thoughts we repeat to ourselves in our mind form our beliefs and values, which drive our motivation and behavior. Only by changing our thoughts, beliefs and values can we experience that the will of God is *"good, and acceptable, and perfect."*

Taking the sense or nuance of the verb one comes to this translation: *"For this [what has already been described] should be habitually or continually your way of thinking, which also was that of Christ Jesus"* (as Paul will continue to describe). In this context, Jesus always considered other people and their needs to be a greater priority than His own human needs (as Phil 2:2-4). He was never personally or selfishly ambitious or conceited, but he *"made Himself of no reputation"* (Phil 2:7) to become our Savior.

This is not an external conformity to legalistic standards, but an internal mind-set of self-sacrifice, self-giving, and selfless love for the benefit of others, which is the new norm in the personal and communal life of believers. In hundreds of ways, believers should be seen serving one another without looking for personal benefits or bragging rights.

In a dramatic conclusion to His life, while the disciples were arguing over who should be the greatest in the Messiah's kingdom (Luke 22:24), Jesus, the King of kings, arose, poured water into a basin, and began to wash the dirty, sandaled feet of His disciples (Jn 13:4–5). How can you serve the ones around you today?

"Dear Jesus, You were willing to sacrifice it all to accomplish Your Father's will. Please give me a willing heart to serve others so that I might be used to accomplish Your purposes for me on this earth."

MARCH 9

Encourage One Another with the Second Coming

1 Thes 4:18—*"Therefore **encourage**~~ **one another** with these words."*

The only way to know what is going to happen beyond the grave is to listen to Someone who has been there and returned to tell us about it. In 1 Thessalonians 4:18, Paul is teaching about what happens after death, as he wrote, *"We want you to know what will happen to the believers who have died so you will not grieve like people who have no hope"* (1 Thes 4:13[NLT]). Aren't you glad we can know for certain?

Since this command is in the present tense, it is meant to be an ongoing encouragement, not a momentary, after-the-fact word of optimism. The idea is that we are constantly anticipating the parting of this life to be present with the Lord. Paul wrote, *"We are confident, yes, well pleased rather to be absent from the body and to be present with the Lord"* (2 Cor 5:8). This "encouragement" should take place long before the incident occurs; thus we are to be intellectually and emotionally preparing each other.

The believer in Christ is to constantly anticipate and celebrate this homecoming welcome. Peter described it this way: *"Then God will give you a grand entrance into the eternal Kingdom of our Lord and Savior Jesus Christ"* (2 Pet 1:11[NLT]). This theme is to be part of our regular thought life and conversations, as well as our worship and songs.

The original word for *encourage* means "to aid, help, [or] comfort" with the idea of beseeching or entreating someone to be glad and to rejoice about a coming reality. Death is not the end of our existence; rather, it is the beginning of our unending life with Christ.

Believers in Thessalonica wondered about their departed friends who had put their faith in Christ: would they be raised as well? Paul had just assured his readers that *"the dead in Christ"* will be resurrected first, followed by an amazing event in which all living believers would be transformed instantly into their glorified bodies without ever dying; then they would be taken up together to rendezvous with Christ in the air. This is the *"blessed hope"* for those who are alive when Jesus returns. Paul lived *"looking for the blessed hope and glorious appearing of our great God and Savior Jesus Christ"* (Titus 2:13). No believer will be left behind. Can you cry out from your heart, "Come, Lord Jesus"?

"Heavenly Father, what a celebration Your children have to look forward to! Thank You for that promise. Help me always anticipate Your return and encourage others to live as if this were their last day on earth."

MARCH 10
Build Up One Another

1 Thes 5:11—*"Therefore **encourage**~~ **one another** and **build up**~~ **each other**, just as you are in fact doing."*

"Therefore" refers back to Paul's clear statement that *"God did not appoint us to suffer wrath, but to obtain salvation through our Lord Jesus Christ"* (1 Thes 5:9) and that *"we should live together with Him"* (5:10). Believers will never experience the terror of God's wrath against unbelieving sinners on the day of judgment and their sentence for eternity in hell.

The first command is to *"be continually encouraging one another,"* which uses the same word as in 1 Thessalonians 4:18, but here the emphasis is on mutual exhortation. This command is bonded to the second—*"be continually building up each other"*—which comes from a verb meaning "to construct houses, or erect," thus to "to establish, edify, make stronger, or embolden."

The self-centered mind can take the promise of Christ's imminent return to mean that time is too short to start anything for God. Thus we are exhorted not to *"sleep [a metaphor for being useless for the kingdom], as others do, but let us watch and be sober,"* always acting in *"faith and love, and . . . hope"* (1 Thes 5:8). There are people to love to the cross and unsaved multitudes to guide to salvation who have never heard the gospel once. We cannot quit yet.

To develop this level of mutual commitment to His word and His model of service requires constant encouragement and instruction from everyone to everybody. Human frailty will never cease to need encouragement. Every day, count the number of times you encourage someone to trust and be faithful. Then increase that number regularly.

Paul ends this command saying, *"as indeed you are doing."* Paul had just written, *"We urge and exhort in the Lord Jesus that you should abound more and more"* (1 Thes 4:1) and *"You yourselves are taught by God to love one another; and indeed you do so toward all the brethren . . . But we urge you, brethren, that you increase more and more"* (4:9–10). Let Christ's return interrupt a thousand plans of yours and your church for reaching the lost of this world!

"Lord Jesus, I know I need to help reach the world with Your message and encourage other believers to follow Your example. Help me do so with the same loving care You so willingly exhibited to Your disciples."

MARCH 11

Esteem Workers Highly in Love; Be at Peace

1 Thes 5:13—*"and to esteem them most highly in love because of their work. Be at peace~~ among yourselves."*

Paul had just asked the believers to *"honor," "recognize,"* or *"appreciate those who labor among you and are over you in the Lord and admonish you"* (1 Thes 5:12). The relationship between the body of believers and their pastor(s) must be a healthy respect, or it detours into dead-end squabbles and suspicions.

Church leadership is called by interchangeable terms. The most common term is *elders*: those who are spiritually mature and wise leaders (1 Tim 5:17, 19; 1 Pet 5:1, 5). The word *overseer* or *bishop* is used interchangeably in Titus 1:5 and 8 to reflect the spiritual oversight and authority in the church. A third term—probably the most common in usage today—is *pastor*, which is a leader whose responsibility is to feed and protect the believers (Eph 4:11–12). The fourth term, *leader*, refers to those who teach and give guidance from the word: *"Remember those who rule [root of the word for* leader*] over you, who have spoken the word of God to you, whose faith follow"* (Heb 13:7; see also 13:17).

In 1 Thessalonians 5:13, evidently, some there were reluctant to obey their leaders, provoking Paul's exhortation to *"esteem [workers] most highly in love"* and *"be at peace among yourselves."* They were to *"hold them in the highest regard"* (lit. "to esteem them hyper-abundantly").

In 1 Thes 5:12, these leaders were fulfilling three responsibilities. First, they were *"laboring,"* meaning "to be worn out, weary, or faint." Paul asked *"that you submit to such, and to everyone who works and labors with us"* (1 Cor 16:16). Second, they were *"over you in the Lord,"* meaning "to stand before, to preside, lead or rule." Third, they were *"admonishing"* the church—literally, "to put in mind, to warn, or correct by discipline, counsel." They were teaching the church to obey the commands.

Then Paul gives the key to the unity of the church: *"[continually] be at peace among yourselves."* The verb implies the end of hostilities, quarreling, or fighting. One is reminded of the command, *"Let the peace of God rule in your [plural] hearts"* (Col 3:15)—that is, do everything possible to allow peace to reign among the body of believers. Are we "peacemakers" in our church?

"Dear Lord, You have given us pastors and teachers to help us learn to live for You. May I always respect and honor, as You have commanded, those You have given as spiritual authorities over me."

MARCH 12

Admonish, Comfort, Help, and Be Patient toward Others

1 Thes 5:14—*"And we urge you, brothers and sisters,* **admonish~~** **the undisciplined, comfort~~ the discouraged, help ~~ the weak, be patient~~toward all."**

The primary task of the pastoral leadership is to *"equip the saints for the work of the ministry"* (Eph 4:12). The "ministry" to which all believers must be trained by their pastors comprises four areas: evangelism, discipleship, mentoring, and counseling. At Thessalonica, three groups needed special counseling: the disorderly, the fainthearted, and the weak.

In our text, the first present-tense command is to *"continually be admonishing the undisciplined [or disorderly]."* To *admonish* means "to warn, [or] exhort"— literally, "to put in mind." In this case, they are to warn the *"undisciplined"*— literally, the "not-orderly," or the "lazy or neglectful of duty." This was a military term applied to the soldier who does not remain in the ranks and hence is out of order. This group had violated the pattern for the believers (2 Thes 3:10): *"For even when we were with you, we commanded you this: If anyone will not work neither shall he eat. For we hear that there are some who walk among you in a disorderly manner [same word], not working at all, but are busybodies. Now those who are such we command and exhort through our Lord Jesus Christ that they work in quietness and eat their own bread."*

Second, all believers are to *"continually be comforting the discouraged,"* which means to "come alongside with helpful instruction and insight." The *"discouraged"* refers to someone of "small soul," thus someone who is "fretful, fainthearted, worried, or timid." These people easily become worried, imagining their failures as inevitable. They need their fellow believers to calm their fears and build up their confidence, self-esteem, and personal value to the body of believers.

Third, we are commanded to *"be continually helping the weak,"* which means to "wrap arms around, hold on to or cling to" the *"fainthearted."* They need to be cheered up, stimulated to press on. Do we care enough?

Fourth, we are commanded to *"continually be patient with everyone."* Never expect people to be perfect: *"Love suffers [is patient] long and is kind"* (1 Cor 13:4). Some require more energy, but God gives more grace to serve others. Can you learn these commands with others?

"Father, Your Son Jesus embodied all these aspects of living to please and honor You. Guide me as I try to practice admonishing, comforting, helping, and showing patience to those You lead across my path each day."

MARCH 13
Do Not Try to Get Even

1 Thes 5:15a—*"See~~ that no one pays back evil for evil to anyone."*

Retaliation is a natural response to unfair treatment, as when someone is hurtful in personal relations. Christians injure others by wicked words (Prov 15:2, 4: *"The mouth of fools pours forth foolishness ... perverseness in it [the tongue] breaks the spirit"*) or by the pain of gossip or slander (11:13: *"A talebearer reveals secrets, but he who is of a faithful spirit conceals a matter"*).

Personal revenge and "getting even" are strictly forbidden to Christ's followers. Jesus said, *"But I tell you, Do not resist an evil person. If someone strikes you on the right cheek, turn to him the other also ... But I tell you: Love your enemies and pray for those who persecute you"* (Matt 5:39, 44NIV). Instead of demanding your personal rights or fairness, trust God for grace to endure injustice or cruelty.

Regardless of whether it is a political, business, or personal offense, we are generally prohibited from hurting any other person in proportion to how much we think they have hurt us. Peter wrote, *"Do not return evil for evil or insult for insult, but instead bless others because you were called to inherit a blessing"* (1 Pet 3:9).

Paul would reiterate this principle in Romans: *"Repay no one evil for evil ... If it is possible, as much as depends on you, live peaceably with all men. Beloved, do not avenge yourselves, but rather give place to wrath; for it is written, 'Vengeance is Mine, I will repay,' says the Lord"* (Rom 12:17–19).

The only thing to fear is being under the hand of God when He takes His vengeance. Nahum wrote, *"God is jealous, and the Lord avenges; the Lord avenges and is furious. The Lord will take vengeance on His adversaries, and He reserves wrath for His enemies."* However, *"The Lord is slow to anger and great in power, and will not at all acquit the wicked"* (1:2–3a).

The problem with getting even is that we do not know the whole story, and in our anger, our response is likely to be exaggerated. Therefore, we cannot be just. *"The wrath of man does not produce the justice of God"* (James 1:20). We can never determine what is fair or "even," so we are to let God make those choices. Can you trust Him to know how to bring justice to every cruel or painful injustice that you experience?

"You know, dear Lord, when we are treated badly by others and have taught us not to get even. Only You have the wisdom to repay a sinner for his ways. Help me remember that only You are God."

MARCH 14

Pursue Good for Others

1 Thes 5:15b—*"[Rather than vengeance taking (15a)] . . . always pursue~~ what is good for one another and for all."*

The command to *"pursue what is good for one another and for all"* has been one of the hallmarks of biblical Christianity. The imperative *pursue* is in the present tense, which means we are to be continually or habitually acting in this manner. The verb means "to pursue with earnestness and diligence in order to obtain." The literal rendering of the verse is *"but always be constantly pursuing the good"* for others with the emphatic position given to *"always."*

Here the word *"good"* is not meant in an abstract sense of being innocent or moral; rather, it is meant in the concrete sense of being "helpful, useful, or beneficial" to others. This is an action to be pursued constantly as a way to bond believers to each other and as an evangelistic strategy, even in a hostile environment. Paul wrote, *"If your enemy is hungry, feed him; if he is thirsty, give him a drink; for in so doing you will heap coals of fire on his head. Do not be overcome by evil, but overcome evil with good"* (Rom 12:20–21).

This action is not an "insider" perk just for fellow believers; it is a general attitude we should have toward everyone we meet in our sphere of influence. Seeking to benefit others is our new nature in Christ. The church at Thessalonica was already doing this well, but because this is an area of spiritual growth and a symptom of maturity, Paul wrote, *"May the Lord make you increase and abound in love to one another and to all, just as we do to you"* (1 Thes 3:12). This is the prescription for being transformed into the likeness of Christ by creatively designing new ways to benefit each other.

In 1569, Anabaptist Dirk Willems, fleeing over a frozen lake, turned back to save his pursuer, who had fallen through the ice. He was captured by his pursuer and burned at the stake, a horrible injustice. He was convinced that obeying the commands was more important than his very life. James put it this way: *"The wisdom from above is first pure, then peaceable, gentle, accommodating, full of mercy and good fruit, impartial, and not hypocritical"* (James 3:17). Would you have turned back to help your pursuer, knowing it would probably cost you your life?

"Dear God, help me learn to do good to others regardless of how they may treat me. I know I can always lean on You to help me do the right thing in each circumstance."

MARCH 15

Exhort One Another Every Day

Heb 3:13—*"But **exhort one another**~~ **each day**, as long as it is called 'Today,' that none of you may become hardened by sin's deception."*

The entire book of Hebrews was written to persuade either young Jewish believers or those close to putting their entire trust in the Christ-Messiah. The author lays down a command for the soul-winner and discipler: *"Be continually exhorting one another every day."*

The word for *"exhort"* means to "come alongside" of a person to "comfort, help, encourage, or challenge." It should be noted that when Jesus told about the Holy Spirit who would soon come to permanently dwell in every believer, He used the title *"Paraclete,"* which is the same word. The Holy Spirit is our comforter, helper, encourager, and challenger. When we comfort or encourage someone, we join with the Spirit. This is the *filling* of the Spirit.

This is the ministry of all the body of Christ to each other in a local church. We are to care for one another daily. We are to teach and admonish one another with all wisdom: *"Let the word of Christ dwell in you richly in all wisdom, teaching and admonishing one another in psalms and hymns and spiritual songs"* (Col 3:16). Paul went to great lengths to walk throughout Asia, Macedonia, and Greece so he could be *"strengthening the souls of the disciples, exhorting them to continue in the faith, and saying, 'We must enter the kingdom of God through many tribulations'"* (Acts 14:22).

The main reason for gathering together as a church body is to exercise this mutual ministry, *"not forsaking the assembling of ourselves together, as is the manner of some, but exhorting one another, and so much the more as you see the Day approaching"* (Heb 10:25). *"The Day"* refers to the end of the church age and the coming of the day of His wrath (Rom 2:5; Rev 6:17).

We must take advantage of every conversation, every encounter, if we care about others we'll help each other stay true to the Word. Anyone can become *"hardened by sin's deception."* Only when a godly friend cares enough to get involved to exhort, encourage, and instruct another can anyone keep true to the Lord. We need each other. Do we care about the body of Christ enough to take on this responsibility of caring for and learning how to exhort one another?

"Heavenly Father, may Your word be so ingrained in me that Your Spirit can freely prompt me to bolster another believer whenever I perceive a need."

MARCH 16
Do Not Slander One Another

James 4:11—*"Do not speak~/ against one another*, *brothers and sisters.* *He who speaks against a fellow believer or judges a fellow believer speaks against the law and judges the law. But if you judge the law, you are not a doer of the law but its judge."*

It is easy to condemn someone for addiction to drugs or pornography, but the most destructive vice is to *"speak against one another"*—that is, to slander and malign a "brother or sister." There is a malicious delight of being on the criticizing side of the slander and gossip that builds a corrupt, self-justifying, and secret society that breeds an inevitable addiction to slander. The damaged victims eventually are fired, run off, or just disappear, and no one cares how deeply they have been hurt or crushed in spirit. These addicts to slander just begin their search for another victim, and the slanderers feel righteous about getting rid of an objectionable brother or sister.

It is much worse when the perpetrator does not care that he is destroying a part of the body of Christ! Godly people are *"those who refuse to gossip or harm their neighbors or speak evil of their friends"* (Psa 15:3[NLT]). David declared God's attitude, *"Whoever secretly slanders his neighbor, him I will destroy"* (Psa 101:5).

Paul said the problems in the church at Corinth were caused by *"quarreling, jealousy, intense anger, selfish ambition, slander, gossip, arrogance, and disorder"* (2 Cor 12:20). He wrote to the Ephesians, *"Let all bitterness and wrath and anger and clamor and slander be put away from you, along with all malice"* (4:31). Peter likewise ordered, *"Get rid of every kind of evil, every kind of deception, hypocrisy, jealousy, and every kind of slander"* (1 Pet 2:1).

The most maliciousness thing about slander is that there is no intent or effort to help the victim, either to counsel, to advise, or to encourage. The verb means to "speak against," and it refers to "mindless, careless, critical, derogatory, untrue, or exaggerated speech directed against others," who are often seen as a possible threat. The tense of the verb suggests that slandering was already going on in the church and it had to stop. Can you help stop the plague of slander and gossip?

"Dear Jesus, may Your Spirit bring quick and deep conviction in me any moment that I may be tempted to speak evil of another believer. Help me recognize how deeply You and others are hurt when I give in to such behavior."

MARCH 17

Do Not Grumble against One Another

James 5:9—*"**Do not grumble~/ against one another**, brothers and sisters, so that you may not be judged. **See~~, the judge** stands before the gates!"*

Gripers and complainers are miserable company. Everyone is wrong except them. They only build their case for getting even. The danger of griping is how contagious it is. Like yawning or coughing in a group, once someone starts it, everyone is doing it. The venom of resentment and bitterness spread like wildfire.

The root causes of *"grumbling"* (lit. "a sigh or groan; a complaint or discontent directed against another, griping") are resentment, envy, and jealousy. All three are cancerous, contagious plagues

Israel played the "blame game," accusing Moses of causing the death plague (Num 16:41), and they griped to Moses about the lack of water and their miserable desert conditions (20:2). They grumbled in their tents against God: *"The Lord hates us."* Israel never learned contentment or thankfulness in their circumstances.

Paul commanded, *"Do all things without complaining [about things] and disputing [with people], that you may become blameless and harmless, children of God without fault in the midst of a crooked and perverse generation, among whom you shine as lights in the world"* (Phil 2:14). The world may gripe, but believers cannot.

James put our present life into eternal perspective when he added, *"Behold, the Judge is standing at the door!"* God takes His word very seriously: *"For all the people have seen my glory and my signs that I did in Egypt and in the wilderness, and yet have tempted me now these ten times, and have not obeyed me, they will by no means see the land that I swore to their fathers, nor will any of them who despised me see it"* (Num 14:22). Israel is not a good model to follow.

We are to live as though Jesus, the judge, is just outside the door listening to our thoughts, hoping to find something for which He can praise us. May we give Him pure thoughts of trust and thankfulness for whatever He has decided to provide and how He leads us in our pilgrimage.

"I am afraid I have a great tendency, dear Lord, to gripe and complain when I think others who should know better are doing wrong. Please put within me a searing sensitivity to quickly quell those evil desires before I speak."

MARCH 18
Love One Another

1 Pet 1:22—*"You have purified your souls by obeying the truth in order to show sincere mutual love. So **love one another***~ **earnestly** from a pure heart."*

What an amazing, giving, sacrificing God we discover in the Scripture. Earlier, in 1 Peter 1:20, His word tells us that *"before the foundation of the world,"* it was *"predetermined"* that Jesus would become the perfect substitute for sinful man. This will be the grateful theme of all eternity.

Peter writes to those who *"have purified [their] souls by obeying the truth."* The word for *purified* means "something set apart for a special purpose." This purifying act was completed in the past (perfect-tense form), but it implies the necessity of an ongoing consecration to a mission in order to effect spiritual progress *"by obeying the truth."* The believers began by trusting in the gospel and continued to live it by obeying all the truths in full trust as they learned them. Paul wrote, *"As you have therefore received Christ Jesus the Lord, so walk in Him"* (Col 2:6).

The "so" indicates that the purpose of our new life is *"to show sincere mutual love"* or "brotherly love." Jesus gave a new commandment that would have an evangelistic impact: *"Your love for one another will prove to the world that you are my disciples"* (Jn 13:35[NLT]). This love was to be *sincere*, from a word meaning "without pretense, acting or faking, but genuine or true;" it is a forever, lifetime, family love.

The command to *"immediately begin to love one another"* requires a decisive commitment of the will rather than an emotional response. This love is decided not by the attractiveness of the object but by the desire to benefit another person. We are instructed to love *"earnestly,"* a physiological term meaning "to stretch a muscle or limb to the maximum capacity." Metaphorically, *earnestly* means to do everything possible. The two terms are used in 1 Peter 4:8: *"Above all, keep fervent in your love for one another, because love covers a multitude of sins."* How do you love your brethren?

God is not asking for sacrifices that will be forgotten, *"for God is not unjust to forget your work and labor of love which you have shown toward His name, in that you have ministered to the saints, and do minister"* (Heb 6:10). It will be worth it no matter what it costs.

"Heavenly Father, the world desperately needs to see Your love in action between believers. Please give me the will and wisdom to love my brothers and, in doing so, make a statement to the world of Your great love for everyone."

MARCH 19

Confront a Brother's Disobedience

Matt 18:15–17—"*If your brother sins [against you]*, **go**~~ **and show him his fault***~ *when the two of you are alone. If he listens to you, you have regained your brother. But if he does not listen,* **take***~ **one or two others with you**, *so that at the testimony of two or three witnesses every matter may be established. If he refuses to listen to them,* **tell***~ **it to the church**. *If he refuses to listen to the church,* **treat**~~ **him like a Gentile** *or a tax collector."*

The church is a mutual ministry that includes exhorting, admonishing, encouraging, instructing, loving, edifying, caring, submitting to, and confessing faults or sins to one another. We need to be open to exhortation by fellow believers.

The excuse for tolerance of sin and false teaching can come from a faulty application of Jesus's statement to "*judge not lest you be judged*" (Matt 7:1). If we have a false sense of humility, we feel uncomfortable holding others accountable—but we are commanded to do so.

If a "*brother sins*"—that is, disobeys the commands in Scripture—he or she needs to be confronted directly and privately in a spirit of humility by another believer. The objective is to help restore the offender (Gal 6:1–4). *Sin* means "missing the mark," or an offense against God Himself and His reputation. A brother should confront the disobedient believer as soon as possible.

The word *show him his fault* means to "bring to light or expose." The disobedient person may not be aware of the command that he has transgressed. If done privately, in a spirit of love and confidence, a change of heart is more likely, and a more intimate bond of brotherhood can result.

To avoid misunderstanding, if the person rebels or refuses to obey, then the one exhorting is to return with one or two witnesses, each in the spirit of humility. Should the disobedient believer continue to rebel against the word, then—and only then—should the sinful behavior go public to the church body: "*Those who continue in sin, rebuke in the presence of all, so that the rest also may be fearful of sinning*" (1 Tim 5:19–20). After this third attempt to encourage obedience, then the congregation is told to "*take special note of that man and do not associate with him, so that he may be put to shame. Do not regard him as an enemy, but admonish him as a brother*" (2 Thes 3:14–15). This is "tough love."

"Lord Jesus, because Your Holy Spirit lives in me, fill me with Your love and humility to allow Your Spirit to work in me to help correct a fellow believer who may be sinning against You and other people."

MARCH 20

Rebuke Your Brother and Forgive Him

Luke 17:3—*"Watch yourselves~~! If your brother sins,* **rebuke*~ him**. *If he repents,* **forgive*~ him.***"*

The combination of rebuking and forgiving makes the Christian relationship unique in this world. In Luke 17:1, Jesus had warned, *"It is impossible that no offenses should come, but woe to him through whom they come!"* We are so prone to disobeying that we must watch out for each other and be open to rebuke.

If we all tend to be disobedient (James 3:2), then we should all frequently be rebuked (or be forced to recognize our own sins), repent, ask forgiveness, and be restored. This repeated cycle requires a certain healthy humility and vulnerability.

The progressive command to "continually be watching out for yourselves" can never be ignored. However, this is a plural command, thus it is a corporate command. Jesus commanded us to care for each other: *"Continually be watching one another."*

The command to *"rebuke"* means "to charge someone as being blamable, or strongly censure." It is the task of every one of us to keep each other from being destroyed or from destroying others by sin. Yes, you are your *"brother's keeper"* (Gen 4:9). Such a confrontation requires prayerfulness, humility, a commitment to forgive, and a high respect for God's word.

In the next verse, Jesus said they had to forgive up to seven times *"in a day."* The rabbis taught to forgive three times in a day made a perfect man. After Jesus taught the threefold step of confrontation for sin (Matt 18:15–17), Peter blurted out a question showing he could not believe Jesus should be take seriously: *"How often shall my brother sin against me, and I forgive him? Up to seven times?"* (Matt 18:21).

Jesus must have wanted to chuckle, but He responded, *"Not seven times, I tell you, but seventy times seven!"* (Matt 18:22). He was saying, "Forgive the penitent always, unconditionally, just as I do you!" It was not any easier for Peter then than it is for us today, but we must obey. Are you open to rebuke?

"Lord, when I sin, help me be willing to be rebuked and to take action to change my behavior. Only with this attitude can I be ready to rebuke another as Your Spirit guides me through the word."

MARCH 21

Restore the Fallen; Pay Attention to Yourself

Gal 6:1—*"Brothers and sisters, if a person is discovered in some sin, you who are spiritual **restore~~ such a person** in a spirit of gentleness. Pay close attention [implied imperative] to yourselves, so that you are not tempted too."*

The restoration ministry is technically not the responsibility of the church leadership but that of the *"brothers and sisters"* in the church. This verse deals with a counseling ministry to restore a fallen believer.

A *sin*, means "a lapse or deviation from truth," results from either ignorance or flagrant disobedience. Even with the new nature planted in the believer by the Holy Spirit, sinful desires persist (Gal 5:16–18). This person was *"discovered in some sin"*: the verb is in the passive mode, meaning "to be overtaken, or be caught unawares" (Tim Friberg, *Analytical Greek Lexicon*) Appropriate confrontation, confession, forgiveness, restitution, and restoration will demonstrate to everyone the integrity, transparency, honesty, and commitment to obedience of the church.

The command is to *"continually do everything possible"* to *"restore"* the fallen. The word *restore* means to "set a broken bone, or refit a ship after a difficult voyage for the next voyage." It is a task for the *"spiritual,"* those who *"walk by the Spirit"* (Gal 5:16). Spiritual maturity is evident in *"those who are of full age, that is, those who by reason of use [study and application] have their senses exercised to discern both good and evil"* (Heb 5:13–14), especially by knowing all the commands.

This is a delicate ministry that requires *"gentleness,"* or "mildness," as opposed to a critical, judgmental spirit that usually provokes rebellion and rejection. Paul wrote to Timothy *"in humility correcting those who are in opposition, if God perhaps will grant them repentance"* (2 Tim 2:25).

They were (and we are) commanded to *"pay close attention"*; this means they are to "keep an eye on" or "look out for" sin so that the restoration team is not tempted by it. Paul's advice in Romans 16:19 to be *"simple [innocent] concerning evil"* is a good policy. Keep the issue to the root causes of rebellion, selfishness, pride, or disbelief instead of any tempting details of specific sins that can be too entrapping. Be wise, caring, and committed to honoring His word. Do we care enough about each other to practice this?

"Loving Father, Your children are prone to sin even though we are Christ's followers. Please make me quick to detect sin in my own heart and confess it to You so that I may be ready to help another person in his moment of need."

MARCH 22

Honor Your Father and Mother

Eph 6:2–3—"*"Honor~~ your father and mother,' which is the first commandment with promise: 'that it may be well with you and you may live long on the earth.'"*

The core value of any society is the family. When people conceive negative beliefs that demean and depreciate the importance of the family, our society or our church is doomed to fail.

A major issue with teenagers is their selfish bitterness and disillusionment toward their parents, which provokes them to reject their parents as well as their values and beliefs. Children must learn from whatever wisdom their parents possess and submit to them in order to mature.

A child's twofold responsibility is to learn to be obedient (Eph 6:1) and to *"honor"* his parents (6:2). These two aspects are different. Obedience is an obligation while under the parent's care, but to honor is to respect and love perpetually. This commandment includes the promise *"that it may go well with you"* and that you will have a long life on earth (6:3). Anyone who grows up in a family where obedience, self-discipline, and respect of parents are emphasized will have the keys to all relationships in an ordered and harmonious society.

The word *honor* means "to reverence, to worship, to hold in awe, to value at a high price." This is the learned attitude of slaves (or employees) toward their masters (or bosses; 1 Tim 6:11), of husbands toward wives (1 Pet 3:7), and of everyone toward those in government and leadership (Rom 13:7).

The failure of parents, as well as children, to practice biblical principles is inevitably the cause of family dysfunction and disintegration. If children would learn obedience, respect, and forgiveness in the family and parents would learn patience, caring respect, and how to discipline their children without destroying their self-worth, more families would be healthy.

Children must learn to forgive their parents for hurtful words or acts of embarrassment or abuse, especially when used as a misguided means of correcting a child. How are you honoring your parents or leaders?

"Dear Jesus, I praise You for the parents who teach their children to seek excellence, to be honest, to love and honor God, to be diligent, and to be giving. May I always honor the memory of my own parents by following their example."

MARCH 23

Demonstrate Your Gentleness

Phil 4:5—*"**Let everyone see***~ **your gentleness** [fairness, equitable]. The Lord is near!"*

Whenever someone sees the golden arches, he thinks of McDonald's restaurants. In marketing terms, this is called *branding*. It is an image-to-value association. In Philippians 4:5, Paul is seeking to establish the "branding" of the followers of Christ, where each one contributes to the image-making reputation of the church as being one of "gentleness." The definition of the term is one "that considerate courtesy and respect for the integrity of others which prompts a person not to be forever standing on his rights" (*Theological Dictionary of the New Testament*).

Paul made his argument for the moral will of God to be obeyed on this basis: *"Now I, Paul, myself am pleading with you by the meekness and gentleness [lit. "magnanimity, sweet reasonableness"] of Christ—who in presence am lowly among you, but being absent am bold toward you"* (1 Cor 10:1). John MacArthur Jr. describes the translations as offering a wide variety of meanings to this Greek word: "generosity, goodwill, friendliness, charity toward the faults of others, mercy toward the failures of others, indulgence of the failures of others, leniency, bigheartedness, moderation, forbearance and gentleness are some of the different efforts to translate the rich meaning of this word. Perhaps the best corresponding English word is graciousness; the humble graciousness that produces patience to endure injustice, disgrace and mistreatment without retaliation, bitterness, or vengeance. It is contentment" (MacArthur, *Philippians*, 276).

Every Christian leader must be *"gentle"* and *"peaceable"* (1 Tim 3:30; Titus 3:2). As an encouragement to always act in this manner, Paul gives pause for reflection: *"The Lord is near."* This phrase has two implications. First, the Lord is close at hand as an ever-present help in time of need, and He is keenly aware of a believer's reactions, conduct, and attitudes in every circumstance. The Spirit of God is ever near to give grace. Second, if He is coming soon, He will make all things right, so we can be patient until then. Are we contributing to this branding of Christ's followers, or do we want to be seen as the proud, successful, important, arrogant, get-all-that's-mine, or get-even kind of a person that characterizes the rest of the world?

"Father, You want Your children to treat others fairly in an attitude of meekness and gentleness. May these characteristics be apparent, like a shield, as I interact with others today."

MARCH 24

Be Subject to Elders; Clothe Yourself

1 Pet 5:5—*"In the same way, you who are younger, **be subject***~ **to the elders**. And all of you, **clothe yourselves***~ **with humility** toward one another, because God opposes the proud but gives grace to the humble."*

The treatment of seniors or people of authority is to be an ingrained cultural practice based on biblical principles. In this passage, Peter is dealing with the attitude of church elders toward their flock. Leaders must not be motivated by compensation or the need to lord it over others; rather, they must be an example for others to imitate (1 Pet 5:2–3). Peter instructs the younger people to *"immediately decide to be subject . . . to your elders"* (lit. "to arrange under or be subordinate").

We must decide to submit to our elders, who have been given the responsibility to take care of God's people (Acts 20:28). This is the same word used in 3:1: *"Wives, likewise, be submissive to your husbands."* Wives learn by watching their husbands' submission to their authorities (i.e., to church, job, state, taxes, and God).

To facilitate a healthy relationship, Peter commands them to be *"clothed with humility."* The word *clothed* means "to tie on oneself," coming from the word meaning "an apron of a slave." We are to figuratively dress ourselves as humble slaves. We are to see humility as a beautiful adornment. Unselfishness, the essence of true humility, opens the door to trustworthiness and sincerity.

Peter's imagery is reminiscent of the night when the apostles were arguing about who would be the greatest in the coming kingdom of Christ, when Jesus silently arose to wash everyone's dirty, sandaled feet. Peter concludes, *"Finally, all of you be of one mind, having compassion for one another; love as brothers, be tenderhearted, be courteous"* (1 Pet 3:8).

The pride within us resists this value of humility, so Peter alludes to Proverbs 3:34 to emphasize God's distinct attitude toward the proud and the humble: *"God resists the proud."* In this sense, *resists* literally means "sets Himself against, or ranges in battle against." On the other hand, He *"gives grace to the humble,"* which refers to the special favor God bestows on a person's life. We become what we desire and value. It's our choice. He is listening.

"Dear Lord, You bless Your children when we obey Your principles. Today, guide my thoughts and actions as I seek to humbly submit to those who have spiritual authority over me."

MARCH 25

Remove Your Sins First

Luke 6:42—*"How can you say to your brother, 'Brother, let me remove the speck from your eye,' while you yourself don't see the beam in your own? You hypocrite!* **First remove*~ the beam** *from your own eye, and then you can see clearly to remove the speck from your brother's eye."*

Individuals tend to minimize their own sins while maximizing those of others. Whenever you seek to warn someone else against pursuing a sinful behavior, understand that the person you seek to help could easily see a weakness or failure in your own life as a beam or log while viewing his own sin as a splinter.

This text is obviously a hyperbole—an exaggerated statement—intended to provide a vivid picture of the biblical teaching so we may apply it to our personal lives before we attempt to help others.

Everyone commits sins. John wrote in his First Epistle that the person who does not admit his own sins is deceiving himself, and *"the truth is not in [him]"* (1 Jn 1:8). This is a symptom of an unsaved person—that is, one who does not know the Bible's teachings about sin. Such people fail to see the reality of how awful they appear in the light of God's holiness.

Their focus is so critical toward others that they do not waste time examining their own disobedience. They ignore the inconvenient commands—especially ones that deal with attitudes of service, mercy, loving each other, and being non-judgmental—all the while criticizing and defaming anyone not following their set of rules.

One of the joys of teaching is the opportunity to research the Scripture to determine its meaning in the time in which it was written and then applying the same principle to your own life in a prayerful commitment. This may mean a personal repentance, a reconciliation, or restitution of actions done in the past before the teacher has a sense of the liberty to be free to teach it to others. Anyone who desires godliness or holiness must constantly search the Scriptures to know the commands and adjust his life to a transparent dependency on God's power in order to obey them. The reality is that we are all struggling together to overcome sin. We cannot shoot our wounded.

"Renew a right spirit within me, dear Jesus, and remind me to check my own heart before trying to correct or teach Your ways to another."

Be Merciful

Luke 6:36—*"**Be merciful** ~~, just as your Father is merciful."*

Jude 22—*"And **have mercy**~~ **on those who waver**."*

In some cultures, mercy is seen as a weakness, primarily because of the belief that leadership is empowered by fear. Mercy is seen as the juxtaposition to fear. Jesus comes on the scene teaching that we are to love our enemies (Luke 6:35), which must have provoked the question "What kind of a leader will Jesus be?"

My brother-in-law Larry once spoke privately to a waitress, "Thank you for serving us so graciously during our meal. I have a Friend who gave me a message to tell you. He told me to ask you to think of the worse sin that you ever committed. Something you would not want anyone to ever know about. Are you thinking of that sin now?" She nodded. "He wanted me to tell you that He forgives you that sin and any other that you want Him to forgive. He also said to tell you He loves you." She was teary-eyed and dumbfounded. Larry turned to leave and then turned back to say, "Oh, by the way, do you know my Friend?" She nodded affirmatively and said, "It was Jesus, right?" "Yes, that's Him!" Larry replied. Their eyes met for a moment. "Thank you so much," she said. Then Larry touched her shoulder and left. An unforgettable seed was planted.

In times of failure, one does not need a judge or critic condemning and inducing guilt. One may simply need a helpful person who mirrors our God of mercy (1 Cor 1:3; James 5:11) and forgiveness: "*For the Lord Your God is a merciful God, He will not abandon or destroy you or forget the covenant with your forefathers, which he confirmed to them by oath*" (Deut 4:31).

Sadly, most men are not like our God: "*David said to Gad, 'I am in deep distress. Let us fall into the hands of the Lord, for His mercy is great; but do not let me fall into the hands of men'*" (2 Sam 24:14[NIV]). Four hundred years later, Daniel wrote of Yahweh, "*The Lord our God is merciful and forgiving, even though we have rebelled against Him!*" (Dan 9:9). The goal for the believer is to be as merciful to others as God is to us.

The verse prompts us to imitate the characteristics of our God. If He is merciful, then we, as His children, are obligated to learn to be just as merciful today by His grace and the empowerment of His Spirit. Think of someone to show mercy to today.

"Heavenly Father, what a wonderful thing to experience Your mercy each day! Open my eyes to the opportunities You are giving me to show mercy to others."

Dot Not Judge Food, Drink, or Special Days

Col 2:16—*"So let no one judge~/ you in food or in drink,* or regarding a festival or a new moon or Sabbaths."

Legalism is a controlling theology linked with manipulative techniques of criticizing and judging anyone not conforming to a set of interpretative standards of morality. It forces conformity to man-made spirituality, targeting superficial and external behaviors.

The command in Colossians 2:16 is to *"let no one judge you"*—that is, do not let it bother you. Christ has redeemed the believer from any guilt of the law, which had been a barrier between the sinner and God. Therefore, the believer should not let anyone intimidate him by making him feel guilty (as the Pharisees condemned Jesus's followers for not washing their hands in Matt 15:2 according to their oral tradition).

Paul wrote that *"Christ is the end of the law for righteousness to everyone who believes"* (Rom 10:4), so it is a fruitless and wasted effort to attempt to become more righteous or acceptable by any legalistic system. In fact, *"it was for freedom that Christ set us free; therefore keep standing firm and do not be subject again to a yoke of slavery"* (Gal 5:1). Anytime someone says, "It is not enough to merely have Christ as Savior. You must obey all these man-made laws to be acceptable," you can be sure that such people are legalists seeking to obligate (enslave) everyone to obey their version of Christianity.

Paul wrote to the Romans, *"The kingdom of God is not eating and drinking, but righteousness and peace and joy in the Holy Spirit"* (Rom 14:17). The dietary laws have been annulled, as well as the formerly mandatory festivals and Sabbath days.

All the Old Testament laws were but a *"shadow of what is to come; but the substance belongs to Christ"* (Col 2:17). He alone was the perfect substitute sacrifice for all man's sins. The shadows of the Old Testament are no longer God's plan; rather, they pointed toward a real object, or *"substance,"* that cast the shadows, which was Jesus. Now that the real sacrifice has appeared, putting your faith in the *"substance"* of Christ as God's sacrificial offering for our forgiveness is the only means of acceptance before God.

Now the focus of obedience to His word is not to be more acceptable, but to please the Savior and to demonstrate that you take His word seriously

"Lord Jesus, You provided us a perfect example to live by. Help me today to obey Your commands without fear of what others may think, but also please keep me from imposing my convictions on others."

MARCH 28

Do Not Judge by External Appearances

Jn 7:24—*"Do not judge~/ according to external appearance,* but *judge*~ with proper judgment."*

It is a natural human response to take the appearance of things as reality or to see what we want to see in others. Judging by appearances misleads us, with many negative consequences.

In John 7:24, Jesus had been teaching on the third day of the week of the Feast of Tabernacles that anyone who speaks from himself seeks his own glory, but he who "seeks the glory of [God] is true and has no unrighteousness is in Him." Then Jesus added, *"Did not Moses give you the law, yet none of you keeps the law?"* The crowd prided themselves in appearing to obeying the strictest part of the law. Whoever acted differently was criticized and condemned.

Then Jesus made this "antireligious" statement: *"Stop judging according to external appearance"*—that is, refrain from judging by superficial measures and preconceived conclusions. Since Jesus did not measure up to their expectations, He was rejected long before He clarified His teachings about His deity. His condemnation of their hypocrisy led the religious establishment to a search for a justification for His crucifixion.

Every day, we make decisions to accept or reject potential employees, team members, life mates, friends, and so on, and these decisions are primarily based on appearances. Few people see beyond the externals to value the inner qualities above the external appearance.

We are told to *"judge with proper judgment."* Earlier, Jesus had said, *"Do not judge, or you too will be judged"* (Matt 7:1); He was denouncing those whose critical attitudes condemn others by comparing them to their own "superior" standards. Those not measuring up are discarded. Even the prophet Samuel was surprised when God chose David to be king. He learned that *"God does not view things the way men do. People look on the outward appearance, but the Lord looks at the heart"* (1 Sam 16:7b). *"Proper judgment"* refers to biblical values and taking His commands seriously. The wisdom of God's word contains this *"proper judgment."*

"Give me wisdom, dear Lord, to see others as You see them without jumping to judgments from mere appearances. I want to learn to be patient and give time for Your Spirit to provide biblical insight and understanding as I deal with others."

2

MARCH 29
Save Others

Jude 23—*"Save~~ **others** by snatching them out of the fire; have mercy on others, coupled with a fear of God, hating even the clothes stained by the flesh."*

If truth is truth, then the consequences of not knowing, or rejecting, the truth are catastrophic. The fear of the Lord is primarily the fear that He will do exactly what He says He will do. Either we intervene or we harden our consciences and ignore the plight of others who don't know the truth.

In Jude 23, Jude had just commanded believers to *"have mercy on some, who are doubting"* (Jude 22) due to the influence of false teachers in the church who provoked doubt that God would send anyone to hell. This sounds like the Serpent in the beginning, saying, "You will not surely die" (Gen 3:4), even though God said they would.

Now Jude gives a present-tense command to all believers to *"be continually involved in the saving of others."* Every believer is to have an evangelistic purpose to his or her daily life, because the unbeliever is already condemned and lives under the imminent threat of eternal punishment. John wrote, *"He who believes in Him is not condemned; but he who does not believe is condemned already [perfect tense: 'has already been condemned'], because he has not believed in the name of the only begotten Son of God"* (Jn 3:18).

In 1792, a cobbler in rural England named William Carey wrote a work titled "An Inquiry into the Obligations of Christians to Use Means for the Conversion of the Heathen." Carey believed sinners everywhere have no hope of avoiding an eternal hell unless they encounter a believer during their lifetime who tells them the good news that Christ died for their sins. This motivated him to sail to India to save the Hindus from a Christless eternity and to translate the Bible into forty languages.

Jude commands us to *"snatch them out of the fire."* The verb means to "aggressively grasp something by force." The prophet Amos wrote of Israel, *"You were like a firebrand snatched from a blaze"* (Amos 4:11). Their false beliefs had to be exposed and rejected . Some will listen.

Jesus gave us the example of being patient with people who are doubtful yet searching (Jn 4:10–26; 6:26–59); on the other hand, He frankly warned those committed to false teaching of the gravity of their lost condition (Matt 12:1–37; Jn 8:12–59). Here is a goal: share the gospel five times a week. Count them on the fingers of your hand. Be accountable to a partner.

"Merciful Father, You gave up everything to provide salvation and forgiveness for sinful human beings. Teach me the compassion and commitment to do my part in snatching others from the consequences of their sin."

MARCH 30

Do Everything for the Glory of God

1 Cor 10:31—*"So whether you eat or drink, or whatever you do, **do**~~ everything for the glory of God."*

During the Old Testament times, Israel had caused such embarrassment to God that He allowed them to be captured and dispersed in shame throughout the Middle East, primarily to *"vindicate the holiness of [His] great name which has been profaned among the nations, which [the Israelites had] profaned in their midst. Then the nations [would] know that [He is] the Lord"* (Ezek 36:23).

The church is challenged to see the world in a different light: we are to *"[look] unto Jesus, the author and finisher of our faith, who for the joy that was set before Him endured the cross, despising the shame, and has sat down at the right hand of the throne of God"* (Heb 12:2). He accepted shame as a part of God's purpose. To follow Christ's example means to be willing to be ridiculed, despised, and rejected for how we live and what we believe without yielding to pressure from our culture.

The key to Christ's method of glorifying God is seen in John 17:4: *"I have glorified You on the earth. I have finished the work which You have given Me to do."* Ours is a life of purpose and submission to accomplish Someone else's agenda and to bring renown to Another instead of to ourselves. *"And whatever you do, whether in word or deed, do it all in the name of the Lord Jesus"* (Col 3:17), not to build up your name, fame, or reputation, but rather to build His honor.

In this context, we should glorify God by what we allow ourselves to *"eat or drink"*: we should be willing to give up our rights to any questionable food even though we have the biblical right to consume it. God is glorified by our humility and submission to the preferences of others. Paul wrote, *"You were bought at a price; therefore, glorify God in your body and in your spirit, which are God's"* (1 Cor 6:20). If God is glorified by my willingness to give up my rights, then I must consider it a privilege to do so, especially if it encourages someone to keep walking with Christ and learning from His word. What have you given up for Christ?

"Dear Lord, it is my privilege to relinquish my rights in order to accomplish Your tasks for me on this earth. Help me honor You by being willing to suffer the shame associated with Your death on the cross."

MARCH 31
Do Not Give Offense to Other Cultures

1 Cor 10:32—*"**Do not give offense**~| to Jews or Greeks or to the church of God, even as I try to please everybody in every way. For I am not seeking my own good but the good of many, so that they may be saved."*

The 1958 novel *The Ugly American* sold seven million copies and became a slogan to describe egotistical, self-interested Americans who cared little about other cultures.

Every country or people group will give different meanings to behavior and words. We communicate more by our actions, gestures, and intonation than we do by the words we speak. If we care, we will avoid anything offensive.

This summation of Paul's discussion (1 Cor 10:27–30) explained his attitude toward the cultural norms that defined different ethnic groups. Earlier, he wrote that he adjusted to the Jews, as well as to the Gentiles where he labored (9:19–23).

In spite of Paul's commitment not to offend different cultures, he never failed to share the gospel, even though this might cause offense. He boldly told the Jews and the Greeks to turn to God in repentance and to put their faith in Christ (Acts 20:21). Paul went out of his way not to provoke rejection of him as a messenger so that his message would not be discarded.

Paul never asked for anything for himself, even though he taught that all Christian workers are entitled to financial support (1 Cor 9:12–18). He forfeited his normal right for recompense so that others would never find his motives suspect and discard his message. He would do anything to communicate the gospel to all the cultures of his day.

Paul navigated a variety of cultural norms. He was comfortable with the Jews and many Gentile cultures, in which Greek or Latin were likely secondary languages. Most provinces were of different ethnicities. The distinct practices of the "church of God," with a variety of scruples, forced Paul to adjust his lifestyle without violating any principle in Scripture.

Paul did not seek to benefit himself but to *"please . . . many."* The word for *please* means "to fit, adapt to, accommodate to, or be acceptable to." Big cities in North America may have more than two hundred cultures or languages, which demands an intercultural commitment from today's messenger. Can you make everyone feel comfortable with you?

"Dear God, You want us to uphold Your word at all costs. Therefore, as I take the gospel to other places, I must be sensitive to nuances of meanings in other cultures in order to communicate correctly."

APRIL 1

Recognize Servants of God

1 Cor 16:18—*"For they refreshed my spirit and yours. So then, **recognize~~ people like this**."*

How do you show appreciation to someone, and how often should you show it without "spoiling" that person? In 1 Corinthians 16:18, Paul had just described the contributions of several workers in the church at Corinth.

Stephanus was an early convert who had matured into a ministry leader. His whole household was credited in the commendation: *"They devoted themselves to the ministry [service] of the saints. I urge you also to submit to people like this, and to everyone who cooperates in the work and labors hard"* (1 Cor 16:14–16).

The next group of workers came to Paul from Corinth: *"Stephanus, Fortunatus and Achaicus"* (1 Cor 16:17) were a great asset to Paul: they *"refreshed [his] spirit"* (Gk. "cause to rest") as they had already done to the church at Corinth. What a delight to be around folks who, by their unselfish attitudes and sincere interest in your needs over their own, lift your spirit to rejoicing.

This is a command for the members of the church to *"submit to people like this"* (1 Cor 16:16). Their commitment to serve the church members and others without seeking personal benefit proves they are trustworthy.

The command to *"recognize"* (Gk. "cause to be known") is a double-edged sword. We are commanded to motivate all workers and leaders in the ministry, not just by honor, but by constant reaffirmation of their refreshing spirit and specific benefits. It is not always healthy to make the recognition monetary, because greed is subtle and self-deceiving. We cannot forget the warning that if we attempt to do ministry *"to be seen by [men]"* (Matt 6:1), or to *"have glory from men"* (6:2), then there is no reward for us in heaven! Frequent, private, individual recognition is always good.

In ministering to one another, we can always encourage one another, praise one another, esteem one another, care for one another, serve one another, and submit to one another in the spirit of love and peace. Letting people know how effective their ministry has been to your spiritual life and maturity is always good. Who have you recognized and appreciated recently as being a challenge and a blessing to your walk with Christ?

"Lord, I am so self-centered that I find it difficult to want others to be more recognized and honored than I am. Give me ideas to encourage my leaders and build their reputations."

APRIL 2

Do Not Blame God

James 1:13—"**Let no one say~| when he is tempted**, 'I am tempted by God'; for God cannot be tempted by evil, nor does He Himself tempt anyone."

The human tendency is to blame God for everything, especially misfortune or calamity, thus avoiding any human responsibility. Proverbs puts it this way: "*When a man's folly brings his way to ruin, his heart rages against the Lord*" (19:3).

In James 1:13, James had just declared, "*Blessed is the man who endures temptation; for when he has been approved, he will receive the crown of life which the Lord has promised to those who love Him*" (1:12).

The present-tense verb form "*I am being tempted*" can have two meanings: one positive, "to try to discover the nature or character of something by testing," and one negative, "to entice to improper behavior" (Bauer-Danker Lexicon). The context generally makes the choice for us, as in our text today.

James is dealing with our personal response to our inherent evil. If the believer yields to the temptation of immediate gratification, doubting God's wisdom and instruction, then he reaps the inevitable negative consequences of sin and possibly death (James 1:15). The correct response to temptation leads us to spiritual maturity, wisdom, and blessings.

Blaming circumstances or others for our incorrect decisions or moral failures is only self-deceiving and unhelpful. A poor man's poverty cannot turn him into a thief and thus justify his stealing; the cause is his own greed. An alcoholic might blame his business pressures or family problems for his drinking, and he might continue toward any number of catastrophes, none of which were God's doing.

The command means "everyone stop saying," or telling yourself to justify your own disobedience. Wrong thoughts breed wrong behavior. You can chose to believe that "*no trial has overtaken you that is not faced by others. And God is faithful: He will not let you be tried beyond what you are able to bear, but with the trial will also provide a way out so that you may be able to endure it*" (1 Cor 10:13). As the wind strengthens the trees, so trials give endurance to those who desire to follow Christ.

"Lord, It is so easy to blame You for the bad things that happen in my life and take credit for the good things. When will I learn to repeat to myself the truth that You have nothing to do with evil that happens in my life? I trust You, Lord, for grace in all circumstances."

APRIL 3

Humble Yourself under God's Hand and Wait

1 Pet 5:6—*"And God will exalt you in due time, **if you humble yourselves***~ under his mighty hand."*

The quest for significance drives many to be the best or the most important, admired, powerful, or famous. The command in 1 Peter 5:6 is the opposite of everything our culture tells us we need to be happy.

The connective *"And"* ties this verse to the preceding one: *"God opposes the proud, but gives grace to the humble"* (1 Pet 5:5). Now our verse literally means it is wiser to "immediately decide to humble yourselves," which means "to make low, assign yourself a lower rank below others who are honored or rewarded" or *"to submit oneself in a lowly spirit to the power and will of God."* Instead of striving to be in total control of our lives and destinies, the aorist imperative verb demands an urgent decision to submit to whatever God's will permits whenever He commands it. We must make an internal commitment to trust in the *"mighty hand"* of God to engineer the circumstances and timing He deems are best.

Jesus taught us the importance of this principal: *"Everyone who lifts himself up will be humbled, and everyone who humbles himself will be lifted up"* (Luke 14:11; 18:14).

Humility does not mean depreciating or "running down" your self-worth but replacing your self-centered motivation with other-centered priorities. We must decide that our personal needs, desires, interests, and ambitions will take a lower priority while we make the needs of others our primary mission (Phil 2:2–4). In this context, a God-centered, self-humbling process occurs when one ceases to want to control his life and lets God have it fully. The next verse says, *"[Cast] all your care upon Him, for He cares for you"* (5:7). These imperative participles describe the means of this humbling process. It is humbling to let God have control.

It is vain to believe that you can run your life better than God can and that you can meet your own needs (and desires) better than God can. It is often humiliating to become totally dependent on God's interventions in order to survive. God's way toward exaltation is to give up that control. Can you trust His "mighty hand" to provide for you . . . in His own time? Will you take on a lowly task for God that benefits others and that few may see?

"Lord, my ego is so deceptive that I tend to think of my importance and what I think I deserve in life more than the importance of others and what I can give to them. Teach me to think humbly."

APRIL 4

Live by the Spirit

Gal 5:16—*"But I say,* **live~~ by the Spirit** *and you will not carry out the desires of the flesh."*

What does it mean to "continually be living by the Spirit"? After receiving Christ, the transforming power of the gospel (Rom 1:16), which is the indwelling of the Spirit in all believers, begins to change believers into Christ's likeness. Transformation is possible because we are now *"strengthened with power through His Spirit in the inner man"* (Eph 3:16), which empowers us to become more obedient. Without the Spirit, we are powerless against the flesh.

The Spirit gave the Scripture to guide the believer into a transformed life: *"Let the word of Christ dwell in you richly in all wisdom, teach and admonishing one another"* (Col 3:16). The New Testament commands are not a legalistic set of external rules to demonstrate spirituality; rather, they deal with attitudes of love and care, or duty and sacrifice for others, of self-denial and our relationship to the Spirit, all of which form the inner principles that guide a transformed lifestyle.

Once we learn the commands, the Holy Spirit then guides us in applying them for the benefit of others. The present progressive imperative verb means *"to be continually living by the Spirit"*—that is, "to walk around, conduct oneself in all phases of life" in harmony with how the Spirit has revealed Himself. This is a progressive transformation into harmony with the indwelling Spirit, until He is as perfectly comfortable residing within us as we are comfortable living in His perpetual presence. The command implies our volition or commitment to walk in the light of what the Spirit has instructed believers to value, think about, prioritize, and commit to do in His word.

The command to *"live by the Spirit,"* which results in "not fulfilling the desires of the flesh," is parallel to the command to *"put on the Lord Jesus Christ, and make no provision for the flesh in regard to its lusts"* (Rom 13:14). As soon as the believer learns of and decides to obey the Spirit's inspired instructions, the Spirit empowers him to obey them, creating a new character or heart within the believer that increasingly looks like Jesus's. This is not a mystical experience but a conscious choice to follow the Spirit's revelation of God's will in His word.

"Thank You, Lord, for the Spirit that dwells in me and brings to my mind Your words and commands. As I learn them, help me yield to the Spirit's urging to obey Your word."

APRIL 5
_____

Do Not Grieve the Spirit

Eph 4:30—*"And **do not grieve~/ the Holy Spirit of God**, by whom you were sealed for the day of redemption."*

Can you imagine the hurt that Jesus felt when He was led out of the predawn, drummed-up trial at the Sanhedrin inquest, where He was railed on and beaten by the people He came to save? The deeper hurt came after He left the judgment hall: across the courtyard, His friend and apostle, Peter, had just sworn in a convincing voice that he knew nothing of this Jesus. Just then, they led Jesus past Peter, *"and the Lord turned and their eyes met"* (Luke 22:61). Peter never got over it, because he knew how much he had disappointed Jesus.

Sin is a hurtful offense to God (Psa 51:4), especially when His children, in whom His Spirit dwells, refuse to change their attitudes or old lifestyles and are indifferent to His instructions. God's Spirit "grieves," which means "to cause grief, offend, cause pain," because He is a person, and too often we ignore Him.

In Ephesians 4:30, believers were lying and getting angry with each other, stealing instead of sharing, and speaking damaging words about each other instead of building each other up, all of which deeply hurt the Spirit. The verb implies they were already doing the action and had to "stop grieving" the Spirit.

One of the greatest motives for learning the commands in Scripture is to avoid grieving the Holy Spirit within us. When we chose to *"believe"* in the gospel, we *"were sealed with the Holy Spirit of promise, who is the guarantee of our inheritance until the redemption of the purchased possession"* (Eph 1:13–14). Thus the Spirit is sealed within us, regardless of how comfortable He may be.

When Ananias ignored the Spirit when he pretended to give everything, Peter asked him, *"Why has Satan filled your heart to lie to the Holy Spirit... Why have you conceived this thing in your heart? You have not lied to men but to God."* (Acts 5:3, 4). If we do not obey the Spirit, we are only pretending to love Him. When the Spirit is grieved, He chastises us to teach us to walk in harmony with His values and principles. But even when He is grieved, He will never leave us or forsake us ... Thank You, Lord!

"I cannot imagine how difficult it is for Your Spirit to dwell in my being when I hurt Him and grieve Him by ignoring Him and listen to my interests more than His. Thank You for remaining in my life and for Your patience with my stumbling ways."

Do Not Get Drunk; Be Filled by the Spirit

Eph 5:18—*"And **do not get drunk** ~/ with wine, which is debauchery, but **be filled**~~ by the Spirit."*

When I was a boy, I learned to bodysurf. When you are in the surf and a wave gets about eight to ten feet away, you turn in the direction of the wave and jump in the same direction, the wave catches you, and the ride begins all the way to the shore. Great fun!

However, if you just stand in the water, the wave passes right through you. If you begin to swim in any other direction, you will only go up and down with the wave. Only if you begin to move in the direction of the wave is any power transferred. The filling of the Spirit is the same.

Jesus promised, "*I will ask the Father, and He will give you another Helper, that He may be with you forever; that is the Spirit of truth . . . you know Him because He abides **with** you, and will be **in** you*" (Jn 14:16–17). From the moment you believe in Jesus Christ, the Holy Spirit dwells in you forever, and thus you become the "*temple of the Holy Spirit who is in you*" (1 Cor 6:19).

The two commands in Ephesians 5:18 give opposite results, because the conjunction *but* always introduces the opposite of the first clause. The evil of drunkenness is the loss of self-control, but the filling of the Spirit results in more self-control. One aspect of the fruit of the Spirit is the empowerment of your will over the influence of the flesh.

We are to "*stop abandoning ourselves to uncontrollable or immoral behavior*" and to trust God to fill us with His power to overcome the flesh and to serve the needs of others.

All believers have the "*fullness of the Godhead*," and "*you are complete [filled] in Him*" (Col 2:9–10). You lack nothing of Him, but He may not have full control over you.

The verb "to be continually being filled" means to let His will consciously control you as you choose to obey His word intentionally, not going in a different direction and thus avoiding His power and blessing. Choose to walk in the Spirit's direction today.

"Lord, as I step out to obey Your commands, I trust You for the power to keep obeying. Take control of my life by Your Spirit to conform me to Your Word."

APRIL 7

Do Not Extinguish the Spirit

1 Thes 5:19—*"Do not extinguish [or quench]~| the Spirit."*

When we don't want to hear what someone is saying, we can "tune out" or refuse to pay attention. The command in 1 Thessalonians 5:19 refers to our response to what the Spirit revealed in His Word. The verb *extinguish* means "to quench, stifle, or disregard" what the Spirit says.

God allows us free will to choose to obey Him. His objective is to free us *"so all of us who have had that veil removed can see and reflect the glory of the Lord. And the Lord—who is the Spirit—makes us more and more like Him as we are changed into His glorious image"* (2 Cor 3:18[NLT]). This transformation can be defined in the following steps.

First, the Spirit illuminates the word of God to us, *"for to us God revealed them through the Spirit"* (1 Cor 2:10). Believers can quench the Spirit by ignoring what they understand of its message in their hearts (Psa 119:11) or by not letting it dwell richly within (Col 3:16).

Second, the Spirit draws the believer into intimacy with God, *"for you have not received a spirit of slavery leading to fear again, but you have received a spirit of adoption as sons by which we cry out, 'Abba! Father!'"* (Gal 4:6). Paul yearned for an even more intimate walk with Christ (Phil 3:10); he wanted to *"know Him and the power of His resurrection, and the fellowship of His sufferings, being made conformed to His death"* (Phi 3:10). But this desire could be quenched by refusing to accept God's purpose in our difficulties (James 1:2–3, 12) or by trusting in ourselves instead of seeking His wisdom (Prov 3:5–6). If we question His will, the Spirit is quenched.

Third, the Spirit helps the believer follow God's will by teaching us what His will is (*"Do not be unwise, but understand what the will of the Lord is"*; Eph 5:17) and doing what He commands: *"I will put My Spirit within you and cause you to walk in My statutes, and you will be careful to observe My ordinances"* (Ezek 36:27). This work of the Spirit can be extinguished by self-will, pride, selfishness, indifference, and refusal to obey His commands, which all stem from a lack of trust in God's care, His plan, and His purpose for our lives. Don't let your everyday decisions progressively quench the Spirit's commands.

"Thank You for Your Spirit within me that gives me such delight when I walk in obedience and convicts me when I disobey. Oh, that I would learn to always obey!"

APRIL 8

Obey Your Superiors

Eph 6:5–6—*"Slaves, **obey~~ your human masters** with fear and trembling, in the sincerity of your heart as to Christ, not by way of eyeservice, as men-pleasers, but as slaves of Christ, doing the will of God from the heart."*

In Ephesians 5:21[NIV], we have the foundational principle to *"submit to one another out of reverence for Christ."* From this foundation, each side of every relationship has its responsibilities.

Employment conflicts rage throughout all societies, each side accusing the other of selfishness, unconcern for the other, and unwillingness to compromise selfish interests. Each party is trying to get all he can, and each assumes that the other is holding back.

Paul addressed the slaves who had become Christians so they could understand how their new faith implied a new attitude toward others, especially their "human masters." When God's instructions are obeyed, every relationship improves, but when they are ignored, any relationship deteriorates. Each side of the relationship must deal with its own obedience regardless of the response of the other party.

Slaves were to be *"continually obedient"* to their masters, especially as believers. The only exception would be if they were forced to do something immoral, idolatrous, or illegal. Peter clarified that this command included all masters, *"not only those who are good and gentle, but also those who are unreasonable. For this finds favor, if . . . a man bears up under sorrows when suffering unjustly"* (1 Pet 2:18–19).

Being a Christian who follows God's principles should always result in being a better worker, being more productive and diligent, and being trustworthy and agreeable. Titus adds that subordinates are *"to be well-pleasing, not argumentative, not pilfering, but showing all good faith that they may adorn the doctrine of God our Savior in every respect"* (Titus 2:9–10). As believers, we bear the reputation of God through our behavior. The believer's workplace is his field of service and his primary platform for an impact on unbelievers. Keep thinking biblically and you serve the Lord Himself and prove yourself to be productive and submissive. This is Christ-honoring job security.

"Lord, why do You put leaders over me that are intimidating and hard to please? Please give me the grace today to see my service to them as service to You."

APRIL 9
Give Superiors Full Respect

1 Tim 6:1—*"Those who are under the yoke as slaves **must regard~~ their own masters as deserving of full respect**. This will prevent the name of God and Christian teaching from being discredited."*

If we think it is difficult in some job situations today, can you imagine being a slave in the first century? Historians estimate that 70 percent of the Roman population was slaves; thus the churches had a significant mix of owners, freemen, and slaves.

These social differences inspired many of the New Testament church instructions. For all who have *"put on Christ, there is no longer Jew or Gentile, slave or free, male or female. For you are all one in Christ Jesus"* (Gal 3:28).

As the church gathered, social distinctions disappeared before Christ, but not necessarily back in society. Misunderstandings and presumptions forced Paul to give instructions to the churches (as today's text). Paul had to clarify how they should think about each other in the church and in society, as well as in their new standing before Christ.

Regardless of the culture, the *"masters,"* or modern-day managers, bosses, or superiors, are commanded to *"always and continually . . . [be] regarded as worthy of all honor."* This is an even greater issue than a slave's personal feelings. The whole reputation of the gospel is at stake.

How a believer behaves at work and the attitude he shows, even as a slave, has a powerful impact on superiors, as it speaks to the credibility of the gospel and the power of God to have changed such a person. What kind of God would teach laziness, bad attitudes, insubordination, rebellion, and disrespect of superiors?

Superiors will always protect a subordinate who respects or honors them (e.g., protecting them from rumors and listening well to fulfill whatever is asked). Even when such a superior is not "worthy" of such honor, he must be treated with honor as a fellow human being (Titus 3:1–2); out of a newfound love of God, the superior is to be served as though one were serving Christ Himself. Every believer bears the responsibility for the reputation of Christ by how he treats others, especially his superiors.

"Lord, if leaders need respect and significance, please give me the grace to give them what they inwardly need with sincerity for the honor of Your name."

APRIL 10

Employers, Treat Your Employees with Respect

Eph 6:9—*"Masters, **treat~~ your slaves the same way**, giving up the use of threats, because you know that both you and they have the same master in heaven, and there is no favoritism with him."*

A thousand books are written every year on management principles. However, conflicts persist, and regrettably, it is often not any better (if not worse) in Christian organizations. Some *"masters,"* or today's managers or leaders, believe in the use of fear and threats to motivate or control subordinates, as they would have driven slaves to work for them in the first century.

How should a Christian employer differ from a secular employer? Some even say Christian principles do not work or have no place in the business world. However, Christian administrators must live under the commands of Scripture and meditate on how they should be applied in each situation. Living under His rules is the priority.

The command in Ephesians 6:9 deals with how the master/employer who has become a Christian should treat slaves/employees. The owners were "to be continually treating" their slaves *"in the same way"* as slaves were to be concerned about the well-being of their master (Eph 6:5–8).

Because slaves were considered as mere resources for tasks, they were less than human in the master's mind. Often, threats were seen as the only way to control them; however, such manipulative techniques are prohibited because Christian leaders must continually *"[give] up the use of threats."* The term *give up* means "to abandon" the use of "threatening." When Paul wrote to the Colossians about the same problem, he said, *"Masters, [continually be] treat[ing] your slaves with justice and fairness, because you know that you also have a master in heaven"* (Col 4:1).

The Ephesians passage adds, *"There is no favoritism with Him,"* because there is no master-slave or employer-employee relationship in heaven—we are all equal before God. If there is no *"favoritism"* or partiality with God, then there should not be any with us. Everyone should be treated as a brother, even if he is a subordinate. How can you apply these principles in your job situation?

"Father, Your way with me has taught me how to treat those under my responsibility, and I recognize that I cannot pretend to be anything more special to You than anyone else. May I honor Your name by how I treat others."

APRIL 11

Do Not Distinguish between
Believing and Unbelieving Bosses

1 Tim 6:2—*"But those who have believing masters **must not show them less respect~/ because they are brothers**. Instead they are to **serve~~ all the more**, because those who benefit from their service are believers and dearly loved. **Teach~~ them and exhort~~ them** about these things."*

If it was difficult to be a Christian slave owner, imagine how much more difficult it was for converted slaves with a Christian owner. They would say, "Why does he not give me my freedom?"

Christians serving under Christians can be discordant if either one or both fail to know or follow God's instructions. The principle is that all people retain their social distinctions in society despite their spiritual equality. A slave/employee could be an elder in a church with his converted owner/superior as a disciple.

In such workplace relationships, the believing employee cannot "despise" his believing employer. The verb, *"show less respect,"* means not "to be disrespectful, think down," or undervalue or diminish the authority of Christian employers, especially on the job, merely because they are spiritual equals. A secular job relationship is not a church relationship. We cannot presume to have special privileges; rather, we are to *"serve [them] all the more."* If slaves were to serve even an unbelieving master with their whole hearts, how much more would they serve a Christian master!

Believers are to serve their employers obediently, completing all tasks and respectfully honoring superiors and they are to do so sincerely and voluntarily, not grudgingly, *"as unto Christ,"* diligently, *"not with eye-service,"* or not by showing off; and spiritually, by *"doing the will of God from the heart"* (Eph 6:5–6; Col 3:22–23). What an employee!

Paul demands that the churches *"continually teach and exhort [preach] these principles"* (in 4:11, he said *"command and teach"*). Thus this becomes a foundational concept for the Christian work ethic and evangelism. The obligation to teach these concepts repeatedly suggests few were doing it. Do you practice this command today?

"Lord, keep me focused on my tasks for today, and may I serve my authorities regardless of who they are in order to protect the Savior's name that I claim as my Lord."

APRIL 12

Do Not Neglect Hospitality

Heb 13:2— *"Do not neglect~/ hospitality, because through it some have entertained angels without knowing it."*

Hotels or inns were either few or indecent and dangerous or expensive as a means of temporary housing for itinerate ministers. They primarily stayed in homes along the way, similar to contemporary bed-and-breakfast inns designed to help itinerate ministries.

Jesus and the apostles depended on this hospitality wherever they went: *"Now it happened as they went that He entered a certain village; and a certain woman named Martha welcomed Him into her house"* (Luke 10:38). Hospitality could mean a meal and a brief visit, but it usually implied an overnight or extended stay. *Hospitality* means making others feel comfortable and at home. The objective is to encourage them, sharing truths and testimonies while providing for their needs.

In a series of imperative participles, Paul sums up the serving ministries, *"distributing to the needs of the saints, given to hospitality"* (Rom 12:13). Peter describes how to serve one another: *"Be hospitable to one another without grumbling"* (1 Pet 4:9–10). To emphasize its importance, a bishop/elder or pastor was required to be *"hospitable"* (1 Tim 3:2; Titus 1:8).

The focus of 3 John is the ministry of hospitality, where Gaius is commended: *"You are faithful in what you are doing for the brothers, even though they are strangers to you. They have told the church about your love. You will do well to send them on their way in a manner worthy of God. It was for the sake of the Name that they went out, receiving no help from the pagans. We ought therefore to show hospitality to such men so that we may work together for the truth"* (3 Jn 5–9[NIV]).

By serving the needs of others, we indirectly serve the Lord. Matthew says, *"Truly I say to you, to the extent that you did it to one of these brothers of Mine, even the least of them, you did it to Me"* (Matt 25:40). He went on to describe this ministry as feeding the hungry, being hospitable to strangers, clothing the naked, and visiting those imprisoned for Christ's sake. To ignore these opportunities for hospitality is to turn our backs on Jesus (24:45). Have you ever gone to church looking for someone to invite to your home for a meal?

"Thank You, Lord, for those who cross my path whom we can help in our home. Keep me alert to look today for someone You want us to bless."

APRIL 13

Help the Missionari   104

Titus 3:13–14—*"**Make every effort to help***~ Z*
*Apollos **on their way**; make sure they have what they ...*
*way that our people **can learn** ~~ **to engage in good works** to m...*
pressing needs and so not be unfruitful."

Most Christian ministries were supported by donations so they can make disciples. Our text gives a glimpse into the day-to-day networking and logistics of first-century ministries.

These men were disciples of Paul to whom he had delegated the expansion of the ministry. Paul is writing from Macedonia and decides to winter in Nicopolis, after which Paul may have traveled to Spain.

We know nothing about Zenas, except that he was a lawyer with a Greek name, a professional committed to making disciples in unreached areas. Apollos, mentioned in Acts 18:24 and 19:1, was a Jewish Christian from Alexandria who *"was mighty in the scriptures"* and *"fervent in spirit"* and who greatly desired *"to cross to Achaia"* (18:27). These two were heading into unreached areas.

Paul gives an aorist command to believers to *"urgently decide to make every effort to help"* or *"do everything you can"* (Titus 3:13[NIV]). The purpose was to "help" or to "send forward on [their] journey," with the result *"that they [the missionaries] have what they need"* or *"may lack nothing."* Third John 6 added, *"in a manner worthy of God."*

Another reason for helping this missionary team is the command to *"habitually learn to engage in good works."* Paul wanted the believers to "keep on learning" to meet the "pressing needs" of laborers. To fail in meeting these needs was to be "unfruitful." Churches should be given ample opportunities to participate in the ministries of evangelists and missionaries.

Paul encourages us to sacrifice for the ministry, *"not [to] seek the gift, but [to] seek the fruit that abounds to your account"* (Phil 4:17). Believers should take advantage of every chance to be fruitful by contributing to or partaking in kingdom projects, especially those that help missionaries make disciples in unreached areas. With whom are you involved?

"Lord, thank You for Your servants who come to our church and for their life's labor. Give me the desire to be a partner with them by helping meet their needs whatever they may be."

APRIL 14

Remember Your Leaders and Imitate Their Faith

Heb 13:7—*"Remember~~ your leaders, who spoke God's message to you; reflect~~ on the outcome of their lives and imitate~~ their faith."*

One of the greatest confidence builders in a life of obedience is to witness how God's way of living works the best! The three commands in this verse are all based on the evident results of obedience.

First, believers are to *"continually be remembering"* their leaders, which means "to be mindful of," that is, how their families, personal relationships, and the overall positive impact of their lives left a positive influence. If you respect their lives, then pay close attention to their instructions from God's word as to how they lived out the principles of God's word.

The word *leader*, or "one with authority over," refers to anyone given the privilege of teaching the word. The discipline of studying Scripture to teach it obligates the leader's submission to its precepts. The authority given to our leaders is proportionate to the level of transformation that God's word has effected in their lives.

The second command is to *"be reflecting on the outcome of their lives,"* which means to "look at again and again" or "observe carefully" the effects of their specific applications of God's word. Have they lived what they taught?

The third command is to *"be continually imitating their faith."* The New Testament focuses as much on correct doctrine as on an obedient lifestyle. Paul wrote, *"Join with others in following my example"* (Phil 3:17). Paul lived to be an example in order to demonstrate the value of God's commands. Peter likewise demanded that they lead humbly and by example, *"not lording it over those entrusted to [them], but being examples to the flock"* (1 Pet 5:3). Their example is as much the basis of their authority as their role in the ministry. Followers willingly imitate a leader's godly example as they listen to his words.

The power of a leader lies in the respect and integrity of his lifestyle, which others will want to imitate. This admiration can take years to acquire, and a leader must earn it by repeatedly proving that God's way of living is best. Nothing is more valuable to a teacher than this respect. Are you willing to practice obedience for leadership?

"Thank You, Lord, for putting godly leaders in my path and my church. Their lives have been such an example of the application of Your word that I desire their kind of life. Help me live up to their examples."

APRIL 15

Do Not Be Deceived by Bad Company

1 Cor 15:33—*"Do not be deceived~~: 'Bad company corrupts good morals.'"*

It is so easy to be deceived into believing what is not true or thinking something is harmless when it is dangerous. In 1 Corinthians 15:33, Paul had already warned the Corinthians twice about being deceived (1) by the wisdom of this world, which makes a person think he knows better than God about how to live and think (3:18) and (2) by thinking that how we live is irrelevant to God (6:9–10). It seems apparent that the Corinthians were being deceived, and the command was to "*stop being deceived*," or "seduced and led astray."

Continuous "*bad company*," or "bad associations," tends to cause "*good morals*" or "positive habits and customs" to become "*corrupt*" or "perverse, depraved, or morally ruined." Paul wrote 1 Corinthians 15 to refute the false notion that there was no resurrection, and he ended with this command to stop being deceived by the lies of those who contradicted the Scripture.

If there is no resurrection, then life is hopeless, purposeless, and meaningless. The only thing that matters is the moment, and the only pleasure is sensual, esthetic, or prideful gratification. Paul quoted Isaiah 22:13: "*Let us eat and drink, for tomorrow we die*," which was a widespread slogan of his day (and all time). By eliminating the hope of resurrection with a living God, there is little reason to avoid a life of selfish, corrupt pleasure seeking. The only basis for morality in a secular, naturalistic world is for the sake of societal conveniences, legal license, and relativistic values. In such a world, individuals are left to their intuition and inclinations for self-gratification within these limits, resulting in a society that lives for whatever they can get away with.

Even believers will eventually be corrupted if they spend most of their time with folks who believe there is no afterlife, no resurrection, and no personal judgment. Our primary friends (by choice) must be Bible followers who seek to practice the commands and follow the teachings of God's word while living in anticipation of seeing Jesus face to face the moment they pass from this earthly life. What are you doing to cultivate godly friends?

"Lord, my heart yearns to walk in Your ways and to have Your attitudes at all times. Please give me friends that know and practice Your word."

Remember, Obedient Living Is the Key to Evangelism

1 Cor 15:34—*"Awake~~ **to righteousness, and do not sin~|**; for some do not have the knowledge of God. I speak this to your shame."*

Someone said about the Bible, "This book will keep you from sin, or sin will keep you from this book."

Thucydides, a Greek historian, wrote of his culture that "people committed every shameful crime and eagerly snatched at every lustful pleasure." They denied any afterlife; thus no one would hold them accountable for a self-centered life.

To *awaken* means "to sober up, come to our right senses or a proper state of mind." The idea is to "return to one's self from drunkenness and thus be sober." Anyone who believes in the resurrection knows there is a living God to Whom all persons must render an account of their lives, so the pursuit of meaningless goals or temporary gratification is not an adequate reason for existing.

Paul commanded those deceived by false notions to "cease from their sinning," whatever those addictive sins might be. One commentator wrote, "Paul regularly regards sin less in terms (if at all) of acts (plural) or commission or omission than as an attitude, stance, and state in which the human will is granted 'autonomy' to turn away from God to seek self-gratification as the chief end of human life" (Pannenburg, *Systematic Theology*, 2:231–76).

By implication, Paul states that the primary purpose of ife is to make sure that everyone, everywhere, has *"the knowledge of God."* Those who selfishly live for themselves—as though finding success, pleasure, and happiness were the primary goals of Christians—have little or no interest in the four thousand people groups who have never heard of Jesus and who have no idea of God's revelation in the Bible.

Paul spoke of this to their *"shame,"* which means "a state of embarrassment resulting from what one has done or failed to do." Can God trust you to make contact with an unbeliever to teach him or her how to know God personally? Are you fulfilling your purpose in this life?

"Lord, apathy so easily grips my heart as my desires drift toward selfishness and self-interests. Please bring people into my life to exhort me to stay focused on reaching the lost and eternal values."

APRIL 17

Be Angry, but Do Not Sin, nor Let the Sun Go Down on Your Wrath

Eph 4:26—"*Be angry~~ and do not sin~|; do not let the sun go down~|*
on the cause of your anger."

Most angry people know one Bible verse: "*Be angry*" as a license
to show anger at will. In Ephesians 4:26, the present command to
"be continually angry" does not refer to an impulsive, momentary
rage, nor is it an anger provoked by an inward, seething resentment;
instead, the word means a deep and determined conviction. This is
not a personal response to an offense or hurt but indignation against
a wrong, immoral, or an unjust situation.

This is the anger Jesus felt against the money changers' abuse in the
temple (Matt 21:12; Jn 2:15), but He was never selfishly angered at
anything done against Him personally. Sinful anger is anger for personal
benefit—that is, when one expresses resentment or hurt to another to
get even with that person.

Any form of vengeance done in anger is sin. Anger, even holy indignation,
can degenerate into hatred, dislike, resentment, bitterness, and malice,
all of which are forbidden. For this reason, Paul adds additional
prohibitions: "*do not sin; do not let the sun go down on the cause of your*
anger." Anger is a dangerous response; as James wrote, "*Let every man . . .*
be slow to anger; for the wrath (anger) of man does not produce the
righteousness of God" (James 1:19–20). Emotional responses produce
inequitable punishments. Paul described "*outbursts of anger*" (Gal 5:20)
as the "*works of the flesh*" (5:19).

In angry situations, the believer can demonstrate the filling of the Spirit
by exercising "*self-control*" (Gal 5:23). We are warned, "*A wrathful man*
stirs up strife" (Prov 15:18). Wisdom says it is best to not be friends with
an angry person (22:24). Also, a key symptom of a foolish person is his
constant display of anger (Eccl 7:9).

If, or when, anger does arise within our emotional bank, then we are
commanded, "*Do not let the sun go down on the cause of your anger.*"
Here the word for *anger* refers to a provoked anger—an anger arising
from internal convictions rather than external provocation. Sinful anger
is basically a selfish, undisciplined, and vindictive behavior that has no
place in the Christian lifestyle and destroys peace among brethren.

"Father, teach me to be angry at what angers You and to have grace to
recognize my self-centered anger as sin and manipulation to get my way."

APRIL 18

Do Not Give the Devil an Opportunity

Eph 4:27—*"Do not give~~ the devil an opportunity."*

"Know your enemy" is a strategy of the military, businesses, and sport teams, yet few Christians know the strategies of their archenemy, Satan. Satan is a created being, an extremely powerful angelic being who has chosen to exalt himself above all that is God. He is not omnipresent, omniscient, or omnipotent, thus he cannot read a person's mind—only God can. His primary power is suggestion, but he is limited. He tests us for symptoms of accessibility to our minds and reads us for our openness to his ideas.

Paul warned, "*Put on all of God's armor so that you will be able to stand firm against all strategies of the devil*" (Eph 6:11NLT). One of those strategies is to suggest false ideas or justifications for destructive reactions in relationships: "*Now the Holy Spirit tells us clearly that in the last times some will turn away from the true faith; they will follow deceptive spirits and teachings that come from demons*" (1 Tim 4:1NLT). All Satan needs is a receptive host. This does not mean that a person must be *intentionally* open to satanic power or influence. It merely means Satan can plant suggestions in the mind of the undiscerning or susceptible person. One of the symptoms he looks for is anger.

The negative, *"not,"* is a continuative conjunction that ties this command to the preceding commands about anger. An additional reason to keep your anger short-lived is to avoid *"giv[ing] the devil an opportunity."* J. B. Phillips's translation paraphrased this verse: "*Never go to bed angry . . . and do not give the devil a foothold."* Anger is fertile ground in which to plant perfectly timed thoughts that will justify the propagation of damaging and destructive actions against others.

Nothing attracts demons like an angry person: "*Be sober, be vigilant; because your adversary the devil walks about like a roaring lion, seeking whom he may devour*" (1 Pet 5:8). Let's avoid giving Satan an opening into our minds.

"May the fear of being influenced by demonic suggestions keep me from emotional reactions. Give me insights into Your word to strengthen my self-control."

APRIL 19

Do Not Grumble or Argue

Phil 2:14—*"Do~~ everything without grumbling or arguing."*

Here is some shocking and disillusioning news: there is no perfect church or Christian organization on earth. Evidently, there were some undercurrents of "grumbling or arguing" in the church over unmentioned issues.

Paul's words remind us of Moses's description of the Israelites, who were a *"stubborn, unfaithful people"* (Deut 32:20) because they incessantly complained about their hardships and wished they had never left Egypt (Num 11:1–6; 14:1–4; 20:2; 21:4–5). Paul warned that such complainers had been dealt with severely (1 Cor 10:10).

The command not to *"grumble"* means not to "murmur, complain, [or] express dissatisfaction or annoyance." This includes talking secretly, gossiping, or whispering about someone, which produces discontent, disillusionment, or suspicion among the body of believers.

Paul described the suffering the Philippians were going through for sharing *"the faith of the gospel"* (Phil 1:27). Paul taught them the honor to be *"granted on behalf of Christ, not only to believe in Him, but also to suffer for His sake"* (1:28–30). Perhaps there were complaints to God for allowing their suffering or seeming to be powerless to deliver them or Paul from imprisonment.

The second divisive action among them was *"arguing,"* which means to "dispute, or have different opinions." Paul exhorted Euodia and Syntyche to *"be of the same mind in the Lord"* (Phil 4:2), Such disagreeable attitudes provoked Paul to write, *"Let nothing be done through selfish ambition or conceit"* (2:3), both of which generate arguments.

All such divisive attitudes must be conquered in order to accomplish the mission of the community of believers to *"become blameless and harmless, children of God without fault in the midst of a crooked and perverse generation, among whom you shine as lights in the world"* (Phil 2:15). All such griping, complaining, and disputing go viral all too fast. These issues discredit its possible impact on lost sinners. We must do everything to keep the "light of the world" shining bright.

"Teach me, Lord, to see how my tendency to gripe and complain about my situation is seen by You as my distrust of and dislike for what You have allowed and provided for my maturity. Forgive me for not accepting Your plan for my life."

Live in Love as Christ

Eph 5:2—*"and **live**~~ **in love**, just as Christ also loved us and gave himself for us, a sacrificial and fragrant offering to God."*

Just as a child imitates his parents, since they have the same DNA and nature, so believers are to imitate the personality and qualities of God (e.g., Luke 6:36: *"Be merciful, just as your Father also is merciful"*). In Ephesians 4:32, Paul had just laid down the command to *"be kind to one another, tenderhearted, forgiving one another, even as God in Christ forgave you."* Then he added, *"Be imitators of God"* (5:1). This sequence of commands is tied to the command in Ephesians 5:2 by the connector *"and,"* which could be translated as "that is." This explains how the believer should imitate God: by walking in love as God does.

The "walk" of the believer is a major focus of Paul's writings to the churches: we are to walk worthily (Eph 4:1), different from the world (4:17), in the light (5:8), and in wisdom (5:15). Our text focuses on walking in love and sacrificing to bring sinners to Christ.

Just as a child learns to draw an object by tracing it until he can reflect the original image accurately, so the believer is to pattern his life and priorities after the original likeness of Christ as seen in the Scripture. The mold of our model is seen in 2 Corinthians 3:18: *"But we all, with unveiled face beholding as in a mirror the glory of the Lord, are being transformed into the same image from glory to glory, just as from the Lord, the Spirit."*

The love of Christ was placed in our hearts (Rom 5:5) to lead us to the sacrificial giving of ourselves to others and to demonstrate the amazing truth of Christ's love for them. The mandate is that we give of ourselves for the spiritual benefit of the undeserving, undesirable, and uncared-for people around the globe.

Nothing is as sweet or pleasing to our God as a free-willed child who gives up his or her life for the benefit of others, just as Jesus did when He came to earth. Walking in the love of Christ is unique to Christianity.

"Lord, I confess that I tend to think so much about my needs and wants that I seldom give a thought to the needs of those around me. Today, Lord, I want to be Your hands and feet to care about the people in my life."

APRIL 21

Clothe Yourself with Mercy, Kindness, Humility, Gentleness, and Patience

Col 3:12—*"Therefore, as the elect of God, holy and dearly loved, **clothe yourselves*~ with a heart** of mercy, kindness, humility, gentleness, and patience, [toward others]."*

Anytime we are invited to a special event, one of our first questions is "What is the appropriate dress for the occasion?"

The command to *"clothe yourselves"* is a plural aorist imperative to bring out the command's urgency. The verb is placed at the beginning of the original to emphasize how your behavior identifies you as a true believer.

Paul described the clothes of the *"old man"* (the typical preconversion dress) that believers are commanded to *"put off,"* including *"anger, wrath, malice, blasphemy, filthy language out of your mouth. Do not lie to one another"* (Col 3:8–9). The *"new man"* is given a new knowledge ("experiential knowledge") that teaches him not to make a distinction between race or social status within the church body (3:10–11).

No legalistic or specific behavioral actions are commanded because we are expected to take the corporate principles and apply them to our individual situations. The church is to be characterized by *"a heart of mercy, kindness, humility, gentleness, and patience."*

We are to be merciful—not quick to condemn, gossip, criticize, or ostracize one another. We choose to act in grace, favoring those who do not deserve it. In humility, we put the needs of others before our own and we choose not to be angry when others hurt us.

The plural command refers to body of believers as the *"elect of God, holy and dearly loved."* Thus the church is the *"elect of God."* Our identity in Christ is to be seen not individually but corporately as a "holy people." Peter writes, *"You are a chosen people. You [pl.] are royal priests, a holy nation, God's very own possession. As a result, you [pl.] can show others the goodness of God, for he called you [pl.] out of the darkness into his wonderful light"* (1 Pet 2:9[NLT]). All these instructions are given in the plural for the entire church and only secondarily to individuals as they are a part of a functioning body of believers. Are you helping your church fulfill this command?

"Lord, it is so hard to be like You. When people interfered with Your plans or offended Your righteousness, You were always gracious, kind, and patient. Make me more like You."

APRIL 22

Let the Peace of God Control Your Hearts

Col 3:15—*"**Let the peace of Christ be in control**~~ **in your heart** (for you were in fact called as one body to this peace), and **be thankful**~~."*

The quest for God to tell us His will specifically and subjectively or mystically within our spirit has led to the "heart-peace" principle—that is, if you have peace about a subject, it must be the will of God. A misunderstanding here has led to a subjective focus in discerning God's will rather than letting scriptural commands, principles, and examples be our guide.

After giving a series of instructions to the church at Thessalonica, Paul declared that because of their obedience *"the peace of God, which passes all understanding, will guard your hearts and minds through Christ Jesus"* (Phil 4:7). Peace is not a signpost that comes and goes, as a green or red traffic light; it is a perpetual part of the new life in Christ and the corporate experience.

The command to let the peace of Christ *"be continually in control"* comes from the same root word used to describe the function of an umpire or arbitrator to maintain the proper playing conditions in an athletic game. The umpire does not tell players what to do but warns when they have violated the rules. The goal is to play in peace within the liberty of the rules. Paul gave the following guidelines to the church for this rule of peace: *"The things which you learned and received and heard and saw in me, these do, and the God of peace will be with you"* (Phil 4:9). Paul taught the church to *"[endeavor] to keep the unity of the Spirit in the bond of peace"* (Eph 4:3).

The command to allow peace to be in control means we should maintain a peaceful spirit within the body of Christ, instead of a conflictive, argumentative, or antagonistic spirit among our brethren. Anything that disturbs the peace among our brethren must be dealt with quickly to restore the peace within the body of believers.

The conclusion of the verse confirms the corporate sense of the command: *"You were in fact called as one body to this peace"*—that is, the rule of peace is for the body of believers, and we are to "be continually thankful" for our privilege to be a part of such a peaceful church. Are you a peacemaker among your brethren?

"Lord Jesus, Your church is a refuge each week as my brothers and sisters gather to learn more about You. Teach us to practice Your principles and live together in Your peace."

APRIL 23

Take Pride in Your High Position in Christ

James 1:9—*"Now the believer of humble means **should take pride**~~ in his high position [as a believer and coheir with Christ]."*

Few people understand the theology of poverty. Jesus said, *"The poor you will always have with you"* (Mark 14:7). We should do everything possible to help the poor survive a temporary situation and to let them know that others care for them, especially God.

The early church practiced a common generosity toward the poor. Believers *"sold their possessions and goods, and divided them among all, as anyone had need"* (Acts 2:45). As the need arose, the church gave a helping hand. *"Nor was there anyone among them who lacked; for all who were possessors of lands or houses sold them, and brought the proceeds of the things that were sold"* (4:34).

This has nothing to do with "Christian communism," or the equal distribution of wealth, or the elimination of poverty. The people gave as generous volunteers to help refugees and others in temporary emergencies, such as famines, wars, or plagues.

Some will always have more than others, but it is sinful for the less fortunate to *expect* that the better off must give to them or that they owe it to them.

God's word for the poor does not promise prosperity or wealth; rather, the commands focus on *contentment*, which means "to have enough, or be satisfied." Jesus commanded, *"Be content with your wages"* (Luke 3:14). Every believer must learn *"if we have food and clothing [shelter], let us be content"* (1 Tim 6:8). The writer of Hebrews said, *"Keep your lives free from the love of money and be content with what you have, because God has said, 'Never will I leave you, never will I forsake you'"* (Heb 13:5)—that is, God says, "Let Me fill your heart, instead of things and money." The Apostle Paul said, *"I have learned how to be content with whatever I have. I know how to live on almost nothing or with everything. I have learned the secret of living in every situation, whether it is with a full stomach or empty, with plenty or little"* (Phil 4:11–12^NLT). Instead of living for more, be thankful now for what you have.

"Lord, the honor of being Your child and the privilege of having a purpose with You are beyond imagination. My situation now is incomparable with what I will share with You forever. Thank You."

Honor All People; Love the Family of God

1 Pet 2:17—*"Honor*~ all people, love~~ the family of believers, fear~~God, honor ~~ the king."*

How are Christians to live in a pagan, perverse, and antagonistic world? This world has never been a friend of the true church. James warned that a *"friendship with the world means hostility toward God"* (James 4:4). Should we show hostility to worldly people to demonstrate that we have no *"friendship with the world"*?

Such *"friendship"* implies a mutually gratifying relationship that supplants or extinguishes a love for the Lord. We do not need friendship with the world, but we must represent our Lord to this antagonistic world. The theology of our earthly citizenship is given in a fourfold rapid fire of a series of practical commands.

The aorist command to *"immediately decide to honor all people"* or to "esteem or respect" them emphasizes the urgency of beginning this now and continuing the action. The original emphasis is on the word *all*. Paul repeats this command: *"Render therefore to all their due: . . . fear to whom fear, honor to whom honor"* (Rom 13:7).

The second command is for believers to *"always be loving the family of believers [brotherhood]."* John emphasized that this command was a sign of the possession of eternal life: *"This commandment we have from Him: that he who loves God must love his brother also"* (1 Jn 4:21). Do believers you know love each other? How should this love be continually demonstrated?

The third command is for believers to *"continuously fear God,"* meaning to be "frightened." Anyone who is not afraid of what God might do if He is disobeyed will eventually yield to temptation. Satan used this lie to deceive Adam and Eve so they would not be afraid: he convinced them that God would not do what He said. God will chasten any child of His who ignores His commands (Heb 12:5–8).

The fourth command gives believers their imperative for political leaders: *"be continually honoring the king."* We are to be *"subject to the governing authorities"* (Rom 13:1), even if we disagree with them. Christians are to be the best citizens in any setting to avoid bringing disrepute to our Savior's name. How will you honor someone today?

"Lord, thank You for making life simple and practical. Keep me repeating Your values in my heart every day."

_____

Strive to Be Found at
Peace and without Blemish

2 Pet 3:14—*"Therefore, dear friends, since you are waiting for these things,* **strive*~ to be found at peace***, without spot or blemish, when you come into his presence."*

Knowing how the story ends takes all the drama out of a book or movie. If *"the heavens will be dissolved, being on fire, and the elements will melt with fervent heat"* (2 Pet 3:12), then it makes no sense to live for earthly things. Who cares how much you own if it is all going to be burnt up?

Most Bible believers see the coming of Christ as imminent. *"Since you are waiting for these things"* sets the stage for the command: *"immediately begin to strive [be diligent] to be found by Him in peace"* (2 Pet 3:14a). Believers should not waste time with the temporary; instead, they should invest in the eternal purposes of God.

The phrase *"urgently strive to be found [by Him],"* or "do your best," is a sobering reminder that our lives are being evaluated, and someday the Lord Jesus Himself will expose His verdict. His omniscience misses nothing but *"will both bring to light the things hidden in the darkness and disclose the motives of men's hearts"* (1 Cor 4:5). His objective is not to embarrass us but to praise us for everything He can. Our seriousness to please our Lord by our obedience to His word determines our faithfulness.

Peter mentions three areas of personal character development. The first is *"peace."* This refers to the *"peace"* of mind from trusting in God's word and the power of God in practical situations. This peace requires focus: *"Be anxious for nothing, but in everything by prayer and supplication with thanksgiving let your requests be made known to God. And the peace of God, which surpasses all comprehension, will guard your hearts and your minds in Christ Jesus"* (Phil 4:6–7).

The next two character traits come from living in light of the soon-appearing Christ, which motivates us to be *"spotless and blameless, when [we] come into His presence."* The character of the believer is to be *"spotless,"* meaning to "be of highest quality" and *"blameless,"* which is to be "innocent, or irreproachable." It requires diligence to say "no" to many temptations. The measure of your diligence is how frequently the thought of Christ's imminent return gives you reason to resist sin and selfishness.

"Come soon, Lord Jesus. My heart yearns to be in Your presence forever. Keep me conscious of Your imminent return so I will keep my priorities fixed on Your word."

APRIL 26

Bear in Mind the Patience of Our Lord

2 Pet 3:15—*"And* **regard*~** *the patience of our Lord as salvation, just as also our dear brother Paul wrote to you, according to the wisdom given to him."*

Thankfully, the Lord has delayed His return until now. The longer He delays His coming, the more people all over the globe will be turning to faith in Christ as never before in history. Much of the growth of Christianity has been in restricted countries where it cannot be publicized.

In Nepal, there were 25 believers in 1960, but by 2010, there were more than 1 million! In China, there were an estimated 1.5 million believers in 1970, which grew to an estimated 100 million by 2010. Estimates project that this will grow to more than 120 million in 20 years. The proportion of Christians in Africa is approaching 50 percent. While Christianity is barely holding its own in the West, it is exploding around the world.

Strange as it may seem, a strong emphasis on the second coming of Christ can be a motivation for world evangelism, or it can be twisted to discourage evangelism. The "what's the use" excuse, or "It's too risky or difficult in these 'end times'" alibi, keeps some from the unfinished task of the church.

Peter uses the command *regard*, which means "to think or lead the way." The thought that follows in the text should be a dominant motivating and guiding principle of your life. In this text, it refers to the delaying of the second coming of Christ (2 Pet 3:9), the purpose of which is the salvation of millions of new believers. Now is not the time to delay sacrificing to finish the Great Commission.

The only biblical reason for His delay is to give the church the time to fulfill Revelation 5:9 at the opening of the seven-sealed scroll marking the beginning of the tribulation. There will be believers *"from every tribe and language and people and nation."* He waits for the church to finish this task.

Peter declares that Paul wrote with the same emphasis, as God gave him wisdom to express the continued passion of Christ for the lost of the world. Let the passion of our Lord for evangelizing the last people group be your guiding principle. Is this a concern of yours?

"Thank You, Lord, for Your patience with me in bringing the gospel to my mind and heart. Why did it take me so long to hear Your word? Are You waiting for me to share Your salvation with my friends? Give me courage today."

APRIL 27

Eliminate Any Cause of Temptation

Matt 5:29–30—*"If your right eye causes you to sin, **tear it out****~ *and* ***throw it away****~*! It is better to lose one of your members than to have your whole body thrown into hell. If your right hand causes you to sin, **cut it off****~ *and **throw it away****~*! It is better to lose one of your members than to have your whole body go into hell."*

Jesus had just made one of the most condemning statements in the Bible: *"Everyone who looks on a woman [or man] to lust for her [or him] has committed adultery with her [or him] already in his [or her] heart"* (Matt 5:28). Sin begins with the lustful thought of a sinful act: "Sow a thought and reap an act. Sow an act and reap a habit. Sow a habit and reap a character. Sow a character and reap a destiny."

Job said, *"I have made a covenant with my eyes; how then could I gaze at a virgin . . . If my step has turned from the way, or my heart followed my eyes, or if any spot has stuck to my hands, let me sow and another eat, and let my crops be uprooted"* (Job 31:1, 7–8).

The phrase *"[your] eye causes you to sin"* translates *skandalizo*, which means to "set a trap or a stumbling block," which describes how a person is led to sin or violate his conscience by what he allows his eyes or mind to desire. The noun form of the verb is the trigger or spring of a trap on which the bait is placed, which, when touched by the animal, causes the trap to close and ensnares the animal. If sin begins in the mind and heart, then we must program our minds to desire and love what Christ honors.

Even the elimination of external harmful influences will not change a lustful, covetous heart into a pure heart, but it can prevent the continual feeding of lust and the vicarious enacting of sinful acts until they become inevitable.

Paul saw the solution to controlling our thoughts: *"We demolish arguments and every pretension that sets itself up against the knowledge of God, and we take captive every thought to make it obedient to Christ"* (2 Cor 10:5). We control our thoughts by what and whom we listen to, read, or watch. Our heart dictates these decisions by what we believe to be most fulfilling. Be honest. Confess. Forsake. Plan to fill your time with thoughts that honor Christ.

"Lord, teach me to be as offended by sin as You are. Give me the commitment to take the steps to eliminate and avoid every source of temptation to violate Your word in my life."

APRIL 28

Do Not Be Deceived about Sin or God

James 1:14b–16—*"But each one is tempted when he is drawn away by his own desires and enticed. Then, when desire has conceived, it gives birth to sin; and sin, when it is full-grown, brings forth death. **Do not be led astray~|**, my dear brothers and sisters."*

The self-deception for being led astray starts in the heart and mind. *"Desire"* is a neutral word that is translated as "lust, longing or craving" for something. It is neutral because a good object or a sin could be equally desired. When sinful benefits and pleasures are allowed to become enticing and are not counterbalanced with any thought of consequences, we can easily be *"led astray."*

To enhance the enticement, the mind engages in pleasurable or viral visualization of the sinful activity. Perhaps you have not seriously thought about taking action yet, but already the enticing desires have become more pleasurable than your reality, and God is seen as an obstacle to your enjoyment in life. Apathy begins. It seems private, harmless, and secret.

There are two symptoms of this phase of self-deception. The first is a growing discontent with any present situation, possessions, or relationship. Along with this growing unhappiness begins the thought that one deserves better. Mutual satisfaction decreases, arguments abound, and dislike grows.

The second phase is the attraction of "greener grass on the other side of the fence." One begins to formulate "what-if" plans.

The third phase is the formulation of a plan to get away with fulfilling one's desires at least occasionally. By the time an opportunity to be unfaithful or disloyal actually arises, the person has already deceived himself into believing that this sinful action is essential to happiness in life and that God's way cannot provide this satisfaction. In fact, the person might blame God for his present problems. The self-deceived person feels he has to do it his way to be happy.

As this process continues, the fourth phase is inevitable: regardless of the consequences, warnings, or hurts to others, selfish desires bring forth a violation of God's commands and horrible consequences. No one can escape them. Sin is never fulfilling. Tempting thoughts will always come, but we are not forced to follow them. God's way is always best.

"Lord, why is it so easy for me to believe that I need 'stuff' or pleasures at any cost or that I can only be satisfied if I secretly sin? I am so unlike You, Lord. Teach me to despise sin and to trust Your word as my guide always."

APRIL 29

Flee Sexual Immorality

1 Cor 6:18—*"Flee*~~ *sexual immorality!* '*Every sin a person commits is outside of the body'– but the immoral person sins against his own body."*

Sex is a beautiful and essential part of God's plan for marriage. It is the most intimate, private, pleasurable, healthy, wholesome, and privileged aspect of married life. Any violation of this mutual trust hurts deeper and longer than any other offense. When God's word marks what is allowed and what is prohibited, and men ignore His instruction, they question God's character.

Equally as damaging as sexually transmitted infections and the threat HIV/ AIDS is how the immoral participant *"sins against his own body."* There are other sins against the body, such as gluttony, smoking, drugging, or drunkenness, but none compares with the effect of sexual sins on memory, personality, psychology, emotions, attitudes toward relationships, and the soul: *"Whoever commits adultery with a woman lacks understanding; He who does so destroys his own soul. Wounds and dishonor he will get, and his reproach will not be wiped away"* (Prov 6:32–33).

Paul's instruction in 1 Corinthians 6:18 begins with the present-tense command to *"be continually fleeing from immorality,"* meaning to "continually or habitually move hastily away from the danger of immorality." Do not be curious about it or seek to experiment. This is not a skill to master before marriage. The command is to be proactive by immediate and total avoidance. In human nature, there is a point at which your impulses become irresistible, driving you to self-destruction. Avoid even getting close to that point.

"Do you not know that your body is a temple of the Holy Spirit, who is in you, whom you have received from God, and you are not your own?" (1 Cor 6:19). If you are a believer, then your body is not yours to destroy and pervert from its created purpose. Sex is more than a mere physical act like shaking hands or kissing. It is the union of the souls and physical beings of two people, which is why it is only beautiful in a marriage.

The Corinthians were exposed to paganism that sanctioned sex in worship, and our society has made a virtual religion of worshipping sex. The obedient believer must make choices every day to remain pure for and within marriage.

"Lord, make my spirit sensitive to sins that offend Your Spirit and give me the conviction to avoid every sensual temptation so my heart is only full of all that You love. Thank You for Your patience and forgiveness."

Be Separate from the World

2 Cor 6:17—*"Therefore '**come out****~ **from their midst**, and **be separate***~,' says the Lord, 'and **touch no unclean thing**~/, and I will welcome you.'"*

Paul had just commanded believers negatively: *"Do not be unequally yoked together with unbelievers"* (2 Cor 6:14)—that is, do not partner with unbelievers. Now in 2 Corinthians 6:17 he lays out the positive command to *"be separate"* from anything *"unclean,"* sinful, or unbelieving. Paul is demanding that believers separate themselves from the immorality of the unsaved around them, while promising, *"I will welcome you."*

The command to *"urgently come out from their midst"* demands a decisive action of withdrawal from the sinful attitudes and practices of unbelievers. To make it clearer, the believer is to *"be separate"* (which likewise demands an immediate and decisive decision). This is followed by a third imperative, this time a present negative imperative, which means to "cease or stop touching the unclean thing." Holiness means to be separated for God's purpose.

This does not mean we should isolate ourselves from the unsaved: *"I wrote you in my epistle not to keep company with sexually immoral people. Yet I certainly did not mean with the sexually immoral people of this world, or with the covetous, or extortioners, or idolaters, since then you would need to go out of the world. But now I have written to you not to keep company with anyone named a brother, who is sexually immoral, or covetous, or an idolater, or a reviler, or a drunkard, or an extortioner—not even to eat with such a person"* (1 Cor 5:9–11).

Separation from the world is not a matter of keeping our distance from sinners, or refusing to know them or befriend them; rather, we should keep ourselves from loving the same things as sinners: *"Love not the world, or the things that are in the world. If anyone loves the world, the love of the Father is not in him"* (1 Jn 2:15). It has always been God's will for His people to be distinct from unbelievers: *"Therefore, having these promises, beloved, let us cleanse ourselves from all filthiness of the flesh and spirit, perfecting holiness in the fear of God"* (7:1). As you read these verses does the Spirit speak to your conscience about some specific sins that you know offend His holiness? Now what are you going to do?

"Father, with all my heart I long to honor You with my life because of Your grace to me. Keep me pure and untainted by the corruption all around me. Make me a distinct light for You in the midst of the darkness of my world."

MAY 1

Do Not Allow Sexual Immorality or Impurity

Eph 5:3–4—*"But among you **there must not be~/ either sexual immorality, impurity of any kind, or greed,** as these are not fitting for the saints. Neither filthiness, nor foolish talking, nor coarse jesting, which are not fitting, but rather giving of thanks."*

In spite of our Creator-Savior-God's self-sacrificing love for people often they behave in lustful, self-indulgent, selfish, egotistical ways. In the previous verse, Paul told us to *"walk in love"* (Eph 5:2), and now he clarifies what impedes this command in our lives. Paul lists six vices among believers that *"there must not be,"* meaning to "stop being."

The first vice is *"sexual immorality"*; this word is the origin of the word *pornography*, which refers to all sexual activities outside of marriage: *"This is the will of God, your sanctification: that you should abstain from sexual immorality"* (1 Thes 4:3). Satan has long used sexual sins of believers as a tool.

The second is *"impurity of any kind,"* which refers to "moral filthiness, lewdness, unnatural perversion, obscenity." This word is used ten times in the New Testament to describe immoral thoughts and sexual fantasies that corrupt morality.

The third is *"covetousness,"* the word for *greediness*, which is the desire to have more than your due, or whatever motivates an illegitimate action to acquire more things. It is pure selfishness.

The fourth sin is *"filthiness,"* or "shamefulness, obscenity, indecency," "dirty talk," or "filthy language," as in Colossians 3:8.

The fifth sin is *"foolish talking,"* which means "silly talk, stupid or low obscenity, gutter talk," or the language of the street.

The sixth sin is *"coarse jesting,"* meaning "facetiousness or making fun of others." This refers to turning any trait or a statement of others into a joke or teasing, sometimes with a suggestive sexual innuendo. Never ridicule others.

Rather, the believer is to engage in the *"giving of thanks"* for having received the undeserved grace of full forgiveness and true, effective wisdom. Now the believer is to show the same grace to others.

"Wonderful Savior, I recognize all my lustful thoughts of sin and greed are spawned by selfishness. Help me have a grateful heart for Who You are and for the wonders You have done in my life."

MAY 2
Get Rid of All Hatred

Col 3:8–9—*"But now you yourselves are to **put off***~ **all these**: anger, wrath, malice, blasphemy, filthy language out of your mouth. **Do not lie~/ to one another,** since you have put off the old man with his deeds."*

You can tell a child of the king because he tends to act like a king. This second list of unacceptable sins in Colossians 3 deals with the mistreatment of others. These actions can never be justified.

"Anger" is a state of constant irritation and displeasure, which results in resentful bitterness. Whatever the provocation, this reveals a person's anger toward whatever has gotten in the way of his selfishness.

"Wrath" is a tumultuous, impulsive outburst of anger like the burst of flame, which flares up quickly and then is gone. This reaction is listed as one of the deeds of the flesh (Gal 5:20), and it is unjustifiable (Eph 4:31). Anger and wrath are closely related.

"Malice" refers to "all kinds of wickedness against an object, or an evil disposition to do premeditated harm." *"For we ourselves were also once foolish, disobedient, deceived, serving various lusts and pleasures, living in malice and envy, hateful and hating one another"* (Titus 3:3). The believer is to be different.

"Blasphemy" refers to any slander, including any word or action that insults, mocks, or devalues another person or God or heavenly beings. Slander or putting others down is unacceptable.

"Filthy language out of your mouth" is "abusive, vulgar, obscene or derogatory speech that is intended to hurt or wound another person." Being put down, shamed, or crudely ridiculed can be more painful than a physical blow.

The command to *"[stop lying] to [or about] one another"* refers to making false statements about others to destroy their credibility or acceptance. The present negative imperative implies that they were lying but now are commanded to stop. In this context, it refers to the malicious gossiping and exaggeration of facts designed to provoke rejection or to justify future action against someone.

The flesh in Christians can be vicious: 2 Corinthians 12:20 describes *"contentions, jealousies, outbursts of wrath, selfish ambitions, backbiting, whisperings, conceits, [and] tumults."* May these sins break our hearts as they do God's heart.

"Dear Lord, You have commanded that I put away anger and all that it leads to. I praise You, because You enable me to experience victory over this kind of sin through the power of Your Spirit."

MAY 3

Love Jesus or Be Accursed

1 Cor 16:22—*"Let anyone who has no love for the Lord be accursed~~. Our Lord, come!"*

Some find it hard to believe that there are serious consequences to not knowing and loving the Lord Jesus. Many parents cannot bring themselves to spank their children, so how could God condemn any of His children? Many hold that no one is ultimately accursed from God forever but will be given a second chance, just as we give our children second chances for everything. This is a concept of a make-believe god, not the One who is there.

In 1 Corinthians 16:22, Paul gives a passionate warning of what happens when his readers follow false teachers. Later he writes: *"I fear that somehow your pure and undivided devotion to Christ will be corrupted, just as Eve was deceived by the cunning ways of the serpent. You happily put up with whatever anyone tells you, even if they preach a different Jesus than the one we preach, or a different kind of Spirit than the one you received, or a different kind of gospel than the one you believed"* (2 Cor 11:3–4[NLT]). They were passive because they thought God was passive, but He is not.

On the other hand, those who love the Lord are promised God's intervention in their lives: *"We know that God causes everything to work together for the good of those who love God and are called according to his purpose for them"* (Rom 8:28[NLT]).

The present imperative verb tense in 1 Corinthians 16:22 means this is a continual, unending action of being *"accursed,"* which indicates the condemnation of the unsaved. John declared, *"He who believes in Him is not condemned; but he who does not believe is condemned already, because he has not believed in the name of the only begotten Son of God"* (Jn 3:18). Paul is warning those in the church that are pretending to be followers, not for the love of the Lord Jesus, but for personal interests, that they are already cursed and condemned. This should warn us that pretenders are not saved even though they come to church. They are the tares among the wheat (Matt 13:38). What are we going to do about it?

The cry of the church is *"Maranatha"*—that is, *"Our Lord, come!"*

"Dear Father, Your kind of love is so far from the human way of thinking that it takes us a lifetime to begin to understand it. Thank You for Your Spirit and Your word that work in me as I am open to Your teaching. I trust You, Lord, to help me love You more each day."

Die to Your Old Nature

Col 3:5—*"So **put to death***~ whatever in your nature belongs to the earth: sexual immorality, impurity, shameful passion, evil desire, and greed which is idolatry."*

In Colossians 3:5, Paul has just laid out the principles for believers to begin preparing their minds for a heavenly life with Christ. We are to think like our Master and act like heavenly citizens while we await our Savior's return.

The word *So*, or "therefore," ties this verse to the preceding ones (Col 3:1–4), with the conclusion that we need to rid ourselves of all aspects of life that are incompatible with Christ and heaven.

The key imperative is to *"decide immediately to put to death"* sin; this is a concept stemming from the medical atrophy of parts of the body that cease to function due to disuse in sickness. We must *"put to death"*—that is, cease to use—these earthly vices that are common to the unsaved.

This can be accomplished by *"setting your mind on things above, not on things on the earth"* (Col 3:2). When heaven is your focus, everything else atrophies. May these sins offend us as they do God.

"Sexual immorality" originally referred to sexual relations with a prostitute (which is from the root word *porneia*, from which we also get the word *pornography*), but it covers any sexual relations outside of marriage. These evil deeds are birthed in evil thoughts of the heart, which is first defined as *"impurity,"* or the morally perverse desires of the heart. These desires erupt into *"passion,"* which is "emotional and uncontrolled lust." This mind-set is linked with *"evil desire,"* which is "a great longing or craving for what is forbidden." It is called the *"desire of the flesh"* (Rom 13:14), and *"youthful desires"* (2 Tim 2:22). Colossians 3:9 describes the worldly "old man" who has to die as *"greed,"* which is an "insatiableness, covetousness, or the desire to have more," especially in the context of sexual addictions.

Paul concludes by identifying greed as *"idolatry,"* as in Ephesians 5:5: *"Know that no . . . covetous man, who is an idolater, has any inheritance in the kingdom of Christ and God."* Greed is a form of idolatry because it teaches that acquiring things and striving for personal satisfaction—instead of knowing God—are fulfilling goals; thus pleasure and material goods become our joys and idols. Can you be honest with yourself?

"Lord Jesus, You say I must "put to death" the desire for evil in my life. Right now I am deciding to obey You by denying those desires and instead working to 'put on' the 'new man' who loves and serves You and others by Your power."

MAY 5
Stay Away from Forms of Evil

1 Thes 5:22—*"Stay away~~ from every form of evil."*

Discernment is a lost art. The text does not tell us what evil is, because it has a multiplicity of forms throughout different cultures.

The present-tense command in this verse is to *"continually or habitually be staying away,"* which means to "abstain or refrain from, or to avoid contact with something." The previous verse had just commanded us to *"test all things; hold fast to what is good"* (1 Thes 5:21); thus followers of the Scripture are not to be naïve, uninformed, or easily impressed with new ideas.

We are to avoid *"every form,"* which means "the shape and structure of something, or the external appearance." The verb form of this word means "to look upon or to contemplate, to see in order to know, to have personal acquaintance and relationship with something." This exposure is dangerous.

The *"evil"* to be avoided is "wicked in a moral or spiritual sense, that which corrupts others, malicious, or malignant." There is an evil that comes from within every person that must be recognized and controlled. Jesus said, *"What comes out of a man, that defiles a man. For from within, out of the heart of men, proceed evil thoughts, adulteries, fornications, murders, thefts, covetousness, wickedness, deceit, lewdness, and evil eye [jealousy], blasphemy, pride, foolishness. All these evil things come from within and defile a man"* (Mark 7:21–22). Human nature is neither innocent nor good; rather, it is self-centered, selfish, and egotistical. Only the simpleminded believe man is good.

We are to *"abhor what is evil. Cling to what is good"* (Rom 12:9). Believers are never supposed to expose themselves to evil. This is foolishness. Evil is too deceitful and, sadly, too appealing and addictive to our evil nature.

This is a general call for believers to discern truth from error, good from evil, and to separate from false teachings, influences, and behaviors that displease our Savior. We are to *"be wise in what is good, and simple concerning evil"* (Rom 16:19). These commands are the means for fulfilling our objective: *"Now may the God of peace Himself sanctify you completely"* (5:23)—that is, may He "separate you" from evil. We are all struggling here. Where are you resisting?

"Mighty God, Your way is the best way! I want to learn daily how to stay away from sinful thoughts and practices by focusing on Your word and being obedient to the guidance of Your Holy Spirit."

MAY 6

Keep Away from Love of Money, but Pursue Godliness

1 Tim 6:11—*"But you, as a person dedicated to God,* **keep away from** *~~ all that [i.e., the love of money; 6:10]. Instead* **pursue** *~~ righteousness, godliness, faithfulness, love, endurance, and gentleness."*

When people can be made to believe that certain things or experiences will bring happiness, security, and significance, they can be manipulated to buy or try anything. We are told that *"contentment is great gain"* (1 Tim 6:6) and that the *"love of money is the root of all kinds of evil"* (6:10), but everything in our society says, "Greed is the key to motivation for prosperity" and "Money will bring happiness and security." Choices must be made. *"Some"* in the church where Timothy was pastoring had already *"strayed from the faith in their greediness, and pierced themselves through with many sorrows"* (6:10). The world's way promises much but delivers little.

If we want to follow God, and to be used by God, we must change our normal values and priorities. We are told to *"habitually keep away from"* certain things. This means "to seek safety in flight [and] move hastily from danger" that results from being *"obsessed with disputes and arguments . . . , envy, strife, reviling, evil suspicions, [and] useless wrangling . . . [of those] who suppose that godliness is a means of gain. From such withdraw yourself . . . those who desire to be rich fall into temptations and a snare, and into many foolish and harmful lusts which drown men in destruction and perdition"* (1 Tim 6:4–9). Keep away from these kinds of people.

On the contrary, *"continually or habitually be pursuing"* six qualities or characteristics: *"righteousness, godliness, faithfulness, love, endurance, and gentleness,"* which are the fruit of the Spirit (Gal 5:22–23). *"Righteousness"* comes from a heart and life in harmony with God's commands, which leads to *"godliness,"* the motivation for an obedient lifestyle. *Faithfulness* refers to reliable trustworthiness in life and trust in whatever God says. *Love* is an unselfish care for and commitment to others. *Patience* refers to an enduring ability to stay true to the faith and God's purpose for one's life. Finally, *gentleness* is kindness in dealing with others. This defines a man who walks with God . . . one that others respect and want to be their leader.

"Loving Lord Jesus, You lived humbly on this earth, showing us the way. Help me love You and Your precepts more than money or fame or any other selfish notion that may want to take Your place."

MAY 7
Turn Away from Evil

2 Tim 2:1—*"However, God's solid foundation remains standing, bearing this seal: 'The Lord knows those who are his,' and 'Everyone who confesses the name of the Lord **must turn away***~ **from evil.**'"*

Deviation from the teachings of God's word plagued the first-century church, since few had access to the New Testament text."*God's solid foundation remains standing*," Paul wrote in AD 64. Orally it had survived the first thirty years. Most of the recorded documents for keeping the church true had been written by this time.

Paul described the foundation in this manner: "*You are . . . fellow citizens with the saints and members of the household of God, having been built on the foundation of the apostles and prophets, Jesus Christ Himself being the chief cornerstone*" (Eph 2:19–20). The task of the apostles and prophets was to lay the foundational teachings and then record them through inspiration for all the ages. The foundational task was complete in the first century. Now evangelists, teachers, and preachers explain, exhort, and apply what was delivered to us by the first-century apostles and prophets. False teaching causes others to deviate from this foundation.

God's seal of ownership is on the body of true believers: "*The Lord knows those who are His.*" Jesus warned, "*Not everyone who says to Me, 'Lord, Lord,' shall enter the kingdom of heaven, but he who does the will of My Father in heaven. Many will say to Me in that day, 'Lord, Lord, have we not prophesied in Your name, cast out demons in Your name, and done many wonders in Your name?' And then I will declare to them, 'I never knew you'*" (Matt 7:21–22). The issue is not whether we think we know Him but whether He knows us. Jesus later said, "*My sheep hear My voice [His word], and I know them, and they follow Me . . . and I give eternal life to them*" (Jn 10:27–28). Does He know you listen to every word He says?

The second seal on the church is evident through personal sanctification: "*Everyone who confesses [names] the name of the Lord must turn away [abstain] from evil.*" True believers respect the commands and instructions given by the true apostles and prophets and turn away any teacher or thought that deviates from them. Are you afraid to disobey Scripture? This is the healthy "fear of the Lord."

"Dear Lord, as we build our knowledge You gave us in Your word, we will have the ability to 'turn away from' evil. Thank You for Your word, which gives me all I need to be successful in living my life for Your purposes."

MAY 8

Keep Away from Youthful Passions

2 Tim 2:22—*"But **keep away from**~~ **youthful passions, and pursue**~~**righteousness, faithfulness, love, and peace**, in company with others who call on the Lord from a pure heart."*

Paul had been training Timothy for the past fifteen years, challenging him to be a *"proven worker who does not need to be ashamed, teaching the message of truth accurately"* (2 Tim 2:15) and a *"vessel for honorable use, set apart, useful for the Master, prepared for every good work"* (2:21). Paul kept the vision before Timothy of what he could be for God.

He told Timothy to *"flee also youthful lusts."* The imperative to *flee* means to "escape, shun, or avoid" something damaging or destructive. The word *youthful* refers to the characteristics of adolescents. *Passion* is a "craving, longing, desire for what is forbidden, lust" for what you think you need. The word can refer to not only sexual passions but also childlike ambitions, curiosity, or selfishness.

Regardless of the specific issue, immaturity is to be avoided, and maturity is to "habitually be pursued"; *pursue* means to "do something with an intense effort and with a definite purpose or goal." Timothy was to seek "righteousness, faithfulness, love, and peace"—a composite of traits of the mature Christian that command respect.

Righteousness refers to actions of moral commitment to the moral will of God as expressed in the commands, progressing in a virtuous life pursuing obedience. This is not legalism, but godliness.

Faithfulness is "reliability," and it appears in a list of virtues (as in Galatians 5:22). People respect their leaders when they can depend on what they say.

Love is an unselfish commitment to benefit others. A feeling cannot be pursued, but a self-sacrificing strategy to give of yourself for others can be.

Peace refers not to the search for an internal peace with God but to the pursuit of tranquil and harmonious relations among the church body.

These are not to be merely Timothy's objectives; he is to associate with (*"in company with"*) *"who call on the Lord from a pure heart"* in a mentor-protégé relationship. The primary method to achieve maturity is to strive together in mutual accountability or mentorship. Who is your mentor?

"Heavenly Father, guide me to find godly people to whom I can be accountable. Help me avoid immature passions as You guide me to be righteous, faithful, loving, and at peace with others and therefore effective in building the body of Christ."

MAY 9

Remove Evil People from among You

1 Cor 5:13—*"But God will judge those outside.* **Remove*~** *the evil person from among you."*

Immorality in the church has always been a challenge to conquer. The Corinthian church was trying to cover it up, deny it, or make it seem normal.

In an earlier personal letter, Paul told them *"not to keep company with sexually immoral people"* (1 Cor 5:9), but he clarified that this did not mean with *"sexually immoral people of this world"*—that is, unbelievers, since we have to live in this world and must win such sinners to Christ (5:10).

However, we are to refuse close, intimate friendship with *"anyone named [or who calls himself] a brother, who is sexually immoral, or covetous, or an idolater, or a reviler ['slanderer, insulter or blasphemer'], or a drunkard, or an extortioner ['swindler']—not even to eat with such a person"* (1 Cor 5:11).

Believers do not have to be perfect, but they do have to respond to biblical exhortation or correction and repent when justly rebuked by a brother. Discipline is reserved only for those who refuse to recognize their sin.

God judges those outside the church, but the believers are to judge those "who are inside," or who claim to be Christ's followers, when they deviate from God's commands, especially in a damaging or public manner causing others to stumble into disobedience. By doing nothing, the church communicates that open sin is insignificant to God and obedience to the commands is optional.

The command is clear: *"Remove the evil person from among you."* The plural imperative refers to action by the whole church body. We are commanded to *"be blameless and innocent, children of God above reproach in the midst of a crooked and perverse generation, among whom [we] appear as lights in the world"* (Phil 2:15). Regeneration breaks the power of sin, but believers can still choose to sin and develop sinful patterns unless we help each other.

If done properly in love, discipline is designed to cause contrition and the desire to return to fellowship with the brethren. When sinners do repent, we should gladly and thankfully *"forgive and comfort"* them back into fellowship (2 Cor 2:7).

"Dear Jesus, thank You for the opportunity to confess my sin, forsake it, and receive complete forgiveness. May I ever be open to exhortation by godly fellow believers, and may I have wisdom to avoid those who will not accept correction."

MAY 10

Have Tough Love for the Disobedient

2 Thes 3:14–15—*"But if anyone does not obey our message through this letter,* **take note~~** *of him and* **do not associate closely~/** *with him, so that he may be ashamed. Yet* **do not regard~/** *him as an enemy, but* **admonish~~** *him as a brother."*

"Tough love" is the ability to teach the negative consequences of disobedience without showing rejection or changing the relationship. If a child does not learn by experience that disobedience is painful, he will have to learn correction as an adult, which is far more hurtful.

Paul makes it clear that *"if anyone does not obey our [instructions] in this letter,"* he must be corrected. Believers are to understand the commands and decide to obey them. Paul's writings under inspiration are treated as God's Words. Thus the commands are meaningless if there are no consequences for disobedience: *"God promises that He will punish the disobedient child of His . . . No discipline seems pleasant at the time, but painful. Later on, however, it produces a harvest of righteousness and peace for those who have been trained by it"* (Heb 12:10–11[NIV]).

The first consequence is that the entire congregation is to literally *"continually be taking note of that person and stop associating with him,"* which means "stop mixing with or mingling" with him socially.

Since Paul warned him twice on the issue of idleness in his first letter (1 Thes 4:11; 5:14), this third step in church discipline is to teach that those who refuse to obey the commands *"will be put to shame,"* which means to "reflect on their action; to be embarrassed or ashamed of themselves." It is to help them see themselves as rebellious, self-willed, and self-centered sinners who have acted unworthily of Christ's name and to urge them to repent with a change in their behavior. Discipline is the means to the goal for a godly character.

Since this is not yet the fourth and final step as Jesus taught (Matt 18:17), the other members of the church must *"stop regarding him as an enemy;"* rather, the entire congregation is to *"admonish him as a brother"* or to "warn and exhort." The congregation must have been carefully taught this process previously: *"If anyone is caught in any trespass, you who are spiritual, restore such a one in a spirit of gentleness; each one looking to yourself, so that you too will not be tempted"* (Gal 6:1). Do you love the family and brethren enough to exhort and discipline?

"Loving Lord, Give me wisdom to recognize those who will not receive correction and humbly treat them as You command."

Reject Foolish and
Ignorant Controversies

2 Tim 2:23—*"But **reject**~~ **foolish and ignorant controversies**, because you know they breed infighting."*

Timothy evidently needed exhorting to not be argumentative or to not take personally every question that arose in a new church. His task was previously stated to *"pursue . . . peace along with those who call on the Lord out of a pure heart"* (2 Tim 2:22).

False teachers have always been a problem in the churches. Some of their false teachings were more dangerous (heretical) than others (e.g., mistaken misinterpretations or erroneous teaching). Paul commanded Timothy to *reject*, or to "excuse oneself or avoid," such *foolish* ("silly, stupid") and *ignorant* ("untrained or undisciplined") types of *controversies*, or "speculations or themes highly disputed, with no certain basis of truth." Paul was not demanding that Timothy have no contact with the false teachers who were influencing the church, since he had told him to rebuke them.

Great maturity is required to maintain the rule of *"the peace of God"* (Col 3:15) in the midst of the congregation. Controversies only breed division.

Earlier, Paul advised, *"If anyone teaches otherwise and does not consent to wholesome words, even the words of our Lord Jesus Christ, and to the doctrine, which accords with godliness, he is proud, knowing nothing, but is obsessed with disputes and arguments over words, from which come envy, strife, reviling [abusive language], evil suspicions, useless wrangling [constant friction] of men of corrupt minds and destitute of the truth"* (1 Tim 6:3–4).

Once someone is convinced of a false doctrine, there is little hope of changing his mind, unless there is an openness to believe everything revealed in the written word of God.

Paul was quick to discuss and to prove the gospel, but he wasted no time discussing extra biblical revelations. Anything that distracts from the authority and value of the written word is man's imagination and has no healthy benefit. Avoid it.

"Dear God, I pray for insight and understanding of Your word so that I may avoid needless contentions in my relationship within the body of Christ. I know You want Your children to live in peace with each other as much as is possible."

MAY 12

Avoid People Who Repudiate the Power of the Gospel

2 Tim 3:5—*"They will maintain the outward appearance of religion but will have repudiated its power. So **avoid~~ people like these.**"*

There are certain people whom it is best not to befriend. Proverbs 13:20 warns, *"He who walks with the wise grows wise, but a companion of fools suffers harm."* Pick your close friends carefully, because you will become like them.

Paul had just described the foolish nature of the end-time generation: *"Men will be lovers of themselves [self-centered, narcissistic], lovers of money, boasters, proud [arrogant], blasphemers [slanderers, verbally abusive], disobedient to parents, unthankful, unholy, unloving [heartless], unforgiving, slanderers, without self-control, brutal, despisers of good, traitors [disposed toward betrayal], headstrong [disposed toward recklessness], haughty ['puffed up'], lovers of pleasure rather than lovers of God, having a form of godliness but denying its power"* (2 Tim 3:2–4).

The standing order for true believers is to *"continually avoid people like these."* The verb *continually avoid* means to "turn away from or shun," and not only is this to be a constant action, but it is in the middle form, which means to "make yourself avoid" these people. The implication is that this is not an easy decision to practice, so we have to *make* ourselves obey it.

The context is dealing with liberal or false teachers whose teachings can take the form of sacramentalism, ecumenism, scientism, subjectivism, experientialism, mysticism, pragmatism, rationalism, or philosophies that sound reasonable and pious. Since their beliefs do not come from the Scripture, they inevitably contradict the written word of God, playing it down as less important than their "fresh" revelation. All believers must be taught to recognize and avoid such teachings.

The harshness of this command must be balanced with the earlier command: *"A servant of the Lord must not quarrel but be gentle to all, . . . correcting those who are in opposition, if God perhaps will grant them repentance, so that they may know the truth"* (2 Tim 2:24). Our enemy is astute and loves to create error and division among the family of God. Lord, keep us true to Your word.

"Dear Father, thank You for giving us such clear teachings about the kinds of people we should avoid as we live to give You glory. Help me not to be blind sided by those who reject You."

MAY 13

Reject Divisive People

Titus 3:10–11—*"**Reject**~~ **a divisive person** after one or two warnings, knowing that such a person is warped and sinning, being self-condemned."*

The church is not a social club that serves only as a gathering point for learning and worship. Rather, it is an organism in which all the saved share the same Spirit and new birth and are fused together with Christ such that they are collectively called *"the body of Christ and members individually"* (1 Cor 12:27). The church is so bonded together with Christ we become inseparable. The church is to be protected as though it were the person of Christ Himself.

All Christ's followers should unite around learning and obeying the revealed word of God. Any deviation from the original apostolic teachings as revealed in recorded Scripture only creates divisions and distrust among the brethren. Divisive teachers demand conformity to their views.

Paul wrote in his last letter to the churches, *"For the time will come when they will not endure sound doctrine, but according to their own desires, because they have itching ears, they will heap up for themselves teachers; and they will turn their ears away from the truth and be turned aside to fables"* (2 Tim 4:3–4)—that is, imaginary, usually miraculous, stories that prove their extra biblical concepts.

The unity and peace of the church are such priorities that anyone disrupting this harmony must be *"rejected,"* which means to "shun, or avoid." This is a *"divisive"* person, which is the origin of the word *heretic.* This word appears in the list of words that describe the *"works of the flesh,"* such as *"immorality, impurity, sensuality . . . outbursts of anger, disputes, dissensions, factions,"* and so on (Gal 5:19–21). Division in the church is not allowed.

Many Christians are neither discerning enough to detect when a teacher deviates from Scripture nor courageous enough to warn him, much less to separate from him if he does not cease. Do you love the church enough to protect its bond to the Scripture only?

"Heavenly Father, please help me recognize a divisive person and avoid friendship with him. I want to help edify Your church, not to be a part of dividing it."

MAY 14

Don't Partake with Disobedient Unbelievers

Eph 5:7—*"Therefore **do not be~| partakers** with them."*

There is a move today within evangelical Christianity to focus on building relationships with the unsaved, learning to like them, and making ourselves less offensive to them or sharing in their culture and activities.

The believer is to *"know with certainty, that no immoral* [anyone having sex outside of marriage], *or impure* [anything the Lord hates], *covetous man* [greedy for more stuff], *who is an idolater, has any inheritance in the kingdom of Christ and God"* (Eph 5:5). These are the characteristics of unsaved persons; *"the wrath of God comes upon the sons of disobedience"* (5:6).

Sadly, religious people pretend to be Christians, but refuse to repent or see anything wrong with continuing in their sinful lifestyles. Stay away from such people! *"For the grace of God has appeared, bringing salvation to all men, instructing us to deny ungodliness and worldly desires and to live sensibly, righteously and godly in the present age"* (Titus 2:11–12).

Therefore, as a result of the foregoing truths about the wrath of God on the *"disobedient,"* believers are commanded, *"Do not be partakers with them."* The imperative *"do not partake,"* or do not be "joint partakers," has the connotation of intimate participation with the unsaved, especially in their immoral behaviors.

How far is this separation to be taken? This is not a distancing from contacts or friendships but an abstinence from the love of the world, from the sensual values of the world and the disregard for the commands of Scripture. We are to be the "light" in the darkness and the "salt" in the emptiness of the world without participating in unbiblical behavior. Paul wrote, *"Have no fellowship* ['participation'] *with the unfruitful works of darkness"* (Eph 5:11).

God's attitude toward any sexual activity outside of marriage (fornication) has not changed. Sometimes His wrath is immediate, but He often patiently waits for sinners to repent and seek His forgiveness. We should never get comfortable, thinking we are exempt from the *"wrath of God* [that] *comes upon the sons of disobedience"* (Eph 5:6). If you care at all for them, confront them about their need of a Savior. Beware of selfish interests in such marginal relationships.

"Dear Lord, help each of Your dear children wisely choose with whom we will spend our time and our lives. May we not partake in any kind of sinful lifestyle simply to be accepted by those who may not know You."

MAY 15
Do Not Become
Partners with Unbelievers

**2 Cor 6:14—*"Do not become~/ partners* with those who do not believe,
*for what partnership is there between righteousness and lawlessness, or
what fellowship does light have with darkness?"***

Becoming a biblical Christian is not merely about repeating a prayer or
reciting a creed; it is an entirely different worldview that inevitably affects
all aspects of your life. Paul described the new believer as one *"for whom
the old things have passed away; behold, all things have come new"* (2 Cor
5:17). The believer is now in an entirely new realm of reality with new
values, beliefs, guidelines for life, purposes, attitudes, motives, and hopes.

Any agreement between believers and nonbelievers can only be temporal
and external. We may be in the same family, work together in the
marketplace, or be friendly neighbors; however, on the emotional and
spiritual level, we live in two different worlds. Believers are told, *"Do not
love the world nor the things in the world. If anyone loves the world, the love
of the Father is not in him"* (1 Jn 2:15). Relationships with unbelievers must
be limited, with the hope they can be open to the gospel message.

The Corinthians found it difficult to break with their pagan, idolatrous past, and
they brought some of their immoral past experiences into the normal Christian
lifestyle. False teachers and pagan associations brought a syncretistic form of
Christianity that mixed pagan mysticism, Jewish legalism, and secular morality
with the ecumenical church. Separation was the only solution.

The negative present command means to *"stop becoming partners with
those who do not believe."* Our text is not explicitly discussing marriage,
but Paul earlier told widows to marry *"only in the Lord"* (1 Cor 7:39), so
the application to marriage is implicit.

The context focuses on any binding relationship with non-Christian religious
groups or individuals, which can open the door for satanic deception or
worldly influence. The redundant questions that follow indicate there is no
"partnership" (mutual partaking) nor *"fellowship"* (sharing or participation)
with unbelievers. Jesus was friendly and helpful to everyone but confronted
them all with the truth and challenge to follow Him alone. He must always
be the point of separation. Are you willing to make Jesus an issue?

*"Loving Lord, guide my life that I may never be bound to a relationship that
would not honor You or would harm my relationship with You and keep me
from accomplishing Your will."*

MAY 16

Do Not Worry about Your Life

Matt 6:25—*"Therefore I tell you, **do not worry~| about your life**, what you will eat or drink, or about your body, what you will wear. Isn't there more to life than food and more to the body than clothing?"*

Worry is a paralyzing and debilitating mental process that cripples many believers into apathy and isolation. Fear of failure, doubts about our needs being met, insecurities from a variety of sources (e.g., criticisms, risks, losses, or rejection), or unpopularity are but a few of the possible root problems that cause worry or anxiety. However, these problems all stem from our basic distrust of God's ability to intervene helpfully in life's affairs. Can we trust Him?

Matthew 6:25 begins with *"therefore,"* looking back to where Jesus had just declared a reality of life: *"No one can serve two masters; for either he will hate the one and love the other, or else he will be loyal to the one and despise the other. You cannot serve God and mammon"* (6:24). This means "wealth, a personification of riches, the comprehensive word for all kinds of possessions, earnings, or the god of materialism." Everyone will direct his energy, talents, ambitions, time commitments, emotional focus, and desires toward what he believes will meet his primary needs in life.

The question is, who can meet these needs? If it all depends on me and my performance in various areas of life, then worry and anxiety are normal. Can I say that it matters more to me to please God than to please myself? The belief that money will give us security is idolatry.

Therefore the command to *"stop worrying,"* means not to "be anxious, or be (unduly) concerned" about any and all aspects of your life; live thoughtlessly, though not foolishly, in regard to your basic needs.

What is Jesus asking of us? He is asking us not to consider our personal security, or any other need we may have, when contemplating how we will obey the command to *"seek first the kingdom of God"* (Matt 6:33). He promises to provide everything we will need. Jesus is looking for men and women willing to serve Him without fear of what it may cost. With no thought of what you may lose, or how you may live, could you trust Jesus for what you will "need?" Will "stuff" keep you from giving your life for the gospel's sake?

"Lord Jesus, You are the blessed controller of all things! You are trustworthy! There is no justification for me to worry about my life as long as I am seeking to obey Your word and to accomplish Your purpose each day. Thank You, Lord."

MAY 17

Watch Out and Guard Yourself from All Greed

Luke 12:15—*"Then he said to them, '**Watch out**~~ **and guard yourself** ~~ **from all types of greed,** because one's life does not consist in the abundance of his possessions.'"*

Christian teachings from the first century included warnings against the seven deadly sins: wrath, greed, sloth, pride, lust, envy, and gluttony. All are corrupt and insatiable—they promise satisfaction, but the soul is never content.

Greed enters our lives camouflaged as innocent ambition to be the best, but the masquerade hides the desire to be better, wealthier, or famous— and to own more or better things—than anyone in our circle of friends. This quest for acceptance, respect, or honor is motivated by the belief that this is the way to find fulfillment and satisfaction in life. Greed usurps the place of God in our lives, yet is a poor substitute, however enticing.

When Jesus was asked about a man's inheritance, He knew the man was preoccupied with getting his hands on the wealth that he thought he needed and was due to him. Jesus took the occasion to explain the vice that turns our hearts against the will and purpose of God. He gives two commands asking us to be alert against being deceived or blind sided. We are told to *"continually be taking heed,"* "perceiving with the mind," and to "continually be keeping ourselves on guard," or "be aware of" traps or vices of *"greed"* or covetousness—that is, the "constant desire or thirst to have more and more."

How do you know if greed has taken root in your heart? The first symptom is discontent with whatever you have and the willingness to sacrifice everything or anyone to acquire more. As soon as one item is acquired, you are already thinking of something else you need.

The second symptom is the anger felt when someone or something impedes your acquisition of what you believe is necessary for your happiness. When you believe you need a sizable bank account balance to feel secure about your future, then whenever a preacher mentions tithing or generosity, your emotions will flare up. Anger is a reaction to something or someone that interferes with what you think you need for security or success. Do you resent being asked for your help?

"Dear God, thank You for supplying all I need to live according to Your will. Thank You also for all the wonderful things You have freely given us to enjoy. Help me never to want more than You want me to have."

MAY 18
Pursue Christ's Kingdom Priority

Luke 12:31—*"Instead, **pursue~~ his kingdom**, and these things will be given to you as well."*

One of the advantages of becoming a Christian is that you now have a purpose in life. Jesus called for a complete reorientation of life's values, objectives, and purpose.

Everyone needs to put bread on the table, but Jesus demands that His followers *"not seek what you should eat or what you should drink, nor have an anxious mind"* (Luke 12:29). He then states, *"For all these things the nations of the world seek after"* (12:30). Jesus expects us to live with a different motivation and purpose. Neither survival nor comfort is to be our driving impulse.

Luke introduces this command with *"instead"* to emphasize the opposite focus from the previous verse for the believer. Jesus said, *"The Father knows that you need these things"* (12:30). To begin with, can we trust Him? Can we rest securely in the awareness that He knows our needs?

If we trust in Him, we are free to focus on His temporal and eternal purposes. He commands us to *"be continually or habitually pursuing His kingdom."* The kingdom needs never end.

This was an introduction to the Great Commission: *"Go and make disciples of all nations"* (Matt 28:19). Christ's kingdom is extended by multiplying individual converts and leading them to surrender to the lordship of Christ on this earth.

How obedient are you today in this task? What is more important: your job, home, or business venture? What if His commitment to meet your needs were proportional to your commitment to Him? God does not promise riches, but He does promise to meet the needs of His servants who are reaching and building disciples in His kingdom.

He must be King of your life as well as your Savior. His will must control your finances, work ethic, ambitions, relationships, thoughts, and daily plans. As Creator, He promises to take care of you if you are useful to His kingdom now.

"Dear Lord, as I execute my daily tasks, guide me to set my sights on Your eternal purposes. Help me contribute to and prepare for Your coming kingdom so that others may know You and learn to glorify You as well."

MAY 19

Do Not Be Anxious, but Tell God

Phil 4:6—*"**Do not be anxious~/ about anything**. Instead, in every situation, through prayer and petition with thanksgiving, **tell** ~~ **your requests** to God."*

In a world where Christianity is suspect or persecuted as a dangerous sect and the loss of possessions, or even life, is not uncommon (Paul was writing from prison), it may seem ridiculous to command, *"Stop worrying about anything."* However, we must stop being concerned about things over which we have no control.

Jesus said, *"Unless a kernel of wheat falls into the ground and dies, it remains by itself alone. But if it dies, it produces much grain. The one who loves his life destroys it, and the one who hates his life in this world guards it for eternal life"* (Jn 12:24–25). You must learn to give up any claim to your life, yielding it fully to Jesus; it belongs to God. He can do what He wants with His property. This is freedom.

Paul's solution to their *"anxious"* feelings was that they pray *"without ceasing"* (1 Thes 5:17). This prayer was to be *"with thanksgiving"* (Gk. *eucharistia*). When God condemned our sinfulness, He described mankind as, *"they did not glorify him as God, or give him thanks, but they became futile in their thoughts and their senseless hearts were darkened"* (Rom 1:21), a state resulting in other grievous sins. Thankfulness is our expression of trust in His providential care, even if it means being fed to the lions.

Here is the remedy for worry: prayer, supplication, and making requests to God. We need to share with God our innermost feelings. He knows what is happening, but He wants us to express our trust and thankfulness to Him. Believers are to *"cast all [their] anxiety on Him, because He cares for [them]"* (1 Pet 5:7).

The sin (not the disease) of anxiety is simply a failure to trust in God's control and His absolute wisdom. Thankfulness springs from confident faith in God's control. Can you thank Him for your difficulties? Your family? Your health? Think of how this trust could help you mature and grow into a simple life of faith and obedience. Rest in this promise: *"All things work together for good to those who love God"* (Rom 8:28). Can you thank God for every part of your life?

"Dear Jesus, I praise You that at any moment of the day or night I may run to You with any concern I may have and You are there to listen and help. I do not have to be anxious or worried, because I can lean on You in times of trouble."

MAY 20

Have Courage; Do Not Be Afraid

Matt 14:27—*"But immediately Jesus spoke to them: '**Have courage~~**! It is I. **Do not be afraid~/**.'"*

It was a normal trip across the northern end of the Sea of Galilee. For some reason, Jesus had remained on the east side and ordered the disciples to go ahead of Him. They were confused, perhaps disillusioned, and disappointed that Jesus sent them off without explanation. It was a dark and stormy night, and they were alone. The last time they were in a storm, Jesus stood up and calmed the storm (Matt 8:26), but now He was not with them. They were afraid. The *"fourth watch"* (14:24) is three to six o'clock in the morning. They had been sailing all night.

Jesus waited, allowing the situation to worsen to see if they would turn to the Lord in their hearts. He knew what their response would be, but they needed to know their limitations and see His ability. This was a test. They would later have to face things far more intimidating and dangerous.

In the midst of the story, they all saw Jesus walking on the water. According to Mark's Gospel, Jesus *"would have passed them by"* (6:48), but the disciples were pushed beyond their limits when Jesus appeared. Fear changed to panic.

"Take courage continually, it is I" (lit. "I am"), Jesus said. Regardless of our situation, He is with us and expects us not to be intimidated or frightened. Paul learned this truth: *"The Lord stood with me and strengthened me, so that the message might be preached fully through me,"* (2 Tim 4:17). We will never be in a circumstance where Christ is not with us.

As a jungle pilot, I once had an engine failure over the Colombian rain forest and had to crash into a canopy of sixty-foot trees. I remember praying, "Lord, I gave you my life. It is Yours. You can do with it whatever You wish. If you want to take me now, that is fine! If you want to protect me through this crash, I'll thank you forever." God's peace was immediate as I descended from four thousand feet to almost certain death. When I hit the trees, the floats caught in a large tree, which bowed over, cushioning the blow as the plane struck the earth vertically. I was not harmed! I got out of the plane, fell to my knees, and thanked God for His amazing protection. That day marked a renewed life of confidence in God. Never be afraid to do His will.

"Thank You, heavenly Father, that we do not have to give in to fear. We can trust in Your love and Your presence in all circumstances. Thank You for standing with us when life gets tough."

MAY 21

Stand in the Lord in This Way

Phil 4:1—*"So then, my brothers and sisters, dear friends whom I long to see, my joy and crown,* **stand ~~ in the Lord in this way,** *my dear friends!"*

Paul was concerned that the Philippians might *"set their minds on earthly things"* (Phil 3:19). Satan is astute at providing the right temptation, the wrong way of thinking, arguments justifying bitterness, or various convincing reasons to become a spectator or bystander in the kingdom of God.

Paul gave them the key to faithfulness: make heaven their primary citizenship. Anticipating the second coming of Christ, we should not waste time on anything that does not please Him (3:20), and we should know that *"He is able even to subdue all things to Himself"* (3:21). Jesus can be trusted (Rom 8:28), and being faithful is reasonable.

Helping new believers was Paul's passion, as when he and Barnabas decided to return to Asia, *"strengthening the souls of the disciples, encouraging them to continue in the faith, and saying, 'Through many tribulations we must enter the kingdom of God'"* (Acts 14:22).

Paul exhorted his friends with endearing phrases: *"my brothers and sisters, dear friends whom I long to see, my joy and crown."* He loved the believers in Philippi. They were his family. Do our fellow believers feel they are our family? The Philippians were *"dear friends"* that Paul longed to spend time with. Do we spend time with our church members, disciples, or Bible study group? Paul also saw them as his *"joy and crown."* His hope for reward at the judgment seat of Christ was to be with the ones he led to Christ.

He asked them to *"stand in the Lord in this way"*—that is, persevere. Verses 2–9 describe seven practical principles for spiritual stability: harmony among believers, an attitude of joy, contentment, rest in faith, prayer, godly virtues, and obedience.

The phrase *"in the Lord"* refers to obedience to the commands of His word. Earlier, Paul had told them to *"let [their] conduct be worthy of the gospel of Christ . . . striving together for the faith of the gospel, and not in any way terrified by your adversaries"* (Phil 1:27–28a). How would you measure your stand for Christ, His word, and His purpose?

"Dear God, There are times when it is not easy to stand up for Your honor and Your word. Too often I am more concerned about this world's opinion of me than I am about Yours. Help me live for the day when I'll see You."

MAY 22
_____
Do Not Be Distressed; Believe in Christ

Jn 14:1—*"Do not let your hearts be distressed~|. You believe in God; believe~~ also in me."*

This was to be the last time Jesus would share a meal with his disciples, but they did not know it. In fact, they were wondering if Jesus would announce His glorious intentions as Messiah. He said, *"Now the Son of Man is glorified, and God is glorified in Him"* (John 13:31). This must have excited the disciples, who did not realize that His glorification meant His crucifixion, not His coronation. *"Little children, I shall be with you a little while longer"* (13:33).

Surely they thought, "What did He mean? We are just ready to get started." Peter said, *"Lord, why can I not follow You now? I will lay down my life for Your sake"* (Jn 13:37). Jesus said, *"Will you lay down your life for My sake? Most assuredly, I say to you, the rooster shall not crow till you have denied Me* ['disowned me'] *three times"* (13:38). Can you imagine the shock and disillusionment? Earlier in this same evening Jesus had told them that one of them would betray Him (13:21–25). Was Jesus now saying that Peter was a traitor? How this must have hurt! They were all bewildered and discouraged.

Nothing ever works out quite the way we want. When Jesus spoke of glorifying the Father, He referred to a cross (Jn 12:23–25) and dying to personal gain by giving his life for the benefit of others. Spiritual fruit often is the result of an inconspicuous, sacrificial investment in others with no personal benefit.

During this emotional evening (Jn 13–17), Jesus announced that He was going to the Father to prepare a special place for them. He told his disciples that Satan was at work in their minds (Luke 22:31–32) and that they would all abandon Him (Matt 26:31). After three brief years, these young men must carry on alone.

Jesus said, *"Cease from letting your hearts be distressed,"* implying that every believer is personally responsible for the condition of his heart. *"Let your heart keep my commands"* (Prov 3:1); *"keep your heart with all diligence, for out of it spring the issues of life"* (4:23). Wrong thinking—that is, selfish thoughts and delusions of grandeur—leads to disillusionment. The solution? *"Continually be believing [trusting] in me."* Rest in His purpose in all circumstances of your life. Stay faithful to His purpose no matter what.

"Lord, help me learn good thinking habits in order to be ready for the upsets that will inevitably come. Help me believe in You instead of giving in to worries or complaints."

MAY 23

Make Christ Your Lord and
Take the Consequences

1 Pet 3:15—*"But **set Christ apart***~ *as Lord in your hearts and always be ready to give an answer to anyone who asks about the hope you possess."*

Persecution against Christians is a common experience. Peter commanded his readers, *"Do not be afraid of their threats or be troubled"* (1 Pet 3:14).

Rather than being afraid, we are to "immediately and definitively set Christ apart as Lord in your hearts." Some translations use the word *sanctify*, but the meaning is to "consecrate or set apart for exclusive use."

Paul described this heart decision as one to *"put on the Lord Jesus Christ, and make no provision for the flesh, to fulfill its lusts"* (Rom 13:14). Earlier he commanded, *"Do not be conformed to this world, but be transformed by the renewing of your mind, that you may prove what is that good and acceptable and perfect will of God"* (12:2). It makes sense to make the will of God our priority: *"The world is passing away, and the lusts of it; but he who does the will of God abides forever"* (1 Jn 2:17).

My first summer camp experience ended with a bonfire dedication service. I had memorized a quick testimony to say that I had just accepted Christ and was so grateful. Each one of us had a stick of wood to throw into the fire, which I thought was strange. Just as I stepped into the circle, another young man stepped forward and began to speak. He said, "I accepted Christ a few months ago, and I want this stick to represent my whole life. I want to publicly let it be known that I have not broken off any splinter to keep in my pocket, but wish to throw every bit of it, as my whole life, into the fire to be consumed in the will of God." Wow! Just then, a small, still voice said to me, "Don, that is what I want. Are you willing?" In that instant, I understood the issue, and I said, "Yes, Lord, You can have all of my life."

The *"heart"* is the seat of our deepest emotions. Allowing Christ to reign here unseats fear and replaces it with the desire to please God and obey His commands regardless of earthly consequences.

A humble yet bold explanation of how Christ has changed your life is powerful. Have you made your heart ready to tell the story?

"Dear Father, give me the wisdom to allow You to reign in my heart no matter what kind of persecution may come. May I be ready, through Your word, to speak out for You."

MAY 24

Guard against Sinful Distractions

Luke 21:34—*"But **be on your guard**~~ so that your hearts are not weighed down with dissipation and drunkenness and the worries of this life, and that close down upon you suddenly like a trap."*

The human mind is corrupt—even in the nicest person. When you tell an unsaved person that God loves him, he could be thinking, "Of course, I am a wonderful person and my self-esteem is great; why wouldn't God love me?" Or maybe, "Well, if God loves me, He would never send me to hell, so I will not worry about death." In regard to the second coming, a person can argue that He has not come yet, and will not come anytime soon. Even believers can become skeptical about the urgency of the hour, as is evidenced by their apathy in world evangelism and personal discipleship. They have failed to guard their hearts and thus have opened themselves to crippling and entrapping sins.

Luke 21:34 tells us, *"Be continually on your guard."* We are to look forward to Christ's return as part of our everyday activities. Regarding the signs of His coming, Jesus had just said, *"This generation will by no means pass away till all these things take place"* (21:32). His disciples were not to let anything interfere with their primary task of getting the gospel to *"the regions beyond"* (2 Cor 10:16) where it presently exists. A thousand things would distract them.

When asked when He would return, the primary answer He gave is in Matt 24:14: *"This gospel of the kingdom will be preached in all the world as a witness to all the nations, and then the end will come."*

When a Christian begins to accept the lie that his life does not matter or that he cannot do anything to make a difference in someone's life or speed the completion of the Great Commission, he can be tempted to live selfishly. His sinful heart will be attracted to fleshly attractions. Christians can be guilty of the worst sins and justify them with psychological or philosophical arguments. Watch your heart!

When Jesus returns, there will be no warning or time to change. In whatever spiritual state is yours at that moment, you will face the judgment seat of Christ with all its consequences. Do not let this world *"close down upon you . . . like a trap."*

"Dear Lord, give me the fortitude to always be on guard against anything that would keep me from honoring You and accomplishing my part in the Great Commission."

MAY 25
Think about Your Call

1 Cor 1:26—"***Think~~ about the circumstances of your call***, brothers *and sisters. Not many were wise by human standards, not many were powerful, not many were born to a privileged position.*"

The thirst for respect from a critical world has been a perpetual temptation. However, many come to know the Lord in childhood, or from backgrounds of poor and working classes, yet become great leaders, so that His power is evident and He receives the glory.

The gospel seems foolish to those who want to be acceptable through their own self-righteous efforts. It is offensive to pluralistic thinkers, since the Bible says the gospel is the exclusive way to become acceptable to a holy God.

All societies have exalted power, influence, and wealth, especially in religion; however, biblical Christianity's values are humble servanthood, self-sacrifice, and generosity. These opposite values seem absurd to the world. Jesus said, "*I thank You, Father, Lord of heaven and earth, that You have hidden these things from the wise and prudent and have revealed them to babes*" (Matt 11:25). It is not that the wise of the world cannot believe but that their self-pride and their confidence in their own accomplishments and goodness keep them from the kingdom.

Paul never wants us to forget where we came from before we met Christ. Our salvation has nothing to do with our importance. He urges us, "*Be thinking about the circumstances of your call.*" When you responded to God's call in salvation, He did not accept you because you were famous, wealthy, educated, influential, or powerful; He accepted you because you surrendered your life to the Savior. Paul told the Corinthians that they should be glad that "*not many were wise by human standards, not many were powerful, not many were born to a privileged position.*" He was building a new set of values into the church.

Beware of thinking that important, powerful and wealthy people are the key to the success of the church. According to Jesus, one of the greatest men who ever lived was John the Baptist. (Matt. 11;11) He had no formal education, no trade or profession, no money, no social status, no prestige, and no important position. However, God used him to change a nation because he was fully obedient to God's will. May his tribe increase.

"*Holy God, the call to eternal life involves all of me in every way. Help me see where I am wasting time in activities that do not contribute to Your kingdom.*"

MAY 26

Boast in the Lord

1 Cor 1:31—"*so that, as it is written, 'Let the one who boasts, **boast** ~~ in the Lord.'*"

You can carry on a conversation with anyone by simply asking questions. For some, it is very important that others have a high opinion of them, so they make sure of it by talking about themselves at length . . . and they don't even realize what they are doing!

The wisdom of God in providing unmerited and undeserved salvation was that "*no flesh should glory in His presence*" (1 Cor 1:29). Braggarts are out of sync with God's ways. Through an incredible, ingenious, and inconceivable plan, our God designed a way that everyone could receive the same level of "*righteousness, sanctification and redemption*" (1:30) as a gift! Not a single religion or philosophy ever dreamed up a plan that could explain how sinful man could be made fully and absolutely acceptable to a holy God forever. Amazing!

Paul commands us to "*boast in the Lord.*" This verb means "straighten up your neck or carry your head in a proud manner." Because this concept is so important, Paul repeats this command verbatim in 2 Corinthians 10:17. When Paul referred to himself, it was not to flatter himself: "*If I must boast, I will boast in the things which concern my infirmity*" (2 Cor 11:30). How unlike Paul we are!

We tend to talk about our accomplishments, our successes, or something we have done to impress others. We tend to brag about the wrong things and are proud about what means nothing to God: "*Let not the wise man glory in his wisdom, let not the mighty man glory in his might, nor let the rich man glory in his riches; but let him who glories glory in this, that he understands and knows Me, that I am the LORD, exercising loving kindness, judgment, and righteousness in the earth. For in these I delight*" (Jer 9:23–24).

Have you ever been ashamed to publicly be called a Christian? How could a Muslim or a Hindu be prouder of his religion and freer to talk about it and defend it than believers in Jesus Christ? We have the greatest story ever told and the King of kings as our Savior, whose salvation is man's only hope. Someday it will be so obvious, so grand, and so globally visible that it will be ridiculous not to boast of His reality.

"Mighty God, this life is not worth living if I am not devoting each day to understanding and knowing You better. May I only glory in what You accomplish in and through my life."

MAY 27
Do Not Exalt Mortals

1 Cor 3:21—*"So then, **no more boasting~/ about mere mortals!** For everything belongs to you."*

Exaltation of human leaders—especially one against another when there were multiple leaders in a church—was one of the signs of carnal attitudes in Corinth. Paul wrote, *"It has been declared to me concerning you . . . that there are contentions among you. Now I say this, that each of you says, 'I am of Paul,' or 'I am of Apollos,' or I am of Cephas [Peter],' or 'I am of Christ.' Is Christ divided? Was Paul crucified for you? Or were you baptized in the name of Paul?"* (1 Cor 1:11–13).

Later, he described the situation that limited their exposure to the truths of God's word: *"I fed you with milk and not with solid food; for until now you were not able to receive it, and even now you are still not able; for you are still carnal. For where there are envy, strife, and divisions among you, are you not carnal and behaving like mere men? For when one says, 'I am of Paul,' and another 'I am of Apollos,' are you not carnal?"* (1 Cor 3:1–4). Their preconceived ideas of the Christian life closed their minds and spirits to hearing from anyone but these special teachers.

There will always be a slight difference of opinion or priorities as God guides different teachers or preachers in their application of the Bible. Listeners or students should not exaggerate these distinctions out of proportion, pitting one against another, as long as the word of God is the supreme authority.

However, if the Bible is neglected or considered an ancient, obsolete text and a teacher gives a special or fresh revelation, those followers who consider those teachings as sacred as the Bible have slipped into the carnal attitudes of the Corinthians. When the word of God ceases to be studied carefully with the challenge to obey His commands, self-help psychology or philosophical arguments become the core of the messages. Most people cannot tell the difference.

Jesus said, *"Teach to obey all that I have commanded you"* (Matt 28:20). After leaving a church service, ask yourself, "How am I to obey the word of God this week?"

"Dear Father, help me never to allow another person or human teaching to be more important than that which You have taught in Your word."

MAY 28
Guard against Self-Deception

1 Cor 3:18—*"**Guard**~~ **against self-deception,** each of you. If someone among you thinks he is wise in this age, **let him become***~ **foolish** so that he can become wise."*

Con artists and deceivers count on the fact that most people are naïve and undiscerning. False teachers have learned to wow their listeners with myths, miracles, and marvels that captivate their curiosity and turn followers from the biblical text to fables or intellectual philosophy. Such leaders are so impressed with their own powers of persuasion that they even believe their own lies!

When believers are not well versed in Scripture, they become easily deceived by stories, myths, and phenomena. These leaders so much want to convince people they have the newest insights for the twenty-first century that they stretch the truth to get people to believe their deception.

Striving for intellectual, philosophical, or academic wisdom through the modern educational system and earning master's degrees and doctorates gains prestige and respect for those in positions of influence and power.

The first step to avoid being deceived is to recognize that all human wisdom is *"foolishness with God"* (1 Cor 3:19). Socrates taught that the recognition of your own ignorance is the starting point for the acquisition of knowledge or wisdom. Intellectual pride is the enemy of biblical truth. Once a teacher told me, "If I believe and practice what you are showing us from God's word about people and truth, I must denounce almost everything I have learned during years working to gain my degrees." The special fields of warning are the sciences, education, psychology, religion, and philosophy.

Biblical teachings of child rearing, origins and nature of man, development of spiritual maturity and biblical character, morality, personal relationships, relationship to authority, and so on will all contradict the world's wisdom. Where the Bible is not the supreme authority, division is inevitable. It may seem *"foolish"* to focus on Bible learning more than on worldly wisdom, but it works! God's word makes no mistakes. It brings unity, transformation, and fulfillment. Be a fool for Christ! Focus on His word today.

"Lord Jesus, guide my thinking and keep me grounded in Your word. I want the Bible to always be the supreme authority and direction for my life."

MAY 29

Be Careful Not to Fall

1 Cor 10:12—*"So **let the one who thinks he is standing be careful** ~~ that he does not fall."*

Paul had just explained why some men in the Old Testament had tempted God and griped against Moses, presuming that God would not do anything to them; after all, they were part of the chosen people. However, God sent a plague that killed 14,700 (Num 16:41, 49). Paul just said these stories *"were written for our admonition"* (10:11). They reveal to us God's patience and compassion and His wrath—we are expected to take them seriously.

God's motive for recording the stories of Israel's beginnings was for our *"admonition"* 3,500 years later! Gentile Christians would need to learn the history of Israel to know these valuable lessons. If we fail to learn them, we are condemned to repeat Israel's mistakes and suffer the same consequences.

"So" ties the previous verses with the present command: *"Let the one who thinks he is standing be continually careful that he does not fall."* *To fall* in the Old Testament meant "to die" (Num 14:3). Is a loving God capable of killing people today? It is a horrible thought, but we are warned in 1 John 5:16, *"There is sin leading to death."*

Those who presume to have a relationship with Christ because of what they do or accomplish, may know nothing of God's word and have little interest in being obedient to His commands. Do you really know Him if you never pay attention to Him? The real question is, does He know you?

Faith is based on knowledge of the word of God and a commitment to trust and obey what it says. If you are merely trusting in being good, beware: you may not be standing at all! *"Faith comes by hearing, and hearing by the word of God"* (Rom 10:17). Faith is trust in biblical truth.

The true believer, likewise, needs to *"continually be taking heed"* that his faith and lifestyle are built on the word of God. The fear of God's chastisement is extremely healthy. Believe it and take heed!

"Dear Father, keep me from spiritual pride. Humble my heart to understand and obey the instructions of Your word each day."

MAY 30

Do Not Be Arrogant, but Fear

Rom 11:20—*"Granted! They were broken off because of their unbelief, but you stand by faith. **Do not be arrogant~| but fear~~!**"*

In today's passage, we must identify who is the *"they"* and who is the *"you."* Paul is describing God's sovereign decision to choose the Gentiles of the world (*"you"*), and He has put aside *"some"* of His formerly chosen people, Israel (*"they"*): *"If some of the branches were broken off [Israel], and you, being a wild olive tree [Gentiles], were grafted in among them, and with them became a partaker of the root and fatness of the olive tree, do not boast against the branches"* (Rom 11:17–18a). Paul is teaching the first-century Gentiles that they are not entitled to the gospel but have been "grafted into" the blessings of God. It was because of God's grace that He chose to spread the gospel among the Gentiles.

First, only *"some"* of Israel were broken off. God, as Paul expressed, is still reaching out to anyone who will believe—even Israel. Paul said, *"I magnify my ministry [to the Gentiles] if by any means I may provoke to jealousy those who are my flesh and save some of them [Israel]"* (Rom 11:13–14). God is always gracious to those willing to *"stand by faith,"* not trying to impress God with their goodness.

Second, God changes situations for His purposes. In the future, God will lift the *"blindness in part [that] has happened to Israel until the fullness of the Gentiles has come in"* (Rom 11:25), and then God will turn His focus to His chosen people, Israel. All people matter to God.

God's warns the Gentile believers, *"Stop being arrogant."* This has always been God's attitude: *"All who fear the Lord will hate evil. Therefore, I hate pride, arrogance, corruption and perverse speech"* (Prov 8:13[NLT]). No one is entitled. No one deserves God's acceptance, so we can only be saved by grace alone.

The second command is to *"be continually fearing"*—that is, we should be afraid *not* to do what He says. The arrogant have little respect for others and less respect for authorities, especially for God and His word. Paul's lesson is to overcome the presumption of God's grace and the vain imagination that blessings will always come regardless of a lack of faith and obedience to His word. Don't be presumptuous!

"Dear Lord, keep me from presumptuous sin. Show me when arrogance begins to take over and help me to have a healthy fear of the consequences of straying from Your word."

MAY 31

Remain in Christ's Love

Jn 15:9—*"Just as the Father has loved me, I have also loved you;* **remain*~ in my love.*"**

Modern Christians have romanticized their relationship with Christ. Does this verse mean to "stay in love with Jesus?"

Let's begin by understanding the parts. We need to see the Father's love for the Son, then the Son's love for the disciples, and then the disciples' love for each other (and the church).

"Love" (Gk. *agape*) is a "benevolent commitment to others." It is an action word, not a feeling-based word. If you love someone with this kind of love, you are committed to benefitting him, even if he is your enemy (Matt 5:44). Jesus clarified this concept of love when He said, *"Greater love has no one than this, that a man lay down his life for his friends"* (Jn 15:13).

Live or dwell in the sphere of love. Christ demonstrated, modeled, and taught the disciples that love should be their abode, their overriding life principle, just as it was in Jesus's life. This is not a command to "stay in love with Jesus" but a command to decisively allow the love principle that drove Jesus to the cross to be an unselfish, guiding life principle. The disciples were to model the love of Jesus not only among themselves but to the whole world. They were to get into the circle of self-sacrificing love or commitment to others and never get out of it. This is not a salvation verse but a Christian life principle.

Jesus would never think of doing anything outside the commands of His Father. He trusted the Father, even when it meant a cross. That was something Jesus detested, but He did it anyway. Jesus's commitment to benefit others drove Him beyond His feelings to sacrifice Himself. He told the disciples, *"As the Father has sent me, so send I you"* (Jn 20:21). In other words, he was saying, "The Father sent Me to show His love; now I am sending you out in My love to benefit others."

"If you keep My commandments, you will abide in My love, just as I have kept My Father's commandments and abide in His love" (Jn 15:10). By keeping His commandments, we abide in His love. Are you willing to demonstrate Christ's love to the world?

"Dear Lord Jesus, may I continually live within the sphere of Your love in my responses to Your word and in my dealings with other people. May You be the all-important center of my world."

<hr>

JUNE 1

Glorify God with Your Body

1 Cor 6:20—*"For you were bought at a price. Therefore* **glorify*~ God with your body.***"

In a recent movie, a robot refused to follow the order of its master and began to generate its own directives. Chaos resulted. Though we are not robots, we do have a Creator who created us in His image, with many of His attributes, for a purpose. Just as the Son submits to the will of the Father, so we were created to willingly walk with the Father and submit to His will. When sin entered the human scene, we became like the rogue robot, seeking our own will.

For the sixth time in this chapter, Paul asked, *"Do you not know . . . ?"* (1 Cor 6:18). He asked the church to recall that when they became believers, the Holy Spirit took up residency within their mortal bodies. The Spirit becomes a permanent resident in each of us, such that we are called a *"temple of the Holy Spirit"* (6:19). Paul wrote, *"For in Him dwells all the fullness of the godhead bodily; and you are complete in Him"* (2:9–10). How should we think about our bodies if the fullness of God dwells within us?

The preceding verse ends with a categorical statement: *"You are not your own"* (1 Cor 6:19). To treat your body as a personal, private possession, seeking your own gratification without regard to God's instructions, is simple robbery. He paid for your life so that you would honor Him with your body and your life.

Just as a temple is a place of worship, sacrifice, prayer, and communion with God, so a believer's body should fulfill these lofty objectives. Just as we would never think of desecrating a sacred temple or church, so we should have respect for our bodies. If we are to *"glorify God in [our] body and in [our] spirit, which are God's,"* then we must make them dignified places of prayer, worship, sacrifice, and obedient service, set apart for God's purposes (Rom 12:1–2). Our bodies *"were bought with a price"*—that is, the life and blood of our Savior, paid to redeem us to God, with the result that our body and soul belong to God.

Will you tell God that you will relinquish all rights to your body and yield control to His will, whatever it may be? Do you trust Him that much?

"Lord, I am so thankful for Your grace in covering all my sins and accepting me as Your child that I want to show the world what You mean to me. May all my actions and reactions reflect Your principles and commands."

Be Careful about Your Liberty

1 Cor 8:9—*"But **be careful** ~~that this liberty of yours does not become a hindrance to the weak."*

Can selfish humans be trusted with liberty? The transition from dictatorship to democracy in many countries often breeds vice and corruption. Democracies depend on the honesty, work ethic, and integrity of their constituents. It can take generations for a people to become mature enough to successfully handle political liberties. It is the same with the church.

Spiritual liberty from the guilt of sin is not always the same as practical liberty. Paul is telling us, *"Stop letting sin reign in your mortal body, that you should continually obey it in its lusts"* (Rom 6:12, with author's expansion of verb meaning). An invisible God supervises Christian liberties, so it is easy to think we can get away with sin and selfishness. But as believers, it is foolish to self-destruct and lose your liberty by becoming enslaved again to sin.

First Corinthians 8:9 deals with food offered to idols and then sold on the open market. It was believed that this food remained affected by the false gods and thus should not be eaten. Young believers were still weak in their biblical understanding and felt that eating it would draw them back into perverse, demonic temple worship. The believer with more biblical understanding was at liberty to eat the food; he knew this was all imagination and no harm could result, since those gods did not exist—there are no gods other than the one true God.

The issues differ in other cultures, but the principle is the same. The command to *"be continually being careful"* means "to discern or understand." Paul is saying, "Be guided by a higher principle." The word used here for *liberty* means "permission or right." A person has a right to do things, but it may not be wise to do so.

In the next verse, Paul discusses the *"conscience"* of the *"weak"* brother, which might be overcome by witnessing a *"strong"* brother's liberties. Since the Holy Spirit exercises His conviction is in the realm of the conscience, which in turn is guided by our personal biblical understanding, we must allow time for the weaker conscience to mature by giving up some of our liberties for their benefit. This is love!

"Father, sometimes my freedom as a believer can make me indifferent to some who are strict in their convictions. Grant me Your love even for those who might criticize me, and give me the grace to adapt my life to not offend them."

JUNE 3

Think on What Is True and Respectful

Phil 4:8—*"Finally, brothers and sisters, whatever is true, whatever is worthy of respect, whatever is just, whatever is pure, whatever is lovely, whatever is commendable, if something is excellent or praiseworthy,* **think~~ about these things***."*

What a believer allows himself to think, or how or what he trains himself to think, will determine how he performs in everyday life and relationships.

Philippians 4:8 begins with *"finally,"* tying this passage to the proceeding list of commands that ends with how to think: *"be anxious for nothing"* and *"let your requests be made known to God."* Whatever you think about molds your beliefs and stimulates your motivation.

Choose to think of all that is *"true"* about someone, which means facts—not gossip or exaggerations. Think positively of others.

Think about whatever is *"worthy of respect,"* which means "noble, dignified, or exalted in character." It is not naïve to see positive traits in others.

Think about what is *"just"*—that is, whatever meets God's standards or is in line with His commands.

Think about what is *"pure,"* or "free from defilements or perversions." The challenge of keeping our thoughts unmixed with immorality or selfishness is not easy. We choose our thoughts.

Think about what is *"lovely,"* or "pleasing or acceptable," as opposed to thinking of negative reasons for rejecting a person.

Think about whatever is *"commendable,"* which refers to something "admirable" or "deserving a good reputation." Build up someone's reputation.

Think about what is *"excellent"*—that is, anything that is "pleasing to God, morally excellent, or good."

Think about anything that is *"praiseworthy,"* or worthy of "applause or commendation," and then look for an opportunity to compliment that person.

When you think of someone, focus on all the characteristics in this list. Remember, this is how God thinks of us (2 Cor 4:5).

"Lord, I know my thoughts too easily focus on the faults or negative characteristics of people around me. Give me the discipline to think as You do of all the positive virtues of Your children. Thank You for thinking of what is praiseworthy in my life."

JUNE 4

Keep Seeking Things Above

Col 3:1—*"Therefore, if you have been raised with Christ,* **keep seeking~~ the things above,** *where Christ is, seated at the right hand of God."*

Whenever we travel internationally, there is always the assurance that soon we will be back home. It is amazing what can be endured with this thought.

Paul said that those who followed false teachers and their imposed legalism became *"vainly puffed up by [their] fleshly mind[s]"* (Col 2:18)—that is, self-righteous. Those who focused on detailed regulations *"according to the commandments and doctrines of men"* (2:22) had the facade of spirituality *"but [were] of no value against the indulgence of the flesh"* (2:23).

On the other hand, the attitude that transforms lives is described in Colossians 3:1. It begins with the command to *"habitually keep seeking the things above,"* which means "to desire to have or experience or prioritize" the presence of Jesus as He is in heaven.

People seek what they believe will satisfy their needs and desires. You must make a decision: will you believe the evidence of Scripture about the value of *"continually seeking the things above?"* This means to choose to sacrifice some personal gratifications now in order to live for Christ's kingdom purposes because this will bring far greater satisfaction and meaning to our lives, especially when we see Him face to face. *"Now if we died with Christ, we believe that we shall also live with Him"* (Rom 6:8). To *"live with him"* we choose to make our greatest delight. Are you eager for this day?

Here is the most powerful, important, and majestic person in all creation . . . and we are His . . . and He is our Savior and Lord! We serve the King of kings and Lord of lords.

The believer is to view everything on earth from His heavenly perspective: *"For here we have no continuing city, but we seek the one to come"* (Heb 13:14). The believer chooses to make *heaven* his chief delight—to make the anticipation of seeing Him face to face, being with Him, and pleasing Him life's greatest expectation. This life is but a pilgrimage in partnership with Jesus.

"Oh, Lord, how I long to see You face to face. The thoughts of living with You forever are the greatest delights of my days. Everything on earth fades in comparison."

JUNE 5

Reflect on Scripture

2 Tim 2:7—*"Think~~ about what I am saying and the Lord will give you understanding of all this."*

The human mind cannot retain or recall everything to which it has been exposed. What we learned once, we will need to review often to reapply the meaning of commands like to *"be continually thinking"* about Paul's teaching, which means "to perceive with conscious thought, as opposed to mere contemplative reflection."

Every command of Scripture must be studied to glean the main thought of every verb. This is much more than casually reading the text or memorizing passages. Then we must consider the context as we draw conclusions from each the passage. Finally, the bridge between understanding the meaning and making decisions about what we must do is called "meditation." The key to maturity is the application of the meaning of the word of God.

In 1 Timothy 2:2, Paul had given the command to train faithful men to do the work of the ministry (cf. Eph 4:12). To illustrate the challenge of applying principles of God's word, he used the hardships of a soldier, the rigorous training of an athlete, and the hard work of the farmer to produce a crop. Merely reading a text can be compared to watching a sport: you may learn a lot, but you won't get in physical shape.

Sadly, many never spend the time to reflect on the meaning and seldom ask, "What am I to do today?" The one who *"finds pleasure in obeying the LORD's commands; . . . meditates on his commands day and night"* (Psa 1:2); he is the one who is *"like a tree planted by flowing streams; it yields its fruit at the proper time, and its leaves never fall off. He succeeds in everything he attempts"* (1:3).

Does this verse describe your life? A growing Christian is devoted to learning and following every principle in God's word, by denying your selfish interests, considering your life as an opportunity to serve Christ, and keeping away from worldly entanglements. If you seek both the meaning and the application of all of Jesus taught then*"the Lord will give you understanding of all this."* This is how you will finish God's plan.

"Father, as I reflect on Your words to us, it is amazing to me that the King of kings has given us His wisdom and instructions to live by. Help me understand them correctly and to have the conviction to live faithfully by them today."

JUNE 6

Do Not Complain

1 Cor 10:10—*"And **do not complain**~/, as some of them did, and were killed by the destroying angel."*

Life is not perfect, nor are circumstances on earth going to be paradise. People tend to think they deserve to be treated better than they are or to have more than they do. When expectations are not satisfied, the human tendency is to gripe and complain.

Our text refers to when the Israelites were in the desert after leaving Egypt. It was a difficult time, but complaining only made it much worse. Moses wrote, *"With most of them God was not well pleased"* (1 Cor 10:5). Of almost a million men, only two—Joshua and Caleb—survived the forty years in the desert to enter Canaan.

In spite of daily miracles providing their essential needs, the Israelites refused to be thankful, content, or obedient. For this reason, they became *"disqualified"* (1 Cor 9:24, 27) from being useful for God's purposes. It appears that the Corinthians followed their poor example.

The command was to *"stop complaining,"* which means to stop "murmuring, griping, groaning, whining, or complaining." This refers to the constant carping and malcontent of self-pitying "victims" on whom God had laid too difficult a burden. The Israelites felt that God had been unfair to them. They dreamed of their life of entitlements as slaves.

God was so displeased with their griping that he sent a plague, which killed 14,700 people (Num 16:49). Do you think God has changed His attitude?

If we believe that God providentially arranges the circumstances of our lives, then we must learn contentment, thankfulness, and wisdom to let Him use our lives as He sees fit. He makes no mistakes. If the mouth expresses what fills our heart (*"For whatever is in your heart determines what you say"*; Matt 12:34^NLT), then griping reveals that the heart is filled with dissatisfaction and distrust. This is a sin He does not take lightly. Can you thank the Lord for your trials and blessings?

"When I think of how Your heart must ache when You hear the griping and complaining of Your children, I want to be one voice that says 'Thank You, Lord,' for everything in life. May my heart be a refreshing encouragement to You."

JUNE 7

See to It That No One
Has an Unbelieving Heart

Heb 3:12—*"**See to it** ~~, brothers and sisters, that **none of you has an evil, unbelieving heart** that forsakes the living God."*

God could have provided all the evidence to make obvious the truth of the His word, but He chose to reveal just enough to require the element of faith on our part. Even in a court of law, absolute proof is not required to secure a conviction. It is only necessary to provide proof beyond a reasonable doubt. Biblical faith is not blind: we are not asked to believe something unreasonable that does not make sense or has no logic to support it. Circumstantial evidence could be compiled to build a plausible case for an evolutionary world, but with a lot of speculation. The same evidence could be used to make the case for creationism.

The bottom line is, which view does a person want to believe? If a person is honest about the evidence for creation and evolution and wants to find reasons to believe in God, he will find sufficient evidence to justify his faith. If he wants to finds reasons not to believe, he will find them as well. The basic issue is not the evidence; it is a heart issue. This is why the greatest sin is unbelief: some people do not want to believe regardless of the proof provided.

The writer of Hebrews warned these Jewish communities, *"Be continually seeing to it ... that none of you has an evil, unbelieving heart that forsakes the living God."* The challenge is given in the plural because they were responsible for each other. The next verse gives the command to *"exhort one another daily ... lest any of you be hardened through the deceitfulness of sin"* (3:13).

We are to help each other find enough evidence to reasonably justify trust in God's word and then believe it with all our heart. We must ignore the criticism of those who have chosen to reject His word and cling together in the bond of faith in all that He has revealed to us.

Only the willingness to believe immense lies, self-pride, or the temporal desire for approval of men could motivate someone to turn his back on the *"living God."* To turn away from Jesus is to turn away from the only One who has life. The record of Israel's terrible history was given to teach us the terrible price of refusing to trust in and obey God's word. Is your heart committed to trust Him always? Do you know someone who needs encouragement in the faith?

"Lord, sometimes You seem so far away and solutions take so long in coming that I am tempted to doubt if You even care. Thank You for Your word and for faithful friends who continually encourage me to trust You in everything."

JUNE 8

Consider the Word of God

1 Cor 10:15—*"I am speaking to thoughtful people. **Consider***~ what I say."*

The test of a wise person is how he responds to correction and commands: *"The fear of the LORD is the beginning of knowledge, but fools despise wisdom and instruction"* (Prov 1:7). In 1 Corinthians 10:15, Paul is addressing his readers as *"thoughtful people,"* which means those who are "prudent or wise." Paul is being very kind and using positive motivation to get his readers to apply the commands to their lives—but is anyone listening? *"Hear, O My people, and I will admonish you! O Israel, if you will listen to Me!"* (Psa 81:8).

In our text, Paul had just given the command to *"flee from idolatry"* (1 Cor 10:14). Idolatry is much more than praying to an idol. Whatever you center your life on (pleasure seeking, possessions, prestige, financial security, or success) becomes your chief desire, which is your god. It may not be wrong in itself, but if you love it more than you love Jesus, it is an idol, and it must go. *"Where your treasure is, there will your heart be also"* (Matt 6:21): beware that your treasure is not yourself! In one list of sins, Paul writes of a *"covetous man, who is an idolater"* (Eph 5:5; Col 3:5). Materialism entraps modern Christians into subtle idolatry, just as Israel engrafted idolatry into their lives while remaining religious. They lived out the Frank Sinatra song "Doing it My Way."

The command is to "immediately consider what I say"—that is, to "judge or discriminate between what is good or evil," not what we like or dislike.

According to Proverbs 15:5, *"A fool despises his father's instruction, but he who receives correction is prudent"*; thus a fool is recognized by his refusal to listen to wisdom from authorities in his life. Furthermore, *"fools have no interest in understanding; they only want to air their own opinions"* (Prov 18:2[NLT]). A fool *"trusts in his own heart"* (Prov 28:26)—that is, he trusts only in what he wants, regardless of what God says. A fool *"will despise the wisest advice"* (Prov 23:9[NLT]), primarily because it disagrees with what he wants. Even worse is *"a man wise in his own eyes. There is more hope for a fool than for him"* (Prov 26:12).

How people respond to the commands and advice of Scripture reveals their character. Do you appreciate correction? Do you always seek advice?

"Lord, it is not easy to be corrected or constantly exhorted by Your word and faithful servants, but I yearn for Your will to be done. I want to be like You so much that I beg You to keep giving me corrections and teachings from Your word."

Get Your Mind Ready for Action

1 Pet 1:13—*"Therefore, get your minds ready for action by being fully sober, and* **set your hope*/ completely on the grace** *that will be brought to you when Jesus Christ is revealed."*

Our text sounds like the beginning of a race toward purposeful action. Peter had just described the price the prophets paid to *"testify beforehand about the sufferings appointed for Christ"* (1 Pet 1:11): *"they were serving not themselves but you"* and laying the foundation for the *"gospel . . . sent from heaven"* (1:12). Now it was the readers' turn to come "stage front" and give the performance of a lifetime.

Peter sounds like a coach giving a final pep talk before launching his team onto the field. He gives five exhortations: (1) prepare your minds for action, (2) be self-controlled, (3) set your hope completely, (4) do not conform to . . . evil desires (1 Pet 1:14), and (5) be holy (1:15). Technically, the first, second, and fourth are participles, which have imperative force as they support the commands. Thus Peter is saying, *"Set your hope with a prepared mind and self-control"* and *"be holy by not conforming to evil desires"* (1:14–15).

The first command—*"decide immediately to set your hope completely"*— refers to a decisive military action, but metaphorically, it means to mentally focus on eternal priorities, eliminating anything that would impede you from accomplishing God's will. Meanwhile, most of us have set our goals on a car, a home, a vacation, material goods, savings, or retirement. We live for these goals, think about them every day, and cut any time drain or financial expenditure that would interfere with these "hopes" or goals. Peter's command tells us to make our eternal inheritance our primary goal.

This goal requires mental preparedness. Obedience is a conscious act of the will. To be *"fully sober"* means to "be in control of your thought process," avoiding irrational thinking, while staying "composed in mind and focused" by choosing the urgent priority of the *"hope"* of the *"grace that will be brought to you when Jesus Christ is revealed."*

This hope is to be *"completely,"* or "entirely, unreservedly," the center of our lives. By His grace we will stand before Jesus at His revelation, having partnered with Him in life to make Him known throughout the world.

"There are times, Lord, when I want my way, my will, and my pleasures now. It is painful to have to wait, but nothing on earth can compare to what awaits Your children. We cannot imagine what You have prepared for us. Thank You, Lord."

JUNE 10

Do Not Show Prejudice

James 2:1—*"My brothers and sisters, **do not show prejudice~| if you
possess faith in our glorious Lord Jesus Christ."*

Learning of God's qualities changes our moral perspectives. Of His many
attributes that humans can imitate (such as justice, grace, love, mercy,
faithfulness, goodness, etc.), impartiality has an essential impact on
human relationships.

Humans tend to classify or categorize each other by looks, mannerisms,
dress, intelligence, race or ethnicity, and especially success, wealth, and
power symbols (possessions and positions). We often classify people to
selfishly determine whom we want to associate with, whom can we use,
whom we need to impress, or who can help us advance our agenda.

God revealed Himself in the Old Testament as *"the Lord your God . . .
the God of gods . . . who does not show partiality nor take a bribe"* (Deut
10:17). Wisdom declares, *"To show partiality in judgment is not good"*
(Prov 24:23). The Old Testament concludes with God's description
of Israel's unfaithfulness: *"I also have made you despised and abased
before all the people, just as you are not keeping My ways but are
showing partiality in the instruction"* (Mal 2:9).

The New Testament revealed the concept of the body of Christ, where
every member partakes equally of God's Spirit and is bonded to each other.
Yet prejudice and favoritism crippled the advance of the gospel for years.
Gentiles were virtually excluded from the Jewish Christian church (see Acts
11:19) until Acts 15 (AD 49). The church knew better: Peter preached to
Cornelius that *"in every nation whoever fears Him and does what is right is
welcome to Him"* (Acts 10:35), but their emotions betrayed their judgment.

James eloquently condemns social snobbery and partiality in the church and
toward outsiders because it contradicts the character of God. The key is to
see others as Christ sees them: equally needing a Savior. Jesus taught, *"Do
not judge according to appearance, but judge with righteous judgment"* (Jn
7:24). How open are you to accepting others outside of your group? Do you
love people of all nations? How often do you help the poor or less privileged?

*"Lord, it is so easy to judge people or categorize them as inferior or unwor-
thy. Oh, to learn to think of people as You do, without rejection or criticism!
Help me see people as Your creation and to value how they are, even when
they are different from me."*

JUNE 11
Think of Christ's Suffering

Heb 12:3—*"Think*~ of him* who endured such opposition against himself by sinners, so that you may not grow weary in your souls and give up."*

Discouragement is inevitable for anyone who wants to serve the Lord. Families will not understand. Acquaintances will think you are crazy. You might be accused of being a proselytizer, a fanatic, a heretic, a bigot, or worse. It is not easy to stay faithful.

In April 2007 in Malatya, Turkey, five Muslims attended an Easter service pretending to be "seekers" and agreed to meet with a missionary named Tilman Geske and two converted Muslim believers, Necati Aydın and Uğur Yüksel, to discuss Christianity. They entered the room and assaulted the Christians, tied them to chairs, and then tortured them for more than two hours, stabbing each of them more than a hundred times and finally slitting each of their throats. When hearing of her husband's fate, Tilman's wife responded, "I forgive them. They know not what they do," as Jesus said.

A missionary to India, John Hyde, years ago wrote a booklet on prayer. In it, he described his daily practice of remaining on his knees before the Lord until, in his words, "Calvary was in my mind fresh once again." He knew that in difficult, dangerous, and discouraging times, nothing helps more than to reflect on all that Jesus suffered in going to the cross. It was the Father's plan to punish His Son for the sins of all mankind. It was all worth it to Him.

The writer to Hebrews had just commanded, *"Let us lay aside every weight and the sin which so easily ensnares us, and let us run with endurance the race that is set before us" (Heb 12:1).* The readers of this letter suffered horrible losses, but they were asked to *"recall the former days . . . , you endured a great struggle with sufferings: partly while you were made a spectacle both by reproaches and tribulations, and partly while you became companions of those who were so treated; . . . knowing that you have a better and an enduring possession for yourselves in heaven"* (Heb 11:32–35). Knowing that their situation might not get any better, they needed to turn their focus from their pain and loss to the companionship and partnership they shared with Jesus by suffering with Him.

"As my mind's eye flashes back to Mt. Calvary, I can't imagine how You never retaliated when rejected and beat upon by cruel men. Thank You for enduring all You suffered for me, and give me the grace today to never give up in serving others."

JUNE 12

Remember the Teaching and Obey It

Rev 3:3—*"Therefore, **remember~~ what you received** and heard, and **obey it~~, and repent*~.** If you do not wake up, I will come like a thief, and you will never know at what hour I will come against you."*

Only the book of Revelation specifically offers a special *"blessing"* for *"he who reads and those who hear the words of this prophecy, and keep those things which are written in it"* (Rev 1:3). However, this blessing is contingent on reading with a willing understanding and then obeying whatever the text commands. It is not mystical, or magical, but practical.

The early first-century church had the appearance of a Christian church but was already declared *"dead"* by Jesus (Rev 3:1), though a few believers remained. The congregation was mostly filled with fake Christians. This happens when teaching becomes more social than biblical and when people become more concerned about popularity than being broken before the Lord, more concerned about liturgical form than true faith and repentance, and more concerned about repeating creeds or confessions than knowing the word of God in order to obey it.

Jesus declared they had to *"continually be remembering"* what they had *"received and heard"* of the teaching of the word. By the end of the first century, they needed a reminder of the truths of salvation by grace and sanctification by obedience.

They were to *"continually be obeying it."* Jesus commanded, *"Teach [others] to observe [obey] all things that I have commanded you"* (Matt 28:20). It does little good to know theology without seriously obeying the commands. How often are commands disregarded and disobeyed when arguing for distinctive theologies? Shouldn't we agree on what to obey?

Finally, the church was to *"repent,"* as they recognized that their lives were not lived according to the instructions and commands of Scripture. With broken and contrite spirits for how they had offended their Savior, they were to turn from their disobedience to follow the teachings— especially the commands—of the Scripture. Anything less would bring Christ's chastisement, which could come at any time. Do you believe He means what He says? How would Jesus evaluate us or our churches?

"Thank You, Lord, for the constant reminders to obey all You have commanded. Keep me faithful to review and repeat Your instructions to myself today."

JUNE 13
Be Subject to Human Institutions

1 Pet 2:13—*"**Be subject*~ to every human institution** for the Lord's sake, whether to a king as supreme."*

It is hard to submit to other people. People don't like to be told what to do . . . or even to have to read instructions! Since his origin, man has naturally resisted submission to authority at any level. Therefore, this command flies in the face of every natural independent instinct of man. We want to be our own authority. It is the human way.

First Peter 2:13 commands us to *"immediately decide to be submissive"*; this originates from a military term meaning to "arrange yourself in formation under the commander." Everyone is called on to be submissive in a number of areas: couples are to be mutually submissive to each other (Eph 5:21), parents are to be submissive to the needs of their children (6:4), believers are to be submissive to their church elders and pastors (1 Pet 5:5), and employees are to be submissive to their masters or bosses (Col 3:22). Now they are also called on to be submissive to human authority in institutions and governments.

Loyalty to Christ does not give us license to rebel against ungodly, unfair, and cruel pagan authorities. It is not the Christian's responsibility to be subversive or to overthrow governments, especially in the name of Christianity. There is no perfect government, since all men are sinners—even in democracies. Followers of Christ are to be a society within a society.

The reason for Peter's mandate is *"for the Lord's sake"*: submission honors the sovereign power of God to raise up and put down leaders according to His ultimate purpose: *"There is no power [authority] but of God"* (Rom 13:1).

Respect for God is reflected in how we demonstrate respect for government leaders. Neither Jesus nor Paul ever advocated demonstrations against slavery or abuse of justice, nor did they engage in any act of civil disobedience. Instead of focusing on social or political reform, Christ kept the focus on His kingdom (Mark 1:15; Acts 1:3).

Peter declared submission to be *"the will of God"*; by being model citizens, Christians can *"put to silence the ignorance of foolish men"* (1 Pet 2:15) and open the door to permit others to listen to the gospel.

"Lord, why is submission to authority, and especially unfairness, so hard at times? Teach me how my reactions can reflect well on Your reputation. I want to honor Your name before all who are above me at every level."

JUNE 14

Show Inner Beauty, not External Beauty

1 Pet 3:3—*"Let your beauty not be external~/—the braiding of hair and wearing of gold jewelry or fine clothes—but the inner person of the heart, the lasting beauty of a gentle and tranquil spirit, which is precious in God's sight."*

Because Jesus is the Light of the World, when we tell people that Jesus is our light or source of life and allow them to observe our good works or changed life-style of living for others, we validate our faith.

Peter had been describing principles for society (1 Pet 2:13–17) and the workplace (1 Pet 2:18–25). Now he directs his commands to the family (3:1–7). The context is a Christian wife and an unsaved husband: the wife's new faith becomes her motivation for submitting to her husband (3:1) whether he is harsh or gracious.

Roman society was built on the gods; upsetting this religious structure was a threat to the family and society. Christians were frequently blamed for public calamities because they upset the status quo of the empire.

First, a *"woman who has an unbelieving husband, and he consents to live with her, she must not send her husband away [or divorce him]"* (1 Cor 7:13, 39).

Second, she is to *"be submissive to [her] own husband, so that even if any of them are disobedient to the Word, they may be won without a word by the behavior of their wives, as they observe [her] chaste and respectful behavior"* (1 Pet 3:1–2).

Third, the wife's *"adornment must not be merely external . . . , but let it be the hidden person of the heart . . . a gentle and quiet spirit"* (1 Pet 3:3[NKJ]). This is not an exclusive command (as the word *"merely"* indicates), but it does imply a change of priority for the believing wife that makes her different and actually more attractive.

Christian women should devote themselves to manifesting their transformed lives and intentionally demonstrating attitudes of love, joy, peace, and hope. Outward adornment should be respectable, but not ostentatious.

Which is more important to you: outward or inward beauty? How can you let your *"light shine"* to be *"precious in the sight of God?"* (1 Pet 3:4).

"Lord Jesus, the beauty of Your character has captured my heart, though I have no idea what You look like. Teach me to reflect Your values and beauty of heart over the façade of fading fads."

JUNE 15

Give to Caesar and to God

Matt 22:17–21—*"'Tell us then, what do you think? Is it right to pay taxes to Caesar or not?' 'Show me the coin used for the tax.' So they brought him a denarius. They replied, 'Caesar's.' He said to them, 'Then **give*~ to Caesar** the things that are Caesar's, and to God the things that are God's.'"*

The Pharisees came to Jesus with a question: "*Is it right to pay taxes to Caesar?*" Jesus asked for a Roman silver coin with the emperor's image. He asked the Pharisees' disciples, "*Whose likeness and inscription is this?*" They answered, "*Caesar's.*" Jesus replied astutely, "*Then render to Caesar the things that are Caesar's; and to God the things that are God's.*"

Paul reworded Jesus's command in Romans 13:7: "*Render therefore to all their due; taxes to whom taxes are due.*" This makes it mandatory for believers to pay taxes to any government over them, regardless of its political, religious, or moral stance. Caesar could demand a percentage of their money, but not their souls.

Our financial commitment to and prayers for our government authorities are "*in order that we may lead a tranquil and quiet life in all godliness and dignity. This is good and acceptable in the sight of God our Savior*" (1 Tim 2:2–3). This is our duty to our leaders today. Christians must be the most honest taxpayers in the region for the gospel's sake.

The question remains: what is our duty to God? Jesus taught, "*Woe to you, scribes and Pharisees, hypocrites! For you pay tithe . . . and have neglected the weightier matters of the law: justice and mercy and faith. These you ought to have done, without leaving the others undone*" (Matt 23:23). In other words, Jesus said not to stop tithing.

Because we were "*bought with a price*" (1 Cor 6:20), we are to "*present our bodies as a living sacrifice . . . which is your reasonable [liturgical or worship] service*" (Rom 12:1). God owns everything we have! Financially, we are to continue doing right (taking care of our families) and giving a tithe to support God's ministry. Beware: wherever you invest your treasure reveals what your heart desires most (Matt 6:21). How do you demonstrate that Christ's kingdom is important to you?

"Father, You have placed me in a country that increasingly asks for more of my income. If paying my government its due is pleasing to You, then I will be faithful and bring You delight."

JUNE 16

Pay Everyone What Is Owed

Rom 13:7—*"Pay everyone what is owed*~: taxes to whom taxes are due, revenue to whom revenue is due, respect to whom respect is due, honor to whom honor is due."*

By paying taxes we avoid scandalizing our Savior's name and making the gospel irrelevant. In biblical times, the tax collector was the least respected person in society, yet Jesus called a *"tax collector"* (Luke 5:27), Levi, to be one of His disciples and then was bitterly accused of associating with his friends (5:29–30). However, Paul referred to tax collectors as *"God's ministers"* (Gk. *leitourgos*, from which we get our word *liturgy*, or "religious service"), which is the same title given to Christ in His high priestly function in the *"true tabernacle"* (Heb 8:2), and Paul calls himself *"a minister of Christ Jesus to the Gentiles"* (Rom 15:16). These officials owe their authority to God, thus Paul says,*"this is why [we] also pay taxes"* (13:6).

The command is a financial integrity issue: *"immediately pay everyone what is owed"* means to "throw off a weight" and therefore have all debts up to date, taxes paid without cheating, and salaries paid to employees in full and on time.

The command is also a relationship issue: *"respect to whom respect is due, honor to whom honor is due."* To *respect* (Gk. *phobos*) means "to fear," a concept that varies from "respect" to "terror"; respect is demonstrated by listening to what is said and seeking to obey the instructions of an authority with a submissive attitude. The fear aspect in relations with governments is real, as Romans 13:4 indicates: *"He is God's minister to you for good. But if you do evil, be afraid; for he does not bear the sword in vain; for he is God's minister, an avenger to execute wrath on him who practices evil."*

The command is also a political issue: *"honor to whom honor"* refers to respect for the "rank and state of office" regardless of who holds that office. Respect is vital in society.

It is supposed that Paul's objective was to ensure that Christians would not provoke undue governmental reaction against the church, limiting its aggressive evangelistic thrust. Every businessman knows how to cheat on taxes, but the Christian must refuse to be disobedient regardless of the temptation. We must commit ourselves to never do anything that would discredit the gospel or our Savior before the world.

"Lord, there are times when my greed or desire for things has put me over my ability to repay. Teach me the foolishness of my selfishness and give me the grace to sacrifice whatever it takes to pay every debt for Your name's sake."

JUNE 17

Owe No Man Anything

Rom 13:8—*"**Owe~| no one anything**, except to love one another, for the one who loves his neighbor has fulfilled the law."*

Debt can be an evil taskmaster. Proverbs warns, *"If you can't pay it, even your bed will be snatched from under you"* (Prov 22:27^NLT). *"The borrower is slave to the lender"* (22:7^TNIV), so we must minimize debt. When we recognize the risk of loans, it motivates our need for wisdom.

Jesus taught, *"Love your enemies, and do good, and lend, expecting nothing in return; and your reward will be great"* (Luke 6:35). The uniqueness of believers is their willingness to live to benefit others now, while trusting in a heavenly reward later.

First, borrowing should be a temporary measure to secure the minimum items needed to continue a business or income flow.

Second, we must carefully calculate to ensure we can repay our debts, because *"evil men borrow, but do not repay their debt"* (Psa 37:21). In difficult times, when income cannot be ensured, debt should be kept to a minimum.

Third, borrowing for unnecessary items is out of the sphere of wisdom living and is usually due to covetousness: *"He covets greedily all day long, But the righteous gives and does not spare"* (Prov 21:26). Does generosity limit your freedom? Do you borrow to show off or brag about new possessions? Wisdom warns that *"the wicked man boasts because he gets what he wants"* (Psa 10:3).

Fourth, borrowing can feed the evil of greed: *"Greedy people try to get rich quick but don't realize they're headed for poverty"* (Prov 28:22^NLT).

A mutual love (not a one-way love) results in a healthy sense of debt to each other in Christ. God loves us, so we repay that love by loving each other, and we have *"a great sense of obligation to people in both the civilized world and the rest of the world, to the educated and uneducated alike"* (Rom 1:14^NLT). Because we have received God's love as a gift through grace, we owe it to those who have never heard His word. Is there a financial parallel with this principle? Meditate on it and tell the Lord your answer.

"Father, give me the conviction and wisdom to get out of debt and to live within the means You have provided."

Share Goods with the Needy

Luke 3:11—*"John answered them, 'The person who has two **tunics must share***~ **with the person who has none**, and the person who has food must do likewise.'"*

Paul wrote, *"The love of money is the root of all evil"* (1 Tim 6:10), and generosity—not getting and hoarding—is one of the clearest signs of a transformed life and a Christlike attitude.

John had been preaching to the crowd to bring awareness of their sinfulness and to generate repentance from the false idea that they were good because they were religious. They did not practice the disciplines that showed that God's love had changed their lives. None of John's teachings were meant to result in the acquisition of any special merit or grace: righteousness is only granted on the basis of a heart-based faith in the grace of God (Eph 2:8–9).

Three groups of people asked John, *"What shall we do [to demonstrate faith and repentance]?"* (Luke 3:10, 12, 14). To the crowd, he said to share with the needy. To the tax collectors, he said to be just and collect *"no more than is appointed to you."* Finally, to the soldiers, he said to not practice intimidation or make false accusations and to be content with their salaries.

The lesson in our text is not restricted to a *"tunic."* When God providentially brings needy people into your life and you have an extra *"tunic"*—or anything else—your new spirit should respond with a generous, wise, and voluntary sharing of resources. Paul gave us the principle for the spiritual gift of giving: *"If your gift is . . . giving, give generously"* (Rom 12:8[NLT]). Generous believers become the models for the body of Christ and demonstrate the joy of giving.

We often want to be appreciated for what we give out of pride or ego. This attitude feeds the flesh by attempting to satisfy an expectation of immediate recompense, even if only by way of appreciation. If your emotional response is anger or hurt feelings when there is little or no appreciation or acknowledgement for a gift, then you know the flesh is seeking satisfaction. If you are giving out of love, then your motive is purely to meet someone else's need, not your own.

"Lord, my selfishness so easily shows itself when my rights or my possessions are threatened. Teach me to be giving rather than clinging and to be a servant rather than an egotist who wants everything for himself."

Give to Those Who Ask

Luke 6:30—*"Give~~ to everyone who asks you, and do not ask for your possessions back from the person who takes them away."*

When we see materialism as the means to happiness and success, any hint of giving is met with emotional denial. We have become idolaters.

No one spoke more about giving generously than Jesus. In Luke 18:22, Jesus challenged a rich, young ruler who mistakenly thought he was obeying the Ten Commandments: *"You still lack one thing. Sell all that you have and distribute to the poor, and you will have treasure in heaven; and come, follow Me."* The young ruler sadly walked away. He was very rich and had put his trust and affection in his wealth. He was a covetous (tenth commandment) idolater (first commandment) and did not know it.

If you feel agony over giving, this is a symptom of misdirection of your affection and trust. If you believe that God will provide all you could need—especially if you provide for the needs of others—giving away your resources should not be so hard. When the Philippian church sent Paul an offering, he knew the sacrifice behind their generosity. This prompted him to write an eternal principle: *"And my God shall supply all your need according to His riches in glory by Christ Jesus"* (Phil 4:19). The *"need"* referred to in this verse resulted from their sacrificial gift, *"a sweet-smelling aroma, an acceptable sacrifice, well pleasing to God"* (4:18). This is not a promise to provide whatever you may need (or want); rather, it is like a reimbursement for generous giving.

Our text tells us to *"habitually and be continually giving to everyone who asks you."* Obviously, this does not happen every day, but when it does, it should not encounter a resistant spirit from your heart. It is not whether or not you should give, but how much you can give.

Furthermore, you are to give without any hope or expectation of being repaid in any manner, *"and do not ask for your possessions back."* Give it up and let it go. Learn to be a giver and enjoy it. Don't forget: you still have Jesus! Rejoice in Him.

"Lord, it is hard to give of one's resources continually. Don't let me think of being generous to get a future favor in return. How self-centered I am! Make me more like You."

JUNE 20

Give and It Will Be Given to You

Luke 6:38—*"Give* ~~, *and it will be given to you: A good measure, pressed down, shaken together, running over, will be poured into your lap. For the measure you use will be the measure you receive."*

A giving spirit flows from a free, forgiving spirit. Luke had been discussing a series of sacrificial, caring, and accepting principles that flow from the heart of God: *"Love your enemies . . . lend, hoping for nothing in return . . . for [God] is kind to the unthankful and evil. Therefore be merciful, just as your Father also is merciful. Judge not . . . Condemn not . . . Forgive"* (Luke 6:35–37). Now Luke writes, *"Give, and it will be given to you"* (6:38).

This command doesn't just tell us how to respond to personal injuries and to be forgiving. It asks even more: give to fulfill the needs of others, with the promise of a divine reward. Luke declared that if we do good (by serving or giving) to our enemies, without hoping for recognition or anything *"in return,"* then *"[our] reward will be great"* (Luke 6:35). The benefit of giving is so great that only a fool would be stingy or selfish.

This principle is derived from the extreme generosity of God to give in abundance. There is both a promise and a strict condition, as in 2 Corinthians 9:6–7: *"He who sows sparingly will also reap sparingly, and he who sows bountifully will also reap bountifully . . . for God loves a cheerful giver."*

Our text promises, *"It will be given to you."* You cannot lose, though you may feel that you will lose. That feeling of loss comes from your selfish nature. When you meditate on the promise and believe that God will repay you *"a good measure, pressed down, shaken together, running over,"* that feeling of loss will disappear. You will feel like you made a deposit into your eternal savings account.

If you could choose, when would you prefer to receive your wealth and reward in the present or in eternity, where you will enjoy it forever? Actually, you are choosing, whether you know it or not. The greatest reward will be to share it all with Jesus, as He tells you how much He appreciated your labor and sacrifice for Him.

"Jesus, do I trust You? Will You really give back at some point whatever we give away now? If You provide it, I will give whatever I have for Your kingdom's purposes. My trust is completely in Your providence toward me."

JUNE 21
_____

Set Aside Income Weekly in Church

1 Cor 16:1–2—*"With regard to the collection for the saints, please follow the directions that I gave to the churches of Galatia: on the first day of the week, each of you **should set aside**~~ **some income** and save it to the extent that God has blessed you, so that a collection will not have to be made when I come."*

From the intensely rich doctrinal discussion on our resurrection (1 Cor 15), Paul goes back to the practical resurrected life. God has a plan for storing *"treasures in heaven"* while we remain on the earth (Matt 6:20).

The text begins, *"With regard to the collection for the saints,"* which implies that Paul is answering questions sent to him in a letter (as in 1 Cor 7:1; 8:1; and 12:1). Paul had been teaching the churches how to respond generously to emergencies. Now he was collecting the fund for the Jerusalem church, which was suffering a famine and poverty: *"For it pleased those from Macedonia and Achaia to make a certain contribution for the poor among the saints who are in Jerusalem"* (Rom 15:26).

Later, Paul wrote one of the greatest commendations to a generous church: *"Moreover, brethren, we make known to you . . . their deep poverty abounded in the riches of their liberality [in giving]. For I bear witness that according to their ability, yes, and beyond their ability, they were freely willing, imploring us with much urgency that we would receive the gift and the fellowship of the ministering to the saints. And not only as we had hoped, but they first gave themselves to the Lord, and then to us by the will of God"* (2 Cor 8:1–5).

Giving should be done *"on the first day of every week,"* which implied both a Sunday meeting and that a planned offering was part of the worship service as a demonstration of grateful commitment to God's work as stewards of all He has given us.

"Each of you" implies that everyone is a steward of whatever God has entrusted to him. We are all to *"set aside some income and save it"* in a treasury for dispensing of the offerings—that is, the church.

The amount to be given was *"to the extent that God has blessed you."* Typically, the tithe has been the starting point for giving (long before the law was given). Our giving demonstrates the thankfulness that our praises declare.

"Lord, why is my heart so rebellious against regularly giving to Your kingdom plans? You have blessed me so much. Give me the grace to bless others as I have been blessed."

Do Not Neglect to Do Good and Share

Heb 13:16—*"And **do not neglect~| to do good** and to share what you have, for God is pleased with such sacrifices."*

The psalmist said, *"I will worship toward Your holy temple, And praise Your name For Your lovingkindness and Your truth; For You have magnified Your word above all Your name"* (Psa 138:2[NKJ]). It is wonderful to exalt His name in praise, but He wants His word exalted in serious obedience, even above His name!

The writer of Hebrews had just described the beauty of praise, saying, *"Through Him then, let us continually offer up a sacrifice of praise to God, that is, the fruit of lips that give thanks to His name"* (13:15[NKJ]). The psalmist wrote, *"I will praise You, O LORD, among the peoples, And I will sing praises to You among the nations"* (Psa 108:3[NKJ]).

Paul said that one of the purposes of a transformed life is the capacity to generate more income than before coming to Christ, so that giving generously becomes a goal: *"The one who steals must steal no longer; rather he must labor, doing good with his own hands, so that he may have something to share with the one who has need"* (Eph 4:28). The main reason God will help someone prosper is to make him a source of giving or an example of sacrifice in order to help the rest of the body of Christ.

Just as Jesus's life of praise to the Father would have meant little to the world were it not for His sacrifice on the cross, so our vocal praise will mean little to God or to the world unless we sacrifice ourselves to benefit others.

It was unimaginable that a Jewish worshiper in the Old Testament times would come to the temple without offering a grateful sacrifice to God for His blessings and presence. This principle carries over into the New Testament with this call to generously sacrifice and share whatever God has given to you. The command to *"stop neglecting"* literally implies the readers had neglected this phase in their worship style.

Worship is not music; it is sacrifice! David refused to *"offer burnt offerings to the LORD [his] God with that which costs [him] nothing"* (2 Sam 24:24). Empty worship is mere words or songs without sacrifice, but genuine worship is sung from a cross . . . your cross!

"Lord Jesus, keep me alert today to the needs of those around me. With every contact, make me curious to how each person might be helped. May my devotion to others seem as a sweet savor to You."

JUNE 23

Consider Elders Worthy of Double Honor

1 Tim 5:17—*"Elders who provide effective leadership **must be counted worthy~~ of double honor** ['be paid well'^{NLT}], especially those who work hard in speaking and teaching."*

Paul challenged the church elders of Ephesus, saying, *"Take heed to yourselves and to all the flock, among which the Holy Spirit has made you overseers, to shepherd [pastor] the church of God which He purchased with His own blood"* (Acts 20:28). The Son of God paid a high price for the church to exist, so it must be protected and highly valued.

The responsibility to *"take heed"* of the church primarily falls on the shoulders of the elders who serve as overseers and shepherd-pastors of the congregation of believers. To *"take heed"* means to "bring near, bring a ship to port, turn the mind to, or attend to." The elders were to lead and train the church to fulfill its function as *"a chosen race, a royal priesthood, a holy nation, a people for God's own possession, that [they] may proclaim the excellencies of Him who has called [them] out of darkness into His marvelous light"* (1 Pet 2:9).

Leadership is a fragile position. One cannot demand, manipulate, or intimidate to receive authority in the eyes of the congregation. Authority must be given voluntarily to a leader who has proven trustworthy by his example. He must be *"counted worthy"*—that is, he must be given *"honor,"* which has a broad meaning from "respect" (as in 1 Tim 6:1) to the *"privilege of financial support,"* as was to be given to the widows (1 Tim 5:3, 9–10).

In our text, the congregation is mandated to *"honor,"* especially by financial support, the elders who *"provide effective leadership"* or, literally, "have been ruling well": this is from a word meaning "to preside, lead, shepherd, or guide." The leaders have the responsibility to minister and therefore must be given the authority to lead. Other believers must *"continually count them as worthy"* or "reckon them as deserving or meriting something."

This honor is *"especially"* to be given to *"those who work hard in speaking and teaching."* To *"work hard"* is to "work to the point of exhaustion"; *"speaking"* (Gk. *logos*) means a "speech" or public proclamation of the truth in exhortation and admonition. *"Teaching"* implies the doctrines of the Scripture *"once delivered to the saints"* (Jude 3). This labor is spent in preparation for both preaching and teaching (as evident in content, clarity, and application) as well as multiple meetings proclaiming the word. How do you show your honor to your leaders?

"Thank You, Lord, for the leaders You have placed in my life and for their commitment to teach and practice Your word as an example to me."

JUNE 24

Do Not Separate a Married Couple

Matt 19:6—*"So they are no longer two, but one flesh. Therefore what God has joined together, **let no one separate~/.**"*

The Pharisees attempted to trap Jesus again with a divisive question: *"Is it lawful for a man to divorce his wife for just any reason?"* (Matt 19:3). This question stems from a misunderstanding of Deuteronomy 24:1–4, where Moses appeared to encourage divorce. Jesus clarified Moses's instruction by explaining that Moses permitted a divorce only because of the *"hardness of [their] hearts."* Even Jesus's disciples reacted in shock to His teaching against divorce: *"If such is the case of the man with his wife, it is better not to marry"* (19:10). They could not imagine a bond of love or mutual submission being more powerful than a threat of divorce for uniting a marriage permanently.

Jesus answers with an intimidating question: *"Have you not read . . .?"* (Matt 19:4). God expects us all to read and know correctly all the instructions He has revealed to us.

Jesus goes on to explain four reasons why divorce was never God's plan: First, Adam and Eve were created as man and woman. It was God who brought them together.

Second, they were to cleave to each other. The word for *cleave* means "to glue one thing to another." God has designed marriage as a total commitment to one another.

Third, *"the two [were to] become one flesh."* Married couples live together and do things together; they are lovers and refuse to think of anyone else. They are one body, inseparable until death. They are one in thought, goals, desires, direction, commitment, and submission to God.

Fourth, every marriage in the world is engineered by God's intervention: *"God has joined [them] together."* Marriage is always the work of God, and divorce is always the work of our own rebellion. Thus the command is to literally "stop separating or divorcing," with only a few exceptions. Always follow God's principles in marriage to resolve conflicts and stay bonded together.

"Lord, every day I meet couples struggling in their marriage. Give me wisdom to engage them in dialogue and help them work through their conflicts. May we seek to avoid divorces as much as You despise the breakup of marriages. Thank You for Your grace always."

JUNE 25

Husbands, Love Your Wives

Eph 5:25—*"Husbands, **love~~ your wives** just as Christ loved the church and gave Himself for Her."*

Adam and Eve chose to follow the deceit of immediate gratification, which Satan promised would fulfill their deepest cravings, only to find it brought only bitterness, disillusionment, isolation, and the loss of God's partnership.

Eve was seduced by Satan to believe that God was not interested in her needs. Satan said Adam and Eve would not die if they disobeyed, because God would not keep His word. Finally, Eve thought their happiness was only possible if they ignored God's way and followed Satan's false promises of happiness.

When God confronted the Eve, He said, *"I will greatly multiply your sorrow and your conception; In pain you shall bring forth children"* (Gen 3:16); thus God permanently changed her physically, making childbirth a painful experience.

God added, *"Your desire shall be for your husband, And he shall rule over you"* (Gen 3:16). This sounds romantic, but it is part of the curse, the consequence, of sin. It is a prediction of how sinners will react to each other, especially in marriage. Only the New Living Translation has the right translation: *"You will desire to control your husband"* (3:16[NLT]). Just as she manipulated Adam to partake of the forbidden fruit, so her nature (and the nature of every woman from then on) was changed so that she would seek to control and manipulate others. The Hebrew is repeated almost verbatim in Genesis 4:7. Unconsciously, every women attempts to control and manipulate her husband, while he attempts to dominate his wife by intimidation and threats, which are prohibited (Mark 10:42–45).

The only hope is for a couple is to recognize these damaging natural responses and resist them. The wife must learn submission and a trusting respect for her husband (Eph 5:24), while he must learn to mutually submit (*"submit to one another out of reverence for Christ"*; Eph 5:21) and to care for his wife *"as Christ loved the church and gave Himself for her"* (Eph 5:25). Both are the opposite of their fallen natures.

The husband's focus in marriage is to commit unconditionally to meeting his wife's needs. Just as Christ poured Himself out to others, winning their hearts and commitment to Him till death, so the husband is to learn from this model to give himself in personal sacrifice for his wife. This is the only way to love!

"Lord Jesus, it is hard to imagine what it cost You to give Yourself for her. Teach me to lose my self-interests and my demands for my needs to be met first. Make sacrificing for my spouse a reflection of Your love for the church."

JUNE 26

Husbands, Love; Wives, Respect

Eph 5:33—*"Nevertheless, each one of you must also **love~~ his own wife** as he loves himself, and the wife must respect her husband."*

God's love for us is the model of love for a successful marriage. He commands us to love in the same manner because, as believers, He has placed His love in our hearts (Rom 5:5). This love does not depend on the attractiveness or responsiveness of the object of that love.

We are initially attracted to many appealing characteristics of a mate. Such admirable traits can disappear in time, but the covenant to love your mate never changes. A spouse needs a selfless, giving, forgiving, sacrificing, and edifying love built not on emotion but on a willing commitment to live to benefit the other person without regard to personal advantages gained from the relationship.

Paul's instructions for marriage give priority to the husband's obligation to *"love his own wife as he loves himself."* Loving yourself is all too natural, *"for no one ever hated his own flesh, but nourishes and cherishes it, just as the Lord does the church"* (Eph 5:29). This love is not measured by how you feel about yourself; rather, just as you selfishly do things to care for, provide for, satisfy, and please yourself, you are to provide the same care for someone else. Just as you please yourself, you must now please the object of your love: your spouse.

Likewise, the command that the *"wife must respect her husband"* comes from a word (Gk. *phobeo*) meaning to "fear." The church's commitment to respect Christ's word is the wife's model for her respect to her husband (Eph 5:23). One listens to and follows what one respects. A key for the wife is to focus her thoughts on positive features: *"Fix your thoughts on what is true, and honorable, and right, and pure, and lovely, and admirable. Think about things that are excellent and worthy of praise"* (Phil 4:8[NLT]). Look for only these traits in a mate, because *"love covers a multitude of sins"* (1 Pet 4:8). Build your case for respecting your spouse. Husbands need wives who recognize them as significant and respect them for their strengths while overlooking their faults. Wives need husbands who willingly sacrifice what they want to meet their needs.

"Lord, it is easy to see how much I love and care for myself, but now You ask me to take my self-centered love and make it a spouse-balanced love. Show me how to make my spouse feel valued, loved, and cared for as You care for us both."

Do Not Be Embittered against Your Wife

Col 3:19—*"Husbands, **love~~ your wives and do not be embittered~/
against them.***"

What is love? The verb used here in Colossians 3:19 and in most of
the New Testament is *agapao*, which is a self-sacrificing love in which
you give of yourself for the benefit of another. The verb is a present
imperative, so it means to continually be loving your wife.

To define *love*, let's look at the opposite of love. It is not *hate*, because
that is an emotional response. If *agapao* meant an emotional reaction,
then it would be impossible to *"love"* your enemy (Matt 5:44). The word
for romantic love—*eros*—is not used in the New Testament.

The best word to express the opposite of biblical love is *selfishness*. Love
always seeks to benefit someone else, without regard to personal benefit,
whereas selfishness causes the person to always seek to benefit him/
herself. When in doubt, simply ask yourself, who is the beneficiary?

What do you do if there is no response from your spouse? The believing
husband is to habitually do caring things for his spouse, regardless
of the response or lack of response he receives. Any resulting hurt or
resentment must be countered quickly or it will generate bitterness
and a desire for vengeance. The command is to *"stop being embittered,"*
implying that this was a common response that had to cease.

There is no justification for disobedience, especially in marriage:
*"Watch out that no poisonous root of bitterness grows up to trouble
you, corrupting many"* (Heb 12:15^{NLT}). Bitterness is often cloaked
in the garb of loss of personal rights: what we think we deserve
and need has been denied or ignored. Selfishness rears its head up
again, and the results can be ugly: *"Get rid of all bitterness, rage,
anger, harsh words, and slander, as well as all types of evil behavior"*
(Eph 4:31^{NLT}). A deteriorating relationship is only changed by a
conviction to forgive, as Jesus forgives you (Eph 4:30) and a renewal
of your commitment to your spouse, no matter what happens. His
grace is sufficient for you.

*"Lord, not everyone we seek to love and benefit responds in appreciation to
our care for them, but neither did the people of Your time always respond
positively to You. May my heart learn from Your example to always forgive
and never become embittered, no matter how they may respond to me."*

Husbands, Live Wisely with Wives

1 Pet 3:7—*"Husbands, likewise, **dwell with**~~ **them** with understanding, giving honor to the wife, as to the weaker vessel, and as being heirs together of the grace of life, that your prayers may not be hindered."*

In 1 Peter 3:7, *"dwelling with them,"* refers back to the wives of verses 3–6, completing the imperative *"be continually"* in verse 3. The conjunction *"likewise"* or *"in the same way"* ties this verse to the previous verses—that is, husbands are to be submissive to serve their wives, and their wives are to be submissive to the needs of their husbands.

The husband's responsibility is to *"dwell with them"* in an intimate and mutually satisfying manner. The key to success is to live with *"understanding"* (Gk. "clear and exact knowledge," as opposed to an intuitive knowledge, or following what one thinks or feels like). It becomes the husband's responsibility to learn about his spouse. Women are different from men in their interests, sexual drive, view of romance, priorities, and source of fulfillment.

Not only does it take new understanding, but men must *"be continually giving honor to the wife"*; this is Peter's way of saying you must love your wife. *Honor* means "the amount at which something is valued, thus respect, esteem." Honor is given to Christ or high dignitaries, as well as wives. The husband is to make her feel like the most important person in his life.

"As the weaker vessel" does not imply that there is anything inferior about women intellectually or spiritually; rather, the meaning is primarily physical and perhaps emotional. Thus husbands must be protective and caring and provide for her needs.

The couple is to celebrate *"being heirs together of the grace of life"*—not the grace of God, but God's special gift (grace) to man. This is the richest bond in this life, but it only works when the principles of the Creator are followed.

Finally, our intimacy to God is no better than our relationship with other believers—especially our spouses. Ignoring God's instructions in marriage has serious implications: *"so that your prayers will not be hindered."* It pays to take God's word seriously.

"Lord, You did not make it easy, putting two imperfect and different people together in a marriage. Grant me the ability to understand my spouse and know how to meet her needs and to accept her for how You made her."

JUNE 29

Wives, Submit to Your Husbands

Col 3:18—*"Wives, **submit**~~ **to your husbands**, as is fitting in the Lord."*

Just as the commands for the husband to be mutually submissive (Eph 5:21) and sacrificially love his wife (5:25) are contrary to his selfish dominant nature, so the command for the wife to be submissive is contrary to her controlling nature. All women were changed because of the fall in the Garden (Gen. 3:16).

God gives a command to a wife that is contrary to her old nature: *"be continually submitting,"* which is the translation of a word meaning "to place under in an orderly fashion." The verb form means to "acknowledge someone's authority over you." The word is also used to describe Jesus's submission to His parents (Luke 2:51), demons' submission to the disciples (10:17, 20), the spiritual mind's willing submission to God's commands (Rom 8:7), and man's submission to governing authorities (13:1).

Often inconvenient passages such as this one are ignored or outright denied any authority in a woman's life. These passages are mistakenly relegated to a first-century culture and declared to be inapplicable to our own. However, failure to apply this principle to marriage has devastating results. A wife who willingly submits to a servant husband who is committed to her benefit will discover the joy of marriage. Titus 2:5 instructs women to be *"workers at home, . . . being subject to their own husbands, that the Word of God may not be dishonored."* A lot is at stake.

Several misconceptions need to be clarified: First, nowhere is there any insinuation that submission implies inferiority.

Second, obedience is conspicuously absent from the instruction to wives, but it is included for children and servants. Submission focuses on meeting the husbands' needs.

Third, husbands are prohibited from abusing their authority. Jesus said, *"You know that the rulers in this world lord it over their people, and officials flaunt their authority over those under them. But among you it will be different. Whoever wants to be a leader [or husband] among you must be your servant"* (Mark 10:42–43[NLT]). A servant leader is first modeled at home. Nothing compares to the joy of marriage done God's way. Do you trust His way?

"Lord, submission is seldom easy, especially in marriage, where we tend to think our rights and needs are more important than a rule. May what is 'fitting in the Lord' become fitting in our eyes as well."

JUNE 30
Women Must Learn Quietly

1 Tim 2:11—*"A woman **must learn quietly**~~ with all submissiveness."*

Modern thought tends to ignore old ideas. Some Christians think some of the biblical commands are antiquated and should be overruled or tweaked, especially when it comes to women in the ministry. Some commands can become culturally complicated to practice, like this one.

In Greek culture, Aristotle severely limited women's activities, which was the popular view. When Paul wrote that women could *"learn,"* or "be disciples," women were elated to be able to study God's word. This was an unheard-of liberty for Christian women. They were to learn *"quietly"*—that is, "without disturbance, implying voluntary restraint." The phrase *"with all submissiveness"* means "submission to the highest degree," which indicated Paul's concern that their learning might overthrow the leadership roles of men in the church.

Paul then adds, *"I do not permit a woman to teach or to have authority over a man, but to be in silence"* (1 Tim 2:12). Having said this, Paul described several women who were *"coworkers"* with him (Rom 16:1–3) and *"who labored with [him] in the gospel"* (Phil 4:2–3). Women can be disciples, evangelists of women (e.g., in cultures where men cannot speak to women), teachers of women, prayer leaders (1 Cor 11:4), worship leaders, musicians, and helpers in hundreds of ways, but God's word must be respected.

It is apparent that it was God's choice to make men the ones accountable to Him for the church's health and well-being. A pastor was to be the *"husband of one wife"* who *"rules his house well"* (1 Tim 3:2, 4).

Only with a considerable twist of the meaning of these passages could women biblically be considered as pastors. It is a question not of who could fulfill this role the best but of to whom God gave the authority and responsibility.

Elisabeth Elliot, wife of missionary martyr Jim Elliot and well-known author, wrote, "The woman who accepts the limitations of womanhood finds in those very limitations her gifts, her special callings . . . , which bear her up into perfect freedom, into the will of God."

"Lord, grant that all husbands will be learners and teachers of the word to meet the needs of their wives for understanding the word of God. May the priority of peace among the church encourage us to follow Your instructions."

JULY 1

Couples, Do Not Deprive Each Other

1 Cor 7:5—*"**Do not deprive~/ each other**, except by mutual agreement for a specified time, so that you may devote yourselves to prayer. Then resume your relationship, so that Satan may not tempt you because of your lack of self-control."*

Some believed sexual abstinence in marriage was more spiritual, but *"marriage must be honored among all and the marriage bed kept undefiled, for God will judge sexually immoral people and adulterers"* (Heb 13:4). The *"marriage bed"*—a reference to sexual relations—must be *"undefiled,"* or kept "pure from any defilement, thus holy."

Within marriage, sexual relations are as pure as prayer. However, outside of or before marriage, those practicing sexual relations are considered *"fornicators and adulterers"* (Heb 13:4), and they can expect God's judgment.

Within marriage, normal sexual relations are to be practiced regularly. It is a biblical duty to provide mutual sexual satisfaction to one another. God expects the pleasure of marital sexual relations to fully meet the normal needs of both husband and wife, thus eliminating the need for any extramarital relations in fantasy, thoughts, or actions.

Furthermore, women have a very different sexual drive than their husbands. Men tend to be easily stimulated in a sexual relationship, but most women are slow to be stimulated, requiring a quality relationship, intimate conversations, a deep sense of security. The real lovers are not the one-night-stand people but the couples who can maintain a romantic relationship over a forty-year period or more. This is what is beautiful to the Lord.

Each partner must learn the needs of his or her spouse and commit himself or herself to meeting those needs regardless of personal feelings. On the other hand, the driven partner can learn patience and self-control, waiting for the right moment with the spouse. Anticipating the wonder of romance is an exciting part of the give-and-take of a relationship. Only selfish attitudes can ruin God's plan for mutual satisfaction.

"Dear loving Lord, only You understand the full extent of true love, so I ask You to guide me in giving all the love that a human can possibly give to my spouse, so that You might be glorified in all we are able to accomplish together."

JULY 2

Do Not Become Slaves of Men

1 Cor 7:23—*"You were bought with a price. **Do not become~/ slaves** of men. Brethren, let each one remain with God in that state in which he was called."*

Though difficult to understand slavery today the basic principle in 1 Corinthians 7:23 is that no situation can keep a Christian from serving Christ, no matter how unjust, painful, or cruel. The bottom line is that a person can serve Christ even in slavery.

This is an over-arching command with many applications, and it is mentioned in the context of marriage and divorce. It is not an absolute command but a principle that can change with the circumstances.

Paul declares the general principle covering the context: *"Let each one remain in the same calling [marital, religious, or social status], in which he was called"* (7:20) if possible.

Paul instructed the slaves, *"Be obedient to those who are your masters according to the flesh, with fear and trembling, in the sincerity of your heart, as to Christ; not by way of eye-service, as men–pleasers, but as slaves of Christ, doing the will of God from the heart. With good will render service, as to the Lord, and not to men, knowing that whatever good thing each one does, this he will receive back from the Lord, whether slave or free"* (Eph 6:5–8). Can you imagine a slave who wants to serve his master willingly and faithfully, going beyond the minimal duty? What an impact this could have, especially when he declares himself to be a Christian! Light shines brightest in dark, dismal places.

Should circumstances change and he *"can be made free, . . . use it"* (1 Cor 7:21). Meanwhile, slaves should remember that they *"were bought with a price."* The cost of their spiritual liberty was the life and blood of Jesus, which was a far higher price than their earthly master paid for them. Therefore, they should *"not become slaves of men"* inwardly, even though outwardly they remained so. They were inwardly free to serve whom they would, and they should choose to serve their master as a testimony to demonstrate what Christ could mean, even to a slave. One can be free in spirit while a slave in body. Can you see an application to the marketplace ministry today?

"Dear Father, You do not want me to be a pleaser of men, but You do want me to live to love and serve others, as I love and serve You, whether at home or at my workplace. Please help me serve others today."

Do Not Seek Divorce

1 Cor 7:27—*"The one bound to a wife **should not seek~/ divorce**. The one released from a wife should **not seek marriage~/**."*

If a spouse did not convert to Christ, some thought it would be better to divorce the unbeliever. This was a particularly threatening time (1 Cor 7:26)— far worse than the norm. Jesus warned that they would be made *"outcasts"* and that *"an hour is coming for everyone who kills you to think that he is offering service to God"* (Jn 16:2). It was a difficult time for marriage!

Parents had written to Paul asking how or whether to arrange their daughters' weddings, and he responded with some general principles. In this context, the *"one bound to a wife"* (lit. "having been bound") was to *"stop seeking to be loosed"* (Gk. "dissolving of any tie")—that is, the believer should not seek a divorce. In the first place, marriage is a lifelong commitment that—from a biblical perspective—can only be broken by death, adultery (Matt 5, 19), or abandonment or divorce by an unsaved spouse (1 Cor 7:15). All other marital problems are to be resolved. The quicker any issues can be faced and counsel sought, the better the chance of resolution. If the couple waits until there is a "hardness of heart," reconciliation becomes difficult.

If the unbeliever abandons the marriage (1 Cor 7:15), the believer is allowed to *"depart"* (Gk. to "separate completely, dissolve the marriage bond"; Louw and Nida, *Greek-English Lexicon*). If a divorce occurs, *"a brother or a sister is not under bondage in such cases"* (7:15)—that is, the marital bond ceases.

In our verse, Paul writes that those who have chosen to remain single (1 Cor 7:26) or who *"have been loosed from a wife"* (perfect tense; thus the divorce was a completed action in the past) should *"stop seeking a wife"* (7:27). The word *seek* means to "strive to find." This is not an absolute prohibition, but searching for a spouse is not to become a priority.

The next verse clarifies the marriage or remarriage issue: *"If you get married, it is not a sin"* (1 Cor 7:28), where *"you"* refers back to the person who *"has been loosed from a wife"* or the single person (7:25). Paul warns of potential problems in marriage (7:28) that could limit the spread of the gospel and *"how [one can] please the Lord"* (7:32). The proper balance enables each partner to become an asset for the Gospel.

"Lord Jesus, when You bind us together in marriage, we truly become one. May we always see our marriage from Your perspective and work to make our love and relationship grow, even through life's difficulties."

JULY 4

Fathers, Do Not Provoke Children to Anger

Eph 6:4a—*"Fathers, **do not provoke*/ your children** to anger."*

It is not uncommon for children to have bitter anger for the hurt and rejection received from their fathers; however, very relationship is a two-way street. The guidelines begin with commands for children to obey and to honor their parents (Eph 6:1–3), even when they feel hurt.

Following the injunctions to children, God gives special instructions to parents. In first-century Roman society, fathers were granted *patria potestas*, or the authority as the head of the house, which included unlimited power over their children to make them obey without question. Fathers learn how leaders use anger and intimidation to get their will, and then they use the same tactics at home.

Few Christian parents know this type of authority is prohibited among believers. Jesus taught His disciples how to lead by serving others: *"You know that those who are considered rulers over the Gentiles lord it over them, and their great ones exercise authority over them. Yet it shall not be so among you; but whoever desires to become great among you shall be your servant. And whoever of you desires to be first shall be slave of all. For even the Son of Man did not come to be served, but to serve"* (Mark 10:42–45).

Paul wrote, literally, *"Stop provoking your children to anger, lest they become discouraged"* (Col 3:21). The negative aorist command in our verse means "never exasperate or make angry." *Discouragement* means to be "broken in spirit" or "disheartened." Any approach to discipline that attacks a person's spirit or soul (perceived as their self-worth) is cruel and damaging. It is not the child's spirit, but the child's selfish, self-centered will that must be broken—without destroying the spirit of the child.

What kills a child's spirit are feelings of rejection, embarrassment, criticism, and unreasonable anger. Discipline is not punishment; it is a lesson to learn.

Children are provoked to anger because parents use anger as a technique to manipulate, resulting in the feeling of rejection. Parents believe the child will be afraid and cease his or her unwanted behavior. The more anger, loud voices, empty threats, and embarrassing name calling are employed to get a response from the child, the angrier and more resistant the child will become. Anger provokes an angry response and rebellion.

"Dear God, a parent's job is complicated and difficult. Help me learn and practice Your principles of love and respect while allowing You to teach me to be faithful in correcting my children according to Your word."

Raise Children in Discipline and Instruction

Eph 6:4b—"... *raise them up~~ in the discipline* and instruction of *the Lord.*"

Not only are parents not to provoke children to anger, which is Satan's favorite tool to destroy relationships (Eph 4:26–27), but parents must also *"raise up"* children, meaning to "bring to maturity, or educate."

Two techniques are given as the means for helping a child to mature: *"discipline and instruction of the Lord."* The word for *discipline* is the same from which we get the word *pedagogy*, or the training of a child, including the cultivation of mind and morals using correction and chastening. Such chastisement has moral instruction as its objective, not punishment for negative actions. The objective has everything to do with the means and motivation of discipline from the parents.

God gives His wisdom even though it may contradict popular psychology: *"He who spares his rod hates his son, but he who loves him disciplines him diligently"* (Prov 13:24). Often a parent wants to be "loved" by his child, so he refuses to teach him the pain of disobedience. By ignoring this command, parents guarantee that children will behave with the characteristics of a biblical fool: *"Foolishness is bound up in the heart of a child; The rod of correction will drive it far from him"* (22:15).

Not only are correction or discipline necessary to raise up wise children, but also *"instruction,"* or *"admonition,"* which means a "word of encouragement or reproof which leads to correct behavior." The memory of the consequence of disobedience can be indelible.

God gave us the perfect model for the treatment of His children in Hebrews: *"And have you forgotten the encouraging words God spoke to you as his children? He said, 'My child, don't make light of the LORD's discipline, and don't give up when he corrects you. For whom the LORD loves He chastens, And scourges every son whom He receives'"* (Heb 12:4–6). Love and disciple must go hand in hand, but the most important issue is that a parent never should communicate rejection, especially as a threat. When the chastisement is over, intimacy should be restored immediately.

"Dear Father, You have provided the perfect example of parenting. Help me follow You in raising my children in correct discipline and loving instruction."

JULY 6

Children, Obey Your Parents

Col 3:20—*"Children, **obey~~ your parents** in everything, for this is pleasing in the Lord."*

One of the most disliked words in any language is the word *obey*. It goes against our fallen nature, which nearly always makes us do what we shouldn't do. Unfortunately, every social structure is built on obedience. In God's plan, obedience is to be learned in the family.

The word *children* is a general word for "offspring without specific reference to sex or age." The term refers to any child living in the home and/or dependent on the parents. The command form means to "continually be obeying." By definition, the word means to "hear, hearken with stillness or attention, or yield to a superior force, even without necessarily being willing."

Since the passage is directed to the children it is evident that they were meant to listen to this text as it was read in the church assembly as part of the worship service. By learning obedience, honor is given to God's word and to the parents. A submissive response to the word as a family is the most profound of worship attitudes.

Parents are to continually instruct children, who are to listen and obey their wisdom (Prov 1:8): *"My son, keep your father's command, and do not forsake the law of your mother"* (6:20).

One of the characteristics of the unsaved and ungodly, especially at the end of the age, is disobedience to parents: *"Men will be lovers of self, lovers of money, boastful, arrogant, revilers, disobedient to parents, ungrateful, unholy"* (2 Tim 3:2).

The general limitation set in Colossians 3:20 is *"in everything"*—unless a demand is contrary to God's commands in His word.

The motive for learning obedience is to be *"well-pleasing to the Lord."* Practically speaking, one is seldom more obedient to the Lord than he is to his parents. How easy is it for you to yield to authority?

"Our loving Lord, as children, we need Your help to make it our main focus to please You. Please help us be obedient children who honor our parents in all things."

JULY 7

Wives Must Be Dignified, Not Gossips

1 Tim 3:11—*"Likewise also their wives **must be** dignified, not slanderous, temperate, faithful in every respect."*

Sometimes in Greek writing, the main verb is omitted, but grammatically it is assumed to be the same as its preceding verb. In this case, the main verb is in 1 Timothy 3:2—*"The overseer then must be"*—and then in 3:11, it is understood as *"Likewise also their wives must be."* To ensure the same verbal imperative, the adverb *likewise* is injected to confirm the continuance of the imperative idea.

First Timothy 3:11 is thrust into the middle of a discussion of church leadership, bishops or pastors (3:1–7), and deacons (3:8–10, 12–13). Most translations add their interpretation to their translations: for instance, they say *"their wives must be"* when the text merely says *"women."* There is no definite article (*the*) or possessive pronoun (*their*) before the word *women*; thus it is ambiguous, referring to women in the ministry. The word translated as *wives* (Gk. *gune*) usually refers to "married women"; thus it is assumed to be the wives of the deacons, though not necessarily.

All through the New Testament, women are key players in the ministry of church planting. Serving women are to be *"dignified,"* which means they are to "evoke special respect, to be reverent or reputable." This quality attracts and invites people to emulate their character because of their spiritual, self-sacrificing, disciplined life.

Serving women are not to be *"slanderous"* (Gk. *diabolos*), which means "false accusers." They must learn to control their tongues in all conversations.

Serving women must be *"temperate,"* meaning "self-controlled, especially in respect to wine," or "sober-minded, circumspect." This means they should be free from the excessive influence of passion, lust, or emotionalism.

Serving women must be *"faithful in every respect"*—that is, they must be absolutely trustworthy and dependable. God expects all His servants to be seriously committed to His word and His people. Can you be trusted with such a ministry?

"Heavenly Father, help me strive each day to discipline myself and earn respect as I avoid the sin of gossip. Help me work to be self-controlled, trustworthy, and dependable. This will honor You and make my spouse proud and happy."

JULY 8
Stay Alert and Pray
Not to Fall into Temptation

Mark 14:38—*"Stay awake~~ and pray~~ that you will not fall into temptation. The spirit is willing, but the flesh is weak."*

One of the many attributes of Jesus was His ability to be ready for whatever happened. What seemed to hurt Him most was the selfishness or disinterest of His closest friends when He knew they would be tempted and fail Him.

To the very end, Jesus was committed to training His disciples. He was telling them the secret of inner fortitude. Three times Jesus interrupted His prayers to check on His disciples who had lost interest and fallen asleep. Each time, Jesus exhorted all three to *"Stay awake,"* or to stay alert for spiritual dangers, deceptions, or disillusionments. They were to *"pray,"* which expresses total dependence on the power and presence of God.

If you are unprepared in these two steps, it becomes highly likely that you will *"fall into temptation,"* meaning you will be "put to the test." Reaction to small tests indicates your inner fortitude for inevitable greater tests in life.

The word *fall* into temptation, means to "come into." Behind it is the idea of walking unaware into a trap, as in the case of the *"simple"* fool of Proverbs 1:32: *"For the waywardness of the simpletons will kill them and the careless ease of the fools will destroy them."* Once you are in the middle of a situation, it is hard to get out unscathed. Prayerful alertness is the key.

The wise person learns the pitfalls, stays alert for the symptoms of danger, and asks God for wisdom to avoid such situations and courage to turn away, say "no," or stand firm as an unashamed follower of Christ.

The *"spirit,"* which is willing, must be strengthened through prayer to overcome the weakness of the self-interest of the flesh. Have you experienced the presence of Christ in areas of testing? Did you have the courage to be true to Him?   .

"Dear Lord, guide my steps each day and help me to always be watching and praying to keep from being drawn into any temptation to disobey Your word."

Ask, Seek, and Knock

Matt 7:7—*"**Ask**~~ and it will be given to you; **seek**~~ and you will find; **knock**~~ and the door will be opened for you."*

One of the special attractions of the teachings of Jesus was all He revealed about God. Prior to this verse, He had been teaching the principles of relationships. He taught against being so critical of others that you ignore the major faults in your own character. Following this passage, He returned to the subject of relationships.

Our text gives the followers of His kingdom examples of how God responds. Here we see one of His characteristics: He is generous and responsive to us. God's example becomes our model for how to freely respond to those around us: with generosity and love.

The three commands in our verse are present imperatives, meaning they are continuous actions: thus we must "habitually keep on" asking, seeking, and knocking.

This promise is not a blank check to fill out as we wish; it must be understood in the broader context of New Testament revelations: *"Whatever we ask we receive from Him, because we keep His commandments and the things that are pleasing in His sight"* (1 Jn 3:22).

Furthermore, self-interest and selfishness are the wrong motives for applying the promise: *"You ask and do not receive, because you ask with wrong motives, so that you may spend it on your pleasures"* (James 4:3). The whole objective is to be like the Father, think like the Father, and desire whatever the Father desires: *"This is the confidence which we have before Him, that, if we ask anything according to His will, He hears us"* (1 Jn 5:14). To get on His wavelength, we need to know His word, His commands, and His desires and then make them our own. Then we will want just what He wants: *"Let this mind be in you which was also in Christ Jesus"* (Phil 2:5).

The greatest request is for the mind (and heart) of Christ. Tell the Lord you would prefer nothing more in this world than to have His attitudes and to fulfill His desires in every relationship.

"Lord Jesus, I am thankful that You are generous, giving Your loved ones the strength and power to be obedient as we ask, seek, and knock in prayer."

JULY 10

Pray for Laborers

Luke 10:2—*"He said to them, 'The harvest is plentiful, but the workers are few. Therefore **ask*~ the Lord** of the harvest to send out workers into his harvest.'"*

Jesus concluded His ministry in Galilee, seeking disciples. Here we are given a glimpse into Jesus's constant task of recruiting disciples and challenging them to give up their ambitions and follow Him.

Though many (or most?) were focused on their own interests and walked away from Jesus's challenge to them (Luke 9:57–61), He told them, *"No one, having put his hand to the plow, and looking back is fit for the kingdom of God"* (9:61). Half-hearted commitments never last.

Before His final trip to Jerusalem, Jesus selected seventy-two disciples for this final mission. Jesus had been training these men and others, along with the Twelve. Tradition indicates that they became church leaders. This group (Luke 10:1) of seventy-two *"others"* means a "different, not the same," group—one that did not include the Twelve. Is this the ministry model we should follow? Rather than expecting people to wait for a mystical feeling, we should take the initiative and follow the model of Jesus to challenge people to give up their lives for Him and then personally train our own disciples in ministry.

On their first mission to bring in the *"harvest,"* this first group of disciples was taught to pray for more *"workers"* as they began to experience the immensity of the task of sharing the "good news" of the Savior with the world. To this day the vast non-Christian populations (two-thirds of the world) receive virtually no message of Jesus's sacrifice from any of Christ's disciples. Whom are we praying for? Do we pray daily that God will lead us to someone to challenge for discipleship?

Do the unevangelized deserve a chance to hear the gospel? "Certainly," we respond, yet our real answer is betrayed by how little we pray for *"workers"* to go, by how little we care for people who have never heard, and how little we help those who are going. Be warned: as you pray for workers, you may be asking God to send you!

"Dear Lord, there is still much work to be done in getting the gospel to the last people groups. I want to be obedient, and I ask You to send laborers around the world to accomplish that task. 'Here am I, send me'" (Isa 6:8).

Keep Thinking about Things Above

Col 3:2—*"**Keep thinking**~~ **about things above**, not things on the earth."*

Motivation in life comes from our beliefs about what is valuable to us. The Bible teaches that the best satisfaction will be in glory, when we stand before our Savior to receive our recognition from Christ and discover our eternal purpose. This life is only the beginning, the testing ground, the opportunity to demonstrate our value to the kingdom of God both now and in the world to come.

This perspective changes everything. Paul put it this way: *"We do not look at the things which are seen, but at the things which are not seen. For the things which are seen are temporary, but the things which are not seen are eternal"* (2 Cor 4:18). Knowing we are eternal makes God's plan very valuable to us. Paul commands us to *"keep on continually thinking about* [set your minds on] *things above."* He meant for us to be *"transformed by the renewing of* [our] *mind[s]"* (Rom 12:2). This requires us to accept and live by new values and a new worldview.

In Colossians 3:2, Paul was thanking the Philippian church for their generosity when he said, *"Not that I seek the gift, but I seek the fruit that abounds to your account"* (Phil 4:17). Their offering to Paul was being recorded in heaven. Jesus taught, *"Where your treasure is, there your heart will be also"* (Matt 6:21).

One way to ensure that you are fixing your mind on heaven is to begin investing in heaven's purpose and objectives: *"For whoever gives you a cup of water to drink in My name, because you belong to Christ, assuredly, I say to you, he will by no means lose his reward"* (Mark 9:41).

The reason for our kindness and generosity now, even toward people we dislike or who oppose us, is that we are thinking about the eternal consequences: *"But love your enemies, do good, and lend, hoping for nothing in return; and your reward will be great"* (Luke 6:35). We are wise to know the rules for receiving His rewards, and we live for His approval.

"Dear heavenly Father, I ask that You give me the wisdom to fix my mind on Your purposes while I live on this earth. Your word renews my mind and keeps my life on track."

JULY 12

Believe You Have Received It

Mark 11:24—"*For this reason I tell you, whatever you pray and ask for,* **believe~~ that you have received it**, *and it will be yours.*"

Is having a vision of a completed task the same as "*believ[ing] that you have received it?*" Futurists of the New Age movement encourage and teach the technique of "visioning" or "vision casting," which may empower individuals or can be useful for decision making and planning—but it has nothing to do with God.

John quoted Jesus when he taught a similar promise as our text: "*Therefore whatever you ask in My name, that I will do, that the Father may be glorified in the Son. If you ask anything in my name, I will do it*" (Jn 14:13).

How much more encouragement do we need to pray for great things that will honor and glorify the Father through the Son? The Father knows how to help us glorify Christ before we ask, but He waits for us to be concerned enough to ask: "*It shall come to pass that before they call, I will answer; and while they are still speaking, I will hear*" (Isa 65:24). By His response, everyone will recognize it was God's doing.

Don't be misled into thinking that this promise is all about you; it is all about God. James clarifies how to pray, saying, "*You want what you don't have, so you scheme and kill to get it. You are jealous of what others have, but you can't get it, so you fight and wage war to take it away from them. Yet you don't have what you want because you don't ask God for it. And even when you ask, you don't get it because your motives are all wrong— you want only what will give you pleasure*" (4:2–3[NLT]).

Stop a moment and think of all the ways you could glorify God through your life and service. He primarily becomes evident to others by answering the prayers of His servants who want Him to be recognized as a powerful and prayer-answering God. If only His people would call on Him with His purposes in mind. What impossible need do you have that would most glorify God if it were answered? Pray for His glory's sake.

"Lord, we can only believe in what is absolutely true: Your word. I know that if I ask You for what You want, I will always receive an affirmative answer, and my life will count for You."

JULY 13

Ask Whatever You Want

Jn 15:7—*"If you remain in me and my words remain in you, **ask***~ ***whatever you want**, and it will be done for you."*

From childhood, we have all heard stories of a genie who would offer three wishes to his master. The protagonist was always cautioned to take care in making wishes, because he might get what he wants, along with the consequences.

The key to effective prayer is to *know* what to ask: "*Now this is the confidence that we have in Him, that if we ask anything according to His will, He hears us*" (1 Jn 5:14). Knowing what to ask requires, first of all, that we know "His will" as He reveals it in His word.

The first condition in John 15:7 is "*if you remain in me*"; this is the translation of the verb meaning "to dwell, or live" in the aorist tense, meaning a completed, permanent fusion. The surrounding text uses the metaphor of the believer being grafted into the Vine (Jesus is the Vine; Jn 15:1) in an inseparable union, with His life flowing to us, the branches. If we have been bonded together with Christ in salvation, His Spirit flows in us enabling us to think and to be like Jesus (Phil 2:5).

The second condition, "*and my words remain in you*," is the prerequisite of knowing the will of God, which is the basis for effective prayer. The verb is the same permanent bonding between our heart and Jesus's teachings. The Spirit grafts His word into our minds and hearts. Our thoughts and dreams no longer are about our selfish aspirations. His values, priorities, principles, and commands become our guides to think and plan about what God desires.

If we know His will by diligently studying His word and asking for His intervention accordingly, then "*we know that He hears us, whatever we ask, we know that we have the petitions that we have asked of Him*" (1 Jn 5:15). Just as the antennae of any powerful radio transmitter must be cut to the precise length to permit the maximum transmission, so we are responsible to mold our lives according to the values, principles, and commands of God's word—His frequency. It is then possible to think as He thinks and desire what He desires. Do we really want to be that close to God? Remember: somewhere in the shadows of His will is a cross.

"I understand, dear Lord, that I can only know what to ask as I pray if I am inseparably bonded to You and Your word. Help me learn to think as You do, so it will become clear what I should ask for."

JULY 14

Forgive Any Offense before Praying

Mark 11:25—*"Whenever you stand praying, if you have anything against anyone, **forgive him**~~ so that your Father in heaven will also forgive you your sins."*

The bond between Christ and His followers is such that disharmony anywhere breaks down the free flow of God's blessing. It has been said that the relationship between the believer and Christ is no better than the believer's relationship with other believers. If we expect Christ to listen to us, we must listen to what He taught.

Not only is faith required for effective prayer (Mark 11:23), but all relationships must be healed by forgiveness—at least on our part—if we want our prayers to be heard. In Jesus's model prayer (Matt 6:9–13), the fifth element is to *"forgive men their trespasses"* (6:14–15).

"Whenever you stand praying" refers, perhaps, to leading prayer in a public setting. What matters in prayer is our attitude of heart and mind and our conformity to His word. They knew the warning of the psalmist: *"If I had harbored sin in my heart, the Lord would not have listened"* (Psa 66:18).

If we expect God to hear us when we pray, we must have the same attitude He has toward forgiving others. Paul wrote in his Letter to the Ephesians, *"And be kind to one another, tenderhearted, forgiving one another, just as God in Christ forgave you"* (Eph 4:32). Later he wrote, *"bearing with one another, and forgiving one another, if anyone has a complaint against another; even as Christ forgave you, so you also must do"* (Col 3:13).

Does it matter to us if God listens to our prayers? Are we more interested in stewing over an offense against us than in having God's forgiving heart and mind bonding us in communion with Him?

If we are mentally reviewing our grudges, dislikes, resentments, or bitterness toward another person for any cause, then the Lord is not listening to our prayers. When Jesus said, *"if you have anything against anyone,"* He meant we are not allowed to harbor *any* resentment or grudge. There must be an immediate and constant spirit of forgiveness toward everyone who offends us, lest we are sinning far worse than they by not forgiving. How important is it to you that God hears you? Can you forgive anything? Think about what Christ did on the cross.

"Dear God, make me aware of any offense I may have caused another so I may confess it and earn his forgiveness before coming to You with my petitions."

Be Self-Controlled and Sober Minded

1 Pet 4:7—*"For the culmination of all things is near. So **be self-controlled***~ and **sober-minded***~ for the sake of prayer."*

The result the global explosion of Chrisitanity has been a shift in end-time teaching with a general loss of the sense of His imminent return.

However, the unprecedented global turning to Christ can be seen as the *"open door, and not one can shut it"* of Revelation 3:8. The prophecy of the Philadelphia Church, which exists until Jesus returns, is promised: *"Because you have kept My command to persevere, I also will keep you from the hour of trial which shall come upon the whole world"* (Rev 3:10).

This is a reference to the Rapture of all believers before the *"trial"* of the seven-year tribulation period begins; we are at the door! Everything points to the imminent return of Christ.

Peter gives us two commands that affect our prayers in the end times. First, we are to *"immediately and urgently decide to be self-controlled,"* which means "to be sane, of a sound mind, sober-minded, and self-disciplined." We must keep the perspective of living in the light of His imminent return, always obedient to His purposes. We are not to panic when things turn against us.

Failing here can be dangerous: *"Be sober, be vigilant; because your adversary the devil walks about like a roaring lion, seeking whom he may devour"* (1 Pet 5:8). Being irrational, explosive, impulsive, or reactionary only signals your openness to demonic attacks. Believers are to bring *"every thought into captivity to the obedience of Christ"* (2 Cor 10:5).

Second, Peter exhorts us to *"urgently become sober-minded,"* a closely related word meaning to have "sound judgment, or self-restraint." We are not to be naïve or presumptuous, thinking that everything will prosper. Believers are to study God's word to be wise, learn the thinking of fools (Proverbs 1:22, 32; 10:18; 12:15; 13:19; 14:3, 8, 9, 16) learn the truths of Scripture to recognize error, and never allow ideas or practices that would quench our rich communion with God.

"Father, help me live in the light of Your imminent return and determine to be sober-minded and self-disciplined through the teachings of Your word so You will be able to use me to help get the gospel to the ends of the earth."

JULY 16
Pray Constantly

1 Thes 5:17—*"Constantly pray~~."*

The driving force of consistency in prayer is a joyful dependence on God as we acknowledge our own insufficiency. The more we think we can handle our lives and situations, the less we depend on God. Paul needed God, *"rejoicing in hope, patient in tribulation, continuing steadfastly in prayer"* (Rom 12:12).

The imperative command to *"pray,"* which is expressed in the present imperative tense, means to be *"constantly or habitually praying."* This does not mean to live in a monastery, but to live in the presence of God, mentally talking to God as though our thoughts were a two-person conversation. He is part of every thought.

As we learn His word, we understand what He thinks about our plans and dreams. This knowledge enables us to talk to Him about how to apply His word in each of our situations.

Jesus taught, *"Men always ought to pray and not lose heart"* (Luke 18:1). Prayer dispels discouragement, disillusionment, and depression and is also a ministry to others: *"For God is my witness, whom I serve with my spirit in the gospel of His Son, that without ceasing I make mention of you always in my prayers"* (Rom 1:9).

The New Testament is full of examples of Paul's prayers for others: *"We do not cease to pray for you, and to ask that you may be filled with the knowledge of His will in all wisdom and spiritual understanding; that you may walk worthy of the Lord, fully pleasing Him, being fruitful in every good work and increasing in the knowledge of God; strengthened with all might, according to His glorious power, for all patience and longsuffering with joy"* (Col 1:9–11)

Find a prayer partner and begin a prayer ministry for other believers and for the lost around the world. Believe that you can accomplish things for God through prayer. It is much more powerful than you can imagine.

"Thank You, Lord, that You are never far away. Your children can be continually in communication with You wherever we may be. I know we simply need to speak and You will hear."

Give Thanks in Everything

1 Thes 5:18—*"In everything **give thanks**~~. For this is God's will for you in Christ Jesus."*

There are several expressions in the New Testament that specifically described as the "will of God," and they are always related to the commands in Scriptures. Why should God give us more insight into His will when we are negligent concerning what He has specifically declared to be His will? Are we truly thankful in every circumstance?

"Everything" means all that happens, including struggles, hurts, failures, conflicts, testings, opposition, challenges, difficulties, disappointments, and losses. We must give thanks not *for* everything but *in* everything. Bad things can happen to believers, but these things do not necessarily come directly from God. In the midst of negative circumstances, we can be thankful for His presence and that He shares our hurts or losses. He is with us: *"Lo, I will never leave you nor forsake you"* (Matt 28:20).

In Acts 5:41, the disciples *"departed from the council, rejoicing that they were counted worthy to suffer shame for His name."* In Romans 8:28, Paul described the foundation for thankfulness: *"We know that all things work together for good to those who love God, to those who are the called according to His purpose."* Our omnipotent God, whose purpose will ultimately be beneficial to us or to others, controls life's circumstances.

Knowing that He is in control, and that whatever happens is part of a bigger purpose, we can trust Him because He considers us trustworthy to be part of His plan.

Grounded in this perspective, thanksgiving will be an indispensable part of our prayers. Paul wrote, *"Continue earnestly in prayer, being vigilant in it with thanksgiving"* (Col 4:2). Nothing expresses our trust in God more than a thankful heart: *"Out of the abundance of the heart the mouth speaks"* (Matt 12:34). After six years in chains, Paul said at his trial, *"But the Lord stood with me and strengthened me . . . that all the Gentiles might hear"* (2 Tim 4:17). God's purpose makes everything worthwhile. Learn to be thankful . . . and tell Him.

"Father, though our lives may be in turmoil and joy is far from us, we can be thankful that You are present, that You understand, and that You are in control of all things. Because of that, we can rest and draw strength from You. Thank You."

Confess Your Sins to One Another

James 5:16—*"So **confess~~ your sins to one another** and **pray~~ for one another** so that you may be healed. The prayer of a righteous person has great effectiveness."*

John wrote five books of the New Testament. In his First Epistle, he sought to clarify the issue of the security of the believer: *"These things I have written to you . . . that you may know that you have eternal life"* (1 Jn 5:13). He explained how to know you are saved and also how to recognize if you are lost.

One of the "signs" of a lost person is found in 1 John 1:8: *"If we say that we have not sin, we deceive ourselves, and the truth is not in us."* Most people think they are "good." Even murderers blame circumstances or other people for their crimes. Almost everyone believes his "good" outweighs his "bad." We can only get someone to admit he is a vile sinner—one who is guilty of breaking God's rules and is therefore lost— when the Spirit of God brings His convicting power. Jesus said, *"When He has come, He will convict the world of sin"* (Jn 16:8).

One of the most uncomfortable commands in Scripture is to *"confess your sins one to one another."* If we are transparent before God, we can be transparent with each other. It is emotionally and spiritually healthy to confess our sins to one another. When we stop pretending to be better than we really are, the principle *"love covers a multitude of sins"* (1 Pet 4:8) can be practiced in the congregation. We must learn to say, "I'm struggling with greed or lust (and so on). Will you help me by praying for me and make me accountable?"

Sin is most dangerous when it is kept secret. It ferments and rots from within until it destroys. The surrounding text indicates that healing can be accelerated when guilt is relieved by open confession. The word *healing* (Gk. *iaomai*) can mean God's forgiveness as well (Matt 13:15; Acts 18:27). Peter used it to illustrate God's forgiveness, making repentant believers spiritually whole again (1 Pet 2:24). Small groups may be an ideal platform for learning to confess to one another.

"Dear Jesus, please send into my life people who love You and are able to help me through the tough days when I fall into sin. Help me to be willing to confess my sin, find forgiveness in You, and rest in Your promise of being 'cleansed from all unrighteousness'" (1 Jn 1:9).

JULY 19
Ask God for Wisdom

James 1:5—*"But if anyone is deficient in wisdom, he **should ask~~, God** who gives to all generously and without reprimand, and it will be given to him."*

No matter how severe or difficult the trial, the rules for survival apply. The secret is in the wisdom of God, which teaches us how to think about situations from God's perspective. Most people tend to rely on their own intuition and resources when things are going well, to the point that, practically speaking, they do not need God. They have everything under control. It is only when we are desperate that we turn to God in prayer.

Nothing reveals our need for God more than our prayer life. It is a good thermometer of how much we want to or have to depend on God. In the preceding text, James commanded believers to have the perspective of *"joy when you fall into various trials, knowing that the testing of your faith produces patience"* (1:2). The key word here is *knowing*—especially knowing that God's perspective, or wisdom, gives joy, though not necessarily happiness. It is joy to know that an all-powerful God is working in and through our lives to produce His character in us so we can honor His name by being like Him in the midst of rejection and persecution.

James offers a sufficient and necessary remedy to life's maladies: *"ask God"* for wisdom, not as an escape from your problems, but to provide understanding that will motivate your endurance. We are to add to our faith, *"knowledge, to knowledge self-control, to self-control perseverance . . . For if these things are yours and abound, you will be neither barren nor unfruitful"* (2 Pet 1:6, 8). God wants to produce a spiritually fruitful child. This is what we should understand, and we should make it our goal and our focus with a whatever-the-cost mentality. This is wisdom.

The verb *ask* is in the present imperative tense, so this is not an alternative or optional solution but a mandatory and continual commitment to be asking God for this wisdom. If our tests do not motivate us to take a closer walk with God and engage in a deeper prayer life, then, since this is His primary tool for teaching, He is likely to continue and/or intensify these tests until we are driven to the throne of grace and until we get an *"ear attentive to wisdom"* and commit our *"heart to understanding"* (Prov 2:2). There is nothing God wants to give us more than an understanding of His thought process. If you are seeking His wisdom, you will find it.

"Lord Jesus, I need Your wisdom to get through each day and to honor You. I am grateful that I can ask a thousand times a day and You will answer."

JULY 20

Ask in Faith without Doubting

James 1:6—"*But **he must ask~~ in faith** without doubting, for the one who doubts is like a wave of the sea, blown and tossed around by the wind.*"

Team players are picked not just because of their abilities but also because they convey unconditional trust in their coach. There is no time in a game to question the coach. God wants to call the plays in our lives through His commands and give us the wisdom to trust that He allows formidable opposition or difficulties for a purpose.

Inner fortitude to endure the pressures or calamities of life comes from a willingness to understand God's perspective and believe that He has a purpose. We are told to "*be continually asking*" (James 1:5) for God's wisdom, which is not a suggestion, but a command; therefore, it is key to our prayer life to cry out for wisdom: "*If you seek her [wisdom] as silver and search for her as for hidden treasures; then you will discern the fear of the Lord and discover the knowledge of God*" (Prov 2:3–5).

The heart of God wants us to understand Him and His ways, which are not our ways, so we must adjust to Him. Jeremiah said, "*I know the plans that I have for you, plans for welfare and not for calamity to give you a future and a hope. Then you will call upon Me and come and pray to Me, and I will listen to you. You will seek Me and find Me when you search for Me with all your heart*" (Jer 29:11–13). Isaiah wrote similarly, "'*For My thoughts are not your thoughts, nor are your ways My ways,' says the LORD. 'For as the heavens are higher than the earth, So are My ways higher than your ways, And My thoughts than your thoughts*" (Isa 55:8–9). This means we have to adjust to His thoughts. Even more so, we must learn to trust our Lord without question.

When Satan convinced Eve to doubt the character, motive, purpose, and promises of God, he was able to manipulate her into disobedience through temptations. She refused to trust God's wisdom or seek it. She believed a lie and chose to do it her way. On the other hand, Job said, "*Though He slay me, yet will I trust Him*" (Job 13:15).

Some Christians doubt God will provide for them, so they refuse to live by faith. Others become bitter against God for allowing bad things to happen to them, thus missing God's purpose for them. To doubt God is foolish and sinful: "*Without faith it is impossible to please Him*" (Heb 11:6). Whatever happens, God expects us to stay on course and trust His wisdom.

"*Heavenly Father, Your wisdom is like pure gold; it is a hidden treasure that I can only possess if I know You through Your word. Give me the determination to know and trust You explicitly.*"

Do Not Suppose You Will Receive Anything

James 1:7–8—*"For that person **must not suppose**~~ that he will receive anything from the Lord, since he is a double-minded individual, unstable in all his ways."*

Have you ever noticed how easy it is to go from spiritual highs to emotional lows? One who sees God as a kind of a Santa Claus can easily be disappointed. If we attempt to know God through personal experience, doubt and disillusionment are inevitable. God can only truly become known through revelation: *"Faith comes by hearing, and hearing by the Word of God"* (Rom 10:17).

A person who loses confidence in God's purpose (James 1:6) *"must not suppose"*—that is "expect, or consider something to be true," especially— *"that he will receive anything from the Lord."* God does not attempt to convince people by answering skeptical prayers. Those committed to God find His wisdom and provision sufficient.

Faith is not expectation or presumption. Disappointment because of less-than-expected results is not lack of faith. Presumption is a self-convincing effort that acts on what it supposes God is going to do; it is an attempt to ignore doubts by focusing on the positive, as though the effort to eliminate doubt can guarantee the results.

Such skeptical or presumptuous prayers often are selfish, primarily benefiting the person praying. On the other hand, faith is based on trusting God to accomplish His will, regardless of what it is, as He fulfills His purpose through the circumstance. Disappointment or disillusionment are symptom of presumptions instead of a trusting faith.

Two additional characteristics of the doubter are given: first, he is *"a double-minded individual"*—that is, he is has "two souls." He wants to be allied with God, but he refuses to be obedient. He is after something for himself under a religious shroud. His insincerity is evident because he is *"unstable in all his ways."* He experiences highs and lows, being controlled by circumstances. His emotions make him undependable. He is the classic "fool" of the book of Proverbs.

Never attempt to dictate to God. Trust Him and wait! Act on His word and trust Him in all situations regardless of what happens.

"Dear Lord, keep me from presumption as I pray. Help me to know You well in order to pray according to Your perspective and Your plan for this world."

JULY 22

Pray when in Trouble; Sing Praises

James 5:13—*"Is anyone among you suffering?* **He should pray** *~~. Is anyone in good spirits? He* **should sing praises** *~~."*

Why is it that prayer is always the last recourse when we have problems? Is there something embarrassing about having to depend on prayer?

In our text, James has come full circle from commanding us to *"count it all joy when you fall into various trials"* (1:2) to commanding us to *"continually or habitually be praying"* during *"suffering"* (Gk., *kakopatheo*, "endure evil, hardships, or trouble"). In 2 Timothy 4:5, Paul wrote to *"endure afflictions, do the work of an evangelist, [and] fulfill your ministry."*

There is no suggestion here as to what the object of their prayer should be. It could be an exhortation to pray to understand the wisdom of God in the face of loss and horrible pain and to learn to be content. They will never endure without this inner strength from time spent in the presence of God. Humanly speaking, if Christ needed to pray for strength to go through the day of His crucifixion, how much more did they (and we) need the same?

Paul went through not only persecution from without but also physical affliction. Three times he prayed to be freed from it. God answered his prayer by helping him understand that his physical affliction was necessary. God said to Paul, *"My grace is sufficient for you, for My strength is made perfect in weakness."* His response was *"most gladly I will rather boast in my infirmities, that the power of Christ may rest upon me."* The *"power of God"* is defined as the manifested sufficiency of the *"grace"* of God in agonizing situations. This is good.

James also wrote to those who were *"in good spirits,"* or "cheerful." This is not a reference to happiness dependent on circumstances, but "cheerfulness" from the heart, as when Paul and Silas sang in the prison at Philippi (Acts 16:25). *"Continually sing praises"* is what Paul wrote of those "filled with the Spirit"; you should be *"speaking to one another in psalms and hymns and spiritual songs, singing and making melody in your heart to the Lord"* (Eph 5:19–20a). A positive attitude and a trusting spirit are contagious. This is how we are to *"encourage one another"* (1 Thes 5:11).

"Dear Jesus, it is wonderful to be able to ask for Your help when life is difficult. I am grateful that Your grace is sufficient and that You will restore my joy as I cling to You."

Call the Elders to Pray for the Sick

James 5:14—*"Is anyone among you ill?* **He should summon***~ **the elders** *of the church, and* **they should pray***~ *for him and anoint [participle] him with oil in the name of the Lord."*

Christians have generated many beliefs and practices because of misunderstanding, but few have been as misunderstood as this concept. Some want to promise all believers that they will always be healed, but sometimes God keeps us weak and dependent.

The word *ill* or *sick* (Gk., *astheneo*) means "weak, feeble, without strength or powerless." It is used when discussing Christ being *"crucified in weakness"* (2 Cor 13:4), which is not a disease. Paul, describing his endurance in the ministry, said, *"We are weak and you are made strong"* (13:9). The word is also used for physical sickness or debilitation (Matt 25:39; Jn 4:46; 11:1–3, 6; Phil 2:26–27; and 2 Tim 4:20). Which is the meaning in this context?

An indicator is the parallel word in James 5:15: *"The prayer of faith will save the sick."* Here the same word means "to be weary, fatigued, even tired of living." In Hebrews 12:3, we are exhorted to *"consider Him who endured such hostility from sinners against Himself, lest you become weary and discouraged in your souls."* The usage of this word indicates that "weak" would be a better translation than "sick."

The early church lived under threats and persecution; many believers were afflicted, beaten, tortured, or harassed. The leaders were instructed to *"encourage the timid"* and *"help the weak"* (1 Thes 5:14).

In James 5:14, the reader is commanded to *"urgently summon"* the elders or church leaders in the Jewish Christian community to his home to be *"anoint[ed] with oil,"* a Jewish custom used to alleviate pain or sickness. Whatever the medicinal effect, the objective was to communicate that the church cared for hurting individuals enough to go to them, help them in their pain, pray to encourage them, and show solidarity to the hurting, defeated member. The body of Christ is one body; we embrace each other in need. Pray for one another.

"Dear God, You have given us instructions for every eventuality of life, even for when we are ill. I praise You for church leaders who willingly pray for those in need of Your healing touch, whether the need is physical or spiritual."

JULY 24

Pray for the Ministry

2 Thes 3:1—*"Finally, **pray**~~ **for us**, brothers and sisters, that the Lord's message may spread quickly and be honored as in fact it was among you."*

The challenge to make disciples comes back to prayer: *"Pray for laborers for the harvest"* (Matt 9:38), and then we must pray that their ministry will spread the understanding of the word of God. Prayer is the key. If we believe that prayer effects change not only in us but also in others, then we can serve our Savior effectively by praying for His servants around the world.

The command in 2 Thessalonians 3:1 is in the present imperative, meaning to *"be continually or habitually praying,"* which means "to ask, make petition, or request." The verb implies that you are requesting a specific outcome, not a vague "God bless so-and-so." The verb is usually seen with a purpose clause: "pray in order that . . ." Specific results are expected.

Paul wrote, *"I am not ashamed of the gospel of Christ, for it is the power of God to salvation for everyone who believes"* (Rom 1:16). The *"power of God"* is the illuminating, convicting, drawing, and regenerating work of the Spirit. Paul was dependent on the power of God: *"I labor, striving according to His power, which mightily works within me"* (Col 1:29). It enabled him to share the gospel in spite of opposition and risk. It was not Paul's reputation as a loving servant that brought the power of God, but the persuasive teaching or preaching of the word unleashed the Spirit's power to change lives.

The word for *spread quickly* means "to speed on or make progress," as in Acts 19:20: *"The word of the Lord grew mightily and prevailed."* See also Ephesians 6:19: *"Pray on my behalf, that utterance may be given to me in the opening of my mouth, to make known with boldness the mystery of the gospel."*

Paul's concern was that the gospel be *"honored as in fact it was among you."* Paul was there less than a month, but he left a functioning church Do you pray for others to testify to someone every day? To how many people have you told the gospel story? The Savior *"desires all men to be saved and to come to the knowledge of the truth"* (1 Tim 2:4). Is this your desire? Pray for it.

"Dear Father, I want to be faithful in praying for my brothers and sisters around the world who are taking Your good news to those who have never heard it. Help me have a definite plan to pray effectively."

Follow Me

Matt 9:9—*"As Jesus went on from there, he saw a man named Matthew sitting at the tax booth. 'Follow~~ me,' he said to him. And he got up and followed him."*

Jesus knew He had only three years to select and train a team of men who could carry the gospel to the ends of the known world. How would He do it?

Jesus did not expect his disciples to volunteer or make a decision after one of His teaching/preaching sessions. He proactively sought out and confronted individuals who would leave everything and follow Him. We know of the Twelve who led (Acts 6:2) the Jerusalem church. Toward the end of Jesus's ministry, there was another group of 72 disciples. Jesus did not stop recruiting and training disciples. By the time of his resurrection, the number of "disciples" (Acts 1:15) had reached at least 120 and perhaps 500 by the ascension.

When the replacement of Judas was necessary, the apostles insisted that the new man must have *"accompanied us all the time that the Lord Jesus went in and out among us. Beginning from the baptism of John to that day when He was taken up from us, one of these must be a witness with us of His resurrection"* (Acts 1:21–22). Several were selected out of many qualified disciples. We know nothing of all these disciples.

How did Paul get into the ministry? After his amazing conversion (Acts 9:10–19), three years in the desert, and two weeks in Jerusalem (Gal 1:17–18), he returned to Tarsus. Six or seven years later, Barnabas came to seek him out as a partner in the Antioch church (Acts 11:25–26). What about Timothy? Paul recruited him: *"You have carefully followed my doctrine, manner of life, purpose, faith, long-suffering, love, perseverance"* (2 Tim 3:10). Paul learned to make disciples by knowing how Jesus did it. We are to be constantly recruiting disciples.

He told the believers in Corinth, *"Wherefore I beseech you, be ye followers of me"* (1 Cor 4:16). This became the norm among the churches as in Philippi (Phil 3:17) and in Thessalonica: *"You became followers of us and of the Lord"* (1 Thes 1:6). Jesus's last words were to *"go and make disciples."* Are we being trained, and are we training others to follow God's word as Jesus did?

"You have instructed us, dear Lord, to go and make disciples, and You have shown us how to do it. Give me the understanding, knowledge, and wisdom to help develop followers of Christ around the world."

JULY 26

Take Responsibility and Learn from Jesus

Matt 11:29—*"Take*~ my yoke on you and learn*~ from me, because I am gentle and humble in heart, and you will find rest for your souls."*

You never really know a person until you are in a close and prolonged relationship. Jesus, wanting a close relationship with His followers, said, *"Come to Me . . . and I will give you rest"* (Matt 11:28).

Jesus said, *"No one knows the Son except the Father. Nor does anyone know the Father except the Son, and the one to whom the Son wills to reveal Him"* (Matt 11:27[NAS]). Man cannot imagine what God is like. Our finite minds simply cannot grasp the infinite. It must be revealed to us.

In the context of revealing the Father and granting rest to the one who comes to Jesus in trust, Jesus challenges his followers, *"Take my yoke upon you and learn from Me."* The yoke, with regard to animals, means control and submission to your owner, but with humans, the imagery signifies slavery to Jesus and His will.

In the Hebrew world, a student is under the yoke of his teacher, which means he submits to his teachings. This first phrase is then parallel to the second phrase: *"and learn from Me."* The word *learn* means to become a "disciple or learner." There are three reasons why Jesus can be trusted:

First, He said, *"I am gentle [or meek]"* as opposed to being quick to anger.

Second, *"I am . . . humble in heart."* His humility is what attracted His followers. He is not filled with self-importance, but He is other-centered, which earns trust.

Third, *"you will find rest for your souls."* Jesus promised, *"I will give you rest"* (Matt 11:28), and now *"you will find rest."* One is the gift resulting from trust, and this rest is the consequence of learning to be like Him. We are no longer slaves to a legalistic system but are free to learn the attitudes of God. As Paul wrote, *"I delight in the law of God to the inward man"* (Rom 7:22).

As we become like Him, we too become trustworthy, modeling the peace that only truth can bring to a soul. Let's become, and make, disciples like Jesus.

"Dear Father, when Your children are willing to take the responsibility You have given us to reach the world, You give us inner rest. What a wonderful God we serve!"

Make Disciples of All Nations

Matt 28:19–20—*"Therefore go [participle] and* **make disciples***~ *of all nations, baptizing [participle] them in the name of the Father and the Son and the Holy Spirit, teaching them to obey everything I have commanded you."*

As Jesus departed the earth, He gave His five hundred disciples in Galilee this last command. In the previous verse, He stated, *"All authority has been given to Me in heaven and on earth"* (Matt 28:18). He could be relied on to facilitate the mission's accomplishment by guiding and empowering them to make disciples in more than twelve thousand people groups.

There is only one imperative in the Great Commission: *"Urgently decide to make disciples."* The command "means not only to learn, but to become attached to the teacher and be his follower in doctrine and conduct of life" (*Strong's Greek Lexicon*). It is used once more in the New Testament in Acts 14:21, *"when they had preached the gospel to that city and made many disciples,"* which ties together *"preached the gospel"* with *"made disciples"* as their core ministry.

The model of ministry was the life of Jesus Himself. They were to repeat for others what He had done for them. This is our problem today: very few people have been discipled by anyone, so they do not know how to do it for others. Now they pick up bad habits and have no one to correct them.

Three participles describe the process with imperatival force: going, baptizing, and teaching. First, *going* implies that the initiative to evangelize and make disciples is our responsibility. Anywhere there are no disciples, someone must go. No additional commands or "calls" are required. Second, *baptizing* means to unashamedly and publicly announce to the world that those who have accepted the gospel personally belong to Jesus and are committing to become disciples. Third, *teaching* means the commands are to be clarified and we are all accountable to obey them. This implies that we are to be exhorting, admonishing, and encouraging one another to obey the commands left for us by inspiration of the Spirit in the word.

About two thousand people groups remain totally unreached. The primary objective is to make at least some disciples among "all ethnic people" (*ethnos*). What will you do about this command?

"I praise You, dear Lord, that You have promised to be with us always as we step out by faith to take Your gospel to those who have not heard the message. We can go with the assurance that we can do what You have asked."

Deny Yourself, Take Up a Cross, and Follow Jesus

Mark 8:34—*"Then Jesus called the crowd, along with his disciples, and said to them, 'If anyone wants to become my follower, **he must deny himself** *~, **take up***~ **his cross, and follow**~~ **me.**'"*

Despite His popularity today, one has to wonder if anybody is listening to what Jesus said. We like a popular, loving, understanding, and forgiving Jesus. But when He began to talk about His own cross and the surrender of His life for the benefit of others, even Peter rebuked Him! (Mark 8:32). Peter did not sign up to follow someone who wanted to be crucified! He wanted glory, power, prestige, and control, not a cross. Jesus rebuked him sternly: *"Get behind Me, Satan! For you are not mindful of the things of God, but the things of men"* (8:33).

As the crowd gathered, Jesus made the cost of discipleship very clear: *"If anyone wants to become my follower, he must immediately decide to deny himself once and for all."* He was not just correcting Peter; he was talking to all His followers, for all time. He drew the line in the sand.

First, if you are going to follow Christ, you must decide once and for all not to pay attention to yourself, to give up self-interest, and, in effect, to go against your pride or profit. Ouch! When have you given up something for Christ? Paul wrote, *"Such things that once were gains to me these have I counted loss for Christ"* (Phil 3:7).

Second, it was necessary for a disciple to *"take up his cross."* The condemned man was forced to carry his own cross to his execution, as Jesus did. But what the convict did under obligation, the disciple of Christ does willingly. He willingly accepts the hurt, embarrassment, shame, and persecution that inevitably will be his lot if he remains loyal to Jesus.

Third, he must *"keep on continually following [Jesus]."* This means that as Jesus *"suffered for us, leaving us an example, we should follow His steps"* (1 Pet 2:21), especially by obeying His commands (Jn 15:14).

These three actions indicate a true conversion and why the power and filling of the Spirit is indispensable. Will you give up your life to follow Christ?

"Heavenly Father, following You means I must be willing to give up things, people, or places I may think I need. But I know that, with Your help, I can do whatever You ask me to do and there will be joy in doing it. Thank You."

JULY 29

Be Salty and Be at Peace with Each Other

Mark 9:50—*"Salt is good, but if it loses its saltiness, how can you make it salty again? **Have**~~ **salt** in yourselves, and **be at peace**~~ **with each other.**"*

Salt is an indispensable requirement for the body. It is both a tasty condiment and a preservative for food. Jesus told his disciples, *"You are the salt of the earth"* (Matt 5:13). They were to be the life-sustaining element in a dying world that would attract people to the gospel, and they were to be a preservative in a rotting world of sin.

Salt in Israel came from the area southwest of the Dead (or Salt) Sea. This coarse, impure salt from the saline deposits in the shallows of the sea would deteriorate, leaving a residue of tasteless crystals that were of no value to anyone.

Jesus commanded the disciples to "continuously maintain your saltiness in yourselves"—that is, their usefulness to God's purpose in the world. In the preceding text, Jesus had been talking about the characteristics of a disciple. The metaphor refers to the elements of true discipleship: obedience, self-denial, humility, purity, and a willingness to suffer for the kingdom. Such disciples would keep their communities from corruption. As God purified them through the Spirit's conviction of sin (Jn 16:8) and they recognized the need for personal repentance, they kept their saltiness (i.e., usefulness) for God.

Their "salty" impact on society would generate *"peace with each other."* If the disciples had kept the salt fresh in themselves, they would not have been arguing about who would be the greatest in Christ's kingdom (Mark 9:34). Each was lusting to be more important than the other (10:35–45). They were losing their saltiness. Soon the responsibility of world evangelism would be placed in their hands, so peace among them was vital (Col 3:15). To maintain their team spirit and bond of unity, Paul encouraged Christians to *"let your conversation be always full of grace, seasoned with salt"* (4:6). We are to keep each other submissive to His word.

Has sin corrupted your saltiness? Has your self-interest made you disinterested in transforming others? Can you be graciously confrontational?

"Dear Lord, just as salt is only useful if it tastes good or preserves food, I can only be useful to You if I possess the elements of a disciple. Help me be obedi-ent, humble, pure, and willing to do whatever it takes to fulfill Your purpose."

JULY 30

Bless Those Who Curse You

Luke 6:27–28—*"But I say to you who are listening:* **Love~~ your enemies, do good~~ to those who hate you, bless~~ those who curse you, pray~~ for those who mistreat you.**"

God has always wanted His people to stand out as a unique people, not blend in unperceived with the unsaved Gentile world.

This sevenfold description of our obligation to love others shows the characteristics of our heavenly Father (Luke 6:35: *"For He is kind to the unthankful and evil"*). We are expected to reflect the character and attitudes of our God and Savior. Of course, this is possible only by the power of the Spirit as He manifests the presence of God. This is how He is glorified.

Jesus begins by addressing *"you who are listening."* They were all hearing, but not all were listening. First, you are to *"continually be loving your enemies."* This is not an emotional love or a friendly love. It is *agape* love: a decision to sacrifice for the benefit of others regardless of your feelings toward them.

Second, you are to *"do good to those who hate you,"* which amplifies how we are to love our enemies. *Good* means "excellent, appropriate, [or] beneficial."

Third, God says, *"bless those who curse you,"* which means to "speak well of" anyone who "curses" or speaks poorly of you, seeking to damage you.

Fourth, you are to *"be continually praying for those who mistreat you."* You must forgive them and pray that God will clarify to them the gospel's value.

The fifth through seventh commands are not to retaliate (Luke 6:29a), to give freely (6:29b–30), and to treat others they way we would want to be treated (6:31). Jesus's love is unique from the world's (6:32–33). His followers stand out because they care for everyone. Do you really want to be a follower of Jesus? It is costly, but He gives us His grace to do it.

"Merciful God, Thank You for providing a way to forgive and cleanse me of my sinfulness. I want to be willing to love those who hate me because of You and Your message so they may have a chance to know You also."

JULY 31
Listen and Understand

Mark 7:14—*"Then he called the crowd again and said to them, '**Listen~~ to me**, everyone, and **understand~~**."*

Jesus was not just teaching a subject matter; He was communicating truths about life and eternity. His information was urgent, but all too often his hearers only gave Him halfhearted attention.

The first command in Mark 7:14 is to *"continually be listening to me."* This means not just hearing but also giving "special attention to hear with the ear of the mind" (Zodhiates, #191). The elements of the truth must be clear before the dots can be connected.

The second command is to *"understand"* what He was saying. It means to "put it together, comprehend, assembling individual facts into an organized whole." What a perfect definition for inductive Bible study! Jesus was amazed at the lack of skill in his disciples.

Jesus said, *"If anyone has ears to hear, let him hear!"* (Mark 7:16). When He took His disciples to a place apart, He asked them in amazement, *"Then do you also fail to understand?"* They were so blinded by their tradition, prejudices, and preconceived ideas that Jesus's teachings did not fit into any slot in their worldview.

After fifteen or twenty years, the Spirit began to inspire the apostles and prophets to write down Jesus's teachings. He had promised that they would accurately remember them. (Jn 14:26). We can examine the text, analyze the meaning of the verb tenses and definitions, and compare similar verses throughout the New Testament and Old Testament to grasp the inductive meaning of the teachings.

It still takes effort and determination to "understand" exactly what Jesus and the apostles meant (*"By faith we understand"*; Heb 11:3). We must investigate it (*"For we do not write you anything other than what you can read and also understand. But I hope that you will understand completely"*; 2 Cor 1:13). Are you a listener who wants to understand the meaning and implications? How much does your Bible study change your attitudes and purpose in life?

"Dear Lord, You have told us all we need to know about this life and about eternity. Help me have 'ears to hear' Your message and to be ready to teach others who also want to hear."

AUGUST 1

Stand Firm, Show Courage, and Be Strong

1 Cor 16:13—*"Stay alert ~~, stand firm~~ in the faith, show courage ~~, be strong~~."*

As Paul concluded his Epistle to the Corinthians, he gave the Corinthians their final orders. Paul warned the elders he met in Miletus, "*Take heed to yourselves and to all the flock . . . to shepherd the church of God which He purchased with His own blood*" (Acts 20:28).

The first command in 1 Corinthians 16:13—"*be continually staying alert*," or "standing on your guard"—involves being diligent and discerning threats to the truth of the word. Some dangers are divisions (1 Cor 1:10–17; 11:18), pride (3:18–21), misuse of spiritual gifts and resulting disorder (14:40), and mistaken theology (15:12). When human reasoning and feelings have more control over our decisions and attitudes than the word, defeat is inevitable.

The second command is to "*be continually standing firm*," or "be true to what you believe." Paul wrote, "*I declare to you the gospel which I preached to you, which also you received and in which you stand, by which also you are saved, if you hold fast that word which I preached to you unless you believed in vain*" (1 Cor 15:1–2). The Corinthians, like the Ephesians, were being "*carried about by every wind of doctrine*" (Eph 4:14). Because they did not want to appear dogmatic, bigoted, or egotistical, they did not stand for anything. We must evaluate everything by scriptural truths and standards so that we "*may stand perfect and fully assured in all the will of God*" (Col 4:12).

The third command is to "*show courage*," or "be brave," meaning to "act like a man." Paul told the Corinthians, "*Do not be children in your thinking; yet in evil be babes*" (1 Cor 14:20; 3:1–2). Maturity comes by obeying the word (2 Tim 3:16–17).

The fourth command—"*continually be made strong*"—only appears in the passive in the New Testament; that is, it is something that is done to us, the filling of the Spirit. As we trust what God commands and begin to obey, no matter the cost, we become "*strengthened with power through His Spirit in the inner man*" (Eph 3:16). It happens only if we obey. Are you willing to commit to serious obedience?

"Lord, it is not weakness but selfish and indulgent thoughts that cause me to give in to temptation. You tell me such thoughts are harmful; why don't I believe You all the time? Deepen my convictions to follow Your word faithfully."

AUGUST 2
Treat Disciples with Respect

1 Cor 16:10–11—*"Now if Timothy comes, see that **he has nothing to fear**~~ among you, for he is doing the Lord's work, as I am too. So then, let no one treat him with contempt. But send him on his way in peace so that he may come to me. For I am expecting him with the brothers."*

Mentoring is the next step beyond discipleship. Paul wanted all churches to learn how to treat young servants of God.

The command in 1 Corinthians 16:10–11 is not just for Timothy. It is given to demonstrate to us how to treat those who teach us God's word. Timothy and Erastus were sent to Macedonia (Acts 19:22) while Paul remained in Asia.

Timothy had a reputation of being "well spoken of" by other Christians (Acts 16:2–3), and Paul sent him to Philippi with this commendation: *"I have no one like-minded, who will sincerely care for your state . . . you know his proven character"* (Phil 2:20–22).

Paul gives three commands to the Corinthian church concerning helping young ministers. First, the verb means they were to make sure Timothy was "unafraid of what might happen" to him or was "put at complete ease." Timothy was worthy of honor.

Second, no one was to *"treat him with contempt,"* which means "to treat with scorn." He should never be treated as a nobody.

Third, they were to *"send him on his way,"* which means "to fit him out with the requisites for a journey." He was to be sent back to Paul "in peace." John wrote about how to treat those with itinerating or missionary ministries, saying, *"If you send them forward on their journey in a manner worthy of God, you will do well, because they went forth for His name's sake"* (2 Jn 5–7). They were to be honored for the sake of the ministry.

Paul always served in a team effort, considering the others just as essential to the mission as he was. For example, he called Epaphroditus *"my brother, and fellow worker and fellow soldier, who is also your messenger and minister to my need"* (Phil 2:25). The ministry is a team effort, not of one or two, but of all coworkers. Do you build up the value of all your coworkers?

"Lord, teach me not to be critical or intimidating but to be a blessing to all who serve You with their lives. May all Your servants feel appreciated and encouraged because I bless them as I would bless You."

<hr>

AUGUST 3

Dwell in the Word of God

Col 3:16—*"Let the word of Christ dwell~~ in you* richly, teaching and exhorting one another with all wisdom, singing psalms, hymns, and spiritual songs, all with grace in your hearts to God."*

Whatever dominates our thoughts and values controls our lives. Our thoughts should be filled with the *"word of Christ"*—that is, the teachings of Jesus (Matt 28:20), which includes all the commands Jesus taught to His disciples and all the Spirit taught the apostles and prophets after Jesus's ascension, which are recorded in the New Testament.

In Colossians 3:16, we are told to let all that God has revealed to us through Christ and His Spirit to *"be continually or habitually dwelling"* in us (or lit. "to live in, or be at home with" us). We are to be comfortable with the instructions and commands of Scripture. Paul commanded Timothy to *"hold on to the pattern of wholesome teaching you learned from me"* (2 Tim 1:13[NLT]). We are to learn His word and graft it onto our being.

The adverb *richly* is added. It means "abundantly or exceedingly," almost an exaggerated form. All our values and guiding principles of life are to come from biblical directives.

The more richly our minds are saturated with the word of God, the more the Spirit can lead us to do His will, if we want Him to do what He says. In this way, as we mature in the word and it fills us, we become equipped to teach and exhort others.

Two specific consequences are inevitable: *"teaching and exhorting one another with all wisdom."* Earlier, Paul defined the nature and goal of his ministry: *"[Jesus] we preach, warning every man and teaching every man in all wisdom, that we may present every man perfect in Christ Jesus"* (Col 1:28). Paul took responsibility for the maturity of his disciples by warning (or admonishing) them and teaching them the wisdom of God in His word.

The sign that this content has filled our minds and hearts is the emotional response evident in *"psalms and hymns and spiritual songs, with all grace [or thankfulness] in your hearts to God."* This is singing that is full of Scripture and sung in the heart to God for the joy of knowing Him through His word.

"Lord, Your word is so full of meaning and insights that it is my daily delight. Because I cannot remember it all, I will refresh my mind and heart every day with Your wisdom and truths."

AUGUST 4
Examin All Things

1 Thes 5:21—*"But **examine**~~ all things; hold fast~~ to what is good."*

Christ is the head of the church (Eph 5:23), and the church is subject to Christ (5:24)—but how does this work in practical life? What is spoken under the revelation and inspiration of God's Spirit is to be taken as if from God Himself and must be subjected to great scrutiny.

In 1 Thessalonians 5:21, the command to "continue to examine" means to "test for authenticity, put it to the proof." God's followers must distinguish between divine truth and error. In this context, *"all things"* refers to anything claimed to be the word of God. The church at Berea was notable: *"They received the word with all readiness, and searched the Scriptures daily to find out whether these things were so"* (Acts 17:11).

We must ask ourselves if a teaching agrees with what God has already revealed; there must be no contradictions in Scripture or with God. It is the listener's task to make sure that what he hears fits with what God says. Prophets in the early church were limited, and what was spoken had to be examined: *"Two or three prophets should speak and the others should evaluate what was said"* (1 Cor 14:29).

The apostles and their prophetic associates were the unique recipients of divine revelation, which they proclaimed and/or recorded under inspiration. They gave us the *"foundation"* for the church (Eph 2:20). Anyone who gave a prophecy that was not fulfilled was a false prophet. In the Old Testament, this is very serious: *"The prophet who presumes to speak a word in My name, which I have not commanded him to speak, . . . that prophet shall die"* (Deut 18:20). All that deviates from the Bible's text is prompted by *"deceiving spirits"* or demons (1 Tim 4:1). This is how false teaching invades the church and causes division.

On the other hand, we are to *"hold fast"* (Gr. *katecho*), or "to embrace wholeheartedly, or take possession of," the teachings that are "good" (Gr. *kalos*), "genuine, or right," or faithful to all God has already revealed.

The only deterrent to false prophecy is for believers to know well the written word of God and to reject error. Are you testing what you hear by always asking, "Does God's word support this?"

"Father, there are so many contrary views in this world; deepen my conviction in the certainty of Your truth and deepen my understanding of its truths so I may not be swayed by error."

AUGUST 5

Take Care of What You Hear from God's Word

Mark 4:24—*"And he said to them, 'Take care~~ about what you hear. The measure you use will be the measure you receive, and more will be added to you.'"*

When a person exercises consistently, he will grow stronger and stay healthy. Similarly, if we exercise our minds, our thinking and learning processes will improve. We must carefully choose the content of what we listen to because it will mold our thought processes.

The command in Mark 4:24 is to *"continually be taking care,"* or "to watch, examine, [and] notice carefully," with continual attention *"about what you hear."* A person who hears only false teachings or speculations will eventually deviate from the truth. Essentially, human beings tend to conform their thinking to what they are continually exposed to.

In the previous verses, Jesus had given the parable of the sower, describing the differing degrees of response to specific environments. The hearers were listening to different sources that affected their spirits, causing either obedience or resistance to the word.

Following this, Jesus gave a general, unbreakable principle: *"The measure you use will be the measure you receive"* (*"if anyone has ears to hear [i.e., is willing to obey], he had better listen!"*; Mark 4:23). He who listens well, understands, and remains open to obeying Jesus receives more understanding and insights.

This concept is the principle of reciprocity reiterated in Luke 8:18. The more judgmental we are of others, the more we will be judged (Matt 7:2). The more generous we are, the more God eventually returns generously to us (Luke 6:38). The more care we give to hearing, understanding, and properly responding to His commands, the more we will be given to understand and the richer our lives will become. However, if we do not take care to hear and understand His word, what little understanding we had will be lost (Mark 4:25). We will lose interest in pursuing the wisdom of God. If you read (or listen to) this study of the commands with care, you are going in the right direction. Listen to know how to obey His instructions.

"Lord Jesus, with all my heart I want Your word to be my guide through life. In a hundred ways every day, I long to live out Your precepts and insights. Help me to do so."

AUGUST 6

Be Quick to Listen, Slow to Speak, and Slow to Anger

James 1:19—*"Understand this, my dear brothers and sisters!* **Let every person be** ~~ **quick to listen**, *slow to speak, slow to anger."*

The transformed life becomes evident as the believer responds to the instructions revealed in God's word (James 1:19–27). The word is the source of our new life: *"He brought us forth by the word of truth"* (1:18a), and *"faith comes by hearing, and hearing by the Word of God"* (Rom 10:17). A true disciple of Jesus has a deep desire to know and obey God as He is revealed in God's word: *"If you abide in My Word, then you are truly disciples of Mine"* (Jn 8:31).

James heard Jesus teach many times. *"To you it has been granted to know the mysteries of the kingdom of heaven"* (Matt 3:11). What a privilege! True believers *"rejoice in [God's] testimonies [i.e., precepts or commands], as much as in all riches"* (Psa 119:14). Think about these three short commands in James 1:19 as the *"Word implanted"* (James 1:21).

First, we should *"be quick to listen."* Be a good listener who runs toward someone to get it right. Focus on learning, comparing Scripture with Scripture, and being open to personal application. Remember Proverbs 6:33: *"If you love to listen you will gain knowledge, and if you incline your ear you will become wise."*

Second, we should be *"slow to speak."* Take your time and think about what you say. You cannot learn while talking. Remember Proverbs 5:11, *"Be quick to hear, and be deliberate in answering,"* and Proverbs 29:20, *"Do you see a man hasty in his words? There is more hope for a fool than for him."* Be more focused on getting it right than on how to answer or argue a point.

Third, be *"slow to anger."* The word for *anger*, or *wrath*, means a "deep resentment boiling within." In this context, it refers to being angry at a truth in God's word: *"Be not quick to anger, for anger lies in the bosom of fools"* (Eccl 7:9). Allow God's word to expose sinful selfishness without getting angry: *"So have I become your enemy by telling you the truth?"* (Gal 4:16). May God's word continually humble us as we willingly submit to it.

"Lord, why do I want to talk so much and impress others with my ideas and opinions? At the same time, I don't listen to others because I want to tell them what I think. Am I so full of myself that I miss what You are trying to teach me? Help me listen to Your word."

AUGUST 7

Remember to Obey

Luke 17:32—*"Remember~~ Lot's wife!"*

Luke speaks of Lot's wife, who could not resist the attractions of Sodom and Gomorrah (Gen 19:26). The command in Luke 17:32 is to *"remember,"* or "bear in mind," this Old Testament story.

Paul describes the reason these Old Testament stories were recorded: *"Now all these things happened to them as examples, and they were written for our admonition, upon whom the ends of the ages have come"* (1 Cor 10:11). The angels warned Lot, who then attempted to save others, but no one believed him; they refused to leave the place of their pleasure and perversion until it was too late. The angels also warned Lot and his family not to look back at the city (Gen 19:17), *"but Lot's wife looked back, and she became a pillar of salt"* (19:26).

What was so bad about Lot's wife looking back at Sodom? Perhaps she did not take seriously the command not to look back: too many fail to take the commands of the New Testament seriously because they believe there will be no consequences. Perhaps she was missing something in the city and clinging to the past, unwilling to completely abandon the evil of the city and the comforts of her possessions.

In any case, it is apparent that she was more anxious about the things she was losing than the blessing she was gaining by being saved. She surely was *"setting her affections on things below, instead of on things above"* (Col 3:1).

However innocent it may seem, it was a disobedient look. Anyone who refuses to admit his sin and indulges in prohibited things only defiles his own heart. Though Eve's eating of the prohibited fruit might be thought of as a slight offense, it corrupted the whole world. Should this not warn us to take His commands seriously?

Luke 17:33 summarizes the main command Lot's wife violated: *"Whoever seeks to save his life will lose it, and whoever loses his life will preserve it."* Compromising by being disobedient is an effort to save a part of your old life that you decide is more important to you than being obedient to even "insignificant" commands.

"Lord Jesus, when I do not focus my mind on You and my life with You forever, I sometimes want to look back. How foolish! Forgive me even for the thought. Nothing compares with what I have in You. Thank You, Lord."

AUGUST 8

Understand the Importance of Being Ready

Matt 24:43—*"But **understand**~~ this: If the owner of the house had known at what time of night the thief was coming, he would have been alert and would not have let his house be broken into."*

In Matthew 24:43, Jesus commands his disciples to "understand," or have the knowledge of this reality and prepare. The context of this command is Jesus's teaching on the second coming of Christ, with the emphasis on the suddenness of His coming and the impossibility of preparing (1 Thes 5:2; 2 Pet 3:10; Rev 3:3; 16:15).

Christ will return at the end of the seven-year tribulation period. In an instant, He will take away or destroy everything that unbelievers hold precious, bringing an end to the world's most devastating period in all history.

In His mercy, Jesus warns the unbeliever to be ready by accepting Him as Savior. Jesus warned His believers to be ready at all times. The same principle applies to those who are awaiting the Rapture, which will occur so quickly there will be no time to prepare once it starts: *"For you yourselves know perfectly that the day of the Lord so comes as a thief in the night"* (1 Thes 5:2). Jesus's coming will be unexpected and surprising, just as the entrance of a thief. No one can even guess when He will appear. Believers must be constantly prepared, because *"the Son of Man is coming at an hour when you do not think He will"* (Matt 24:44).

Jesus describes the *"faithful and sensible slave"* whom the master finds alert and occupied with the *"charge of feeding the entire household"* (Matt 24:45)— that is, he is found being responsible for priorities. Every believer is given a responsibility to be a steward of his life, strength, talents, spiritual gifts, and circumstances, which are to be used for Christ's purposes and glory: *"Blessed is that slave whom his master finds so doing when he comes"* (24:46).

There is no way of measuring the significance of the "blessedness" that will result from being occupied in God's purposes in the world when the King arrives. Such a person does not have to be told what to do; he just knows what the King wants done and never wastes time in meaningless pursuits. Our only goal in life is for Jesus to interrupt us in the midst of activities for His kingdom.

"Lord, You are coming soon. Everything points to Your prompt return. Help me to always ask, 'Do I want my Lord to come and find me doing this?' I want to live for You today."

AUGUST 9

Be Careful of How You Live

Eph 5:15–16—*"Therefore **be very careful**~~ **how you live**—not as unwise but as wise, taking advantage of every opportunity, because the days are evil."*

Foolishness is not just silliness or making poor decisions. The *"unwise"* or "fool" is a person with a self-centered mind-set, a character deficiency. Believers should learn to identify the symptoms in order not to imitate them. The longer a fool practices his foolishness, the more permanent his destructive character becomes. Eventually, he persuades others to follow him.

"The fool says in his heart that there is no God" (Psa 14:1), and he sets himself up as his own god and *"mock[s] at sin"* (Prov 14:9). Because he does not recognize God, he does not recognize sin in his own life. Believers, however, are to live as *"children of light"* (Eph 5:8), exposing evil. They are to be *"acceptable to God"* (5:10) by reflecting Christ's attributes and attracting others to Him.

The command to *"be very careful"* means to be intentionally obedient. Wisdom living is the exact opposite of the fool's lifestyle, as we "imitate God" (Eph 5:1) and walk in humility, unity with the believers, separation from sin, love toward all, and light of His Word (4:1–5:14): *"You have known the sacred writings which are able to give you the wisdom that leads to salvation through faith which is in Christ Jesus"* (2 Tim 3:15). *"In all wisdom and insight [God] made known to us the mystery of His will"* (Eph 1:8–9); even Jesus *"kept increasing in wisdom"* (Luke 2:52).

When Christians fall into Satan's traps, it is because they choose to be *"unwise,"* or "without wisdom": *"We also once were foolish ourselves, disobedient, deceived, enslaved to various lusts and pleasures, spending our life in malice and envy, hateful, hating one another"* (Titus 3:3).

We cannot waste time. Only the wise see how to make the most of it, especially in times that are *"evil,"* or full of "wickedness or moral corruption." Do you believe wise living is best?

"Father, my daily life is so full of my activities, fun, and plans that sometimes I miss the moments You provide to speak a word for You or to serve someone You want to touch through me. Keep me alert today to see Your hand in my life."

AUGUST 10
Do Not Be Foolish

Eph 5:17—*"For this reason **do not be~/ foolish**, but be wise by understanding what the Lord's will is."*

The world's wisdom is often foolish to God. Ephesians 5:17 presumes we know what a fool is and tells us to *"stop being foolish."* How can we recognize the characteristics of a fool?

• A fool **gossips about others**: *"Hiding hatred makes you a liar; slandering others makes you a fool"* (Prov 10:18[NLT]).

• A fool has **no control over his anger**: *"A fool is quick-tempered, but a wise person stays calm when insulted"* (Prov 12:16[NLT])

• A fool **refuses to respond positively to commands,** preferring to do things his way: *"The wise in heart accept commands, but a chattering fool comes to ruin"* (Prov 10:8[TNIV]).

• A fool **can't be told to do anything** because he has never had to be obedient. This leads him to hate his father's correction. Perhaps the fool's father thought being kind and loving would make his son a friend, but his son's foolishness makes his father an enemy (Prov 15:5).

• A fool **loves to break the rules**. Being obedient seems boring to him: *"Doing wrong is fun for a fool, but living wisely brings pleasure to the sensible"* (Prov 10:23[NLT]).

• A fool **has no fear of risk and is overconfident** about his abilities. He manipulates followers, whom he controls by the fear of his wrath: *"A wise man fears and departs from evil, but a fool rages and is self-confident"* (Prov 14:16).

We must identify all these characteristics and root them out of our hearts and lives. Then we must help others who give in to foolish behavior.

The second command in this verse is to *"be continually being wise by understanding what the Lord's will is."* The measure of our willingness to be wise is evident in our determination to master His commands and be eager to put them in practice.

"Lord, the more I learn about fools in the Bible, the more I see those traits in myself. I never knew how much pride twisted my thinking in so many ways. Teach me Your ways to think and live."

Hold on to the
Traditions You Were Taught

2 Thes 2:15—*"Therefore, brothers and sisters, **stand firm**~~ **and hold on**~~ **to the traditions** that we taught you, whether by speech or by letter."*

There is no greater privilege than to join with Christ in giving our lives to benefit those who may hate us. As we share Christ, we make clear *"the glory of our Lord Jesus Christ"* (2 Thes 2:14). The victory is won. Those who stand with Christ can rest assured, for *"God has not destined us for wrath, but for obtaining salvation through our Lord Jesus Christ"* (1 Thes 5:9).

With the promise of a shared glory and full assurance, Paul exhorts the believer to *"be continually standing firm,"* or *"to persevere, or be faithful no matter what."* Paul's disciples would face severe pressure from persecution, false teachers, temptations, discouragement, and apathy. It might cost them everything, as it did Paul.

They were to *"continually be holding on,"* or *"grasp with all your strength."* The meaning is "keep in mind, give power or rule to" the teachings. Believers always need to be encouraged and exhorted (1 Cor 15:58; 16:13; Eph 6:11, 13, 14; Phil 4:1) not to be weak or vacillating but to continue to follow Paul's example and commands.

Believers were to follow the *"traditions that we taught,"* or "teaching or commandments handed down." They were to obey them *"just as [Paul] delivered them"* (1 Cor 11:2). Paul is referring to divine revelation (2 Thes 3:6; 1 Cor 11:2), especially during the period of the church age before these revelations had been written down under the inspiration of the Holy Spirit. This would be called the "oral tradition," carefully differentiated from the "tradition of the elders," or the practices of the early church leaders.

However, this is not the message of this passage. The Thessalonians were to hold fast to what God had revealed through the apostles as in Acts 2:42, where they met to *"persevere in the doctrines of the Apostles."* Believers must refresh and obey the *"faith which was once for all handed down to the saints"* (Jude 3), which was *"committed to their trust"* (1 Tim 6:20). We are to obey by the power of the *"Spirit who dwells within"* (2 Tim 1:14). Today, renew your commitment to obey the Scriptures.

"Lord, teach me to distinguish between man's legalistic traditions and biblical traditions that Your commands teach us. I love Your instructions; Help me remember them today to honor You."

Continue in the Things You Have Learned

2 Tim 3:14—*"You, however, **must continue**~~ **in the things you have learned** and are confident about. You know who taught you."*

Throughout the ages, there have always been enemies to the faith, both within and outside of the gatherings of believers. Jesus warned, *"The evil one comes and snatches away the good seed of the Word that had been sown in the heart of a hearer"* (Matt 13:19). Satan does this by creating doubts and substituting false teachings.

"Imposters" (Gk. "wailers, howlers," such as sorcerers) are those who pretend to be spiritual with magical powers, deceive by performing phenomena, and attack followers, causing them to abandon practical teachings for the miraculous. Sadly, the undiscerning Christian public will continue to be deceived (2 Tim 3:13). Imposters' claims of new revelations, inexplicable signs, phenomena, and claims of unusual powers distract hearers from the word of God.

Timothy is *commanded to "continue in the things [he has] learned"* (Gk. "abide, or remain.") *Learned* comes from the root word for *disciple.* Timothy had been discipled in the scriptural commands and had become "confident about" the Scriptures as truths that are not to be compromised, diluted, ignored, or superseded.

The last phrase is *"You know who taught you."* Biblical teaching must be evident in the teacher first, making it meaningful and able to be imitated. The word *who* is plural: Timothy had numerous mentors, and all taught the same principles and consistently lived out the commands of Scripture. Symptoms of false teachers are those who always seek something new and "fresh" and speak condescendingly of the "old" revelations in Scripture.

Timothy's early childhood training laid the groundwork for a life of obedience and godliness, from which he never deviated. His learning increased through the years, reinforcing and deepening the values of the principles and commands. Paul laid the validity of his doctrine not only on the clear teachings of Scripture but also on the transformed lives of followers like Timothy.

Rather than seeking the sensational or emotional, will you commit to never be distracted from learning to apply the inspired word of God to your life?

"Lord, You told us how important Your commands are for us, but we forget them so easily. Help me devise a plan for remembering them and for being accountable to someone to obey them today."

Bear with Exhortations

Heb 13:22—*"Now I urge you, brothers and sisters, **bear~~ with my message** of exhortation, for in fact I have written to you briefly."*

Proverbs teaches us to love instruction, correction, and even chastisement because the end result is greater wisdom with all its benefits. The word for *bear* means "to endure, have patience with," and "listen to with care." Paul foretold the time when men would not want to hear the truth of God's word: *"For the time will come when people will not put up with sound doctrine. Instead, to suit their own desires, they will gather around them a great number of teachers to say what their itching ears want to hear. They will turn their ears away from the truth and turn aside to myths"* (2 Tim 4:3–4[NIV]). Believers should practice *bearing*, or patience, in these situations:

1. **Bear with persecution.** *"Being reviled, we bless; being persecuted, we endure"* (1 Cor 4:12); *"We proudly tell God's other churches about your endurance and faithfulness in all the persecutions and hardships you are suffering"* (2 Thes 1:4[NLT]).

2. **Bear with each other.** *"With all lowliness and gentleness, with longsuffering, [bear] with one another in love"* (Eph 4:2), especially with another's mistakes: *"Make allowance for each other's faults, and forgive anyone who offends you. Remember, the Lord forgave you, so you must forgive others"* (Col 3:13[NLT]).

3. ***"Bear with"* or "be open to" exhortations and admonishments from others.** A symptom of an immature believer is an unwillingness to accept moral instruction: *"I fed you with milk and not with solid food; for until now you were not able to receive it, and even now you are still not able"* (1 Cor 3:2).

Whether parents like it or not, they must correct their children: *"Discipline your children, and they will give you peace of mind and will make your heart glad"* (Prov 29:17[NLT])

The *"word [or message] of exhortation"* also appears in Acts 13:15 Are you open to personal application of the Scripture? Be honest with yourself: how much do you want to be instructed to be obedient.

"Lord, my pride is so evident when someone tries to correct me or encourage me to do something You want me to do. Humble me, Lord, to hear Your voice through friends and leaders who care about my spiritual growth."

AUGUST 14
Awake from Your Sleep

Eph 5:14—*"For everything made evident is light, and for this reason it says: 'Awake*~, O sleeper! Rise*~ from the dead, and Christ will shine on you!'"*

Paul explained that all believers at one time were abiding in darkness and had become as *"darkness"* (Eph 5:8a). Now that they had come to the Light, they had become as *"light"* (5:8b), able to see *"what is acceptable to the Lord"* (5:10). Likewise, now that they could see, they were to avoid all forms of darkness; in fact, they were expected to expose such darkness (5:11).

The unsaved have no idea how *"shameful"* their actions (Eph 5:12) are before a holy God. They delight in living *"in secret,"* but believers are to have nothing to do with these *"unfruitful works of darkness"* (5:11).

The light of God's word exposes perverse, vile, and repugnant sinners. How He could ever love us is amazing. He sent His Holy Spirit to *"convict the world of sin"* (Jn 16:8) so that sinners could recognize their true condition and their desperate need for a Savior (Gal 3:24). In spite of how He feels about our sin He loves us..

Paul described his awareness of his sin through the Ten Commandments: *"I was alive once without the law, but when the commandment came, sin revived and I died"* (Rom 7:9). This is what happens when *"all things that are exposed are made manifest by the light"* (Eph 5:13). This preconversion work of the Spirit leads a person to understand he is lost, desperately in need of the Savior, and without any personal goodness to merit salvation.

In Ephesians 5:14, Paul shouts to the world, *"Awake, O sleeper! Rise from the dead."* The metaphor shifts from the darkness of sin to the spiritual deadness of the sinner. The command is a call to repent and turn away from a naïve belief in your own personal goodness or false security of a religion and to trust exclusively in Christ and depend solely on His death as full satisfaction for the payment of sin's debt.

If you trust in Him, *"Christ will shine on you."* Your sins will be forgiven and replaced with the incredible gift of His righteousness. This alone makes us acceptable to God. Call out to the unsaved *"sleeper"* and tell him to wake up to the truth of the gospel. When was the last time you shared the good news of Christ's redemption with a sinner?

"Lord, why are so many of us asleep concerning Your kingdom purpose? Are we so full of our plans that Your plans are crowded out? Make this day count for You."

AUGUST 15

Be Devoted to Prayer

Col 4:2—**"Be devoted ~~to prayer**, *keeping alert in it with thanksgiving."*

For many believers, prayer is a last resort. When all is lost and only a miracle will suffice, we pray. Sometimes this is called a "foxhole prayer."

We have a choice in life: we can attempt to do things on our own or we can join in partnership with God, petitioning His involvement in all that is done for His honor and glory. After all, one of Jesus's last declarations was, *"All authority has been given to Me in heaven and on earth"* (Matt 28:18). If anyone is worth being close to, it is the One who has the authority to do anything He wishes.

Paul began this Letter to the Colossians with prayer, and in Colossians 4:2 he concludes with a command for believers to pray for others. Prayer is the core of the believer's communion with Christ and the source of his power against Satan's demonic forces (Eph 6:18). The command is to *"be continually and habitually devoted to prayer,"* meaning "to endure, cleave faithfully to, or stay close to" the action of prayer.

"Pray at all times" (Eph 6:18) *"without ceasing"* (1 Thes 5:17); *"contin[ue] steadfast in prayer"* (Rom 12:12). The foundation of a balanced ministry is being *"devoted to prayer and the ministry of the Word"* (Acts 6:4), the believer's lifeline to God.

To pray ceaselessly does not necessarily mean we should continually vocalize our prayers to God. Instead, we should share everything with our caring Savior, who *"lives forever to intercede with God on [our] behalf"* (Heb 7:25[NLT]). Jesus taught, *"At all times they ought to pray and not to give up"* (Luke 18:1–8). This attitude is founded on dependence on God and a determination to obey Him fully.

Paul said we should *"be continually keeping alert"* or "vigilant." Prayer should saturate every activity for God. Paul requested prayer because *"a great and effective door has opened to me, and there are many adversaries"* (1 Cor 16:9). We are to be conscious of the needs around us and bring them before the throne, always with *"thanksgiving"* for His powerful presence and willingness to answer prayers and accomplish His will on earth. Stay alert and pray!

"My Father, I confess that my prayers are more selfish than beneficial to anyone else. Teach me to believe that prayer is effective and You hear every thought or request directed to You, especially when praying for others."

AUGUST 16
Remain in Christ

Jn 15:4—*"Remain*~ in me, and I will remain in you. Just as the branch cannot bear fruit by itself, unless it remains in the vine, so neither can you unless you remain in me."*

Jesus is all about reproducing your obedience to Christ in other lives. Eight times in this chapter, John has presented Jesus as a gardener who desires fruit (Jn 15:2 [3x], 4, 5, 8, 16 [2x]). There is a progression in the development of this thought from bearing fruit (15:2), to being more fruitful (15:2), to bearing *"much fruit"* (15:5, 8).

Jesus declares Himself to be the *"true vine"* (John 15:1) into which branches are grafted. The life force in the trunk of the vine flows through the branches and produces the flowering, fragrant, and reproducing fruit from the Source of its life, the Spirit. The lesson of the metaphor is that the gardener's objective is to keep the branches that are bearing fruit, pruning or cleansing them to produce more fruit.

John shifts in 15:3 to a personal application, stating that they had *"already been cleansed by the word that I have spoken to you,"* and he uses the same word for *pruned* in 15:2. Because they had trusted in His word, they were cleansed and ready to bear fruit in their daily lives.

The meaning of the command is to *"once and for all immediately decide to remain in me."* Especially in John's writings, this refers to a relationship in which a person "stands with another . . . , and remains united with him, one with him in heart, mind and will" (Forest Wychopen, *"Abide in Christ,"* p.59). Jesus said to those Jews who had believed Him, *"If you abide in My word, you are My disciples indeed"* (Jn 8:31). Abiding implies more than a superficial acknowledgement of who Jesus is; rather, it is a commitment to bond to Christ forever, and it is far more intimate than marriage. It is a two-way relationship: You abide in Me, and I abide in You. Do you really want Christ in every aspect of your life? There is no privacy for one who abides in Christ.

Paul wrote of the fruitbearing, transforming nature of the new life: *"This same Good News that came to you is going out all over the world. It is bearing fruit everywhere by changing lives, just as it changed your lives from the day you first heard and understood the truth about God's wonderful grace"* (Col 1:6[NLT]). Has the gospel transformed your life? Those who abide in Christ are transformed and transform other lives by sharing the gospel with the lost of the world.

"My heart is filled with an everlasting peace and joy in Your presence. Help me to show how great You are to others. I never want to live without You."

AUGUST 17

Be Imitators of Paul

1 Cor 11:1—*"**Be imitators**~~ **of me**, just as I also am of Christ."*

Someone once said that everyone should be mentored by someone and likewise mentor someone else. Paul had lived with the Corinthians for eighteen months, founding their church and discipling the first believers. He was willing to pay any human price to bring people to Christ (1 Cor 9:19–23). They knew his commitment, and in 1 Corinthians 11:1 he calls them to follow his example.

When Paul wrote about doing *"all to the glory of God"* (1 Cor 10:31), they knew he lived to glorify God, not himself. They saw how he gave up his rights to eat and drink certain things so as not to offend different cultures or distract from the message of the gospel. If people were going to be upset, he wanted it be the offense of the gospel, not his own idiosyncrasies. They saw how he, like Jesus, *"emptied Himself, taking the form of a bond-servant"* and how he *"humbled Himself by becoming obedient to the point of death"* (Phil 2:7–8).

Paul considered it a vital part of Christian maturity to be a mentor, exemplifying the principles and commands of Christ. His goal was to seek the good in others—the basic concept of love. In this regard, Paul gave the command to *"imitate"* him. He wrote, *"For even if you had ten thousand others to teach you about Christ, you have only one spiritual father. For I became your father in Christ Jesus when I preached the Good News to you. So I ask you to follow my example and do as I do"* (1 Cor 4:14–16[NLT]).

Having a mentor was the norm for individuals and churches. To the Thessalonians he wrote, *"You became followers of us and of the Lord, having received the word in much affliction, with joy of the Holy Spirit, so that you became examples to all in Macedonia and Achaia who believe."* Paul lived daily to bring others to Christ, and every decision was made to facilitate this goal.

He was not being boastful or proud, because he knew he was not perfect—nor did he pretend to be (Phil 3:12). He was quick to admit his failures as he laid down the principles he was striving to live by (3:13). Paul took seriously the commands and teachings of Jesus, and this is the attitude he asked all believers to develop. Who is the leader in your life that most models Jesus's life?

"Lord, thank You for the godly leaders You have placed in my life. They challenge me to walk with You daily."

AUGUST 18
Be Imitators of God

Eph 5:1—*"Therefore, **be~~ imitators of God** as dearly loved children."*

A person's behavior betrays his view of God. If he thinks God has an indifferent attitude toward sin, he will adopt the same attitude. If he thinks God is critical and hard to please, he will be critical. If a man's god is himself, his narcissistic attitudes will be evident. The believer will generally follow the pattern of his concept of God.

Paul concluded chapter 4 with a series of commands based on God's nature. *Therefore*, refers back to the previous verses: *"Let all bitterness, wrath, anger, clamor, and evil speaking be put away from you, with all malice. And be kind to one another, tenderhearted, forgiving one another, even **as God in Christ** forgave you"* (Eph 4:31–32).

We are to forgive because God in Christ has forgiven us. Because forgiveness is the primary proof of God's love, it will also become the most convincing evidence of our love for others. Through the power of the indwelling Spirit, His nature is to become our nature and the pattern for our lives. To *"be continually being imitators of God"* means to be "followers or mimics." Earlier, Paul began his exhortations with the command to *"put on the new man, which was created **according to God**"* (Eph 4:24), that is, in the likeness of God's nature.

In Ephesians 5:2, we are told that imitating God means imitating Christ: *"Walk in love, as Christ also has loved us and given Himself for us."*

Because believers have been adopted into God's family (Eph 1:5), we should exhibit a family resemblance. It only makes sense that God's dearly loved child would want to become like his loving Father. Paul commands us to walk so closely with God that He imprints His nature on us.

God's purpose in bringing us salvation is twofold: to redeem us from sin and all its consequences and to conform us *"to the image of His Son"* (Rom 8:29). The blessed hope of the believer is this: *"We know that, when He appears, we shall be like Him, because we shall see Him just as He is"* (1 Jn 3:2). How much do you want to be like God?

"Lord Jesus, thank You for accepting me into Your family. Nothing will please me more than to be like You in all Your ways. Thank You for Your word, which shows me how to imitate You in my life."

AUGUST 19

Watch Those Who Live Like Paul

Phil 3:17—*"Be imitators~~ of me, brothers and sisters, and watch carefully~~ those who are living this way, just as you have us as an example."*

It is not easy living in a fishbowl. Paul did not pretend to be perfect—quite the contrary (Phil 3:12–14). He wanted all believers to join with him, as a struggling sinner, to constantly pursue the goal of becoming Christlike. If Paul had suggested he was perfect, he would not have been an example that others could follow.

In Philippians 3:17, when Paul commands us to *"continuously be imitators,"* he uses a word only found in this text. The prefixes give the meaning "to join together [as a community] in imitating" his life.

We need examples of leaders who are not perfect, who struggle to overcome temptations, imperfections, disappointments, hurts, failures, or disillusionments. How do they handle these problems? Paul was our example for godliness, overcoming the flesh and temptation, worshipping and sacrificial service to God, patience under persecution, contentment, financial management, and relationship building.

In this passage, Paul asks us to take the challenge of following future leaders. The Philippians were commanded to *"be continually and carefully watching those who are living this way, just as you have us as an example."* The Greek word for *watch* means to "mark, spy out, observe, or give attention to"; it comes from a word meaning the "goal-marker," or pacesetter, an athletic term referring to runners, as in 3:14. Paul is saying, *"Focus on those whose daily conduct is according to the correct pattern—the one you saw in us."* The plural *us* implies that Epaphroditus and Timothy were also examples, and probably the "bishops [or pastors] and deacons" (Phil 1:1) were included.

Leaders in the churches are to *"set [themselves as] an example of the believers in speech, in life, in love, in faith and in purity"* (1 Tim 4:12). Every church needs pacesetters in humility, unselfish service, willingness to suffer without complaint, exemplary devotion to Christ's purpose on earth, courage, and dedication to spiritual maturity. Those who teach and preach the word of God have a double responsibility: first, to know accurately what the Bible says, and second, to incorporate its principles and commands into their lives until their obedience becomes evident to all. Live to be an example.

"Lord, it is amazing to notice people who are like You. They demonstrate Your grace and wisdom in all they do and say. Please help to be like those who are so much like You as revealed in Your word."

Obey What Paul Commanded

Phil 4:9—*"And what you learned and received and heard and saw in me,* ***do~~ these things*** *And the God of peace will be with you."*

Paul had just written how godly thinking is essential to establish the believer emotionally and spiritually (Phil 4:8). Now in Phil 4:9, he describes principles for carrying godly thinking into a godly lifestyle. We have no hope of being established in the faith without a disciplined life of obedience to God's commands, ("be continually doing").

The listeners were commanded to "habitually do or practice" what they had learned of God's word. How do we know what to practice? A sole focus on doctrine often overlooks obedience. Paul said that "practice" was to be what his disciples learned, received, heard, and saw.

The word *learned* refers to "teaching, learning, instructing and discipling." Jesus said, "*[Teach] them to obey all things that I have commanded you*" (Matt 28:20). Preaching the truth is not enough. Disciples must understand and be held accountable to practice "all" the commands. Timothy was a learner: "*You followed my teaching, conduct, purpose, faith, patience, love, perseverance*" (2 Tim 3:10; 2:2).

The word *received* refers to an attitude of commitment both to practice and to pass along. Paul wrote to Timothy, "*The things which you have heard from me in the presence of many witnesses, entrust these to faithful men who will be able to teach others also*" (2 Tim 2:2).

They *heard* not only what God had revealed to Paul but how it transformed Paul's character and godly lifestyle. He intentionally lived by principles and commands that God had taught him so he could pass them on to others.

They *saw* Paul's lifestyle when he started the church and knew there was no gap between what he taught and how he lived; this is credibility.

If you practice such obedience, you are promised that "*the God of peace will be with you.*" All worry, and depression will be dissolved when you fill your mind and life with the practice of His commands and delight in His presence.

"Lord, why do I take Your word so lightly? Do I think I can get away with ignorance or neglect? Forgive me for not loving all You have commanded. Today I will search for a command to obey for You."

AUGUST 21
Obey Your Leaders and Submit to Them

Heb 13:17—*"Obey~~ your leaders and submit~~ to them,* *for they keep watch over your souls and will give an account for their work. Let them do [subjunctive] this with joy and not with complaints, for this would be no advantage for you."*

Leadership of God's people through the church is not for everyone. Those who had been honored with recognition as leaders of a congregation were to be remembered and their teachings followed: *"Remember those who rule over you, who have spoken the word of God to you, whose faith follow, considering the outcome of their conduct"* (Heb 13:7).

Leaders are selected with great scrutiny (1 Tim 3:1–7), and their priorities are clear: equip believers for the ministry (Eph 4:12) and teach the flock, helping them be obedient (1 Pet 5:2). Leaders are to preach, reprove, rebuke, exhort, and teach doctrine and obedience (2 Tim 4:2). However, their primary authority does not come from their position, because they are not allowed to "lord it over" their congregation (1 Pet 5:3). It is given to them because of their example.

To fulfill the purpose of the church cooperation is imperative: *"But we request of you, brethren, that you appreciate those who diligently labor among you, and have charge over you in the Lord and give you instruction, and that you esteem them very highly in love because of their work"* (1 Thes 5:12–13).

Hebrews 13:17 begins with the command to *"be continually obeying your leaders"* (Gk. "be persuaded to do something")—that is, as leaders teach the biblical principles, followers are to be persuaded or to yield to what is taught. Likewise, the plural command indicates that the church is to *"be continually being submissive"* (Gk. *hupeiko,* "to yield to someone's authority or to resist no longer"); thus the leaders can *"teach to obey"* (Matt 28:20) to a submissive, obedient church eager to practice the Scriptures.

Leaders must *"keep watch over your souls"* because they *"must give account"* to God, who will reward them for fulfilling their responsibility (1 Pet 5:4) of keeping Christ's church true to His word. Every gathering of the church should teach us how to be more obedient.

"Sometimes my leaders are hard to follow, but I trust You to have placed them in my life, so I will learn submission to them as if it were to You."

Receive Those Who Are Weak in the Faith

Rom 14:1—*"Now **receive~~** **the one who is weak** in the faith, and do not have disputes over differing opinions."*

Paul was meticulous in guiding believers to eliminate sinful practices: *"Let us cleanse ourselves from all defilement of flesh and spirit, perfecting holiness in the fear of God"* (2 Cor 7:1). However, flagrant sin is not the only danger to church life.

Many disputes are not about direct violations of a command, and godly believers might have different opinions on a number of topics. When there are no direct commands, the issue is not a question of sin, but preferences in how to apply a general principle. Wrong attitudes can cause division, rejection, a critical spirit, a rupture of peace, and the destruction of personal ministries. Legalistic beliefs that focus on external or physical issues can result in man-made rules that breed strife, false guilt, judgmental attitudes, and disharmony.

If the commands are not clarified, there can be a heritage of legalism; disputes about hairstyle, makeup, dress, Sunday activities, music style, and so on are symptoms of spiritual problems. Only by the application of biblical principles will the church find harmony.

A person is strong in the faith when he can mingle with unsaved friends without being influenced by them and instead have a positive influence on them. A person's faith is weak when he must avoid certain activities, people, or places so as not to be tempted to fall back into former sinful habits.

The command for the church is to *"receive the one who is weak in the faith,"* which means "to take into one's company, or welcome." Paul repeated the command: *"Receive one another, just as Christ also received us"* (Rom 15:7). Jewish converts had stringent dietary rules and special days, and they were to avoid anything even remotely associated with paganism. Gentile converts had a much simpler faith centered on the Bible and what it commanded, without adding any human traditions. It was easy for both groups to become critical of each other.

Differences in non-doctrinal issues must be respected without straining the *"bond of peace"* and unity in the church (Eph 4:3). Are you critical of others who have stricter convictions than your own or vice versa?

"Even though new believers in my church may have legalistic views or want to change everything, I vow to keep Your attitude of acceptance, forgiveness, and patience toward all believers."

AUGUST 23

Do Not Despise the One Fasting

Rom 14:3—*"The one who eats everything **must not despise~/ the one who does not**, and the **one who abstains must not judge~/ the one who eats everything**, for God has accepted him."*

It is a false concept that righteousness and acceptance before God can be attained if certain requirements are met or specific rites or personal sacrifices are made. Since we are granted His perfect righteousness by faith in Christ (2 Cor 5:21), nothing can improve on our permanent standing.

A second false belief of legalism is the notion that a believer can become more spiritual or acceptable to God by abstaining from certain things or by practicing prescribed behaviors. By grace we are *"accepted in the Beloved"* (Eph 1:6). Christian legalism believes spirituality is defined by how separate (or different) we are from the rest of the world; however, we can never improve on His gift of righteousness to become more acceptable.

The symptom of having succumbed to legalism is finding fault with those who do not follow the letter of the legalists' viewpoint. In Paul's day, Gentile and Jewish believers were critical of each other. For example, Gentiles would not eat meat offered to idols for fear of contamination, but Jewish Christians thought nothing of it (Rom 14:17, 21).

Paul taught principles of personal convictions without a sense of self-righteousness or judgmental feelings toward others. We are prohibited from *"despising"* those who eat everything or those who abstain. There is no justification for legalistic criticism of each other. Such feelings are the result of persistent false beliefs about spirituality.

Paul's second command was for the weaker brother, who refused to be "unspiritual" by eating such food, to *"cease being judgmental,"* which means "to separate or isolate." The word is a legal term used when a person is found guilty of a crime.

The problem of legalism is that we, as believers, accept an attitude different from God's: *"God has accepted him,"* then so should we. Our goal is always to assume God's perspective. It is self-righteous and arrogant for believers with differing opinions not to fully accept each other as brothers and sisters. Let us commit to helping each other be obedient to what we know from Scripture to be true, without despising each other.

"Lord, it is so easy to be critical and to reject believers who I feel are either too strict or too liberal in their lifestyles. Teach me to be open and gracious toward all who want to follow You."

AUGUST 24
Consider Yourself Dead to Sin

Rom 6:11—"*So **you too consider**~~ **yourselves dead to sin**, but alive to God in Christ Jesus.*"

"*If anyone is in Christ, he is a new creation; old things have passed away; behold, all things have become new*" (2 Cor 5:17). Our worldview, attitudes, relationships, commitments, and desires will change when we are united to the death, burial, and resurrection of Christ.

The first secret to this new life is the imperative to "be continually considering yourselves dead to sin." The verb means "to put together with one's mind, to count, or put on someone's account." It refers to knowledge deduced and believed from self-evident truth. The word *so* refers to the previous ten verses, especially the truth that "*we have been united together in the likeness of His death, certainly we also shall be in the likeness of His resurrection*" (Rom 6:5). This is the amazing plan of God, which pays for every man's sinfulness, allowing a holy God to forgive every man while being completely just.

Second, the concept of why Christ had to die for our sins reveals how repugnant our sin is to God, and why the only possible payment required the death of the sinless God-Man. No other payment would suffice. Just one sin had condemned the earth and all mankind to depravity and separation from God. He hates sin, yet He sacrificed the sinless life of Jesus to pay the price for our wickedness. Let this fact change your desire for sin.

Third, by God's grace and power, we have been united to Him: "*Our old man was crucified with Him, that the body of sin might be done away with, that we should no longer be slaves of sin*" (Rom 6:6). Death and sin "*no longer have dominion over Him*" (6:9), and in Him, we are free from their power.

Fourth, this astounding feat of a just payment for all was accomplished in one act on a cross two thousand years ago: "*He died to sin once for all*" (Rom 6:10)

Fifth, because we are "*in Christ,*" we partake of His resurrection and new life: "*The life that He [continually] lives, He [continually] lives to God*" (Rom 6:10).

We are to *consider*, or "reckon," that we are "*dead to sin*" and its power (Rom 6:2) and "*alive to God in Christ Jesus.*" We are to live out each day of the new life we have in Christ. May our bond to Him daily transform us into His likeness.

"*Sometimes everything in my body wants to indulge in some sin, but my spirit despises such sin, and I am ashamed that it even appeals to part of me. I've died with You, Lord Jesus, to the horribleness of sin. May I learn to hate it as You do.*"

AUGUST 25

Do Not Submit Your Body to Sin

Rom 6:12–13—*"Therefore **do not let sin reign~/** in your mortal body so that you obey its desires, and **do not present~/** your members to sin as instruments to be used for unrighteousness, but **present yourselves*~** to God** as those who are alive from the dead and your members to God as instruments to be used for righteousness."*

In Romans 6:12–13, *"Therefore"* refers back to the command to in the previous verse to *"consider yourselves to be dead to sin, but alive to God in Christ Jesus."* Salvation is not just a positional truth but a transformational truth. It is not just theoretical truth; it is also a practical liberation from sin's domination in our lives.

Transformational salvation begins with the confidence of a divine transaction that has taken place on our behalf. However, one of the key signs of the reality of the new birth is the presence of the Holy Spirit within us, which is indicated by a new sense of conviction of sin. Jesus said, *"When He has come, He will convict the world of sin"* (Jn 16:8). The believer experiences a new awareness of sin and a desire for godliness.

With this new presence of the Spirit working in the believer, he is *"strengthened with might through His Spirit in the inner man"* (Eph 3:18). We are promised, *"No temptation has overtaken you but such as is common to man; and God is faithful, who will not allow you to be tempted beyond what you are able, but with the temptation will provide the way of escape also, that you may be able to endure it"* (1 Cor 10:13).

We are to cease doing two things and make one commitment: First, we are to *"stop letting sin reign in [our] mortal bod[ies]."* Sin has no right to reign over a dead person, and we have died and now *"are alive from the dead."* We are no longer *"slave[s] to sin"* (Rom 6:6).

Second, we are to *"stop presenting [our] members to sin,"* which means to "cause to stand near or place nearby." We are told to *"make no provision for the flesh to arouse its desires"* (Rom 13:14). Avoid sinful situations.

Third, we are to *"immediately decide to present [ourselves] to God . . . and [our] members to God as instruments to be used for righteousness."* The command means we are to stay near to God, especially following His word, and keep our bodies and minds occupied practicing His word in service to others. Victory is for the choosing.

"Lord, I will trust You for grace to conquer my most besetting sin, and I will focus on being ready to serve You by serving others You put in my path."

Present Your Members as Slaves to Righteousness

Rom 6:19—*"(I am speaking in human terms because of the weakness of your flesh.) For just as you once presented your members as slaves to impurity and lawlessness leading to more lawlessness, so now **present*~ your members** as slaves to righteousness leading to sanctification."*

An enormous amount of material has been written on how the human mind learns and retains information. In Romans 6:19, Paul presents this principle for man's mind (*"I am speaking in human terms"*), utilizing a metaphor that illustrates the external or living reality in an indelible or unforgettable bridge to the memory or cognitive domains of the mind.

"The weakness of your flesh" can mean "weak or sick" depending on the context. The *weakness* in this context may refer to an inability to comprehend the dangerous consequences of personal sin, which results in an overwhelming attraction to disobedience and wickedness.

In Paul's metaphor, we are slaves to the personification of *"impurity"* (lit. "lewdness, or inward perversion") and *"lawlessness"* (lit. "an outward disobedience"). Paul's readers had essentially sold their bodies in the slave market of a progressively deteriorating and delusive quest for pleasure, lust, and power, and such *"lawlessness [leads] to more lawlessness."*

"Just as you once presented your members as slaves" means to "place beside, or stand near" by intentionally exposing yourself to all forms of perversion, lust, or pleasures by being close enough to wickedness to observe it and providing the opportunity to participate in it at will. But what benefit did that lifestyle bring (Rom 6:21)? Momentary pleasure and illusive dreams of grandeur and prestige only lure the simpleminded into a trap from which there is no escape.

There is another taskmaster to choose: *"So now present your members as slaves of righteousness leading to sanctification."* We are to submit to a personification of *"righteousness"* as our taskmaster. The same verb is used to indicate that this means to choose to be nearby or stay close to everything righteous.

God's purpose in granting us a salvation by grace is not to give us the freedom to do as we please, but to give us the freedom to choose to be as He pleases, obeying His principles of living, fully assured that His way is the best way to live. Choose your friends and activities wisely. Keep the Bible close at hand.

"Lord, here is my body, my life, my dreams, and my ambitions. They are all Yours; I'll never take them back. May my thoughts and actions be Yours in every way."

AUGUST 27

Do Not Be Conformed to This World

Rom 12:2—*"**Do not be conformed**~| to this present world, but **be transformed**~~ by the renewing of your mind, so that you may test and approve what is the will of God—what is good and well-pleasing and perfect."*

When someone accepts Christ as his Savior, Paul wrote that he *"become[s] a new creature"* (2 Cor 5:17), which is true—at least inwardly. This new Spirit, which regenerated our inner lives in our souls by the abiding presence of the Spirit, now seeks to *"work out your salvation"* (Phil 2:12) from the inside out.

In Romans 12:1, the believer is commanded to give control of his body as a *"living sacrifice"* to God as part of his *"reasonable service"* (lit. a "logical worship"). True worship can happen if the believer commits to *"stop being conformed to this present world."* Though his body is attracted to sin, his mind must make the right choices. We either commit ourselves to obedience to God or yield to sensual pleasures.

To *"stop being conformed"* (Gk. "to fashion alike, follow the same pattern") refers to an outward expression that hides what is within. The verb is passive, meaning that we are to stop allowing the world to force us into its mold or lifestyle. Is the world's approval more important than Christ's approval? Instead, you are to *"be continually being transformed by the renewing of your mind."*

The word for *transformed*—that is, "a process within, which eventually becomes external or evident"—was used to describe the transfiguration of Jesus when He revealed His inner nature to His disciples (Matt 17:2). This verb is also in the passive form.

The Spirit works in our lives *"by the renewing of your mind,"* which is "the control center of our attitudes, thoughts, feelings and motivations" (Zuck, *The Bible Knowledge Commentary*, p. 487). This happens when we *"let the Word of Christ richly dwell within [us], with all wisdom teaching and admonishing one another"* (Col 3:16).

We must *"test and approve what is the will of God."* When our minds are transformed, our new spiritual understanding evaluates everything according to the will of God, approving what is *"good and well-pleasing and perfect"* to Him. It begins with knowledge of His commands and our commitment to practice them. Are you with Him in all He says, or are you against Him?

"Lord, it is so challenging to avoid the influence of popularity and fame in the world; help me be humble in my decisions and desires today."

AUGUST 28
Fear Civil Authorities

Rom 13:4—*"For it is God's servant for your good. But if you do wrong,* ***be in fear***~~, *for it does not bear the sword in vain. It is God's servant to administer retribution on the wrongdoer."*

There are two reasons a person might not be afraid of authorities: either he is sure he is obeying the law or he thinks the law will not catch him or not take action. The former is the hope of human government, and the latter is the motive of fools.

God included capital punishment in human government: *"Whoever sheds man's blood, by man his blood shall be shed"* (Gen 9:6). In Romans 13:4, the implication of *"it does not bear the sword in vain"* is that the government can use weapons against disobedient civilians. Government is the establishment of authoritative justice in any society.

The Bible recognizes this authority and tells us to pray that it brings peaceful conditions for the free propagation of the gospel. Paul acknowledged this authority in his trial before Festus in his appeal to Caesar: *"If then I am a wrongdoer, . . . I do not refuse to die"* (Acts 25:11). The command is to fear *"if you do wrong"* ("bad, worthless, harmful"). Human nature is bent toward anarchy, which can only be brought under control by governmental power and punishment.

Paul told Timothy, *"I urge, then, first of all, that requests, prayers, intercession and thanksgiving be made for everyone, for kings and all those in authority, that we may live peaceful and quiet lives in all godliness and holiness"* (1 Tim 2:1–2^{NIV}). To pray efficiently, we must watch officials closely to pray specifically, and whatever they might do that interferes with our ability to live quiet lives of faith should be exposed, confronted, challenged, or appealed in prayer.

When nations fail to function as *"God's servant to administer retribution on the wrongdoer,"* God eventually brings His justice to the nation. The state is charged with the responsibility to be an avenger for the innocent, a responsibility forbidden to individuals (Rom 12:17, 19). Fear of disobedience is a good thing, whether it is disobedience to parents, governments, or to God. None of these can be disobeyed without painful consequences. Remember to pray that all leaders will execute justice in their spheres of influence.

"Lord, teach me to correctly fear disobeying the laws of society You have allowed to be instituted. May my life always reflect attitudes that will bring respect for Your word."

AUGUST 29
Clothe Yourself in Christ Jesus

Rom 13:14—*"Instead, **put on***~ the Lord Jesus Christ, and **make no provision***/ for the flesh to arouse its desires."*

To be a follower of Christ means to be like Jesus as much as possible in everyday life. Paul said, *"Let us live decently as in the daytime, not in carousing and drunkenness, not in sexual immorality and sensuality, not in discord and jealousy"* (Rom 13:13). We are to *"lay aside the old self, which is being corrupted in accordance with the lusts of deceit, and be renewed in the spirit of your mind, and put on the new self, which in the likeness of God has been created in righteousness and holiness of the truth"* (Eph 4:22–24).

All believers who *"[are] baptized [lit. "put into, immersed in"] into Christ have [been] clothed with Christ"* (Gal 3:27). God graciously clothes us with the righteousness of Christ (1 Cor 1:30; Rom 3:22). Because our salvation is secure through justification and the gift of His righteousness by faith, Paul exhorts us to continue to live up to the standing He has given us.

One writer described it this way: "Any athlete may don the uniform and take the name of a championship team, but it is his performance, not his team's uniform or name, that determines his value as a player." (John F. MacArthur Jr., *Romans 9–16*, 17:268.) Our value to Christ and the quality of our belief are determined by our obedience to His word and our influence on others to follow Christ.

After *"putting on"* Jesus Christ, the believer is to put off sin by making *"no provision for the flesh to arouse its desires."* The word *provision* means to take no "forethought or planning ahead." James said, *"Each one is tempted when he is drawn away by his own desires and enticed. Then when desire has conceived, it brings birth to sin"* (James 1:14–15).

Most people do not stumble into sin but *"plan to do evil"* (Prov 24:8). David described the process when *"transgression speaks to the ungodly within his heart; there is no fear of God before his eyes … He plans wickedness upon his bed; he sets himself on a path that is not good; he does not despise evil"* (Psa 36:1, 4).

The *"provision"* for sin begins in our hearts and minds, which are influenced by the desires of our *"flesh."* If we fill our minds with God's thoughts, we do not give our flesh the chance to tempt us to evil. Let's allow the word to root sin out of our hearts.

"Thank You, Lord, for living within me. Help me never to embarrass You with my thoughts or desires. I don't even want to think about sinning against Your word."

AUGUST 30
Do Not Participate in Unfruitful Acts

Eph 5:11—*"**Do not participate**~~ in the unfruitful deeds of darkness, but rather expose~~ them."*

Sometimes it's hard for Christians to believe that sin is always destructive and offers no benefits. Promised pleasure can taste bittersweet, but its poison will accumulate and eventually bring about damaging consequences. Forgiveness does not alter consequences now.

The full sense of the command in Ephesians 5:11 is to *"stop participating in unfruitful deeds."* The believer should not be involved in any way with sinful behavior. The gospel message and the teachings of the New Testament will only be heard if the speaker is committed to the word.

Do children listen to a parent's faith when they witness the parent's repeated unchristian behavior? Will wives want to be submissive to husbands who refuse to be submissive to God's commands, and vice versa? It is inconsistent for believers to live a lifestyle similar to the unsaved world. Paul said of disobedient believers, *"It is shameful even to speak of those things which are done by them in secret"* (Eph 5:12).

Right after I accepted Christ, I wanted all my friends to understand the gospel. Once I overheard a conversation that began the transformation in my life. A friend said, "You know that Don Fanning, he claims to be a Christian now, but he is not any different from the rest of us!" I sincerely wanted my friends to accept Christ, but I was the obstacle to their openness. It finally dawned on me that I needed to be different.

The *"unfruitful deeds of darkness,"* in Ephesians 1, 4, and 5, are the lusts of deceit, falsehood, stealing, unwholesome speech, bitterness, wrath, anger, clamor, slander, malice, immorality, impurity, greed, filthiness, silly talk, coarse jesting, covetousness, and idolatry. These sins bring only hurt, destroyed relationships, trouble, disillusionment, and dissatisfaction. We are to *"continually be exposing them."* Our silence can imply that we approve of such behavior.

Furthermore, by not taking a strong stand against such attitudes, we remain susceptible to their temptation. May your light shine as you lovingly show your friends their need for the Lord. Tell them why you are different. Do you know why?

"Lord, give me Your courage to be different, pure, honest, and as generous and forgiving as You are. I feel so cowardly at times. Give me the boldness to stand up for You in my world."

AUGUST 31

Behave in a Manner Worthy of the Gospel

Phil 1:27—*"Only **conduct yourselves** ~~ in a manner worthy of the gospel of Christ so that—whether I come and see you or whether I remain absent—I should hear that you are standing firm in one spirit, with one mind, by contending side by side for the faith of the gospel."*

Every good parent attempts to instill in the hearts of his children the pride of their family name. The goal is to teach them to enhance their family's reputation by faithful, heroic duty and service.

Paul thought his time might be short on earth due to his coming trial, so he gave a final exhortation to his beloved Philippian church (Phil 4:10–18). He described his hope to return to them for *"the sake of [their] progress and joy in the faith"* so that their *"proud confidence [or rejoicing] in [him] may be more abundant in Christ Jesus"* (1:25–26). Paul would go through anything to encourage them to be consistent and not discredit the gospel message.

Paul begins his exhortation with the word *only*, meaning the "one essential thing" is what follows. He commands them to *"be continually conducting themselves"* (lit. "to live as a good citizen") according to the commands in Scripture. Romans were to live in such a way as to bring honor to the political body they represented—but of course Paul is referring to their heavenly citizenship (Phil 3:20; Eph 2:19).

The best way to live *"in a manner worthy of the gospel"* is to *"please Him in every way, . . . [bear] fruit in every good work, [grow] in the knowledge of God, [and be] strengthened with all power according to His glorious might, so that you may have great endurance and patience, and joyfully [give] thanks to the Father, who has qualified you to share in the inheritance of the saints in the kingdom of light"* (Col 1:10–12).

Paul does not want them to change just because he might come see them; rather, he wants them to do so on their own, just because it is right. He asks them to *"stand firm,"* regardless of the dangers, as soldiers in rank, united with *"one spirit, with one mind"* in attitude and perspective to honor the word as they *"[contend] side by side for the faith of the gospel"* to unashamedly make it known to all. We must ask ourselves what we are doing to *"conduct [ourselves]"* to live *"worthy of the gospel."*

"Lord, if everyone around me knew I was a follower of Christ, I would have to always reflect Your honor. Teach me to never be ashamed of You or Your word."

SEPTEMBER 1
Work Out Your Salvation

Phil 2:12—*"So then, my dear friends, just as you have always obeyed, not only in my presence but even more in my absence, **continue working out~~ your salvation** with awe and reverence."*

Paul wants to dispel mediocrity from Christian thought forever. Paul begins Philippians 2:12 with *"so then,"* introducing a summation from the previous commands: *"conduct yourselves in a manner worthy of the gospel of Christ"* (1:27), *"make my joy complete by being of the same mind"* (2:2), *"Let nothing be done through selfish ambition"* (2:3a[NKJ]), *"each of you should, in humility, be moved to treat one another as more important than yourself"* (2:3b), and *"You should have the same attitude toward one another that Christ Jesus had"* (2:5). Christ exhibited a servant's heart, and we need to help each other live the same way.

The phrase *"just as"* introduces a comparison between past obedience and the present command to *"[work] out your own salvation."* The plural *"you"* refers to the church body. Paul remembered that they *"always obeyed, not only in [his] presence but more in [his] absence"*; this demonstrates the importance of recalling the joy of obeying His commands and being filled with the Spirit as we walk in obedience.

Jesus and Paul emphasized obeying Scripture over knowing Scripture. Salvation is not just something that happened in the past; it is a continuum from the moment we decide to trust Christ's atoning death on the cross and His word through the instructions for living (sanctification) to our eventual face-to-face encounter with Christ and the transformation of our beings (glorification). In the meantime, we are to grow in His likeness daily from the inside out through our increasing obedience to His instructions.

The principle of *"working out your salvation"* demands a personal commitment to obedient living. Salvation is planted within individuals; it is *"not of perishable seed, but of imperishable, through the living and enduring word of God"* (1 Pet 1:23). We must allow this seed of the eternal, regenerated life to gain control of more and more of our lives as He functions within the corporate body, where we work together to encourage, exhort, teach, and admonish one another in an ongoing journey toward spiritual maturity. Whom will you encourage today?

"Dear Father, Thank you for my wonderful salvation, now please guide me as I learn to 'work out' my salvation by learning obedience to Your commands. May my daily living please You and show others how to know You as well."

SEPTEMBER 2

Reject Myths; Train Yourself for Godliness

1 Tim 4:7—*"But **reject~~ those myths** fit only for the godless and gullible, and **train yourself~~ for godliness**."*

There is a strong drive today to prove that God is performing miracles, often motivating us to believe stories that are beyond reality. Paul begins this section by defining how to *"be a good servant of Christ Jesus"* (1 Tim 4:6b) especially by recognizing false teachings that had invaded the churches. Paul discussed false teachers (4:1–5) who unknowingly were inspired by demonically induced ideas that deviated from the Scripture.

The ministry should not be characterized by negative attacks on all who hold different opinions, but this does not mean that teachers should ignore the responsibility to *"[instruct] the brethren in these things"* (1 Tim 4:6a[NKJ]) to prevent believers from being *"tossed here and there by waves, and carried about by every wind of doctrine by the trickery of men, by craftiness in deceitful scheming"* (Eph 4:14).

True teachers focus on *"[nourishing] in the words of faith and of good doctrine, which [they] have carefully followed"* (1 Tim 4:6b); but they must *"reject myths fit only for the godless and gullible"* (4:7). The command to *"reject"* means to "have nothing to do with," and it is used again in 2 Timothy 2:23: *"Avoid foolish and ignorant disputes, knowing that they generate strife."*

Paul refers to *"myths,"* or fables, legendary tales of miraculous proofs that are declared as being true but are both non-historical and untruthful. These false ideas are for those who are *"godless"* (Gk. "profane, or unethical") and *"gullible"* (Gk. "characteristic of old women"), which is a sarcastic epithet used to convey credulity. No person in his right mind would listen to such *"myths,"* though they were very popular. Such myths might be stories of exaggerated miracles or persons fabricated to prove new doctrines (e.g., the ascension of Mary, reported levitations, raising the dead, etc.).

On the contrary, the servant of God is to *"train [himself] for godliness."* The word *train* (Gk., *gumnazo*, from which we get gymnasium) suggests the attitude of an athlete toward disciplined, dedicated, and strenuous spiritual training. Every believer is to exercise *"godliness,"* or the discipline of daily study and committed obedience to the word (1 Cor 9:24–27). Success is irrelevant without such godly discipline.

"Lord Jesus, You want Your church to follow Your word explicitly in order to be trained in truth. Help us be disciplined and dedicated to knowing Your word so we may not be misled by the words of mere humans."

SEPTEMBER 3
Reinforce These Commands

1 Tim 5:7—*"Reinforce~~ these commands, so that they will be beyond reproach."*

Paul expects all believers to listen to all his "team" instructions or "commands," but too many believers choose to disregard the New Testament commands.

The commands in this context direct believers to reach out to those in need, especially within their own households, while maintaining the priority of spreading the gospel message throughout every community. Paul emphatically states, *"Continually and habitually reinforce these commands."* In the previous chapter, he urged specific obedience: *"Command these things and teach them"* (1 Tim 4:11). Leaders and parents must make sure the commands are carefully followed.

In the Old Testament, God is described as a *"Father to the fatherless"* and a *"protector of widows"* (Psa 68:5). God told Israel, *"Do not take advantage of a widow or an orphan. If you do and they cry out to me, I will certainly hear their cry"* (Ex 22:22–23NIV). James defined true religion as taking care of widows *"in their distress"* (James 1:27). The Ephesian church obeyed the command to care for their widows and organized financial support for them. However, the younger widows, who really did not need such help, abused this command. Good intentions can go astray when selfish people take advantage of generous people, but such problems should not quench the desire to do right.

Paul clarified that *"a widow under sixty"* should not be supported (1 Tim 5:9, 11, 13, 14). *"Widows who were really in need"* (5:3) were those who had no children or grandchildren (5:4) who could be responsible for them. Taking care of your elderly parents is *"pleasing in the sight of God"* (5:4–8).

We must make difficult decisions about how to allocate our time and resources, keeping the priority on spreading the gospel, while not ignoring those in need around us. Wisdom and planning ahead can keep us *"beyond reproach,"* or "rebuke, unaccused," so that the lost do not disregard the value of the gospel. The key is constant reiteration of His commands.

"Heavenly Father, I pray for our pastors and teachers of the word. Please give them the wisdom they need to continually teach us Your precepts. May we always remember to teach Your precepts to our children and grandchildren and thus keep Your desires alive in all our lives."

SEPTEMBER 4
Live Out the Message

James 1:22—*"But **be~~ sure you live out the message** and do not merely listen to it and so deceive yourselves."*

Some people have accepted a salvation by grace through faith that means their lives are still their own and they can do whatever they want with impunity. If a person wants to be forgiven of his lusts only to continue to love his sins, he deceives himself. God knows when someone lacks sincere sorrow for their sins or for the hurt they caused Jesus, who paid a terrible price for their guilt (2 Cor 5:21). God also knows when someone has no desire to abandon hypocritical living, and He tends to bring it to their attention.

James just described the true meaning of repentance and faith: *"Lay aside all filthiness and overflow of wickedness, and receive with meekness* [a sense of undeserved favor] *the implanted Word, which is able to save your souls"* (James 1:21). Artimedorus, in the second century, described the root term for "filthiness" (Gk. *hruparian*)—which comes from the "earwax" that must be washed away to allow good hearing. This is a great illustration of how our sins block us from hearing God.

Now James warns believers to *"be continually living out the message."* . One should ask after hearing a message, "What does the Scripture expect me to do now?" The message has failed its purpose if this answer is not clear. Merely listening to a message with no intent or challenge to obey useless. Even worse if one decides not to practice what is commanded, he quenches the Spirit and opens the door to Satanic deceptions.

James says that when someone only listens to the message, we *"deceive [our] selves,"* which means "to cheat or be deceived by false reasoning." In the early church, there were few complete Bibles. Believers gathered to hear the text read from a few precious manuscripts. Today, many fool themselves into thinking that just because they come to church, listen to a message, or enjoy worshipping, yet they can continue to live any way they want.

On the other hand, to live with victory and to live "abundantly" (John 10:10) we must gladly learn the commands and commit to living them out in our daily lives. Will you do it, and will you help others have the same attitude?

"Dear Lord, listening to messages from Your word without deciding to live them out every day is a dangerous position for the believer. Help me to continually look for ways to put into practice what You are teaching me."

SEPTEMBER 5
Become Holy in All Conduct

1 Pet 1:15—*"But, like the Holy One who called you, **become holy***~ **yourselves** *in all of your conduct."*

The seventeenth-century author John Bunyan wrote the following in his Bible: "This book will keep you from sin, or sin will keep you from this book." Our command today is the fifth command in a series from 1 Peter 1:13–16. Three mental preparation commands on the second coming of Christ (*"gird up the loins of your mind"* [prepare your minds for action], *"be sober"* [be self-controlled], and *"rest your hope"* [decide to set it]) are followed by two behavioral commands (*"[do] not [conform] yourselves to the former lusts, as in your ignorance"* and the overall mandate to *"be holy").*

After committing to follow Christ, many are still attracted to their former sinful patterns; however, God came into their lives in the person of the powerful Holy Spirit with the purpose of transforming them into a reflection of God. God is calling all believers to develop the nature of our heavenly Father, who gave us "new birth" (1 Pet 1:3), and He has empowered us to make this a reality: *"As His divine power has given to us all things that pertain to life and godliness, through the knowledge of Him who called us by [His] glory and virtue, by which have been given to us exceedingly great and precious promises, that through these you may be partakers of the divine nature, having escaped the corruption that is in the world through lust"* (2 Pet 1:3–4).

God's *holiness* or His *"divine nature"* means that He is completely separated from sin and evil. Sin is so contrary to His character that He repudiates any aspect of it. His holiness establishes the standard for morality and purity for all His creatures. Thankfully, God has granted us His perfect righteousness by His grace through our faith in His promises. Now He commands us to live as righteously as He has made us by faith: *"become holy yourselves in all of your conduct."* The aorist tense of the verb does not mean that you are not holy and must become holy but rather that you must "immediately decide to show yourself to be holy."

God wants us to be like Him in every aspect of our lives: *"Be holy, because I am holy"* (1 Pet 1:16). Salvation begins our active pursuit of opposing sin and demonstrating how much we want to become like our God and Savior Jesus Christ. Be holy for Him.

"Dear Jesus, because of Your sacrifice, we have been made righteous. To show You our gratitude for this new relationship with You, we want to live righteously; help us decide once and for all to live according to Your holiness."

SEPTEMBER 6
Yearn for Spiritual Milk

1 Pet 2:2—*"And yearn*~ like newborn infants for pure, spiritual milk,
so that by it you may grow up to salvation."*

The simile of babies in 1 Peter 2:2 does not expect us to behave entirely
like babies; rather, as babies have the strong and instinctive longing for
their mothers' milk, so we are to long to understand God's word. Why do
we have to be *commanded* to desire the word and to make it our highest
priority? The continual desire for sin quenches our thirst for God's word.

The aorist command to *"yearn,"* or "desire," means we must give urgency and
immediacy to this action. Peter earlier warned, *"As sojourners and pilgrims,
abstain from fleshy lusts, which war against the soul"* (1 Pet 2:11). Now he uses
the same root word to focus on spiritual nourishment.

Desires are a part of life, and they can motivate us toward good or
bad. As believers, we must choose healthy, godly desires and cultivate
them to assuage the carnal, fleshly desires that lead to corruption and
self-destruction.

But how can we distinguish between good desires and bad desires? The
dividing line is whether the desire is self-centered and selfish or a desire
for God's will. After we consciously decide to reject impure desires and
motives (1 Pet 2:1), we must fill that vacuum with healthy, spiritual food
that generates growth in spiritual maturity and godly living. We are to
crave *"spiritual milk"* (Gk. "unadulterated reason" or rational), which
means we wish to understand God's word and practice its teaching. The
word is also figuratively described as meat, flesh, food, bread, and blood,
illustrating the enjoyable incorporation of the practical elements of the
word into our lives.

This spiritual or conceptual milk is the only means by which we can
"grow up," or "attain great power or authority," in regard *"to salvation"*—
that is, *"receiving the end of your faith—the salvation of your souls"* (1 Pet
1:9). Thirst for understanding the word in order to follow it faithfully
should continue throughout this life. How thirsty are you for His word
today?

*"Dear God, thank You for giving us all the information You want us to know
in the Bible. Give me a growing hunger to know it and put it into practice
every day."*

SEPTEMBER 7
Keep Your Tongue from Evil

1 Pet 3:10—*"For the one who wants to love life and see good **must keep***~ **his tongue** from evil and his lips from uttering deceit."*

If we want to *"love life and see good,"* we must build and protect our relationships. We are tempted to exaggerate, deceive, or abuse with words; therefore, we must *"learn to be content whatever the circumstances"* (Phil 4:11). We don't have to deceive others.

The key to this lifestyle is found in keeping the *"tongue from evil and [the] lips from uttering deceit."* As James tells us, *"The tongue is a fire, the very world of iniquity; the tongue is set among our members as that which defiles the entire body, and sets on fire the course of our life, and is set on fire by hell"* (James 3:6); the last phrase implies that demons can influence our speech, especially when we are in a fit of anger (Eph 4:27).

In 1 Peter 3:10, *"evil"* refers to any type of "vicious, hurtful or harmful" speech that can cause a vengeful reaction from another person. Peter earlier provided us with the solution: *"Be of one mind, having compassion for one another"* and *"love as brothers"* (1 Pet 2:8). This whole section was introduced by the command to put *"aside all malice, all deceit, hypocrisy, envy and all evil speaking"* (2:1). We are to love one another by *"not returning evil for evil or reviling for reviling, on the contrary blessing"* (2:9). Be careful of your reactions, especially with the tongue.

In addition, obedient believers are to *"keep . . . [their] lips from uttering deceit,"* which means to deliberately trick or mislead someone by lying or intentionally giving the wrong impression for personal advantage: *"Whoever hides hatred has lying lips, and whoever spreads slander is a fool"* (Prov 10:18). No one will trust a deceiver. Once broken, a relationship is very difficult to rebuild.

The tongue should build up, not tear down:*"There is one who speaks like the piercing of a sword, but the tongue of the wise promotes health"* (Prov 12:18).

Let us commit to being honest, transparent, and protective of each other. When we inadvertently hurt someone, let us have the courage to admit it and ask forgiveness. Nothing is as valuable as the bond of believers. If you love life, protect your relationships.

"Lord Jesus, I commit myself to be honest and transparent before You and to carefully protect others by speaking to them with kindness. I need Your wisdom and understanding to benefit others with my words and physical expressions."

SEPTEMBER 8
Add to Your Faith

2 Pet 1:5—*"For this very reason, make every effort to **add***~ **to your faith** *excellence, to excellence, knowledge."*

When a person receives a significant inheritance, the greatest care must be taken to preserve it and make it grow for future generations. In 2 Peter 1:5, *"For this very reason"* refers to the preceding context: We have received everything we need for a practical, godly lifestyle. Now Peter describes a sevenfold personal development plan to keep us from squandering God's investment.

We are to *"urgently determine to make every effort"* to incorporate these seven attributes into our lifestyle. This is a translation of the Greek verb *spoude*, which means "to speed, hasten, or apply diligence." To *"add to your faith"* means to "bring to bear alongside of," thus to incorporate these seven attributes to your character.

The seriousness of our commitment to our Personal Development Plan is evident in the steps we take to ensure that these traits become permanent characteristics of our lives.

These qualities begin with saving faith, to which a new believer is expected to *"add,"* or "to supply lavishly or generously" seven qualities. Each attribute flows out of the former, thus *"supplement your faith with a generous provision of moral excellence"* (2Pe 1:5 ᴺᴸᵀ).*"Virtue,"* or "moral excellence," speaks of heroic deeds demonstrated in normal living: *"You received from us how you ought to walk and to please God"* (1 Thes 4:1b).

To *"excellence,"* we are to add *"knowledge,"* or an "intellectual grasp," of God's word (2 Cor 6:6 and 8:7). Next comes *"self-control"* (1 Pet 1:6), which means to "hold oneself in"; to that, add *"perseverance,"* which means "endurance in what is right, resisting temptation while enduring trials and difficulties." This leads to *"godliness"*—that is, a special "reverence for God or true worship." *"Brotherly kindness"* (1:7) is a commitment to other believers as family. Finally, we are to add a selfless and sacrificial *"love"* that reflects Christ's character (Phil 1:9) in benefiting others. Let us encourage each other in these virtues.

"Dear Father, every day is an opportunity to continue to add to my self-control, perseverance, godliness, brotherly kindness, love, and knowledge of Your word. Only as I decide to obey Your commands can these characteristics truly become part of my life."

Be Sure of Your Calling and Election

2 Pet 1:10—*"Therefore, brothers and sisters,* ***make every effort*~ to be sure*** *of your calling and election. For by doing this you will never stumble into sin."*

Peter tells us to *"urgently make every effort"* to be certain that we have a genuine salvation relationship with Christ. In this context,the command is to *"be sure"* that our virtue and godliness give evidence of a true salvation. The word *"make"* means "to produce something new, using materials already in existence," thus the objective is to "urgently use reliable resources to make ourselves absolutely sure" that we have biblical confirmation of what we profess to believe in.

This is not a command to make sure we have been elected to salvation before time began, which makes no sense, because we weren't there! Instead, we are commanded to be certain that the fruitful purpose of coming to the *"knowledge of our Lord Jesus Christ"* (2 Pet 1:8) is fulfilled in our lives. The context of 2 Peter 1:10 deals with fruitfulness, vision, and motivation to serve out of a grateful spirit generated by the knowledge that God has forgiven our sins. Now our energy is spent making His sacrifice for us worthwhile.

Paul told the Thessalonian believers that they were *"called . . . by our gospel, for the obtaining of the glory of our Lord Jesus Christ"* (2 Thes 2:14). By responding to the gospel message, they were, in effect, responding to God's call. Likewise, their *"election"* or "being chosen" is related to their response to the gospel message Paul preached: *"We know . . . that he has chosen you, in that our gospel did not come to you merely in words, but in power and in the Holy Spirit and with deep conviction . . . when you received the message with joy that comes from the Holy Spirit"* (1 Thes 1:4). God reaches out to sinners through the preaching of the gospel, bringing the conviction of sin and drawing the sinner to seek Christ's forgiveness. In this way, He calls us to Him and chooses us to be fruitful.

Peter makes two promises to the believer who makes every effort to continually practice these principles: First, *"you will never stumble,"* (using the strongest negation in Greek) or "trip," or "fall away" (NLT) Second, in the next verse, Peter promises a *"rich welcome into the eternal kingdom"* (2 Pet 1:11[NIV]). Let's make growth in Christlikeness our priority so that we may fulfill His eternal purpose for our lives.

"Lord Jesus, Your word says that if we believe we will have eternal life. . Thank You. Please help me be faithful to demonstrate what you mean to me."

SEPTEMBER 10

Grow in the Grace and Knowledge of Jesus Christ

2 Pet 3:18—*"But **grow~~** in the grace and knowledge of our Lord and Savior Jesus Christ. To Him be* [understood imperative] *the honor both now and on that eternal day."*

Virtually every profession requires life-long-learning. Christians are also to *"continually be growing in the grace and knowledge of our Lord and Savior Jesus Christ."*

Peter warned his readers about false teachers or prophets who *"twist to their own destruction"* the teachings of the Scriptures (2 Pet 3:16). These false teachers tend to be *"untaught,"* relying on impressions, traditions and their imaginations considered as new prophecies instead of studying the revealed word of God. They are also *"unstable"* (Gk. "without being established"), which means they have "the tendency to change and waver in [their] views and attitudes." The main symptom of false teachers is they always seek new prophecies, unsatisfied with the Bible alone.

The command *"to always be continually growing"* means "to grow to the extreme limit, to advance." We must perpetually increase in two areas. First, we are to grow in the *"grace . . . of our Lord."* The word *grace* has broad meanings. In a context of salvation, it is the grace of God, the basis of God's acceptance of undeserving sinners.

Second, His gracious acceptance of us and promise to never leave us, but be with us through all life's turmoil is an encouraging partnership. Through Him and with Him, we can overcome undesirable situations, physical conditions, or poor responses to difficult people. When Paul prayed three times for God to heal his physical condition, God said, *"My grace is sufficient for you"* (2 Cor 12:9). He becomes all we need.

We are also to *"be growing in the . . . knowledge of our Lord,"* which Peter earlier saw as the result of learning more about God: *"Grace and peace be multiplied to you in the knowledge of God and of Jesus our Lord"* (2 Pet 1:2). If you are established in the knowledge of the faith, you are protected from being misled by false teachers and misapplications of Scripture. Are you growing in *"grace and knowledge"* of Christ?

"Dear Father, I want to be willing to endure any adverse circumstance You send my way so that I may grow in Your grace. Only through extensive knowledge of Your word is that kind of growth possible. Thank You for allowing me to depend on Your help as I seek to know You."

SEPTEMBER 11

Walk as Children of Light

Eph 5:8—*"For you were at one time darkness, but now you are light in the Lord. Walk~~ as children of the light."*

Paul thought that the unique quality of the transformed life of a believer should be apparent to all. If you are not different from an unbeliever, you have no message to give, and you make the statement that Christ makes no difference.

Before meeting Christ, every person lived in ignorance of the truth, lacking spiritual life (Eph 2:1) and being enslaved to sin (2:2–3). The first verb phrase, *"were at one time darkness,"* is in the past tense, meaning this previous condition is no longer a reality. All believers were previously living in darkness. Paul described this dark life in Ephesians 4:17–19: *"You should no longer walk as the rest of the Gentiles walk, in the futility of their mind, having their understanding darkened, being alienated from the life of God, because of the ignorance that is in them, because of the blindness of their heart; who, being past feeling, have given themselves over to lewdness, to work all uncleanness with greediness."* Believers must demonstrate a changed life from this.

Jesus said He is the *"light of the world"* (Jn 8:12): *"God ... commanded light to shine out of darkness, who has shone in our hearts to give the light of the knowledge of the glory of God in the face of Jesus Christ"* (2 Cor 4:6). Because we, as believers, have the Light of the World *"in our hearts,"* we have become transmitters of this light. Jesus said,*"You are the light of the world"* (Matt 5:14), hence the command to *"be continually or habitually walking as children of light."*

In Ephesians 5:9–10, Paul amplifies the meaning of walking in the light, *"(for the fruit of the Spirit is in all goodness, righteousness, and truth), finding out what is acceptable to the Lord."* If we are born anew as children of light, then we are to be consistent with what we have become. Paul told us to *"walk worthy of the calling with which you were called"* (Eph 4:1)—that is, walk in obedience to His word today and you will be different, pointing people to the Light of lights.

"Dear Lord, thank You for giving us the understanding of who You are and how You want Your children to live. What a difference from the selfish kind of life I was living! My great desire is to constantly live in a manner that makes me worthy of being called Your child."

SEPTEMBER 12

Show Your Faith without Works

James 2:18—*"But someone will say, 'You have faith and I have works.'*
Show*~ me your faith *without works and I will show you faith by my works."*

Just as love without an active response is meaningless, so faith without action according to God's word is empty. A transforming faith should be evident in new behavior.

When a baby is born, the doctor sometimes spanks the newborn, if necessary, to make it cry, thus indicating it is alive and breathing. Without the sign of this first cry, the doctor suspects the baby is not alive. Crying does not generate life in the baby, but it does indicate that the baby already has life. James stated, *"Thus also faith by itself, if it does not have works, is dead"* (James 2:17). Works cannot generate faith, but genuine faith always shows a changed life as evidence of the new birth.

In James 2:18, James has created a hypothetical person who argues that faith and works are entirely unrelated. But God says that actions without faith are meaningless, just as faith without obedient responses to His word is meaningless. This case is illustrated by Jesus's warning: *"Why do you call Me, 'Lord, Lord,' and do not do what I say?"* (Luke 6:46). John saw the same issue: *"The one who says, 'I have come to know Him,' and does not keep His commandments, is a liar, and the truth is not in him; but whoever keeps His word, in him the love of God has truly been perfected. By this we know that we are in Him"* (1 Jn 2:4–5).

The opposite is just as deceiving: one might presume to have faith because of his works and trust that God will approve of him because of those good works, but *"not everyone who says to Me, 'Lord, Lord,' will enter the kingdom of heaven, but he who does the will of My Father who is in heaven will enter. Many will say to Me on that day, 'Lord, Lord, did we not prophesy in Your name, and in Your name cast out demons, and in Your name perform many miracles?' And then I will declare to them, 'I never knew you; depart from me, you who practice lawlessness'"* (Matt 7:21–23). Such a person believes in God, but his heart is filled with his own sense of self-worth rather than with Jesus' merciful grace.

The *"will of [Christ's] Father"* (John 6:40) is clear: *"For this is the will of my Father– for everyone who ... believes in him to have eternal life, "* No one can trust God's promises for salvation without being changed. How has the gospel changed your life?

"Heavenly Father, thank You for Your gracious salvation and for the desire it has given me to love You by daily putting into practice the things You have said."

SEPTEMBER 13
Do Not Love the World

1 Jn 2:15—*"**Do not love~| the world** or the things in the world. If anyone loves the world, the love of the Father is not in him."*

First John was written so *"that you may know that you have eternal life"* (1 Jn 5:13): the whole epistle describes the characteristics of true believers and contrasts them with false believers. The sign of a true believer is that he begins to change his beliefs, values, priorities, and commitments to conform to God's word.

First John 2:15 is written to those who struggle with craving what the world offers to satisfy their deepest needs and wants. They were told to *"stop or cease loving the world"* and the accompanying senseless lust for possessions, power, prestige, and pleasures. Satan attempts to persuade us that such things will satisfy us more than our relationship with Christ and being obedient to His word. Here we are being taught a new lifestyle.

In verses 16–17, John clarifies what he means by *"all that is in the world"*: *"the lust of the flesh, the lust of the eyes, and the pride of life."* It is the passion to find fulfillment and meaning in life apart from Christ—satisfying the flesh instead of the heart, which only Christ can fill. A person worships the things he believes he needs to feel secure or fulfilled in life. The world promises a mirage, because *"the world is passing away, and the lusts of it; but he who does the will of God abides forever"* (2:17).

First, we cannot love God and love the world simultaneously: *"No one can serve two masters; for either he will hate the one and love the other, or else he will be loyal to the one and despise the other. You cannot serve God and mammon"* (Matt 6:24). Both masters demand loyalty and obedience.

Second, it is futile to trust the world to satisfy your cravings: *"He who loves silver will not be satisfied with silver; nor he who loves abundance, with increase. This also is vanity"* (Eccl 5:10). The world promises satisfactions, but only the fool believes such lies.

We are not commanded to abandon the world or to never enjoy the things in the world; we are commanded not to love things, show them off, or brag about them to demonstrate our importance. God knows the heart of man. Do you love things more than God's will? God knows the answer, but He will test you to bring you out of your denial. Are you ready?

"Dear Lord, it is possible for the heart of a believer to be enticed by the things of this world; therefore I run to You and Your word to help me set my affections on heavenly things so I may not be drawn away from You."

SEPTEMBER 14
Be What You Really Are

Rev 22:11—*"The evildoer **must continue to do evil***~, *and the one who is morally filthy **must continue to be filthy***~. *The **one who is righteous must continue to act righteously***~, *and the **one who is holy must continue to be holy***~."*

An amazing characteristic of God is that He allows a person to be whatever he wants to be. If he wants to live without God, He will grant him his desire, now and forever. Of course, the opposite is also true.

In Revelation, an angel told John, *"Write in a book what you see, and send it to the seven churches"* (1:11). Two thousand years ago, he wrote describing events—some quite terrifying—that remain in the future to this day. This message is certain; we who believe this prophecy owe it to the world to make it known to them.

In spite of cataclysmic global events that will nearly bring an end to mankind in a brief period (seven years), and even though men will recognize that God is behind the judgments, they will refuse to repent, ask for mercy, or recognize their own wickedness. Rather, men will persist in increasing wickedness until they are destroyed. Unbelievers will refuse to believe God's prophecies and *"continue to do evil."* The *"one who is morally filthy must continue to be filthy."* Men will harden their hearts as they determine to be increasingly wicked, persuading others to join them in their filthy living. They will continue in their sin, knowing that what God says about the future will come to pass. Their lostness will become increasingly evident.

On the other hand, those who have put their trust in Christ, receiving His perfect righteousness as the free gift of God, will continue to practice righteousness and *"continue to be* [or keep themselves] *holy."*

Depending on our response to God's warnings, our character is progressively fixed forever. In a sense, we determine our own destiny. Sinners are warned not to rebel and harden their hearts (Heb 3:15; 4:7), but if they consistently reject the truth, God will abandon them to their *"reprobate mind"* (Rom 1:18–32) and the eternal consequences of their own choices (1 Cor 1:18). People must hear the truth while there is time. Are you making it possible for them to hear?

"Dear Jesus, because of Your saving grace, I can rely on You for the power to live righteously, honoring You by setting apart my life for Your purposes. I know I can trust You as I do my best to show others the way to eternal life in You."

SEPTEMBER 15
Continue to Live in Christ

Col 2:6—*"Therefore, just as you received Christ Jesus as Lord, **continue to live~~ your lives in him**."*

Once an organization starts on a certain philosophy of ministry, it is very hard to change its direction. Likewise, how a person begins the Christian life will determine how he lives it out daily.

Paul was deeply concerned about the believers at Colossae because many had not seen him in person (Col 2:1) but had heard the gospel through his disciples. He wanted to make sure that they had *"all the riches of the full assurance of understanding"* (2:2) of their newfound faith and the *"treasures of wisdom and knowledge"* (2:3). Paul wrote the command in Colossians 2:6 because there were some that would *"deceive [them] with persuasive words"* (2:4), distracting their focus on the *"steadfastness of [their] faith in Christ"* (2:5).

"Therefore" ties this verse to the previous thought. There is a continuum from how these believers received Christ to how they continued to live in Him. The presentation of the gospel is described in several passages. Paul wrote to the Thessalonians of their conversion: *"When you **received** the Word of God which you heard from us, you **welcomed** it not as the word of men, but as it is in truth, the Word of God, which also effectively works in you who **believe**"* (1 Thes 2:13). To the Ephesians, he said, *"In Him you also **trusted**, after you **heard** the word of truth, the gospel of your salvation; in whom also, **having believed**, you **were sealed** with the Holy Spirit of promise"* (Eph 1:13). The common threads include hearing God's word (His teachings and promises), understanding what it means, and making a conscious decision to trust His word. Thus the believer receives Christ as his new life focus, submitting to whatever His word says and allowing it, through the Spirit, to transform his life.

By "continuing to live their lives in Christ" they would be *"rooted and built up in Him and established in the faith, as [they] ha[d] been taught, abounding in it with thanksgiving"* (Col 2:7) This is not a mystical feeling but a continual growth in the knowledge of God's word as it explains how we are to live as followers of Christ. Then we must commit ourselves to live His way and to honor Him in every detail of our lives.

"Dear Father, I have exercised faith by receiving Your message of salvation in Your Son Jesus. Now, to fulfill Your will, help me live each day by faith in Your word, focusing on being obedient to what You have written there."

SEPTEMBER 16

Convince Yourself about Personal Conviction

Rom 14:5—*"One person regards one day holier than other days, and another regards them all alike. Each **must be fully convinced~~ in his own mind**."*

As believers, sometimes we can be judgmental and critical, thinking that we are more spiritual than others. We might demean other people in order to support our own internal sense of righteousness.

Parts of Scripture are "grey areas": they give one the liberty to choose. Typically, those who take more restrictive positions think of themselves as more spiritual, seeing those with more liberal views as carnal or disobedient. Paul wrote Romans 14:1–15:13 to diffuse these divisive and destructive legalistic attitudes.

The first issue in the debate Paul was addressing was which day of the week should be given special significance: *"One person regards one day holier than other days, and another regards them all alike."* Believers with many scruples and convictions wanted a special day (i.e., Sabbath) dedicated to rest, family, and worship. They also wanted to be separated from pagan festivals and to eat only certain foods.

Paul warned the Colossians, *"Let no one act as your judge in regard to food or drink or in respect to festival or a new moon or a Sabbath day"* (Col 2:16). Paul did not prohibit such practices, but he also insisted that they had no spiritual benefit.

The command that *"each must be fully convinced in his own mind"* means we should "be completely certain of the truth." This is a settled conviction that a pattern of conduct is the will of God (Rom 12:2).

Paul asked the Romans, *"Why do you condemn another believer? Why do you look down on another believer? Remember, we will all stand before the judgment seat of God"* (Rom 14:10). We are to be *"like-minded, having the same love, being of one accord, of one mind"* (Phil 2:2), but this doesn't mean we must agree on minutia. Absolute conformity of opinion in areas of liberty is never demanded. We must humbly make a commitment to honor and serve one another (2:3–4). Do you "agree to disagree" while still loving others as your family?

"Dear Lord, the Bible is our guide to knowing You and having 'the mind of Christ' as we learn how to govern our daily lives. Give me the wisdom to stand firm on what You have made clear and to show love and tolerance to others in areas where Your word is not so clear."

Do Not Judge One Another

Rom 14:13—*"Therefore we must not pass judgment on one another* [subjunctive of prohibition, 'Don't ever start'], *but rather* **determine~~ never to place an obstacle** *or a trap before a brother or sister."*

Paul warns, *"Each of us shall give account of himself to God"* (Rom 14:12). We have no business playing the role of God by judging one another. Whatever the personal convictions of another believer, we are not to judge his activities or his motives.

Christ said, *"Take heed that you do not do your charitable deeds before men, to be seen by them. Otherwise you have no reward from your Father in heaven"* (Matt 6:1–4). God alone knows our motives, but if you are only motivated to do good when your actions are seen, recognized, or praised by others, God will not reward you, no matter how great the deed. To pretend to have God's omniscience to accurately judge a person's inner motivation is pretentious and presumptuous.

Paul uses the same Greek verb for *judge* twice in Romans 14:13, yet it carries two different connotations. We must *"not judge one another"* refers to condemning someone, as in 14:3–4, 10. The second phrase, *"but rather determine,"* refers to making a decision. We must decide not to be *judgmental*, but we should *judge*—that is, evaluate how we will live to benefit others. One involves being critical, and the other involves discerning how to help.

We are warned, *"Take care lest this liberty of yours somehow become a stumbling block to the weak"* (1 Cor 8:9). Remember that your liberties could motivate another's excess or cause him to violate his conscience, thus leading him to sin. The mature Christian will be sensitive to any weakness in a fellow believer and abstain from anything that could cause him to revert to sinful behavior. This may mean giving up your own rights for the sake of others. Do we just pretend to love others?

"Dear heavenly Father, make me acutely aware of critical, judgmental attitudes toward others so I may quickly confess when I fall into this pit. On the other hand, keep me from allowing my liberty in Christ to cause another to stumble."

SEPTEMBER 18

Do Not Cause Someone to Sin

Rom 14:15–16—*"For if your brother or sister is distressed because of what you eat, you are no longer walking in love.* **Do not destroy~/ by your food** *someone for whom Christ died. Therefore* **do not let what you consider good be spoken of as evil~/.***"*

When personal rights create division and disharmony, it might be better to give up our rights. In certain regions of the world, or among certain groups of people, it is offensive to eat certain foods that are not offensive in other cultures (e.g., pork in a Muslim community). What should a Christian do in these questionable areas? What should guide our choices?

There are two over-arching principles: always act in love (i.e., seeking the benefit of others) and maintain peace in the body of Christ (Col 3:15). Paul declared, *"No food is unclean in itself"* (14:14), but not all believers agreed. The Jerusalem Council (Acts 15 in AD 49) asked the Gentile churches not to eat meat from animals that had been sacrificed to idols. Paul agreed to communicate this opinion to the Gentile believers because it was not worth dividing over.

Flaunting liberties can create division. If our liberties cause others to be *"distressed"* (i.e., "hurt, grieved, causing pain"), we *"are no longer walking in love."* Wounding another's conscience could destroy his faith (Rom 14:13, 21). Love always avoids this consequence.

Paul establishes that everyone needs to follow his or her personal convictions in areas not clearly commanded (Rom 14:5, 14a, 22–23) under the love principle: *"Walk in love, as Christ also has loved us and given Himself for us"* (Eph 5:2). Have convictions but don't separate over them.

Jesus has a huge investment in every believer, so the issue is that your liberties might hurt not just *another person* but a person *"for whom Christ died."* Furthermore, He is bonded to that person in such a way that anything done to him or her is perceived as having been done to Christ Himself (Acts 9:4–5; Matt 25:40). Be careful!

Paul's final command is to stop letting *"what you consider good to spoken of as evil."* In unclear areas, believers are free to partake or abstain. Our liberty must be limited by the commitment to protect others and Christ's reputation. The question is, how much do others matter to us?

"Dear Father, I ask You for help in making decisions about Christian convictions. You want us to be a blessing and a help to others on their life journey, so provide me wisdom ,to allowing pride or selfishness to take control."

SEPTEMBER 19

Do Not Allow Your Freedom to Cause Another to Sin

Rom 14:20—*"**Do not destroy**~~ **the work** of God for the sake of food. For although all things are clean, it is wrong to cause anyone to stumble by what you eat."*

What motivates a new or weaker brother to give up and return to a sinful behavior? For some, any excuse will suffice. The mature believer strives to live *"above reproach"* (1 Tim 3:2) so as not to become an excuse for a new believer to fall back into sin.

Paul lays the foundation for relationships within the church. Believers must *"pursue the things which make for peace and the things by which one may edify another"* (Rom 14:19). They must be *"diligent to preserve the unity of the Spirit in the bond of peace"* (Eph 4:3).

The Roman Christians were doing just the opposite. They were told to *"stop or cease destroying the work of God for the sake of food."* Just as in the Corinthian church, their *"meetings [did] more harm than good"* (1 Cor 11:17ᴺᴵⱽ)! The command to *"cease destroying"* (Gk. "demolish or dissolve") implies the destruction was already happening. Some were flaunting their right to eat whatever they wanted, while others were just as adamant about criticizing and judging those who ate such food as unworthy of the name of Christ.

Paul clarified that both sides were equally sinful. In the first place, *"all things are clean,"* so the believer has the right to eat any food, even the food ceremonially unclean to Jews. God declared such food now to be *"clean." "What God has made clean, you must not consider ritually unclean!"* (Acts 10:14–15). Ten years after the ascension, Peter still did not feel free to eat certain foods, in spite of a specific command from God! Apparently, many in the church at Rome still had Peter's attitude, so the issue against Gentile believers must have been merciless.

Paul condemned this selfish thinking as *"evil"* (i.e., "troublesome, injurious, destructive") and concluded, *"It is good neither to eat meat nor drink wine nor do anything by which your brother stumbles or is offended or is made weak"* (Rom 14:21). Thus the principle is far broader than just eating meat: *"Now food will not bring us close to God. We are no worse if we do not eat and no better if we do"* (1 Cor 8:8). When we choose to judge and believe we are more spiritual than another because of our practices, we only deceive ourselves and bring chastisement upon ourselves.

"Lord Jesus, thank You for loving each of us to the extent of giving up the glory of being God to save us. In that same attitude, I am seeking Your guidance to avoid causing a brother to sin because of my liberty in Christ."

SEPTEMBER 20

Be Strengthened in the Lord

Eph 6:10—*"Finally, **be strengthened~~** **in the Lord** and in the strength of his power."*

Once you are branded as a Christian, the forces of evil charge you, trying to extinguish your desire to live for God.

Paul began his summary of important concepts with *"Finally"* to introduce the beginning of the end. MacArthur tells us, "If we are walking worthy of our calling: in humility rather than pride, in unity rather than divisiveness, in the new self rather than the old, in love rather than lust, in light rather than darkness, in wisdom rather than foolishness, in the fullness of the Spirit rather than the drunkenness of wine, and in mutual submission rather than self-serving independence, then we can be absolutely certain we will have opposition and conflict" (MacArthur, *Ephesians*, p. 331).

Jesus demonstrated the power of prayer to strengthen Him in the garden of Gethsemane. He urged His disciples to do the same. Non-praying believers will either compromise or hide.

The command is to *"be [continually] strengthened in the Lord,"* which means "to be made capable." We gain our strength *"in the Lord,"* not by human strength. Paul prayed that believers would know God's *"incomparably great power for us who believe"* (Eph 1:19). This power was used to raise Jesus from the dead (1:20), and this same power flows in us.

Next, Paul adds, *"in the strength of His power"*—that is, "in the manifested power of His inherent might," a description of majesty and insurmountable strength. This power is sufficient to help us stand true to Christ despite any threatening opposition, as we see in the church of Philadelphia: *"because you have a little power, and have kept My Word, and have not denied My name"* (Rev 3:8). They stayed faithful even with *"a little power."*

Paul's final words to Timothy were, *"Therefore do not be ashamed of the testimony of our Lord . . . be strong in the grace that is in Christ Jesus"* (2 Tim 1:8; 2:1). Being saturated with His presence brings inevitable power, but it flows as we obey Him and stand up for Him.

"I praise You, Father, that Your power is made evident through our weakness. I need to cling to You in prayer, saturate my mind with Your teachings, and continually learn to obey You so that, when the trials and opposition come, You will be glorified in my words and actions."

Clothe Yourself with the Armor of God

Eph 6:11—*"Clothe yourselves**~ **with the full armor** *of God so that you may be able to stand against the schemes of the devil."*

God never wants a believer to go into battle unprepared (the task of the church) and unprepared (personal disciplines). We are commanded, *"Decide urgently now to clothe yourself with the full armor of God."*

The word for *"full armor"* refers to every kind of defensive and offensive piece of weaponry provided to each Roman soldier. Remember, Paul was writing this letter while chained to a Roman soldier!

Our enemies are the demonic forces in the unseen world who manipulate the political powers that serve them unknowingly (Eph 6:12–17). This explains the irrational opposition of evil leaders against biblical Christianity. They are pawns in a battle beyond their knowledge, and we Christians are to pray for them (1 Tim 2:1-2) so we can live in peace.

The *"armor of God"* is vital in a raging battle and is sufficient to enable the believer to *"stand against the schemes of the devil."* Satan is bent on destroying all that belongs to God. Satan *"takes away the Word from their hearts, so that they may not believe and be saved"* (Luke 8:12).

He empowers *"false christs and false prophets [who] will arise and will show great signs and wonders, so as to mislead, if possible, even the elect"* (Matt 24:24).

Peter gives the battle cry, *"Be sober, be vigilant; because your adversary the devil walks about like a roaring lion, seeking whom he may devour"* (1 Pet 5:8); he adds, *"Resist him, steadfast in the faith,"* then *"after you have suffered a while, [He will] perfect, establish, strengthen, and settle you"* (5:10).

It won't be easy, and the hardships of slander, ridicule, and persecution are unavoidable, if we remain faithful to Christ and His word, but the *"glory which shall be revealed in us"* (Rom 8:18) makes whatever our suffering to pale into insignificance. Be brave for God today!

"Dear Mighty God, our spiritual battle ramps up daily, and I am very thankful for Your power, which I wear as armor. Help me be disciplined by Your word and prepare to honor You in each opportunity to stand up for You."

SEPTEMBER 22

Take Up the Helmet and the Sword

Eph 6:17—*"And **take***~ **the helmet of salvation** and the sword of the Spirit, which is the word of God."*

We need all of God's armor to withstand Satan's onslaughts (Eph 6:14–16). In the preceding verses four participles—*fastening, putting on, fitting,* and *taking up*—indicate the means by which believers can take their stand. Metaphorically, we are to *"fasten the belt of truth around [the] waist"* (6:14a). We are to be certain that our reliance is on the truth of God's word, not on men's opinions (Jn 14:6), so as not to be defeated by doubts and false arguments.

We *"put on the breastplate of righteousness"* (Eph 6:14b). We have been given the righteousness of Christ (2 Cor 5:21) to withstand the accusations of Satan (Rev 12:10), who delights in proving how unworthy and undeserving we are of Christ's faithfulness to keep us covered with His righteousness (Rom 3:22).

Our *"feet"* are to be *"fitted with the readiness that comes from the gospel of peace"* (Eph 6:15[NIV]). If we are clear on the gospel message and are eager to share it, we can stand firm in battle with an inner peace: *"The peace of God, which surpasses all understanding, will guard your hearts and minds through Christ Jesus"* (Phil 4:7).

Likewise, we *"take up the shield of faith"* (Eph 6:16), whereby we have confidence in and rely upon God. The *"flaming arrows of the evil one"* (6:16)— doubt, temptation, anger, lust, despair, vengeance, trials, or impossibilities— should not move us. We are assured that *"whatever is born of God conquers the world. And this is the victory ... our faith"* (1 Jn 5:4). His word never fails.

Now the imperative *"take"* in verse 17 communicates another means by which to stand firm in battle. Every soldier had a helmet that the enemy's sword could not penetrate—the *"helmet of salvation."* The believer is to *"put on the hope of salvation as a helmet"* (1 Thes 5:8). This hope assures us that we will be protected against any attack. No matter what might happen, we have no need to fear, because our salvation is sure.

Likewise we are to "take" the "sword of the Spirit, ... the word of God" is our only offensive weapon. The Spirit proclaims God's word, penetrating the inner consciousness, convicting us of sin, and healing the very wounds it causes. Develop the discipline of mastering the word as a sword.

"Thank You, Father, for the hope and assurance Your salvation supplies to each believer. May I always be aware of all that it means as I live each moment for You."

SEPTEMBER 23

Work for Your Living

2 Thes 3:10—*"For even when we were with you, we used to give you this command: 'If anyone is not willing to work, **neither should he eat~~.'"***

Cultures have typically denigrated the value of work, delegating it either to the lower classes or to slaves. For the biblical Christian, every activity is a spiritual duty, an opportunity to give glory to God (1 Cor 10:31).

Paul elevated the concept to working directly for the Lord: *"Slaves [like employees], be obedient to those who are your masters according to the flesh [as employers], with fear and trembling, in the sincerity of your heart, as to Christ; not by way of eye service, as men-pleasers, but as slaves of Christ, doing the will of God from the heart. With good will render service, as to the Lord, and not to men"* (Eph 6:5–7). Christ perceives the motives for our work.

In Thessalonica, some refused to work, obligating the congregation to support them. Taking advantage of Christian hospitality, kindness, and generosity merited Paul's stern reprimand. Anyone *"not willing to work"* (Gk. "desire, implies active volition and purpose") suggests that the person had the choice to work, but refused.

Lazy men did not want take the commands of God's word seriously. In 2 Thessalonians 3:6, Paul said, *"Now we command you, brethren, in the name of our Lord Jesus Christ, that you keep away from every brother who leads an unruly life"* (i.e., "out of line, disorderly, doing nothing, or undisciplined"). Any command recorded in the New Testament is given with the full authority of Christ and is to be obeyed unquestioningly.

This does not mean we should not help those with disabilities or those who lack job opportunities (Matt 6:2–3; Gal 2:10; Heb 13:16). Paul is referring to those who are *"not willing to work"* and seek to exploit others. Those who do work should pay no entitlements to those who will not work: *"A worker's appetite works for him, for his hunger urges him on"* (Prov 16:26). Let us pray for those who need skills and opportunities to earn a living so that God's people can be respected for obeying the principles of His word.

"Dear Lord, being resourceful and working for a living gives direction and meaning to our lives, to say nothing of putting food on our tables. I am thankful for the strength and ability to accomplish good things."

SEPTEMBER 24

Do Not Get Angry about the Lord's Discipline

Heb 12:5—*"And have you forgotten the exhortation addressed to you as sons? 'My son,* **do not scorn~|** *the Lord's discipline or* **give up~|** *when He corrects you.'"*

God wants us to conform to the image of Christ through personal study and application of God's word; He will exhort us by various means or persons. If this fails to get our attention, he will personally discipline and correct us. This can be a painful experience.

When God's word is neglected, it is easily forgotten. The readers of Hebrews 12:5 had *"forgotten the exhortation,"* which led them to two negative consequences. Let's learn from them.

First of all, the believers were to *"cease from scorning,"* which means having "little esteem for something, be[ing] careless about, or despis[ing]." They despised the providential suffering, seeing no benefit in it. They were *"careless"*—that is, they did not care about or value whatever God's purpose might be. They were spiritually indifferent.

Suffering can discourage one's faith, provoke uncertainty, create doubts of God's power, or lead to despair. What might appear as God's neglect or abandonment might actually be His *"discipline"* (Gk. "instruction to children, chastening, or correction"). How can we determine if the situation is discipline from the Lord or attacks by Satan? We cannot! Because God controls our circumstances, everything is a learning experience. We must treat our difficulties as lessons on how to grow in His wisdom and grace. We should examine our motives, our behavior, our decision making, the quality of our relationships, and our integrity in doing God's will.

Second, believers are commanded to *"stop giving up when He corrects you."* Giving up is a product of our modern concept of permissiveness and an anti-punishment psychology. God takes disobedience seriously and punishes sin. Society says that such chastisement is "cruel and unusual punishment." In spite of our self-centered reaction to His correction, God never rejects us or ceases to love us. His punishments have a purpose. He promises to *"never leave [us] or forsake [us],"* so He goes through our sufferings with us. Let's hold His hand and learn wisdom, always honoring the Savior.

"Heavenly Father, thank You for showing Your great love for me by chastening me when I need it. Help me to always recognize Your loving hand in all that happens to mold my life for Your purposes."

SEPTEMBER 25
Endure Suffering as Discipline

Heb 12:7—*"**Endure~~ your suffering** as discipline; God is treating you as sons. For what son is there that a father does not discipline?"*

Elisabeth Elliot wrote, "God will go to any lengths to bring us to acknowledge who He is" (Elliot, *A Lamp unto My Feet*, p. 21). If He is your Father, Savior, and Lord, it should be no surprise when He treats you accordingly. Being a "son" or "daughter" of God does not mean that you are exempt from chastisement and suffering. It just means He is with you.

The ability to endure suffering is to be learned through the parental process of discipline. Only a parent can and should discipline children. Children need loving parental care for their personal development. Biblically, parents are obligated to discipline their children. If they do not, the children will inevitably have to learn from the harsh, cruel world.

When disciplined properly—without anger or rejection—children *"respect [their parents] for it"* (Heb 12:9). Children learn that they are punished *"for a little while as [their parents] thought best"* (12:10). After the punishment is over, life goes on with another lesson learned and the family bond intact.

Sometimes parents want their children's friendship and affection so much that they refuse to inflict any pain in punishment. The closing argument of Hebrews 12:7 is a rhetorical question: *"Today, what father never disciplines his son?"*

One of the most glaring conflicts between the Bible and psychology is found in Proverbs 13:24: *"Those who spare the rod hate their children, but those who love them are diligent to discipline them."* Likewise, in Proverbs 29:15, *"a child who gets his own way brings shame to his mother"* and to the rest of his family. So it is in the family of God. He dares not allow us to be "spoiled children."

God promises to undertake the responsibility to break our will—but not our spirit—in order to make us humble and obedient in our walk with Him. We are to *"continually endure our suffering as discipline."* A wise man once said, "The measure of your character is what it takes to stop you" (from a sermon by Bob Jones Sr.).

"Dear Lord, You are our loving Father who will not allow us to stray far from Your plan. I praise You for the security Your discipline affords."

SEPTEMBER 26

Put Away Filth and
Welcome God's Word

James 1:21—*"So **put away***~ **all filth** and evil excess and humbly **welcome***~ the message implanted within you, which is able to save your souls."*

Our corrupt flesh reaches its ugly tentacles into the life of every believer. James 1:21 is written to the *"dear brothers"* (1:19) who are to urgently decide to *"put away all filth and evil."* The aorist-tense verb indicates a once-and-for-all decision to quit justifying our sinful behaviors and to just "strip them off as a garment."

Paul taught the same principle to the Ephesians: *"You were taught with reference to your former way of life to lay aside the old man who is being corrupted in accordance with deceitful desires, to be renewed in the spirit of your mind"* (Eph 4:22–23). Then he wrote to Christians in Colossae, *"Put them all aside: anger, wrath, malice, slander, and abusive speech from your mouth"* (Col. 3:8–10).

We are to shed all moral evil or *"all filth"*—the root word for *earwax* that must be cleaned out for good hearing. Moral filth impairs our hearing and understanding of God's word and extinguishes our interest in change.

We are also to shed all *"evil,"* or "moral wickedness and corruption," which is composed of deliberate, planned sins that can reside in the heart as lustful or greedy fantasies long before our sins become a reality. Whether acted on or not, the damage to our character and motivation for God is the same. This evil is modified by the adjective *"excess,"* meaning our "preference." The believer is to *"lay aside every weight, and the sin which so easily ensnares us"* (Heb 12:1).

We are to *"humbly welcome the message implanted within."* The *"message"* (Gk. "word") has already been *"implanted,"* as a seed in the *"good soil"* (Matt 13:8,23) of our hearts and minds at the time of our salvation; the implication of the aorist tense is that we must decide *from now on* to *"welcome"* all of the word into our lives.

The word has the power to *"save [our] souls"* because it is the basis of our saving faith (Rom 10:17; Eph 2:8). Its instructions will save us from the dominion of sin, and it will eventually bring us to glory. Do you love the word?

"Loving Lord, everything we do that does not honor You is 'filth' to You. Help me to understand this concept fully and truly believe it, so I may want only what You want."

SEPTEMBER 27

Watch Out for the
Doctrine of the Pharisees

Matt 16:6—*"'Watch out~~,' Jesus said to them, 'beware~~ of the yeast of the Pharisees and Sadducees.'"*

It only takes a small amount of yeast to make a large mound of dough rise and change into leavened bread. During the Passover celebration, Jews were not allowed to use any yeast, nor was it permitted to be anywhere in their homes (Ex 12:14–20). Yeast was used as a metaphor for evil teaching and hypocritical leaders. Bad teachings and attitudes can lead an entire group down a wrong and dangerous trail.

In Matthew 16:6, we are commanded to *"be continually watching out"* for false concepts. The disciples had been trained to follow and respect their leaders, and now Jesus was warning against them. The warning is repeated in verse 11, with a clarifying statement in verse 12, referring to *"the teaching of the Pharisees and Sadducees."* The *"Pharisees and Sadducees"* were considered as a group. They were enemies of Jesus's teachings and attempted to manipulate the population with fear, ostracizing or even killing opponents to protect their power base. Jesus prohibited such tactics (Mark 10:42–44).

Jesus saw the Pharisees, who were legalistic interpreters of the Jewish law with thousands of traditional applications they could not keep (Matt 23:13–36). The Sadducees were the religious, politically correct members of the aristocracy. Though they accepted the five books of Moses, they did not believe in the resurrection (22:23–33) or angels (Acts 23:6–10).

An incorrect view of morality had led the Gentile Corinthians to allow perverse *"sexual immorality"* to remain unchallenged within their congregation. Paul said, this *"is not good. Do you not know that a little leaven leavens the whole lump? Therefore purge out the old leaven, that you may be a new lump, since you truly are unleavened"* (1 Cor 5:6–7).

The true disciple is to be alert to the destructive influences of judgmental legalists and weak, politically correct deniers of biblical truth and morality. Both of these views teach a critical, retaliatory attitude toward anyone who opposes their traditions. New Testament instructions and commands are ignored and their value minimized in favor of the legalistic traditions and politically correct power struggles of intimidating leaders. We are never to tolerate fear, threats, and intimidation among us.

"Lord Jesus, I want to be alert to destructive beliefs. Guide my daily learning through Your word so I may not allow 'little' ideas to sneak in and corrupt Your truth."

SEPTEMBER 28
Beware of the Legalist

Luke 20:46—*"**Beware**~~ **of the experts** in the law. They like walking around in long robes, and they love elaborate greetings in the marketplaces and the best seats in the synagogues and the places of honor at banquets."*

If we believe that prestige in this world is equivalent to prestige before God, we will strive to be important and revered by people. This attitude reveals a set of values that corrupts a godly character.

In Luke 20:45, Jesus spoke publicly to His disciples and to *"all the people"* listening in on His teachings as He listed a series of symptoms of a deeper problem in the beliefs and values of their spiritual leaders. Jewish leaders had ceased to serve to benefit others and had become self-seeking, self-gratifying, and self-glorifying by pretending to be more important than they actually were.

In Luke 20:46, He describes the *"experts,"* "scribes," or teachers in the schools and synagogues, who considered themselves authorities in the law of Moses. Theirs was a superficial doctrine with little heartfelt obedience or worship. Their lives were full of greed, pride, and self-righteousness. They could not handle anyone being respected more than they thought they should be. Jesus gave a description of their narcissism that can speak to leadership in any culture.

Pride motivated them to wear special clothing that set them apart as prestigious and pompous religious leaders to be recognized and respected. They sought to gain attention by *"lov[ing] . . . greetings in the marketplaces"*; their egos were enhanced when they flaunted their positions in public. Their conversations were all about themselves. They always sought prominence by claiming *"the best seats . . . and places of honor."* They constantly pushed themselves into the limelight, jealous when anyone else was honored. They were always after more money, even taking from those who had little (i.e., widows), probably for favors or religious benefits (Luke 20:47a). They worked to appear spiritual by *"making long prayers"* (20:47b).

The command is not only to be weary of such self-centeredness in other leaders but, more important, to *"beware"* not to fall into the same superficial, hypocritical leadership style. Stay humble as the Master!

"Dear Master, pride and selfishness are so powerful that they can make my life unprofitable for Your plan. Teach me to be humble, as You are, while I do my best to serve others, not myself."

SEPTEMBER 29

Beware of Dogs and Evil Workers

Phil 3:2—*"Beware~~ of the dogs, beware~~ of the evil workers, beware~~ of those who mutilate the flesh!"*

Paul warned the church at Philippi concerning the coming false teachers (Phil 3:1), and in 3:2 he repeats his warning three times, with the present imperative to *"be continually beware,"* of *"dogs," "evil workers,"* and *"those who mutilate the flesh."* He did not mince words or show any compassion for false teachers. Who were these people, and what did they teach?

Dogs refers to scavenger dogs that roamed in packs, feeding on garbage. They were despised, hence the derogatory connotation to these Jewish teachers.

The false teachers prided themselves on their supposed goodness, fasting, and religious ceremonies, but they actually were *"evil workers,"* denying a gospel of unmerited grace. Teachings of sacraments or rituals to save you is false.

The phrase *"those who mutilate the flesh"* refers to Judaizers who wanted believers to become circumcised Jews in order to be saved. However, the term used here is used in the Septuagint (the Greek Old Testament) for pagan religious mutilation in Leviticus 21:5 and 1 Kings 18:28. Paul is stating that religious circumcision—or any external rite or ceremony—is as meaningless as a pagan ritual. They have no benefit for salvation.

Though circumcision is not an issue today, many people trust in their baptism, church membership, communion, or good deeds to others as a way to earn God's approval. Many try to keep the Ten Commandments to be good enough for God, but no one can keep them perfectly. James declared, "the one who obeys the whole law but fails in one point has become guilty of all of it"(Jas 2:10[NET]). Even Abraham was saved by faith alone (Gen 15:6) before he was circumcised (Rom 4:10). Good works cannot erase sin.

The New Testament believer seeks to be obedient out of a heart of gratitude for forgiving grace received by faith. Paul continues stating his own religious accomplishments, only to declare, *"What things were gain to me, I have counted as loss for Christ . . . and count them as rubbish . . . and be found in Him, not having my own righteousness, which is from the law, but that which is through faith in Christ, the righteousness which is from God by faith"* (Phil 3:7–9). Rejoice that you know the truth of the gospel by faith!

"Dear Jesus, it is not our own goodness but Yours that makes this life worth living. Help me to recognize and avoid following leaders who only desire to point others to their own greatness. Thank you for your grace to forgive."

SEPTEMBER 30

Be Careful of Philosophy

Col 2:8—*"Be careful~~ not to allow anyone to captivate you* *through an empty, deceitful philosophy that is according to human traditions and the elemental spirits of the world, and not according to Christ."*

When a person comes to Christ, *"all things have become new"* (2 Cor 5:17).The new transformed life also requires a new set of beliefs about life and reality and a new set of values. *"Do not be conformed to this world, but be transformed by the renewing of your mind"* (Rom 12:2); we must learn to think biblically.

We should *"beware of the false prophets, who come . . . in sheep's clothing, but inwardly are ravenous wolves"* (Matt 7:15). False teachers can convince believers of wrong values, priorities, and errors: *"You therefore, beloved . . . , be on your guard lest, being carried away by the error of unprincipled men, you fall from your own steadfastness"* (2 Pet 3:17).

God's warning is *"not to allow anyone to captivate you."* Due to ignorance of God's word, we can be unaware of our susceptibility to the attractions of false teachings. This deceit and its captivation come through *"empty, deceitful philosophy"* (used only here in the New Testament): speculations, miraculous arguments, or deductive logic to formulate theories to unanswerable questions not found in the word of God.

The two sources of these philosophies are *"human traditions and elemental spirits of the world."* The first source is man's additions of traditions to Scripture that become sacred. Jesus was asked, *"Why do Your disciples not walk according to the tradition of the elders?"* (Mark 7:5). False Christianity likewise trusts in teachings contrary to the Bible because they are traditions.

The second source, the *"elemental spirits of the world,"* or "basic parts," refers to simplistic, childish thoughts. Galatians 4:3 refers to the unsaved as being *"held in bondage under the elemental things of the world,"* or the simplistic notion that a person must be or can be good enough for salvation. Every false religion teaches this. These foolish ideas are *"not according to Christ,"* who *"has forgiven us all our trespasses by canceling the record of debt that stood against us . . . This he set aside, nailing it to the cross"* (Col 2:13–14[ESV]). Access to forgiveness is only by faith in Christ alone. False teachers focus on new revelations or traditions that distract from God's word. Develop a plan to study and know His word to recognize error. Trust the Scriptures alone.

"Heavenly Father, help me only to be captivated by Your love and truth rather than allowing my thinking to be clouded by the deceitful ways of this world."

OCTOBER 1

Watch Out for Dissension

Rom 16:17—*"Now I urge you, brothers and sisters, to watch out for those who create dissensions and obstacles contrary to the teaching that you learned. **Avoid them***~!"*

In warfare, especially spiritual warfare, the enemy does not identify himself. The enemy is without and within. Once identified, they must be avoided.

Paul was greatly concerned that the Roman churches have correct doctrine, a clear understanding of their responsibilities to each other, and peace and unity within the body. In the midst of growing persecution, any internal fighting, disagreements, or divisions were unacceptable. Christ provides forgiveness with His own blood (Acts 28:20), indwells believers through the Spirit, and makes them members of each other and of Him (1 Cor 12:12, 25). Creating divisions and dissonance in this sacred body is the highest offense against our Lord Jesus.

Paul was *"continually urging"* (i.e., to "ask for something earnestly") the brethren in Rome to *"watch out for those who create dissensions."* The verb means to "mark, spy out, examine or look critically at." From the Greek word, we get the word *scope*, as in microscope or radarscope. Thus they were (and we are) to watch anyone who would seek to undermine or contradict the *"teaching"*—that is, the divinely revealed apostolic teaching and divinely inspired record of that teaching in the New Testament.

False teaching always creates *"dissensions and obstacles."* These two words refer to "divisions," which means "discord, tearing apart, disunion," and those who *"create ... obstacles,"* which means "a trigger in an animal trap, a hidden consequence, an enticement to conduct which could ruin the person in question."

Questioning the integrity or validity of God's word or teaching heresy while pretending to be a Christian must be dealt with scripturally (Matt 18:16–17). We are to *"decide to avoid"* those people. There is to be no debate. John also warned us, *"If anyone comes to you and does not bring this teaching, do not receive him into your house and do not give him any greeting"* (2 John 10). If we love God's word more than our own lives, we will protect its teachings. If we love His church, we will keep her true to His word and not allow divisive people to destroy her. Pray for biblical unity of your church.

"Lord, I love Your church so much that I do not want to have anything to do with creating dissension by fighting over new prophecies. I want to be a peacemaker, but I will not tolerate those who contradict Your word."

OCTOBER 2

Know the Welcome in Heaven
Is Worth It All

Matt 25:21—*"His master answered, 'Well done, good and faithful slave! . . .* **Enter*~ into the joy** *of your master.'"*

Of all the commands in the New Testament, this is the easiest to obey: *"Enter into the joy of your master."* Although this is the conclusion to the parable of the talents, it is the hope of all believers to hear these words as they enter God's paradise.

Being a slave in the first century was a thankless task. Jesus said, *"Does [the slave master] thank that servant because he did the things that were commanded him? I think not"* (Luke 17:9). A slave owner may have noticed competence and diligence and might have rewarded a slave (as in Matt 24:46) or perhaps given him greater responsibility (Matt 24:47), but to praise a slave was rare—but not so with God.

In this parable, the "master," or owner, is away for an indefinite period, implying that his return will not be immediate (Luke 19:11). Upon returning, he would determine which of his slaves were faithful and had been useful for his purposes. Jesus implied that His return soon, for that would quench their motivation for zeal and long-term planning for global evangelization. Jesus expected them to begin a strategy and make it happen, and He would not return until they finished the task of getting the gospel to every language and culture on earth (Matt 24:14).

According to the parable, the master's return would be sudden and unexpected. Just as in the parable, Christ will evaluate every servant according to what and how he has contributed to the main purpose of the church: making disciples in every people group on earth (Matt 28:19–20). He only told them what to do, not how to do it.

Paul wrote to Timothy, *"I have fought the good fight, I have finished the course, I have kept the faith; in the future there is laid up for me the crown of righteousness, which the Lord, the righteous Judge, will award to me on that day"* (2 Tim. 4:7–8). Our Master will honor those who took the initiative to fulfill His desire to tell everyone what He has done and how great He is. As the hymn says, "It will be worth it all when we see Jesus!" (hymn by Esther K. Rusthoi).

"Lord, Thank You for gifting me and investing so much in me; my life now only finds meaning in living for Your kingdom and the purpose of making You known in this world."

OCTOBER 3
Become Like a Servant (Slave)

Luke 22:26—*"So Jesus said to them, 'The kings of the Gentiles lord it over them, and those in authority over them are called "benefactors." Not so with you; instead the one who is greatest among **you must become***~ **like the youngest**, and the leader like the one who serves.'"*

One of Jesus's most remarkable teachings concerned His view of leadership. He marked a distinction between how the believer leads and how the unsaved world leads: in the world, some *"lord it over,"* or control by *"authority,"* but this was not the way His followers were to lead their families and ministries.

One has to wonder if the disciples responded to this teaching as they did to His teaching on a very limited right to divorce: *"If this is the situation between a husband and wife, it is better not to marry"* (Matt 19:10). The threat of divorce was their means of control over their wives. Did they now think the same way about His form of leadership? When you think of all the leaders you know, do some stand out as servants, or do most seem like strong leaders, micro-managers, controlling every decision and refusing to delegate?

The events of Luke 22:26 occurred on the eve of Jesus's crucifixion. The disciples assumed Jesus would take control of the city, and they wanted to know which of them *"was to be regarded as the greatest"* (Luke 22:24) in this new kingdom that surely Jesus was about to begin. Their heads were filled with grandeur, importance, and power.

Jesus did not say there would be no leaders in His new order, but he said they would lead from entirely different principles. The only way a person can be a leader is if someone is following him! The question is, why do people follow any leader? Is it out of fear or anger or public criticism? Is it the charisma, importance, wealth, or popularity of a leader that attracts others to blindly follow him? Or is it due to the selfless, caring acts and edifying commitment of a servant-leader who seeks what is best for his followers rather than himself?

The "patron" syndrome of paternalistic dominance, as a father over a preschool child, is not the model Jesus sought to replicate in His disciples. Jesus's leadership model takes the attitude of a "servant" with no extrinsic authority. He is granted increasing authority as others learn how faithful, wise, and committed he is to them. Which kind of leader do you want to become?

"Lord, put me behind the cross and give me Your eyes to see the needs of others, if I'm willing to give up my personal interests to benefit others."

OCTOBER 4
Test Yourself

2 Cor 13:5—*"**Put yourselves to the test**~~ to see if you are in the faith; **examine yourselves**~~! Or do you not recognize regarding yourselves that Jesus Christ is in you– unless, indeed, you fail the test!"*

Paul had chosen to adopt Jesus's example of leadership: *"He was crucified in weakness, yet He lives by the power of God"* (2 Cor 13:4). This power-in-weakness model required patience, exalting righteousness and obedience without crushing others through harshness or a demanding superiority. The Corinthian church needed Paul's discipline. It grieved him so much that he canceled a third visit (1:23–2:4), hoping that they would respond to this letter as they had his earlier letter (7:8–13) so he could rejoice with them and not deal with divisive issues.

False teachers had introduced legalism, fostering a false sense of self-righteousness while hiding a bitter, critical, dissenting spirit that would set believers against believers and discredit Paul's apostleship, which he had been defending for several chapters. Paul said, *"For I fear lest, when I come, I shall not find you such as I wish, and that I shall be found by you such as you do not wish; lest there be contentions, jealousies, outbursts of wrath, selfish ambition, back biting, whispering, conceit, tumult"* (2 Cor 12:20). Self-righteous legalism often covers unrepentant, contentious attitudes. He waited to let them respond.

In 2 Corinthians 13:15, Paul challenges them to turn their critical attitudes inward, to *"put [them]selves to the test to see if [they were] in the faith."* They needed to take the beam out of their own eyes before criticizing the splinter in another's (Matt 7:1–5).

The two commands for believers are *"to test,"* or "learn the character of someone" (Louw and Nida, *Greek-English Lexicon*, p. 46.), and *"to examine,"* means "to approve a thing whether it is worthy or not" or "to learn the genuineness of something by examination" (Louw and Nida, *Greek-English Lexicon*, p. 45). They were to test themselves to see whether they were *"in the faith,"* the evidence being their response to Paul's exhortation.

Before sharing in the Lord's Supper, *"a man must examine himself, and in so doing he is to eat of the bread and drink of the cup ... But if we judged ourselves rightly, we would not be judged"* (1 Cor 11:28, 31). Practice examining yourself. Is there any area of disobedience in your life you must deal with today?

"I am appalled at my unworthiness, and I am desperate for Your mercy and gracious gift of righteousness. Without Your promise, I'd have no hope of eternal life. I am so grateful my whole life is Yours."

OCTOBER 5

Do Not Be Subject to Legalism

Gal 5:1—*"For freedom Christ has set us free.* **Stand firm~~***, then, and* **do not be subject~~** *again to the yoke of slavery."*

Slavery to pagan religion or the legalistic system of Judaism is the subject of Paul's declaration in Galatians 5:1: *"For freedom Christ has set us free."* Christ is the great liberator who sets the believer free from bondage to sin's dreadful addiction; laws that are impossible to keep (Gal 3:24); or worse, the bondage of man-made traditions and rules that foster fake spirituality.

Christ wants us to live on an entirely different level, guided by principles and empowered by the Spirit, marking a broad circle in which we are free to make decisions that honor Him. Paul describes our liberty within limits this way: *"For you, brethren, have been called to liberty; only do not use liberty as an opportunity to indulge your flesh [as partially defined in Gal 5:19], but through love serve one another. Christ's liberty does not mean a license to sin"* (Gal 5:13).

When a person is united to Christ through the baptism of the Spirit—that is, by *"putting him into Christ"* (1 Cor 12:13)—his spirit is bonded with Christ's, making him a new creature (2 Cor 5:17). The presence of the Spirit progressively produces Christlikeness (Gal 5:22–23a). This godly character is much better than pretended obedience to the law. Paul declares, *"Against such things [qualities or "fruit"] there is no law"* (5:23b), thus it is never wrong to practice the fruit of the Spirit.

As he says in Romans, *"God be thanked that though you were slaves of sin, yet you obeyed from the heart that form of doctrine to which you were delivered. And having been set free from sin, you became slaves of righteousness. I speak in human terms because of the weakness of your flesh. For just as you presented your members as slaves of uncleanness, and of lawlessness leading to more lawlessness, so now present your members as slaves of righteousness for holiness"* (Rom 6:17–19).

He commands that we *"continue to stand firm"* in liberty, choosing to be a slave of Christ, where real freedom is enjoyed. Evidently, many were tempted to add legalistic works to their faith in their vain attempts to become more acceptable to God. How foolish, for the gift of His perfect righteousness makes us forever acceptable!

"I have an overwhelming sense of freedom since trusting in You as my Savior. Thank You for accepting me just as I am. I don't have to impress You. I just want to please You with my life and avoid doing things just to please men."

OCTOBER 6

Be Strong in Grace

2 Tim 2:1—*"So you, my child,* **be strong**~~ **in the grace** *that is in Christ Jesus."*

The key to any athletic involvement is strength building through daily exercises. Likewise, spiritual strength building will require daily disciplined practices designed to stretch our commitment until it hurts and increase our endurance for understanding God's wisdom and how He governs our life circumstances and relationships.

When Paul sent Timothy on a mission to build up the churches, Timothy ran into many problems and conflicts that may have caused him to question his gifts and the sufficiency of God's intervention. Timothy was challenged to "rekindle God's gift that you possess" (2 Tim 1:6[NET]). He did not need more of God; he only needed greater wisdom and confidence to use his gifts without hesitation. The Spirit of God, which was not a *"spirit of fear, but of power and of love and of a sound mind"* (2 Tim 1:7), dwelt within him.

Timothy had to forget the notion of popularity, stop being ashamed of *"the testimony of the Lord,"* and commit to *"suffering for the gospel according to the power of God"* (1:8), just as Paul was doing. Timothy needed to *"retain the standard of sound words which [he had] heard from [Paul], in the faith and love which are in Christ Jesus"* (1:13). In addition, he had to avoid some faithless church members, like Phygelus and Hermogenes (2 Tim 1:15) and associate with faithful believers, like Onesiphorus and his household (1:15–16).

Timothy was commanded to *"be strong,"* or "be enabled, capacitated, strengthened," especially "in the grace that is in Christ Jesus." The actual grace that is *"in Christ Jesus"* is to become the grace motivation for our actions as well. This transfer of grace occurs when we act like Him in obedience by forgiving those who hurt or disappoint us. Grace is received by resting in the *"comfort we ourselves have received from God"* (2 Cor 1:4) to endure all things.

In Paul's worst moment, he knew Christ was with him, as in his trial before Caesar: *"The Lord stood at my side and gave me strength, so that through me the message might be fully proclaimed and all the Gentiles might hear it"* (2 Tim 4:17). Someone once said, "One with Jesus is a majority." With our Partner at our side, we can take on any task or any foe. How can you be strengthened by grace today?

"Lord, the grace that filled Your life is flowing in my life as well, according to Your word. I believe I can endure and persevere in my situation by Your grace and presence with me. Thank You, Lord."

Make Every Effort to Be Approved

2 Tim 2:15—*"**Make every effort***~ **to present yourself** before God as a proven worker who does not need to be ashamed, teaching the message of truth accurately."*

There is a vast difference between being accepted and being approved. It is one thing to be accepted into college but an entirely different thing to graduate summa cum laude. As we accept God's promise of salvation by faith, we are accepted entirely without merit, and our heart's desire is to be approved by our Savior, not for ourselves, but to show Him honor.

In 2 Timothy 2:15, Paul commanded Timothy (and us as well) to *"make every effort to present yourself before God."* The imperative means "to do one's best, be diligent, or desire eagerly"—that is, we must persevere to accomplish a particular objective. The point is "to decide from now on to present yourself before God," "to stand alongside of or before God," or to live in His presence. We should do things to be accountable to God for whatever and however we seek to serve Him.

A believer's goal is to become *"a proven worker"*—that is, we should be able to pass a careful examination to be counted as worthy. Just as great athletes bring honor to their coaches, so great students of God's word bring honor and respect to their Savior and Lord. The diligent worker is one who labors long and hard at a task, as a farmer or an artisan, to teach something correctly and efficiently.

The phrase *"who does not need to be ashamed"* refers to false teachers who inject their own ideas into their teachings. It implies that they will be brought to shame. The purpose of the diligent teacher is always to please God and seek His approval, especially in the way he teaches God's word. Paul wrote to the Galatians, *"For am I now seeking the favor of men, or of God? Or am I striving to please men? If I were still trying to please men, I would not be a bond-servant of Christ"* (Gal 1:10). Just as Jesus warned us not to be men-pleasers (Matt 6:1), Paul sought approval only from *"God to be entrusted with the gospel, so we speak, not as pleasing men but God, who examines our hearts"* (1 Thes 2:4).

The thrill of accurately discovering the original sense of God's mind through the divinely inspired authors is worth every effort. Do you love His word enough to be diligent in studying and teaching it?

"Your word, Lord, is so important to me that my heart's desire is to diligently explain it as You meant for men to understand it. Keep me disciplined to master Your meaning as You want Your church to know You."

OCTOBER 8
Avoid Profane Chatter

2 Tim 2:16—"*But avoid~~ profane chatter, because those occupied with it will stray further and further into ungodliness.*"

The believer is to accurately understand the meaning of God's word and teach it with clarity (2 Tim 2:15), avoiding "profane chatter" with those who are willing to accept false ideas, myths, or stories of angelic encounters that lead them to views that differ from the text itself. When people are unwilling to limit their knowledge of God and truth to the recorded, inspired, and inerrant word of God, they will argue that their "miraculous" experiences are genuinely from God. False teachers always look for impressive and convincing experiences that cannot be analyzed or confirmed but give the impression of their spiritual elitism.

Paul advised Titus to be careful of these same issues: "*Shun foolish controversies and genealogies and strife and disputes about the Law; for they are unprofitable and worthless*" (Titus 3:9). Certain conversations with false teachers are to be avoided. Paul wrote to Timothy, "*Reject profane and old wives' fables, and exercise yourself toward godliness*" (1 Tim 4:7), and "*Guard what was committed to your trust, avoiding the profane and idle babblings and contradictions of what is falsely called knowledge*" (6:20). Arguing over the validity of dreams and impressions is useless.

In 2 Timothy 2:16, Paul is instructing believers about how to deal with heretical views that distort biblical truth, which if allowed to become the subject of discussions throughout the church will "*lead to further ungodliness*," or "lack of reverence, neglect or violations" of God's commands. When these views are entertained, there is less interest in discovering the true meaning of Scripture and obeying what it says. Christians who are weak in the faith might feel that these ideas are better than Scripture. This is dangerous! Peter faced a similar problem: "*Many will follow their sensuality, and because of them the way of the truth will be maligned*" (2 Tim 2:2). Small errors in understanding can lead to broad deviations in practice.

Some Christian institutions, once biblical in their beliefs, have become distorted by false doctrine. Such popular and appealing concepts become viral and "*will spread like gangrene*" (1 Tim 2:17). We must always work to protect God's word.

"Lord, I get confused at times with all the differing opinions about some interpretations of Your word and the passion with which some argue their point. Help me to only be persuaded by the clear meaning of Your word, not by men."

OCTOBER 9

Be Self-Controlled;
Do the Work of an Evangelist

2 Tim 4:5—*"You, however, **be self-controlled**~~ in all things, **endure hardship***~, **do an evangelist's work***~, **fulfill***~ your ministry."*

It is amazing how susceptible people can become to false views and emotion-based errors. Paul just warned Timothy (1 Tim 4:3) that for some *"the time will come when they will not endure sound doctrine"* or *"healthy teachings"* (Gk. *hugiaino*, from which we get the English word *hygiene*). People will choose teachers *"according to their own desires"* (the word for *"lusts,"* or a *craving* for emotional experiences), *"because they have itching ears"* (a metaphor for wanting to feel good or boost their self-image), *"they will heap up for themselves teachers"* (4:3). Self-help and sentimental preachers are always popular.

Paul gives four imperatives in response to these circumstances. First, he commands Timothy (and us as well) to *"be self-controlled"* (lit. "free from intoxicants,") or *"sober-minded, watchful,"* that is, well balanced and in control of our thoughts and actions. In the midst of a world in contradicting ideas, fables, and persecution, we are to be calm and balanced *"in all things,"* avoiding fads and the sensational.

Second, Timothy was to *"definitively decide to endure hardship"* (i.e., to "suffer misfortune, evil or affliction"). Any biblically based ministry or person will inevitably be persecuted. Part of being *"self-controlled"* is to know that difficulties will come and to decide the proper reaction. There is no greater privilege than to suffer for His name's sake (Acts 5:41).

Third, Timothy was to *"urgently decide do an evangelist's work."* He is not gifted as an "evangelist," but he is commanded to evangelize, just as any other member of the church. Everyone is to help unbelievers become aware of their sinfulness and to show them how Christ Jesus alone can resolve their sinful issues with God.

Fourth, Timothy was to *"decisively commit to fulfilling"* his ministry. The verb means to "bring to completion." Paul's passion is summarized in Acts 20:24: *"I consider my life worth nothing to me, if only I may finish the race and complete the task the Lord Jesus has given me."* May God give you the commitment to finish His purpose for your life (Eph 2:10).

"Lord, I know the path You have chosen for me is not an easy one; please keep my heart burning for the souls of men to see them turn to trust You."

OCTOBER 10

Rebuke Mistaken Teachers

Titus 1:13—*"Such testimony is true. For this reason* **rebuke~~** *them sharply that they may be healthy in the faith."*

"Tough love" is never easy. The early church was prey to many false ideas because there were few biblical texts. Many teachers would appear claiming to be prophets or apostles.

In a letter to Timothy, Paul wrote, *"The Spirit explicitly says that in later times some will fall away from the faith, paying attention to deceitful spirits and doctrines of demons, by means of the hypocrisy of liars seared in their own conscience as a branding iron"* (1 Tim 4:1–2).

Titus was warned that these people were *"insubordinate, both idle [or empty] talkers and deceivers, especially those of the circumcision"* (Titus 1:10). Their words were appealing, but they said nothing, and they wrapped their falsehoods in distorted concepts and took biblical references out of context. Titus's responsibility concerning these false teachers was to ensure they were *"silenced because they [were] upsetting whole families, teaching things they should not teach"* (1:11).

In Titus 1:13, Titus is commanded, *"For this reason rebuke them sharply,"* which means to "expose, shame, disgrace, or prove one in the wrong." The word *sharply* means "severely, cutting off, or [to] show harshness." False teachers are hazardous to the faith of many and must be cut out of the leadership and any influential roles to demonstrate the seriousness of the danger of incorrect doctrine.

Paul commanded us to be strict with those who contradicted the commands (*"if anyone does not obey our message through this letter, take note of him and do not associate closely with him"* [2 Thes 3:14]). This seems harsh in our politically correct society, but deviating from God's word has damaging effects in lives. Leaders must be courageous.

Paul's objective is *"that they may be healthy in the faith"*; this is tough love. Paul's concern always was for obedience to truth without concern for whether people liked him or not. This is what makes leaders.

"Lord, teach me to be as willing to give exhortation and correction as to receive the same, especially when I deserve it."

OCTOBER 11

Practice Consistent Behavior

Titus 2:1—*"But as for you, **communicate**~~ **the behavior** that goes with sound teaching."*

How can we change a society or nation? Genuine change can never be imposed or forced on people—legalistic systems never change the heart. Paul sought not to change his society's system but to change believers from within. Only then could behavioral transformation occur.

False teachers *"profess to know God, but in works they deny Him, being abominable ['abhorrent, detestable'], disobedient [lit. 'unwilling to be persuaded'], and disqualified [or 'unapproved, worthless'] for every good work"* (Titus 1:16). They distracted people from knowing and obeying the word of God, convincing them to submit to their rules, revelations and visions.

The first word in Titus 2:1, *"but,"* introduces a contrast from the theme of the previous verses (1:10–16). *"As for you"* (i.e., the teachers faithful to God's Word) directs the change from addressing the false teachers to addressing the true leadership of the church. True teachers are commanded to "continually be communicating ['intellectually and with reason'] the behavior that goes with sound teaching." What we think, believe, and value directly affects our emotional motivation toward consistent behavior. The foundation of biblical understanding is vital for godliness. Paul did not write about the "behavior" or the "traditions" (1 Cor 11:2; 2 Thes 2:15; 3:6), but he insisted upon them.

True teachers are to *"teach the older men to be temperate, worthy of respect, self-controlled and sound in faith, in love and in endurance"* (Titus 2:2), not by saying it, but by living it: *"encourage the young men to be self-controlled. In everything set them an example by doing what is good. In your teaching show integrity, seriousness and soundness of speech that cannot be condemned"* (2:6–8). They are to *"remind the people to . . . be ready to do whatever is good, to slander no one, to be peaceable and considerate and to show true humility toward all men"* (3:1–2). None of this is legalistic. None of this curriculum is mere intellectual knowledge; rather, it is taught through a personal display of godly, practical living. These are the teachers we need. Are you becoming one?

"Father, with all my heart I want to live a life that reflects all Your commands and instructions so I can teach the principles of life to others. Show me the way."

OCTOBER 12
Encourage Self-Control

Titus 2:6—*"Encourage~~ younger men** likewise to be self-controlled."*

How do we teach "self-control"? Self-control was so important that it was the only virtue Titus was required to teach the *"younger men"* (i.e., the "inexperienced, immature," and, by implication, typically impulsive men). Maturity, not age, is the issue. It seems that human nature is the same everywhere. Young men tend to be impulsive, selfish, easily angered, emotional, and sometimes arrogant, getting themselves into many kinds of trouble and being lured by a variety of temptations. When these men bear the name of Christ, His reputation is at risk.

In Titus 2:6, Titus is to be *"continually being encouraged"* (or "aid, help, exhort, beseech") the immature. He is primarily to teach these values to *"show [himself] in all respects to be a model of good works and in [his] teaching [to] show integrity, dignity"* (2:7). Coaches spend considerable time teaching their athletes to be self-controlled, lest their anger or reactions ruin the team effort or eliminate them from games. Paul wrote, *"Everyone who competes in the games exercises self-control in all things"* (1 Cor 9:25).

Ephesians 5:18 tells us not to exalt losing control of ourselves. The command *"not [to] be drunk with wine, in which is dissipation, but [to] be filled with the Spirit"* does not compare drunkenness with being filled with the Spirit; rather, the word *but* introduces a contrast or an opposite concept. Drunkenness is wicked because it causes us to lose self-control. In contrast, by the filling of the Spirit, the believer gains *more* self-control (Gal 5:22). Uncontrolled, impulsive reactions are characteristics of the immature, not the Spirit-filled, believer.

As young people experience their first taste of freedom, they face many decisions, just as new believers who understand the freedom of grace. Paul warns, *"For you were called to freedom . . . only do not use your freedom as an opportunity for self-indulgence"* (Gal 5:13). Peter likewise urges, *"As servants of God, live as free people, yet do not use your freedom as a pretext for evil"* (1 Pet 2:16). These principles should be learned early in life, especially in the family, and as a last result in the church ministries. In which areas do you need self-control?

"Lord, teach us to understand that we are all together in the struggle against sin and selfishness so that our encouragement to each other will be accepted by all."

Communicate, Exhort, and Rebuke

Titus 2:15—*"So communicate~~ **these things** with the sort of exhortation **or rebuke~~ that carries full authority. Don't let anyone look down*/ on you.**"*

Probably nowhere in Scripture is the Christian life defined more succinctly than in the preceding four verses. *"For the grace of God that brings salvation has appeared to all men, teaching us that, denying ungodliness and worldly lusts, we should live soberly, righteously, and godly in the present age, looking for the blessed hope and glorious appearing of our great God and Savior Jesus Christ, who gave Himself for us, that He might redeem us from every lawless deed and purify for Himself His own special people, zealous for good works"* (Titus 2:11–14).

Titus, and every reader of this epistle, is charged with *"continually communicating these things"* (i.e., to "talk at random, talk much"), to each other, to children, to friends, and to neighbors why you live the way you do. You should be unashamed about what is important and proactive in discussing your love for Jesus. We must *"be continually exhorting"* (i.e., "beseech, plead, or encourage") believers to understand the implications of their salvation by grace and God's purpose for their lives.

Some will persist in their addiction to sinful behavior and require *"continuous rebuking"* (i.e., "to shame, disgrace, prove one in the wrong"). People must recognize where God draws the line. If we are to live in the blinding light of God's presence by His grace, we must understand His hatred for sin. To have received His grace in salvation yet persist in the same, or worse, sins as before knowing Him is the most grievous of offenses. He sacrificed His life, not so we could sin with impunity, but so we would live always in the light of His presence.

This kind of communication should be performed *"with all authority,"* which means "a command imposed upon someone." It is everyone's responsibility to explain the commands of Scripture to others and to obey them. Titus was to stop letting people intimidate or *"look down"* on him ("disregard" or "despise" him). Stand for the truth and godliness of God's word no matter what the response from others.

"Lord, I cannot live for myself isolated from other believers. Give me the courage and skill to exhort those needing encouragement and rebuke those walking in disobedience. Help me care enough for others to risk their rejection when I speak the truth."

OCTOBER 14
Do Not Boast or Tell Lies

James 3:14—*"But if you have bitter jealousy and selfishness in your hearts, **do not boast~| and tell lies~| against the truth**."*

Concluding his discussion on the difficulty of controlling the tongue, James described *"wise and understanding"* believers (James 3:13a). We should all seek to become persons whose attitudes and actions are *"done in the meekness of wisdom"* (3:13b). If Biblical knowledge does not change lives it is meaningless.

Two attitudes will mark those who are not motivated by wisdom: first, *"bitter jealousy,"* or a "sharp" kind of "fervent rage against another because he does not have what another person has." This kind of person demands to be respected, and anyone else is put down, criticized, or defamed. Second, such people will display "selfishness in [their] hearts," which means they will "[seek] their own benefits or ambitions," which inevitably leads to "contention, strife, rivalry and scheming for personal advantage." These inner attitudes become self-evident in behavior.

James is telling believers to "stop or cease boasting" (or "being arrogant or rejoicing against someone," especially "to degrade someone"). Boasting is so normal that it is almost expected. People say, "If you don't toot your own horn, nobody will." Arrogance often is seen as self-confidence. Most people, especially leaders, want to boast of their accomplishments, importance, and successes.

James commands us to "stop or cease telling lies against the truth"—that is, do not "cheat, defraud, falsify, [or] speak deceitfully." Inevitably, when one is ambitious to be the best, or the most important person, his need for self-promotion will cause him to exaggerate, fabricate falsehoods, and deceive, *"for where envy and self-seeking exist, confusion and every evil thing are there"* (James 3:16[NKJ]). Such foolish people talk on and on about themselves to anyone who will listen.

James concludes, saying, *"This wisdom [i.e., this way of thinking] does not descend from above, but is earthly, sensual, demonic"* (James 3:15); *"but the wisdom that is from above is first pure, then peaceable, gentle, willing to yield, full of mercy and good fruits, without partiality and without hypocrisy"* (3:17). Don't worry about being great; value humility and fulfilling His will.

"Heavenly Father, I want to be accepted by others so much that I find myself bragging, exaggerating, and pretending to be better than I know I am. Make me conscious of how sinful this behavior is to You."

OCTOBER 15

Know That Soul-Winning Saves Souls

James 5:20—*"He should **know~~** **that** the one who turns a sinner back from his wandering path will save that person's soul from death and will cover a multitude of sins."*

In Scripture, we are commanded to *"be continually knowing"* (i.e., "come to know, receive a knowledge of") the facts of reality, and we are to live in the light of this knowledge. James concludes his epistle with the believers' responsibilities to each other (James 5:13–18).

In James 5:19, James identifies a group of needy people (*"if any among you wanders from the truth"*) that at least professed to be saved and were part of the church. We are responsible for those who *"wander from the truth"* (a passive form meaning "cause to wander, be led astray, cause to err, [or] be seduced into rebellion"). Jesus uses the same word when he says to the Sadducees, *"You are mistaken not understanding the Scriptures nor the power of God"* (Matt 22:29). Paul also uses this term to describe our foolish unbelief: *"For we also once were foolish ourselves, disobedient, deceived [same word]"* (Titus 3:3).

These people strayed *"from the truth,"* which in general applies to the word of God but more specifically applies to the gospel of salvation (James 1:18). Failing to understand the gospel can lead to a legalistic attempt to be better or to presume upon God's love while living in sinful habits, eventually giving up any pretense of being a Christian at all. The wanderer is a *"sinner,"* unsaved or unregenerate (Rom 5:8; 1 Tim 1:9, 15; 1 Pet 4:18): *"The wicked will not stand in the judgment, nor sinners in the assembly of the righteous"* (Psa 1:5).

In every church, there are many who do not understand the gospel and increasingly feel out of place: *"They went out from us, but they were not really of us"* (1 Jn 2:19). Those who become part of a group of believers but do not understand biblical salvation must be taught the basis of faith. This ministry will *"save [their] soul[s] from death and will cover a multitude of sins."* The believer who knows the horrible destiny of the unsaved has a prime motivation to *"turn a sinner from the error of his way."* Take the time to find a wanderer in your church and help him understand the truth of the gospel.

"Lord, I am staggered by the reality that everyone will live somewhere forever, either with You or in a horrible place of torment. Give me the privilege of turning many to Your wonderful salvation."

OCTOBER 16

Rejoice, for a Great Reward Is Coming

Luke 6:23—*"Rejoice~~ in that day*, *and **jump*~ for joy**, because your reward is great in heaven. For their ancestors did the same things to the prophets."*

Until we face real persecution, it is hard to imagine the discouragement and disillusionment we will experience. But it will be worth it if we stay faithful through whatever opposition or persecution we may have to face.

Jesus knew a day of rejoicing was coming for each of His disciples, so He asked them again to trust in His word. Jesus never spoke to His disciples about fame, popularity, or wealth. On the contrary, He told them that they would experience sorrow, weeping, losses, and suffering. We might not experience these things every day, but they will come to everyone someday, assuming we remain faithful and obedient to His word. Opposition is inevitable: *"Blessed are you when men hate you, and when they exclude you, and revile you, and cast out your name as evil, for the Son of Man's sake"* (Luke 6:22).

An environment or job situation in which men hate believers requires a strong motivation or value for truth. Jesus said, *"The time is coming that whoever kills you will think that he offers God service"* (Jn 16:2). This does not refer to a personality conflict or an action provoked by unethical or inept actions; it is a reaction to the unashamed disciple who openly exposes sin and injustice by sharing the gospel. It will not be easy for the believer.

The opportunity to suffer together with Jesus and the description of a promised reward of disproportionate size are sufficient to motivate faithfulness, even through the agony of persecution: *"I consider that our present sufferings are not worthy to be compared to the glory that shall be revealed in us"* (Rom 8:18). The eventual benefits are so great that we are to *"continuously rejoice"* (see 1 Pet 4:13).

Confidence in God's promise of a reward for faithfulness should make believers "jump for joy," *"for our light affliction, which is but for a moment, is working for us a far more exceeding and eternal weight of glory"* (2 Cor 4:17). Can you demonstrate your boldness and fidelity to Christ without becoming discouraged or worrying about what others think of you?

"May the life we will share forever and the rewards You have planned become my greatest delight and value in life. Lord, may I live with eternity in mind."

OCTOBER 17
_____

Do Not Worry about What to Say

Mark 13:11—*"When they arrest you and hand you over for trial,* **do not worry~/ about what to speak***. But* **say~~** **whatever** *is given you at that time, for it is not you speaking, but the Holy Spirit."*

Most of us will have little fear of being arrested for our beliefs, because we live in the one-third of the world that is nominally Christian.

Fortunately, most of this "Christian" world has withdrawn the power of the state from these churches, but when "Christianity" was in power, any disagreement with their form of religion was cruelly persecuted. In Catholic countries, leaders of the Inquisition tortured and killed hundreds of thousands of non-Catholics. The Anglican Church and Greek Orthodox Church were just as cruel to the evangelical believers, who were burnt at the stake, beheaded, and tortured in the most painful ways because believers merely wanted to obey the Scripture. Only in the past few centuries have we been free to practice the Bible as it reads. As Christians increase in number and influence, the secular world is making laws that will inevitably result in more persecution.

Another third of the world is dominated by non-Christian religions: Islam, Hinduism, and Buddhism. Evangelicals are not always free in these parts of the world to practice their religion, and they live under threats of various degrees, although it might still be possible to creatively communicate the gospel.

The final third of the world population has no knowledge of Christianity at all. Here Christianity has never been spoken in their tongues. Changes to the status quo might be met with violent resistance, but there have been heroic victories in which whole people groups have converted to the gospel.

Jesus gave His disciples instructions for how to respond to inevitable persecution. They were commanded to *"stop worrying"* (implying that they were worrying) and to *"continuously say"* what the Spirit brought to their minds at the time (Jn 14:26). What we have learned of His word will come back to our minds when we need it: *"Now when they saw the boldness of Peter and John, . . . they marveled. And they realized that they had been with Jesus"* (Acts 4:13). Imagine yourself on trial for your faith.

"Lord, help me to never worry about being politically correct; rather, allow me to be bold enough to speak the truth at all times."

OCTOBER 18

Entrust Your Soul to the Creator

1 Pet 4:19—*"So then let those who suffer according to the will of God* **entrust**~~ **their souls** *to a faithful Creator as they do good."*

Why do God's people suffer? Peter gives several reasons to help us accept unfair suffering as part of God's purpose for some believers.

If a believer lives in a hostile environment and is unable to avoid persecution for following Christ, then he must understand God's plan. Peter began his discussion by instructing believers to *"not think it strange concerning the fiery trial which is to try you, as though some strange thing happened to you"* (1 Pet 4:12). He now gives several reasons why this attitude is helpful.

Whatever the degree of suffering, it is a privilege to *"partake of Christ's sufferings"* (1 Pet 4:12a) because we experience a sense of camaraderie with Christ. The Savior will never forget your willingness to stand up for Him amid threats and pain, so rest assured you will *"be glad with exceeding joy"* (4:12b).

His promise, *"Lo, I am with you always"* (Matt 28:20), means that He will be with you through any *"reproach"* (i.e., "defamed, accuse with abusive words").

If you suffer because you have boldly identified with Christ, you can glorify Him (1 Pet 4:14b), but this is only possible when you are *"not ashamed"* (4:16). It seems the more unjust the suffering, the more Christ is glorified.

Now *"the time has come for judgment to begin at the house of God"* (1 Pet 4:17). Suffering for Christ purifies and proves our faith (1:6–7). It is a test, a "judgment" to determine who is genuine. When I asked him if he ever prayed for the cessation of persecution in China, a Chinese believer told me, "Oh no, never! Persecution is how we know who is a true believer." Remember, *"endure hardship as discipline; God is treating you as sons"* (Heb 12:7). Suffering for Christ is an expected and vital part of the Christian life. Whatever He allows is designed with a purpose. Never doubt it. Keep doing right.

"What an honor to be able to trust a Savior who has been through the worst of sufferings and stayed faithful to the end. Thank You, Lord, for the privilege of showing You how I can be trusted in threatening situations to stay faithful to You."

OCTOBER 19

Do Not Be Afraid of Men

Matt 10:29–31—*"Aren't two sparrows sold for a penny? Yet not one of them falls to the ground apart from your Father's will. Even all the hairs on your head are numbered. So **do not be afraid*** | you are more valuable than many sparrows."*

Jesus wanted His followers not to fear what any man could do to them, but to *"fear the one who is able to destroy both soul and body in hell"* (Matt 10:28). We are never to be afraid of being separated from the omniscient and omnipotent God who is so careful of details that He counts every hair on our heads and knows the death of every insignificant sparrow (10:29). He will miss no detail of what happens to His most precious followers.

The world's systems have always used fear as a manipulating tactic. A person will eventually become submissive to whatever he fears the most. Terrorists understand this; they go to extremes to create fear because it is their key to obedience.

The disciples were asked to consider the worst case scenario: all man could do is kill the body. Millions of Christ followers have been unashamed and unafraid to die for Christ through the centuries.

Human evil does not compare to the wrath of God. He can send the body and soul of an unbeliever to a horrible eternity in hell. In Matthew 10:28, Jesus told the disciples to fear the one who determines man's destiny; then, in verse 31, He said, *"So do not ever at any time be afraid."*

There is a healthy fear. Jesus wants us to fear God, meaning that we should be afraid God will do exactly what He said He would do: for the unsaved, this means a destiny in hell, and for the saved, He promises chastisement for disobedience and great reward for faithfulness.

We are never to be afraid of anything that man can do to us, because we can never be separated from God (Rom 8:38–39). Whatever happens to a believer is part of His plan, so faithfulness is highly prized. If He marks the death of a tiny sparrow, how much more will He note the persecution or loss of one of His children? Stay true to Him. It will be worth it all.

"Lord, my fear of what others will think is often greater than I want to admit. Teach me to fear disappointing and disobeying You more than what men can do to me."

OCTOBER 20

Be Aware That the World Hated Jesus

Jn 15:18—*"If the world hates you, **be aware~~ that it hated me first.**"*

Whom do you want as your worst enemy: the world or God? Unfortunately, everyone has to choose. If you love the world, it may treat you well temporarily, but it is a fickle and cruel taskmaster. However, such a compromise with the world makes God an enemy: *"Whoever therefore wants to be a friend of the world makes himself an enemy of God"* (James 4:4). But friendship with God inevitably provokes the wrath of the world system.

A choice between God and the world is imperative because the two options are incompatible. Something happens within a believer that forces a decision: *"No one can serve two masters; for either he will hate the one and love the other, or else he will be loyal to the one and despise the other. You cannot serve God and mammon"* (Matt 6:24).

John described the world system as a social structure manipulated by satanic control and always hostile to God's people. Thankfully, for now, the Spirit of God *"is holding [the antichrist] back, so that he may be revealed at the proper time ... but the one who now holds it back will continue to do so till he is taken out of the way"* (2 Thes 2:6,7b) at the Rapture. Then satanic forces will be unrestricted in their opposition to anyone who dares to follow God's word. Few will survive the horrible persecution of the tribulation period (Revelation chapters 4–19); *"the secret power of lawlessness is already at work"* (2 Thes 2:7a).

Jesus was hated at His birth (Matt 2:13–16) and throughout His ministry. The disciples had to accept inevitable persecution or walk away, just as the seed sown in *"rocky places"* (13:20) is the one *"who hears the word and at once receives it with joy. But since he has no root, he lasts only a short time. When trouble or persecution comes because of the Word, he quickly falls away"* (13:21). We must decide to follow Jesus knowing that it will not be a popular decision.

For a believer, it is an honor to take a hit for Jesus. Any Secret Service officer will step between an assassin and his president. Jesus said, "The world is no friend of mine, nor will they be of yours. Will you stand true to My Word no matter what?" Do not expect any less today. Take courage.

"Lord Jesus, my sinful soul wants to be popular with others, but their price is too high. They demand my conformity to them, but my heart wants to walk with You and to be like You. I prefer Your fellowship whatever the consequences."

Remember, Do Not Expect Better Treatment

Jn 15:20—*"**Remember**~~ **what I told you**, 'A slave is not greater than his master.' If they persecuted me, they will also persecute you. If they obeyed my word, they will obey yours too."*

We humans tend to believe we are the exception to the rule—whatever the rule might be, but John 15:20 introduces us to another rule of life. We are commanded with the present imperative to *"continuously remember that . . . a slave is not greater than his master."* Likewise, God does not make unbelievers react against believers; rather, their sinful nature produces this hostile reaction. Jesus is warning us not to be disillusioned.

This verse implies that the believer is a *"slave"* (i.e., "one who is a permanent relation of servitude to another, his will being altogether consumed in the will of the other"), and he should never expect to be treated any better than was Jesus, his Master.

Jesus had just elevated the status of the disciples from "servants" to "friends": *"No longer do I call you servants, for a servant does not know what his master is doing; but I have called you friends, for all things that I heard from My Father I have made known to you"*
(Jn 15:14). The difference is that servants had to be told what *"[their] master is doing"*—that is, the will of God. But when they committed to know what God had revealed and to do whatever His word commanded, they became known as His friends. Now that they knew God's will, they were accountable to fulfill it, regardless of the risks (Jn 15:18). Remember that this conversation occurred the evening before His crucifixion: Jesus knew what was going to happen, but His disciples did not.

There would be little glory in being an apostle. Paul said, *"For I think that God has displayed us, the apostles, last, as men condemned to death"* (1 Cor 4:9). They knew what they signed up for and gladly paid the price: *"Unless a kernel of wheat is planted in the soil and dies, it remains alone. But its death will produce many new kernels—a plentiful harvest of new lives"* (Jn 12:24[NLT]). They had to die to themselves. Are you willing to do the same?

"Lord, I choose to be a friend of Yours unashamedly. I want to live in Your presence and please You more than I please myself."

.

OCTOBER 22
Take Courage

Jn 16:33—*"I have told you these things so that in me you may have peace. In the world you have trouble and suffering, but* **take courage**~~—*I have conquered the world."*

Most people long for peace of mind. Buried by their conflicts, troubles, and fears, they will do anything for a few moments of inner calm. There is peace knowing for certain that there is much more to our existence than this temporary life. Jesus puts everything into perspective, allowing all who learn His view of reality to live with a peace that He alone can give.

Hebrews gives us an insight into the inner fortitude of Jesus: *"Let us fix our eyes on Jesus, the author and perfecter of our faith, who for the joy set before him endured the cross, scorning the shame, and sat down at the right hand of the throne of God"* (Heb 12:2). Knowing what was waiting for Him on the other side of the cross, He could endure the temporary agony, even suffering the wrath of His Father for man's sins.

Peace is found in understanding the reality of life from God's perspective. Jesus's instructions in John 14–16 on the eve of His crucifixion were given to sustain the disciples and encourage them, because this life is not the end of all things. Jesus promised, *"Peace I leave with you, My peace I give to you; not as the world gives do I give to you. Let not your heart be troubled, neither let it be afraid"* (Jn 14:27). The world's peace is temporary.

As the Father did not abandon Jesus (Jn 16:32), neither would Jesus abandon His disciples. Bruce Barton in his commentary on John quotes Sebastian Valfrè of the seventeenth century in northern Italy, "When it is all over, you will not regret having suffered; rather you will regret having suffered so little and suffered that little so badly." The world will always be hostile: *"in the world you have trouble and suffering."* But our bond to Christ brings *"peace which surpasses all understanding"* (Phil 4:7).

Jesus commanded them to *"continuously show courage"* (i.e., "be bold, daring, [and] courageous"); this is spoken as a coach's final words before a championship game. He said, *"I have conquered the world"* (i.e., to "be victorious, or subdue"). Peace is the consequence of knowing the certainty of the end game and counting on its reality. Does this give you courage today to stand up for the Lord?

"Thank You, Lord, for showing us that this world is not all there is; in fact, it is but a moment in eternity. I choose today to be true to You in every encounter."

OCTOBER 23

Take Your Share of Suffering

2 Tim 2:3—*"Take your share of suffering**~ *as a good soldier of Christ Jesus."*

Paul often used the metaphor of a soldier to illustrate spiritual fortitude: *"Put on the full armor of God, that you may be able to stand firm against the schemes of the devil"* (Eph 6:11). He exhorted the Corinthians to be aggressive against evil and false teachings: *"Though we walk in the flesh, we do not war according to the flesh, for the weapons of our warfare are not of the flesh, but divinely powerful for the destruction of fortresses"* (2 Cor 10:3–4).

A good soldier is willing to suffer hardships. The aorist imperative translates as "immediately decide to start taking your share of suffering," meaning to "suffer hardship, evil or affliction along with someone else." Paul wrote, *"Do not be ashamed of the testimony of our Lord, nor of me His prisoner, but share with me in the sufferings for the gospel according to the power of God"* (2 Tim 1:8). The conflict between truth and evil is inevitable as we stand up for Christ: *"All who desire to live godly in Christ Jesus will suffer persecution. But evil men and impostors will grow worse and worse, deceiving and being deceived"* (3:12–13).

Secularist, nontheistic, and monotheistic religious societies are in direct opposition to biblical truths. In China, the gospel can only be preached legally within the commonly called "3-selfs" registered churches (i.e., self-governing, self-supporting, and self-propagating) that existed before the communist revolution in 1949. Punishments can be imprisonment, torture, or death. More than a hundred million underground believers willingly risk death to share the gospel.

Sadly in the West, many Christians do not want to be soldiers. They do not carry a Bible or gospel tracts. They do not know how to explain the gospel, and they do not want to be considered fanatics. Can you imagine a soldier refusing to carry a gun or ammunition, much less not knowing how to fire a gun? As proudly as a Green Beret wears his cap and uniform, so believers should unashamedly stand for Christ in their spheres of influence. This is a 24/7 task. What can you do today to be a good soldier of Christ?

"I don't like the idea of suffering, but the honor of being a soldier of Christ Jesus in an antagonistic world demands my willingness to take the consequences. I'll take my hits for You today."

OCTOBER 24
Understand That Difficult Times Are Coming

2 Tim 3:1—*"But **understand**~~ this, that in the last days difficult times will come."*

There is a sense of urgency as Paul writes about the *"last days,"* the entire period of the church age since the resurrection of Christ until the Rapture. This period will lead into the seven years of the great tribulation (Rev 4–19) and the unhindered rise to power of the antichrist as he attempts to destroy all who claim to follow God's word. The deceived world will worship him as God (2 Thes 2:3–4). Believers are to "continuously understand" the implications of the last days of the church age.

Throughout the church age, *"the secret power of lawlessness [has been] already at work"* (2 Thes 2:7). Millions have been killed and persecuted merely for daring to follow the commands of Scripture. In *Damned through the Church*, John W. Montgomery (Minneapolis: Bethany House Publishers, 1973, quoted by John MacArthur Jr., *Second Timothy*, Chicago: Moody, 1995, p. l04), describes seven "damnable epochs of church history" from the beginning of the church to the present: (1) sacramentalism, when the church replaced God; (2) rationalism, when reason became a god; (3) orthodoxism, when God was sterile and impersonal; (4) politicism, when the state was treated as a god; (5) ecumenism, when there was uncritical fellowship and cooperation among nominal Christians; (6) experientialism, when our personal experiences became our god; and (7) subjectivism, when feeling and self became our god. This latter period emphasizes mysticism, or determining truths about God by intuition, feeling, and pragmatism.

Paul said to Timothy, *"The Spirit explicitly says that in the later times some will fall away from the faith, paying attention to deceitful spirits and doctrines of demons, by means of the hypocrisy of liars seared in their own conscience as with a branding iron"* (1 Tim 4:1–2). Jesus described these days: "Because lawlessness will abound, the love of many will grow cold" (Matt 24:12). From the ascension until Jesus's return, there were to be periods of great danger for true believers. Things are not going to get better and better, but dangerous times will come and go. The wise believer knows the signs of the times and decides to live for His kingdom no matter what may come.

"In every generation since You came, it has been difficult to follow Your instructions for living, but I want to be part of the 'company of the unashamed.'"

OCTOBER 25

Consider It Joy when in Trials

James 1:2—*"My brothers and sisters, **consider***~ **it nothing** but joy when you fall into all sorts of trials."*

James wrote to the early Christian Jews (1:1) who were "scattered abroad" (Gk. *diaspora*) because of persecution and were coping with the loss of everything, were abandoned by their countrymen as traitors to their ancient religion, and were mercilessly killed or imprisoned by the political regime. They questioned God's involvement or trustworthiness.

James begins his book with a surprising aorist command: *"immediately begin to consider it nothing but joy"* when your whole world falls apart. Was James out of touch with reality? He was no stranger to suffering. His own brother was Jesus!(Gal 1:19) The command deals with how we are to think and the "truth" phrases we are to repeat in our minds. We are warned not to allow ourselves to think false thoughts.

A trial should not be viewed as a punishment, a curse, or an accident without purpose. The verb *count* (*hegomai*) literally means "to be a leader or chief," but metaphorically, it means to "lead out before the mind, [or] to view, esteem, or consider" something to be a certain way. This is a controlling or dominating thought that we allow to lead us through life's difficulties.

The Phillips translation reads, *"Don't resent [trials] as intruders, but welcome them as friends."* We must respond not just with joy but rather "nothing but joy," or literally, "all joy." Happiness is a natural response to pleasant circumstances, but joy is deeper and unchangeable; it is a response to truths about God and His ultimate purposes. Because we have learned to trust Him to forgive us, we can trust Him to never make a mistake or never allow anything in which He cannot be glorified.

A believer can be both sad about circumstances and joyful that God is present and has a plan. To consider these experiences a joy requires a trust and value in God's perspective. Bitterness is symptom of unbiblical thinking. Can you trust Him?

"Lord, Your promises of an eternal purpose through persecution and reward for faithfulness to You help me accept hurt and rejection for obeying Your word. Thank You."

OCTOBER 26

Remember God's Purpose in Suffering

James 1:4—*"And **let endurance have~~ its perfect effect**, so that you will be perfect and complete, not deficient in anything."*

Christ knows there is only one way for the believer to mature and become like Him. Trials and conflicts condition us to demonstrate the grace of God.

In James 1:4, the present active imperative of *"let . . . have"* implies continual submission to progress toward the ultimate goal of Christlikeness. God cannot complete His *"perfect effect"* (from a Greek word for the "completion of a process, or reaching full grown") in us without teaching us *"endurance"* (lit. being "under pressure," or the "capacity to continue to bear up under difficult circumstances"). Alan Redpath said, "For every discouragement has been allowed to come to us in order that through it we may be cast in utter helplessness at the Saviour's feet" (Christian Quotes.com).

The objective of God's "coaching" is to make us *"perfect and complete, not deficient in anything."* Paul's use of the word *perfect* does not mean moral or spiritual absolute perfection; it refers to what is fully developed or matured. Even James admitted, *"We all stumble in many ways"* (James 3:2). Paul confessed, *"Not that I have already obtained all this, or have already been made perfect, but I press on"* (Phil 3:10, 12).

Paul referred to the analogy of suffering the pain of childbirth as part of the process of producing Christian maturity when he wrote, *"my children, with whom I am again in labor until Christ is formed in you"* (Gal 4:19). The word *complete* means "a totality or entirety." This is not a superficial conformity to legalistic standards, but it means that your thoughts, beliefs, values, motivations, discipline, habits, reactions, responses, ambitions, and goals all reflect the principles of God's word. Having learned the application of the word to every one of these areas, each of us is tested until the right responses become more instinctive. Then we will not be *"deficient in anything."*

This we know: *"After you have suffered for a little while, the God of all grace . . . will Himself perfect, confirm, strengthen and establish you"* (1 Pet 5:10). He knows what each of us needs. Trust Him as your coach.

"Lord, why is my maturity so important to You? If becoming like You is good for me, then I'll take whatever circumstance You send me today."

OCTOBER 27

Grieve, Mourn, and Weep

James 4:9—*"Grieve*~, mourn*~, and weep*~. Turn*~ your laughter into mourning and your joy into despair."*

Contemporary evangelism eliminates the first two as being too psychologically harmful and instead emphasizes how much God loves the sinner. The sinner's naturally egotistical mind believes he is not that bad after all, because God still loves him. He is led in a prayer that he repeats verbatim, as though the precise wording is the formula for salvation. After a public announcement as a new convert, he is usually baptized and becomes a member of the church, still thinking he is a pretty good person.

Something is missing from this picture. The convert goes to church thinking he is a pretty good person, learns that God loves him, and goes home unchanged. He often believes that as long as he remains a good person, accepted by the church, he will go to heaven. The commands in James 4:9 show the element missing in most Christians. Are you ever sincerely broken because of your continual sinfulness? Why does sin not break our hearts like it does His?

We are told to *"grieve,"* which means, in the aorist imperative, "to immediately decide to be miserable, lament or mourn." John wrote to the church at Laodicea, *"You say, 'I am rich, have become wealthy and have need of nothing'—and do not know that you are wretched, miserable, poor, blind, and naked"* (Rev 3:17). The New International Version translates 2 Corinthians 7:10 this way: *"For the kind of sorrow God wants us to experience leads us away from sin and results in salvation . . . But worldly sorrow, which lacks repentance, results in spiritual death."* When did you last weep because of your sins?

James sums up the thought: "Immediately begin to turn your laughter into mourning and your joy into despair." Do your sins bother you? Do you take the time to *let* them bother you? James is not forbidding legitimate laughter or joy; rather, he is emphasizing the shady, sensual, sin-condoning, worldly entertainment that unbelievers revel in. James is teaching his readers to grieve over *"the lust of the flesh and the lust of the eyes and the boastful pride of life"* (1 Jn 2:16). Never lose your sense of unworthiness and our refuge in the grace and mercy of our Savior.

"I'm sorry, dear Lord Jesus, for how often I fail to obey You. It hurts me that I hurt You after all You have done for me. I could never deserve Your grace; Thank You so much for Your undeserved mercy toward me."

OCTOBER 28
Be Patient and Strengthen Your Heart

James 5:8—*"You also **be patient***\~* **and strengthen***\~* **your hearts,** for the Lord's return is near."*

Difficult circumstances, conflicts, and abuses are an inevitable part of life in a world infected with sin and evil. Job wrote, *"Man is born for trouble, as sparks fly upward"* (Job 5:7). Jesus warned us in John 16:33, *"In the world you have tribulation."* Paul added, *"Through many tribulations we must enter the kingdom of God"* (Acts 14:22). And Peter exhorted us, *"Beloved, do not be surprised at the fiery ordeal among you, which comes upon you for your testing, as though some strange thing were happening to you; but to the degree that you share the sufferings of Christ, keep on rejoicing"* (1 Pet 4:12–13). How is the believer expected to respond in these trials?

James condemned the rich who took advantage of or persecuted some of the poor (James 5:1–6), and he described the rich as abusing, taking advantage of, and even murdering the disadvantaged (5:6). They knew how to respond passively, as did Jesus, who *"while being reviled, did not revile in return; while suffering, He uttered no threats, but kept entrusting Himself to Him who judges righteously"* (1 Pet 2:23).

Abusive circumstances only escalate when the response is impulsive and reactive. In the previous verse, James mentions a farmer who works to plant the seeds of his crops and then waits patiently for the early and late rains (typical seasons in Israel) before the harvest (James 5:7). Now James exhorts believers to respond to persecution by "immediately deciding to be patient," which comes from a compound word composed of *long* (Gr. *makros*) and *temper* (Gr. *thumos*). The word conveys waiting a long time to demonstrate your temper or angry response, hence our word *long-suffering*. *"Love suffers long"* (1 Cor 13:4); the believer should not take the judgment of the wicked into his own hands but patiently wait for God to avenge.

Abused believers are not to give in to the world or give up in despair; they must "immediately decide to strengthen [their] hearts." This command translates the Greek word *sterizo* (from which we get the word *steroids*), which means "to fix firmly, [or] establish," our commitment to an attitude or conviction. Obedience generates the strength to obey more. The believer's greatest hope is that *"the Lord's return is near."* He will make all things right. We must trust Him and live as though He were coming today.

"Lord Jesus, the thought of Your return to earth is captivating and challenging to me. If You come today, I commit to be engaged in Your work when You call."

OCTOBER 29
Do Not Complain

Jn 6:43—*"Jesus replied, 'Do not complain~/ about me to one another.'"*

Jesus, using the present negative command, demanded His followers to "stop complaining" (*gogguzo* is "an onomatopoeic word derived from the sound made when murmuring or muttering in a low and indistinct voice with the idea of complaint"). The disciples could hardly believe this command. How could they follow such teachings?

There was ongoing "grumbling" because Jesus had said, *"I am the bread that came down from heaven"* (Jn 6:41). They thought this was ridiculous: *"Is not this Jesus, the son of Joseph, whose father and mother we know? How does He now say, 'I have come down from heaven?'"* (6:42).

Jesus made no attempt to clarify the issue or correct their ignorance. He only rebuked their grumbling. It is not unusual for people to misunderstand God's ways. In the Old Testament, the Jews grumbled in the wilderness about the water they had to drink (Ex 15:24), their lack of bread (Ex 16:2), their hardships in the desert (Num 11:1), the conflicts and difficulties in conquering the promised land (14:1–3), and the "manna" God provided to eat (11:4–6). Paul wrote of this generation, *"Nor let us tempt Christ, as some of them also tempted, and were destroyed by serpents; nor complain, as some of them also complained, and were destroyed by the destroyer. Now all these things happened to them as examples, and they were written for our admonition, upon whom the ends of the ages have come"* (1 Cor 10:9).

Following His admonition, Jesus made two remarkable statements: First, *"No one can come to me unless the Father who sent me draws him"* (Jn 6:44). Second, *"Everyone who has heard and learned from the Father comes to me"* (6:45), and *"whoever believes has eternal life"* (6:47). The incarnation has always been a contested issue. How could God become a man? No explanation is given, only the declaration that it happened.

We cannot understand everything about God. His revelations always require an element of trust. Can you take Him at His word, or do you continue to complain that you would do things differently? Choose wisely.

"Lord, sometimes Your ways are hard to understand, and it is easy to complain, but I trust You with all my heart even when I don't understand things."

OCTOBER 30
Follow Jesus No Matter What

Jn 21:18–19—*"'I tell you the solemn truth, when you were young, you tied your clothes around you and went wherever you wanted, but when you are old, you will stretch out your hands, and others will tie you up and bring you where you do not want to go.' (Now Jesus said this to indicate clearly by what kind of death Peter was going to glorify God.) After he said this, Jesus told Peter,* **'Follow~~ me.'"***

Peter was on an emotional roller coaster. Having denied the Lord three times, now he had to openly confess his loyalty to Christ three times. Finally, he was told he would live to an old age and be led by others to *"stretch out [his] hands, and others will tie [him] up and bring [him] where [he] do[es] not want to go,"* which is an early proverbial description of aspects of the crucifixion.

Peter never forgot this prophecy, referring to it in his Second Epistle, when he spoke about his imminent death (2 Pet 1:14).

John adds the parenthetical commentary reflecting their understanding of Jesus's prophecy about Peter, declaring this was *"to indicate clearly by what kind of death Peter was going to glorify God."* How would you like to know thirty years in advance that you were going to be crucified at the end of your life? How ironic: Peter denied he even knew Jesus because of his fear of being crucified. Now he is told that he will be crucified as well! He had his whole life to think about how he would *"glorify God"* in his inevitable death (1 Pet 4:16). Tradition says he wanted to be crucified upside down.

Now Jesus gives His final command to Peter: *"Continuously be following me."* By these words, Jesus is starting all over again with Peter. Three years earlier, near the Sea of Galilee, where they now were standing, Jesus had said to Peter, *"Follow me and I'll make you fishers of men"* (Matt 4:19).

After Peter had been singled out of all the disciples for crucifixion, he looked at John and then asked Jesus, *"Lord, what about him?"* (Jn 21:21). Jesus sharply rebuked Peter for wondering if the same fate awaited his friend John: *"If I want him to live until I come back, what concern is that of yours? You follow me!"* (21:22). Are you influenced by how others succeed or have it easier than you have it?

"What would it have been like to hear You say to me, 'Follow me'? Would it be any different than reading it in Your word? I'll take it that You are saying the same words to me today and follow You however You command."

OCTOBER 31

Face Persecution with Trust

1 Pet 4:19—*"So then let those who suffer according to the will of God* **entrust~~ their souls** *to a faithful Creator as they do good."*

The West is moving from a post-Christian to an increasingly anti-Christian worldview. The early church proclaimed Jesus Christ as the King of kings instead of Caesar. This clash of powers and authority could not be tolerated, so they suffered the consequences. Are we willing to pay the price for following Christ publicly and boldly, to lose our jobs, be heavily fined, or spend time in jail for the sake of Christ? As of 2011, it is estimated that approximately one hundred million Christians face persecution daily in the Muslim world, North Korea, China, and at the hands of Hindu extremism and Islamic terrorism in India. We will be targeted.

To *"suffer according to the will of God"* seems to be contradictory. Naturally, it is easier to trust God's will when life is going well and things are prospering, but then no one can tell the difference between an unsaved, prosperous person and a prosperous Christian. This suffering is not a reference to a downturn in the economy or punishment for the violation of laws. There will come a time when the government closes down Christian ministries and confiscates Christian homes and bank accounts or radical anti-Christian groups attack believers because they dare to follow Christ and His word.

God has a purpose to let sin and evil become so blatant and obvious that it shouts for justice. This is the reason for the seven short years God will let evil be unrestricted: to show how it merits the *"winepress of the wrath of God"* (Rev 14:19). It will be horrible, but God's real purpose for believers will be seen in the millennium and throughout eternity.

Peter said, "continuously be entrusting [your] souls to a faithful Creator." To *"entrust,"* or "commit," means to "place alongside or near someone." Jesus used this word on the cross when He committed His spirit to the Father (Luke 23:46). We are now commanded to commit our souls to the Creator for safekeeping while continuing to *"do good"*—that is, to do "good deeds." The Creator is in control and can be trusted in every circumstance. He makes no mistakes.

"Thank You, Lord, for showing me that this world is not all there is. I want to tell You that I cannot wait to see You face to face. All that I am is fully Yours. Do with it today as You wish."

NOVEMBER 1
Take the Example of the Suffering Prophets

James 5:10—*"As an example of suffering and patience, brothers and sisters, take*~ the prophets who spoke in the Lord's name."*

One of the keys to success in life is to have a mentor. When the church begins to face severe testing, true believers will need to look to heroic mentors as their examples. If the police give you an escalating fine for holding a Bible study in a private home, how will you respond? When you are forbidden to pray or mention Jesus's name in public, what will you do? When these issues become more prevalent, believers will need to take courage by the examples of those who have gone before.

Suffering for Christ was only beginning when James wrote his epistle. To encourage the believers not to compromise or give in to pressure as Peter did at the trial of Jesus, he proposes *"an example of suffering and patience."* The example they were to follow is described by the word *suffering*: a compound word from "evil" and "suffering," meaning "to suffer misfortune, hardship, bearing affliction." *Patience* is also a compound word from "long" and "temper or anger," meaning the ability to not respond emotionally when attacked—that is, your anger takes a long time to appear.

We are instructed to *"take"* these examples seriously. The aorist imperative verb means *"from now on decide to take,"* or to "choose, seize, [or] lay hold of," their example as your model.

These Old Testament prophets were God's spokesmen to faithfully deliver His message. Stephen, on trial for preaching Jesus's word, said, *"Which of the prophets did your fathers not persecute? And they killed those who foretold the coming of the Just One, of whom you now have become the betrayers and murderers"* (Acts 7:52). He would not back down.

Hebrews 11:35b–38a sums up our heroic heritage: *"Others were tortured and refused to be released . . . Some faced jeers and flogging, while still others were chained and put in prison. They were stoned; they were sawed in two; they were put to death by the sword. They went about in sheepskins and goatskins, destitute, persecuted and mistreated—the world was not worthy of them."* We are commanded to follow these examples. The truth of God's word must become worth defending no matter the price.

"Dear Father, You know and preserve those who are willing to suffer for Your sake. Give me the perseverance and wisdom to follow the example of those of whom You said the world is not worthy for how badly it treated Your people" (Heb 11:38).

NOVEMBER 2

Never Stop Rejoicing

1 Thes 5:16—*"Always rejoice~~."*

By divine mandate, all believers must learn to rejoice in every kind of situation. Any negative or judgmental spirit reflects a low regard for the authority of the Scripture, casts suspicion on the character of God, and leads inevitably to sinful disobedience.

Paul faced many kinds of turmoil, frustration, and threats against him while *"serving the Lord with all humility, and with many tears and trials which happened to [him] by the plotting of the Jews"* (Acts 20:19). This is hardly the environment for rejoicing, yet this was precisely when his rejoicing could have a meaningful impact. Paul said the believer lives above his situation where continual joy abounds, *"sorrowful yet always rejoicing"* (2 Cor 6:10).

Some of our calamities are caused by our own ignorance, stubbornness, pride, impatience, or impulsiveness, but some circumstances are beyond our control. For the Christian, a deep sense of victory is rooted in his bond to Jesus Christ, who conquered death and all the evils of this life. Nothing can ever change our relationship with the King of kings (Rom 8:28–30): *"In Your presence is fullness of joy; at Your right hand are pleasures forevermore"* (Psa 16:11).

When the Philippian jailer believed in Christ, he did so with all his household: *"He rejoiced, having believed in God with all his household"* (Acts 16:34). His personal joy was magnified when all his family and servants heard the gospel and believed. This joy is not from this world but *"through whom also we . . . rejoice in hope of the glory of God"* (Rom 5:2)—that is, when Christ will be revealed. I can't wait!

Peter explained it best: *"The genuineness of your faith, being much more precious than gold that perishes, though it is tested by fire, may be found to praise, honor, and glory at the revelation of Jesus Christ, whom having not seen you love. Though now you do not see Him, yet believing, you rejoice with joy inexpressible and full of glory, receiving the end of your faith—the salvation of your souls"* (1 Pet 1:7–9). Literally, 1 Thessalonians reads, *"At all times be constantly always rejoicing."* Whatever your situation, know that God is in control and His purpose for you is beyond your imagination. Rejoice in His promise.

"Lord, please cause my faith to continue to grow and give me the understanding I need to be able to rejoice in any circumstance You allow to come my way. May I not disparage Your character by becoming upset when things go 'wrong.'"

NOVEMBER 3
Let Your Light Shine

Matt 5:16—*"In the same way,* **let your light shine****~ before people, so that they can see your good deeds and give honor to your Father in heaven."*

Whenever a person makes a bold claim, suspicion and curiosity are aroused. Can you imagine being lost in a deep jungle on a pitch-black night with no flashlight, when suddenly you see a flicker of light approaching? Hope of rescue dawns within you, but doubts cause you to investigate the source before committing yourself. Once assured of rescue, the relief erupts in thankfulness as you run to the light.

Jesus said, *"I am the light of the world. He who follows Me shall not walk in darkness, but have the light of life"* (Jn 8:12). However, He was not to be the *"light"* alone, or for very long: *"As long as I am in the world, I am the light of the world"* (9:5). The unsaved are in the dark: *"If one walks in the night, he stumbles, because the light is not in him"* (11:10). The light of Jesus's presence must be within a person. Jesus told His disciples, *"Believe in the light, that you may become sons of light"* (12:36). Jesus further clarified this analogy: *"I have come as a light into the world, that whoever believes in Me should not abide in darkness"* (12:46).

Jesus told His disciples, *"You are the light of the world. A city that is set on a hill cannot be hidden"* (Matt 5:14). How cruel to hide the light from a world in need! So Jesus commands the disciples, *"In the same way decide from now on to let your light so shine before men, that they may see your good works."* When needy people see a corresponding fountain of *"good works"* flowing from the light in a believer, their ideal response is to *"give honor to your Father in heaven"* (*"honor,"* doxaazo, is the origin of the word *doxology*, meaning "to recognize Him for Who and What He is").

However, there is no guarantee: *"judgment is based on this fact: God's light came into the world, but people loved the darkness more than the light, for their actions were evil"* (Jn 3:19^NLT). But *"if you are filled with light, with no dark corners, then your whole life will be radiant, as though a floodlight were filling you with light"* (Luke 11:36^NLT). Those in the light live to validate the genuineness of Christ's light through their sacrificial *"good works"* for those in darkness.

"Lord Jesus, Your Spirit lives in me, giving me the light of understanding through Your word. Guide me to allow that light to shine for the sake of those who do not know You."

NOVEMBER 4
Tell the Story Boldly

Matt 10:27—*"What I say to you in the dark,* **tell*~ in the light***, and what is whispered in your ear,* **proclaim*~ from the housetops***."*

Fear is a paralyzing emotion impeding development in every area of life. Proverbs warns, *"The fear of man brings a snare"*(Prov 29:25). Many Christians live privately, allowing only a few people to know them well, and their fear of criticism, rejection, or ridicule keeps them from boldly telling others about the most important relationship in their lives.

When Christ comes into our lives, all our ideas about what is essential to be happy are challenged and put at risk. Most people believe they deeply need to be accepted and approved by other people. Our mind-set must be challenged and reset to biblical values, and we make these changes by the thoughts we repeat in our minds. This can be an agonizing experience, but it is unavoidable if we want to follow Jesus and be His disciples.

Our life on earth is but a moment. When we come to know the God of heaven through Jesus Christ, He begins to prepare us for an eternity with Him. We must choose to build a future with Christ in His kingdom, not to build our own private kingdom. John wrote, *"If anyone loves the world, the love of the Father is not in him"* (1 Jn 2:15).

Our fears are dispelled when we know we are defended and exonerated by God. The wickedness of the world will be exposed, and our commitment to His word will be praised: *"There is nothing covered that will not be revealed"* (Matt 10:26). Jesus *"will both bring to light the things hidden in the darkness and disclose the motives of men's heart; and then each man's praise will come to him from God"* (1 Cor 4:5). If we believe this and value His praise more than our lives, we will have an increasing motivation for serving the Lord and fearlessly confront our world with His truth.

We must openly and unashamedly tell to everyone we can about what God has taught us in private (*"What I say to you in the dark, tell in the light"*). This is contrary to contemporary views of political correctness that tell us to avoid controversy at any cost for fear of offending someone. How bold is your witness today?

"Dear Father, when it counts most, please give me the boldness to speak to others what You have taught me."

NOVEMBER 5
Go into All the World and Preach

Mark 16:15—*"He said to them, 'Go into all the world and* **preach****~* **the gospel** *to every creature.'"*

In a mission conference, the banner across the front of the auditorium stated, "Don't Take the 'Go' out of the Gospel." We naturally find a myriad of excuses for why we cannot go to preach the gospel.

The resurrected Christ reiterated five times His final charge: *"Go into to all the world."* Christ's death on the cross was to be proclaimed around the world. There is no news more dramatic than this: *"God made him who had no sin to be sin for us, so that in him we might become the righteousness of God"* (2 Cor 5:21).

God asked the question: *"Then I heard the voice of the Lord saying, 'Whom shall I send? And who will go for us?' And I said, 'Here am I. Send me!' He said, 'Go and tell this people'"* (Isa 6:8–9). Was this written merely so we could appreciate Isaiah's courage, or was it a glimpse into the perpetual heavenly issue? God is asking, "Who cares about our agenda for telling the world about Jesus?"

Paul wrote, *"For I have no one like-minded, who will sincerely care for your state. For all seek their own, not the things which are of Christ Jesus"* (Phil 2:20–21). Jesus is searching now, as He was when Isaiah overheard Him saying, "Who is like-minded to Our priorities? Who will care for the lost people groups of the world? How can they not be committed to what their Savior is all about?"

The command in Mark 6:15 is to *"urgently decide to preach the gospel."* The verb means "to herald, announce publicly, or publish." This is not a reference to pulpit preaching, but to telling everyone personally. It is not restricted to gifted or salaried persons, but it is for everyone who knows the truth.

From the beginning in Galilee, these relatively poor Jewish businessmen were to *"go into all the world,"* which they naturally despised, to share the *"gospel"* (the word for "good news or message") to the *"whole creation"* ("all that has been created, the whole of mankind") (Rom 1:14). There is no acceptable excuse not to go. Tell Him, "Here am I. Send me," and see what God does in your life.

"Thank You, Father, that You will always be with Your children as we go and tell the message of Your salvation. You want the whole world to hear it, and it is our job to make sure it reaches the last tribe and nation."

NOVEMBER 6
Do Not Be Afraid

Acts 18:9—*"The Lord said to Paul by a vision in the night, '**Do not be afraid~|, but speak~~ and do not be silent**.'"*

Do great leaders suffer the same fears we normal mortals do? The record indicates that they do. Paul was rejected again in a Jewish synagogue (as in Philippi, Thessalonica, and Berea and by the philosophers in Athens). Whatever the threat, it was enough to cause the apostle to be afraid.

After he boldly proclaimed the gospel at Corinth, the Jews rejected his message and became threatening. He said to them, "Your blood be on your own heads! I am clear of my responsibility. From now on I will go to the Gentiles" (Acts 18:6). Paul felt that it was his "responsibility" to make the gospel clear to his countrymen. Having announced the gospel, he was "clear of [his] responsibility"; he was no longer in "debt" (Rom 1:16). We can see a principle for our day; we are responsible to announce the gospel wherever we can. Paul said, *"I have been faithful. No one's damnation can be blamed on me"* (Acts 20:26^NLT). How does this apply to us?

The Lord Himself encouraged Paul five times in Acts (9:12; 16:9–10; 22:17–18; 23:11; 27:23–24), each time promising to be at Paul's side to strengthen and protect him. Jesus gave the promise of His presence to all believers: *"Lo, I am with you to the end of the age"* (Matt 28:20). He gave the same promise to Joshua in 1:5, 9.

Paul was commanded to *"stop being afraid"* and to *"keep on continuously speaking, and do not keep silent."* If Christians were to remain silent, they could avoid persecution and conflict, but our silence could condemn our friends and neighbors to hell: *"Let each one of you speak truth with his neighbor"* (Eph 4:25). Paul wrote to the Thessalonians, *"Our God gave us the courage to declare His Good News to you boldly, in spite of great opposition"* (1 Thes 2:2).

Times are different, but God has not changed. His work on earth requires that His disciples speak His word to this generation boldly, clearly, and openly regardless of the consequences. If you ever sense the fear of saying a word for Jesus or the gospel, face it and be bold yet gracious, but never silent.

"Loving Lord, when persecution or conflict comes my way, I will trust You to help me respond calmly, speaking Your truth in love. It will be my privilege to honor You with my life."

NOVEMBER 7
Be Reconciled

2 Cor 5:20—*"Therefore we are ambassadors for Christ, as though God were making His plea through us. We plead with you on Christ's behalf, 'Be reconciled*~ to God!'"*

An ambassador is the highest-ranking diplomat who represents a foreign sovereign in another country. His task is to make sure the foreign land understands the values of his country on every issue. Though Paul was a physical citizen of Rome, he had a dual citizenship with a heavenly nation, along with every believer. We *"are no longer strangers and foreigners, but fellow citizens with the saints and members of the household of God"* (Eph 2:19). Not only are we citizens, but we are also called to be *"ambassadors for Christ."* We must represent our sovereign King in an antagonistic world.

We who have become *"ambassadors"* were first the recipients of His grace: *"God was in Christ reconciling the world to Himself, not imputing their trespasses to them, and has committed to us the word of reconciliation"* (2 Cor 2:19). To *reconcile* means to change from a relationship of enmity to one of friendship. When one of the two parties is the holy God, who is so horribly offended by our sinfulness that only the physical death of the God-Man Jesus Christ could appease His wrath against our sin, the value of this reconciliation becomes exponentially greater. Can you imagine a sentence of an eternity in hell justly canceled because God inflicted a far worse penalty of wrath on His beloved Son to satisfy the Father's indignation against sin? Now God is just and willing to forgive all sins because the debt has been paid for all who want it.

Just as Jesus announced His offer of salvation, so we must continue allowing *"God [to make] His plea through us."* Paul wrote, *"He might reconcile them both [i.e., Gentiles and Jews] to God in one body through the cross, thereby putting to death the enmity. And He came and preached peace to you who were afar off and to those who were near"* (Eph 2:17). This is what He is all about.

"For this is good and acceptable in the sight of God our Savior" (1 Tim 2:3). Our mission in life as ambassadors is *"to bring about the obedience of faith among all the Gentiles for His name's sake"* (Rom 1:5).

"Heavenly Father, please make me aware of the sins I need to confess to You; I desire to be used as Your ambassador to take the gospel to the world."

NOVEMBER 8

Preach, Be Ready, Reprove, Rebuke, and Exhort

2 Tim 4:2—*"**Preach***~ **the message, be ready***~ whether it is convenient or not, **reprove***~, **rebuke***~, **exhort***~ with complete patience and instruction."*

As we read this last epistle from Paul, we are privileged to sit in on private conversations between a mentor and his protégé.

The goal of a disciplining ministry is to equip disciples with the knowledge and application of the teachings in Scripture. Timothy believed: *"All Scripture is given by inspiration of God, and is profitable for doctrine, for reproof, for correction, for instruction in righteousness, that the man of God may be complete, thoroughly equipped for every good work"* (2 Tim 3:16–17).

We must learn its contents, doctrines, wisdom, and commands to apply to our own lives, then we can help others do the same. In 2 Timothy 4:1, Paul is *"continually charging"* (present tense), or "earnestly exhorting," on the basis of the coming of Jesus Christ. In the meantime, the "man of God" (3:18) is given five commands to obey.

First, he must *"urgently decide to preach the message,"* or "announce it publicly." Believers must be bold and passionate about the *"message."*

Second, he must *"urgently decide to be ready whether it is convenient or not"* (i.e., "be on duty all the time"). We are to share the word of God everywhere all the time. Was this a weakness of Timothy as suggested in 1:6–8?

Third, he must *"urgently decide to reprove,"* or "correct," especially in public (1 Tim 5:20), those who persist in rebellion. A requirement of a pastor is to correct those living contrary to the word (Titus 1:9, 13) with authority (2:15).

Fourth, he must *"urgently decide to rebuke,* meaning to "express strong disapproval of someone as a type of punishment."

Fifth, he must *"urgently decide to exhort"* (i.e., "to cause someone to be encouraged or consoled," or "to beseech with a strong force"). This was to balance his ministry: *"You know how we were exhorting and encouraging and imploring"* (1 Thes 2:11–12). Political correctness quenches against any effective ministry.

"Lord Jesus, I want to do my part to communicate the 'whole counsel' of God. I know it will include some 'tough love,' and I want to be ready to give it by Your wisdom and power. It is not easy for me to be so confrontational. Deepen my conviction for truth."

NOVEMBER 9
Go the Extra Mile

Matt 5:41—*"And if anyone forces you to go one mile, go~~ with him two."*

Some of Jesus's commands seem unfair, abusive, and unmanly. The Roman army imposed a law that a soldier could obligate any citizen to carry his load for a thousand paces, or a Roman mile as Simon of Cyrene was asked to carry the cross of Jesus to Calvary (Matt 27:32; Mark 15:21). The Jews hated this law because it forced them to demonstrate their subjection to Rome. Peace in the political realm was so important that Jesus commanded His followers to *"be continually going with him two"* miles. The believer is to bear cheerfully what is an interference with his activities or is unseasonable and distasteful, while giving more time and effort than expected.

Paul reiterates this series of responses with the following precepts: *"Repay no one evil for evil. Have regard for good things in the sight of all men . . . live peaceably with all men . . . do not avenge yourselves, but rather give place to wrath; .... Therefore 'If your enemy is hungry, feed him; If he is thirsty, give him a drink'"* (Rom 12:17–20KJV).

Jesus shocked his disciples with His demand *"not to resist an evil person. But whoever slaps you on your right cheek, turn the other to him also"* (Matt 5:39). Another tough command to follow is this: *"if anyone wants to sue you and take away your tunic, let him have your cloak also"* (5:40). Paul took this command seriously for the churches: *"Even to have such lawsuits with one another is a defeat for you. Why not just accept the injustice and leave it at that? Why not let yourselves be cheated?"* (1 Cor 6:7).

Jesus never demanded something of His followers that He did not demonstrate and practice, as *"when He was reviled, He did not revile in return; when He suffered, He did not threaten, but committed Himself to Him who judges righteously"* (1 Pet 2:23). Can you trust God to make things right or to retaliate in His time and manner?

We must not fight for our rights. The believer lives in, and is being prepared for, another kingdom where retaliation will not exist and where forgiveness is as common as daylight. This is what makes a believer in Jesus unique.

"Dear Lord, I trust You to keep records and make things right as I learn to give up my personal rights in order to communicate Your message."

NOVEMBER 10

Love Your Enemy and Pray for Persecutors

Matt 5:44—*"But I say to you, **love~~ your enemy and pray~~** for those who persecute you."*

In Matthew 5:43, Jesus says, *"You have heard it said, 'You shall love your neighbor, and hate your enemy.'"* Jesus taught by stating the common perspectives and then directly contradicting them. *"But I say to you"* now He introduces a stark contrast in how to think about others. Jesus expected His disciples to commit to His commands and a new worldview, changing their lives forever.

It is true you are to *"love your neighbor"* (5:43). Wisdom warns us against vengeful thoughts: *"Do not say, 'Thus I shall do to him as he has done to me'"* (Prov 24:29).

Nowhere in the Old Testament do we see "hate your enemy"; rather, it became a Jewish tradition of thought that brought great animosity and prejudice against anyone with different or opposing ideas. The early Jewish believers used this thought to justify their hatred of the Gentiles and their refusal to give them the gospel message (Acts 10; 11:19). They truly believed God hated the Gentiles as they did. Perversion is an element of truth mixed with demonic lies to destroy what God means to say.

The Greek has four words for "love." These are *philia*, a brotherly love or friendship; *storge*, the love of family; *eros*, desire, feeling, sex, and romance (which word does not appear in the New Testament); and *agape*, a love that seeks the highest benefit for another person without regard to personal benefits or agendas. This final word is the love Jesus refers to in Matthew 5:44. Because it is not an emotional response, but a commitment to a beneficial action toward another person regardless of our own feelings, we can choose to love an enemy. It's our choice. Thus we can love someone we do not like personally.

We are commanded to *"continually be praying for those who persecute [us]."* Even if it does not change them, we are to continue to pray for abusive authorities to show that we care for them regardless of how they treat us. This reaction required the grace of God for Jesus's response, and we must rely on His grace as well. Do you really want to be like Jesus?

"Loving Father, You have shown us how to love those who hate us. Help me follow Your wonderful example, deciding not to return evil for evil but to pray for those who would persecute me."

NOVEMBER 11

Do Good

Rom 13:3—"*(for rulers cause no fear for good conduct but for bad). Do you desire not to fear authority?* **Do good**~~ *and you will receive its commendation.*"

Simply knowing wisdom concepts is not a guarantee of success; rather, each person must choose guiding principles for decision making. Wisdom instructions are not absolute commands because there are always some exceptions to the rules, but they provide wise guidelines.

When leaders are honest and just, people who do right have nothing to fear. However, if citizens are commanded to do something contrary to God's word, a higher priority of submission to God takes precedence over secular laws. When a believer is necessarily disobedient to civil laws, he is not afraid of being caught, because he is "doing good" even if it brings persecution.

Great care must be exercised on this issue. Some Christians do not want to pay taxes, comply with licenses for different ministries, or pay Social Security, etc., believing they are exempt, when in fact, they may not be. Ethical issues can get complex and questionable, so be sure to get the best advice possible. At some point, everyone must draw a line that he will not cross, but often, wise action can avoid the potential conflict.

Even unregenerate civil authorities have a sense of right and wrong. They are required to punish wrongdoers and give the honor of *"commendation"* to those who do good in difficult situations. When evil leaders refuse to recognize the difference between good and evil, it is because they "*suppress the truth in unrighteousness, because that which is known about God is evident within them; for God made it evident to them*" (Rom 1:18–19).

A missionary friend of mine, Bruce Olson, three times has received the nation's highest award in Colombia for civil service in the battle against the communist guerrillas. He was once capture by the guerrillas, chained to a tree for 150 days, and nearly died. His Christian witness during this time changed many lives among them to the point that the guerrilla band disbanded. The gospel faithfully proclaimed is the key to individual and societal transformation. Can God count on us to share the gospel in difficult times?

"Lord Jesus, give me the wisdom to know what is good and the courage to do the right thing regardless of the problems that may come my way because of my actions."

NOVEMBER 12
Make the Most of Opportunities

Col 4:5—*"Conduct yourselves~~ with wisdom* toward outsiders, making the most of the opportunities."

God's commands can imply specific actions for individuals to take, attitudes to maintain, or general principles for living. There are principles to apply among believers and in dealing with the world, or *"outsiders"* (1 Cor 5:12, 13; 1 Thes 4:12; 1 Tim 3:7).

Unbelievers slandered the early Christians. Because the Christians had no visible gods, they were called atheists; because they would not burn incense before the emperor's image, they were called unpatriotic; and because they met behind locked doors, they were called immoral. In a critical world, the gospel's credibility will depend on believers who live in light of what they believe despite the accusations.

Paul's instruction for the response to these false accusations was to *"be continually conducting yourselves with wisdom,"* as opposed to impulsive, foolish responses, or changing standards to avoid criticism. The verb means to "walk, live, or behave in a customary manner." If believers are seen to live as fools, whatever they claim will be seen as meaningless.

The opposite of wisdom living is to be led by foolish thoughts. For example, it is foolish for believers to live for money: *"Those who want to get rich fall into temptation and a snare and many foolish and harmful desires which plunge men into ruin and destruction"* (1 Tim 6:9). Foolishness is common to all men: *"For we ourselves were also once foolish, disobedient, deceived, serving various lusts and pleasures, living in malice and envy, hateful and hating one another"* (Titus 3:3). Society cannot dictate our morality.

Living wisely also involves *"making the most of the opportunities."* As Moses wrote, *"Teach us to number our days, that we may present to Thee a heart of wisdom"* (Psa 90:12). Jesus said, *"Night is coming, when no man can work"* (Jn 9:4); *"Therefore, as we have opportunity, let us do good to all, especially to those who are of the household of faith"* (Gal 6:10). When unselfish living is observed, the gospel gains credibility. Unselfish living reflects an unselfish God.

"Heavenly Father, if Your word 'dwells richly' in me, I will be guided by Your wisdom to be effective in every part of my life and ministry for the sake of those who need to know You. This is my desire to honor Your Name in life."

NOVEMBER 13

Learn to Engage in Good Works

Titus 3:14—*"Here is another way that our people **can learn~~ to engage** in good works to meet pressing needs and so not be unfruitful."*

Fruitfulness, in general, is a value to reproduce in a life. The purpose of fruit in a plant is to provide for germination and reproduction. Metaphorically, it refers to participation in the expansion of the gospel and the reproduction of the character of Christ in other believer.

Believers were to *"be continually learning to engage in good works."* For the third time in this chapter, Paul exhorts believers to do good works (Titus 3:1, 8, 14). Visiting teachers were moving on to other churches: *"Send Zenas the lawyer and Apollos on their journey with haste, that they may lack nothing"* (3:13). One way to be fruitful, therefore, is to facilitate the ministry of itinerating evangelists, missionaries, and teachers. Pastors tended to live in one place with partial or full support.

The traveling missionaries had to learn to trust God's guidance of other believers to provide for their needs as they continued their ministries. Paul had learned to be content (Phil 4:11) whatever his situation, whether he had plenty or could scarcely meet his team's needs. God kept a record of everything the churches gave to meet Paul's needs (*"fruit that abounds to your account,"* 4:17), a heavenly fruit that will never be forgotten.

This participatory giving is to be learned. *"Good works"* can refer to any act motivated by unselfish love to benefit others, especially to *"meet pressing needs"* of itinerating evangelists and teachers. Generosity is a general principle for all believers: *"Let him ... labor, working with his hands what is good, that he may have something to give him who has need"* (Eph 4:28). Believers should be taught to share in each other's ministries and fulfill Christ's purposes in the world encouraged by their eternal consequences and rewards.

Bearing fruit in others is also a high priority for the believer: *"By this My Father is glorified, that you bear much fruit; so you will be My disciples"* (Jn 15:8). Paul wrote, *"Then the way you live will always honor and please the Lord, and your lives will produce every kind of good fruit. All the while, you will grow as you learn to know God better and better"* (Col 1:10). Everything we can do to further the expansion of the gospel will never lose its reward.

"Dear Lord, I want to have a willing heart to be involved in the good works that bring others to know You and become dedicated followers through the guidance of Your holy word."

NOVEMBER 14
Show Your Works

James 3:13—*"Who is wise and understanding among you? By his good* **conduct he should show***~ **his works** *done in the gentleness that wisdom brings."*

Our value system determines every choice we make. James, by asking the rhetorical question, *"Who is wise and understanding among you?"* assumes that we will readily recognize God's models of behavior. The word *wise* (Gk. *sophos*) describes moral insight and skill in its practical application to life's situations. *Understanding* refers to intellectual and scientific knowledge. *"Getting wisdom is the wisest thing you can do! And whatever else you do, develop good judgment"* (Prov 4:7). In the Scriptures, there are two kinds of wisdom: man's wisdom and God's wisdom.

Solomon, full of God's wisdom, wrote of the consequences of worldly wisdom: self-centered, selfish indulgences that result in foolishness, senselessness, frustration and futility. He concluded, *"I set my mind to know wisdom and to know madness and folly; I realized that this also is striving after wind"* (Eccl 1:16–18). Human wisdom is a mirage.

Job asked, *"Where can wisdom be found? And where is the place of understanding?"* (Job 28:12). Then he answers, *"Behold, the fear of the Lord, that is wisdom; and to depart from evil is understanding"* (28:28). True, beneficial wisdom only comes from above. It is not a matter of how much we know but of how much we trust, love, and obey the Lord's words.

Most people believe their understanding is as good as, or better than, others'—this foolish thinking (Prov 12:15) leads them to *"bitter envy and self-seeking [i.e., selfish ambition] in [their] hearts,"* as well as boasting. Denying or lying against the truth *"does not descend from above, but is earthly, sensual, demonic"* (James 3:14–16). What a person trusts to be true determines how he lives.

God's wisdom is evident: *"By his good conduct—his works [are] done in the gentleness [of] wisdom."* Such *"gentleness,"* or meekness, puts other's needs first and self-interest last, which is the objective of God's wisdom: *"Blessed are the meek for they shall inherit the earth"* (Matt 5:5). They will know how to lead in Christ's kingdom when He comes.

"Lord Jesus, I pray You will make my good works evident and give me the wisdom to do them with gentleness and meekness."

NOVEMBER 15
Help Bring Peace among Believers

Phil 4:3—*"Yes, I say also to you, true companion, **help**~~ them. They have struggled together in the gospel ministry along with me and Clement and my other coworkers, whose names are in the book of life."*

It may surprise us to find people in the ministry who become so contentious and disagreeable that they discourage other believers. Paul taught believers to build relationships by making the needs of others a priority (Phil 2:2–3), allowing the *"peace of God to rule in [everyone's] hearts"* and minds (Col 3:15). But harmony in Philippi was on the verge of erupting into conflict.

The two women in conflict here, Euodia and Syntyche, were urged *"to be of the same mind in the Lord"* (Phil 4:2), lest the peace in the congregation be destroyed and people begin to take sides against each other.

Euodia and Syntyche had been instrumental in planting the church at Philippi, perhaps from the very beginning, when Paul met with some women *"by the riverside"* (Acts 16:13). Paul and his evangelistic team stayed at the home of Lydia after her conversion (16:14).

To the Corinthians, Paul wrote, *"Now I exhort you, brethren ... that you all agree and that there be no divisions among you, but that you be made complete in the same mind and in the same judgment"* (1 Cor 1:10). And Peter wrote, *"All of you be harmonious, sympathetic, brotherly, kindhearted, and humble in spirit"* (1 Pet 3:8).

Restoration and harmony are so important in the body of Christ someone had to intervene to help them resolve the conflict. We are not told what the issue was, or who the *"true companion"* (lit. "bound by a common yoke") was, but we know Paul was asked to *"help"* in this conflict. The command means to "bring together, or catch hold of." Whenever there is a conflict seek out a trusted third party to help resolve the issue for the sake of the church body before it gets out of hand and reactions hurt the everyone.

Conflicts among even the most mature, faithful, and serving people can happen when selfish, self-serving interests subtly enter into their thinking (Mark 10:37, 41). When a conflict is perceived, someone must intervene. Jesus wants us all to be "peacemakers" (Matt 5:9) to maintain harmony among believers.

"Dear Father, as I serve You, please help me work to benefit others, bringing harmony and peace to my fellow workers and furthering the ministry of the word."

NOVEMBER 16

Be Hospitable to Those Who Cannot Repay It

Luke 14:12–13—*"Then He also said to him who invited Him, 'When you give a dinner or a supper, **do not ask~/ your friends**, your brothers, your relatives, nor rich neighbors, lest they also invite you back, and you be repaid. But when you give a feast, **invite~~ the poor**, the maimed, the lame, the blind.'"*

It's been said that leadership is all about attitude. Jesus warned us many times that He scrutinizes our attitudes, or motivations, as much as the acts themselves. His judgment is far beyond any human's evaluation of another human, and He never makes mistakes because *"He [knows] all men"* (Jn 2:24).

Insincerity occurs when we do nice things for people who can—and are expected to—return the favor. "You scratch my back, and I'll scratch yours": corrupt governments build their infrastructure on this principle. Corruption rules when returning a favor takes precedence over rules or laws.

Some people are so driven to succeed and become important that they will only associate with people more important than themselves. Pictures of them with important people abound in their homes and offices. This is all part of a vain effort to gain notoriety or favors. Jesus warned His followers not to seek the important seats (Luke 14:8–10) to teach the lesson of life and providence that *"whoever exalts himself will be humbled, and he who humbles himself will be exalted"* (14:11).

We must always ask why we are doing what we do. Someone once said, "The best hospitality is that which is given, not exchanged," because it is about giving love without repayment in mind. Jesus does not absolutely prohibit inviting *"friends, . . . brothers, . . . relatives, [or] rich neighbors"* for a meal, but He does prohibit us from being hospitable just so they will invite us back and repay us. This is important to Jesus because it is the way God thinks, and He expects us to think as He does in our social lives. Jesus said, *"If you love only those who love you, what reward is there for that? Even corrupt tax collectors do that much"* (Matt 5:46).

We are to be hospitable merely to show God's love and encourage others. Can you care for someone like this today or this week?

"Father, lead me to people in need of help and give me the ability to give generously without expecting anything in return."

NOVEMBER 17

Find Someone Open to Truth

Matt 10:11—*"Whenever you enter a town or village,* **find out*~ who is worthy** *there and* **stay*~ with them** *until you leave."*

In the mid-1990's, David Watson, a missionary in India, decided to study Jesus's methodology to determine a new approach to church planting among resistant people groups. He decided to practice what he learned, and he developed at revolutionary approach to missionary strategy!

A worker goes into a village and knocks on every door until someone invites him to come in to hear more of the "good news" about how to know God personally. The worker goes no further in the community, but he returns regularly to this one home, where he continues to teach the meaning of the gospel. Soon the whole family—and many times extended family members, neighbors, and friends—comes to Christ. A church is born under the leadership of the host family.

The worker then only spends time with the head of the household, who guides the young house-church. The process is repeated in other communities, and soon a church-planting movement has begun.

Today, hundreds of thousands of churches are starting in some of the most difficult regions of the world. This is the approach of the underground church. The modern concept of the missionary is that of a nonresident evangelist, teacher, trainer, and mentor to hundreds of non-salaried pastors across a region. All this happened because one missionary decided to take Jesus's instructions seriously!

This approach doesn't require a highly gifted teacher or an eloquent speaker; God simply needs a person who is committed to *"go and make disciples of all nations [i.e., ethnic people groups]"* (Matt 28:19). In Matthew 10:11, he was to find someone *"worthy,"* or "fitting, proper, [or] useful." Luke calls this person a *"son of peace"* (Luke 10:6), referring to God's preparation of an open spirit to know God's truth (Matt 3:8).

The *"worthy"* person is a gift whose home becomes the base of operations for a new ministry. Often this person may seem inadequate for the job, but the missionary should *"stay with [him]"* ("remain, abide") and trust in God's providential leadership, just as Jesus' disciples did.

"Dear Lord, I pray for Your servants around the world who are carrying the gospel to the lost. Guide them to people willing to listen, and help them persevere until the truth is planted in their hearts."

NOVEMBER 18

Be Wise as Serpents

Matt 10:16—*"I am sending you out like sheep surrounded by wolves, so **be wise**~~ as serpents and innocent as doves."*

We cannot imagine the difficulty and risks that accompanied following Jesus. Soon the great miracle worker was gone, and His disciples had to take on the world. They went in separate directions, knowing that their task would mean their death, as it had for their Master. Jesus made it clear in Matthew 10:17 that the *"wolves"* would *"hand [them] over to councils and flog [them] in their synagogues; and [they would] be dragged before governors and kings [Gentiles] because of [Jesus], as a testimony to [themselves] and the Gentiles."* The word *martyr* comes from the same Greek word for "witness" or "testimony."

Sheep must be guided to proper vegetation to avoid eating poisonous weeds. Without a shepherd, a flock usually did not survive, because of their greatest enemy: wolves. Jesus is the Shepherd who loves His sheep and lays down His life for them (Jn 10:11–15), but He sent them out into a Christ-hating world to be rejected.

Though they were called "sheep," they were not to be sheep-like in their attitudes—that is, thoughtless and unprepared. Jesus delegated to them miraculous power (Matt 10:8), but this would not prevent them from suffering at the hands of resistant men. The honor of dying for Christ's reputation meant more than life itself: *"All who desire to live godly in Christ Jesus will be persecuted"* (2 Tim 3:12).

"Serpents" are considered to be *"wise"* ("prudent, practically wise in relationships with others")—that is, shrewd, smart, cunning, and cautious. Jesus was a master at turning the traps of the Jews into unanswerable dilemmas. He was never fooled into condemning Rome's leaders or approving their corruption. He was always one step ahead of his accusers.

The *"dove"* represents purity and innocence, which were characteristics of Jesus's disciples. The clear presentation of the gospel does not need to be done abrasively, inconsiderately, or belligerently. We are to be like our Lord: *"holy, innocent, undefiled"* (Heb 7:26; 1 Pet 2:23). The effective presentation of the gospel requires astute and clever methods to finish the task. He will make it worthwhile.

"Heavenly Father, as we take Your truth to those who may wish us harm, help us be astute and prudent as we deal with them in purity and love."

NOVEMBER 19
Go Far Away

Acts 22:21—*"Then he said to me, 'Go~~, because I will send you far away to the Gentiles.'"*

Paul thought his testimony was convincing to his audience. The Jews knew of his disdain for Christians and that he was a participant in Stephen's martyrdom (Acts 7:58; 8:1a). Surely they would recognize that only divine intervention would have changed his direction. In spite of Paul's conviction that he had a great potential ministry in Jerusalem, God said, *"Go."*

Paul had been converted by Jesus's special appearance on the road to Damascus, where Paul was going to arrest Christians for apostatizing from Judaism (Acts 9). Following his conversion, Paul had a brief ministry in Damascus (9:20–25) and then spent three years in Nabatean Arabia (Gal 1:17–18), during which time Jesus taught him the about the church. Many of these teachings were controversial to the Jews. Christ told Paul to leave Jerusalem, *"for they will not receive your testimony concerning Me"* (Acts 22:18). The Christians learned of a plot to kill Paul, so they rushed him out of the city, sending him back to his home in Tarsus (9:30).

Earlier, Paul was told that he *"[would] be His witness to all men of what [he had] seen and heard"* (Acts 22:15), and now it was further clarified that he was to "continually be going," specifically, "far away to the Gentiles."

God has always desired to communicate His message to every Gentile language, tribe, or people group in the world (Rev 5:10). Christ took this occasion to clarify His final charge to go to *"the ends of the earth"* (Acts 1:8). He wanted believers to get out of their comfort zones to live among very different people to bring them the light of the gospel. Someone had to break the mold of self-centered thinking and take the risk. Paul was chosen, and he said, *"I become all things to all men so that by all possible means I might save some. I do all this for the sake of the gospel"* (1 Cor 9:22–23).

Even to this day, 98 percent of all global Christian ministries target traditional "Christian" populations. Only 2 percent of Christian ministries target the remaining 70 percent of the non-Christian world. God trusts His disciples to read His word and know what must be done, however uncomfortable or unpopular it might be. Will you go?

"Father, You have told all Your children to go with the gospel to the ends of the earth. I pray You will prepare hundreds of thousands of workers to reap the great harvest before You return."

NOVEMBER 20

Do Not Stop Other Ministries

Luke 9:50—*"But Jesus said to him, 'Do not stop~/ him, for whoever is not against you is for you.'"*

Just as Jesus was discussing how greatness is only achieved in His kingdom by being the least important, John, one of the inner circle of three disciples, interrupted to say that a man who was casting out demons was not following Jesus as they were. John wanted the Master to forbid this man; however, Jesus commanded, *"Stop stopping him, for whoever is not against you is for you."*

It appears as though the Twelve saw themselves as the exclusive leaders of God's people. They wanted all the control, so they were jealous of the success of another outside their group. They wanted to micromanage the followers of Christ. They should have rejoiced that the power of God was being manifested on earth by other disciples. This was not a rival or an enemy but a collaborator helping complete the task. The laborers were few, so they should have appreciated every one of them (Luke 10:2).

This concept was expressed in the negative as well: *"The one who is not with me is against me"* (Luke 11:23 and Matt 12:30). Here the emphasis is on deciding to follow Jesus to avoid remaining in opposition to Him by indecision. Whatever his motivation, the person who exorcised a demon in Jesus's name would never turn around and oppose Jesus. At least he had performed an act of mercy for a possessed person and stood against Satan.

A similar situation developed with Moses and the seventy elders (Num 11:25). Joshua wanted Moses to punish the two elders who did not come to the tabernacle by forbidding them from serving. Moses answered Joshua, *"Are you zealous for my sake? Oh, that all the Lord's people were prophets and that the Lord would put His Spirit upon them!"* (11:29).

Paul expressed a godly attitude to the Philippians: *"Some indeed preach Christ even from envy and strife, and some also from good will ... What then? Only that in every way, whether in pretense or in truth, Christ is preached; and in this I rejoice, yes, and will rejoice"* (Phil 1:15–18). Can you always rejoice in the successful ministries of others when the gospel is proclaimed?

"Dear loving Lord, when we have a tendency to want to control or micromanage other people who serve You, help us stop and trust You to guide us all to accomplish Your purposes."

NOVEMBER 21
Let the Children Come

Mark 10:14—*"But when Jesus saw this, he was indignant and said to them, 'Let the little children* **come*~ to me** *and* **do not try to stop~| them,** *for the kingdom of God belongs to such as these.'"*

To understand a person, it is important to know his likes and dislikes. In Mark 10:14, Jesus is said to be *"indignant"* (meaning to "arouse to anger, [be] grieved"). By now, the disciples should have known Jesus's attitude toward those who wanted to know Him. His response reveals His values, His compassion, and His annoyance with their offensive, elitist attitude.

A mute child possessed by a demon was brought to Jesus because his disciples could not cast out the demon. Jesus's response revealed another value: *"O faithless generation, how long shall I be with you? How long shall I bear with you? Bring him to Me"* (Mark 9:19). Unwillingness to exercise faith to aid a helpless soul was intolerable!

In our text, Jesus gave a sharp double command. First, He said, *"Immediately start letting the little children come to me."* The Greek word for *children* (*paidion*) has a range of meanings, from "infant" to "teenager," but the command implies that they were old enough to come to Jesus if not prohibited, and they consciously desired to know Him. There is no presumption that all children are automatically part of the kingdom, but those who desire to come to Jesus will be warmly welcomed. Second, the disciples were commanded, *"Stop trying to hinder them."* Christianity is not just for adults. Anyone who understands God's truth is a candidate for Christ's salvation. A child can understand quite early.

The phrase *"such as these"* refers to all who have childlike characteristics, such as helplessness, insignificance, dependency, and a willingness to trust Jesus's authority. In fact, the next verse declares that everyone who desires to be saved must come with these childlike characteristics.

Were the disciples still thinking that they were important people, working hard to be worthy or good enough for salvation? Was this why Jesus was angry? They still did not understand the simplicity of the gospel that even a child can understand. How important are children in your life's mission?

"Dear Lord, may we never hinder in any way a child coming to You. It is Your Spirit who leads another to faith in Your saving grace, regardless of his age."

NOVEMBER 22

Do Not Be Afraid of Witnessing

Luke 5:9–10—*"For Peter and all who were with him were astonished at the catch of fish that they had taken, and so were James and John, Zebedee's sons, who were Simon's business partners. Then Jesus said to Simon, '**Do not be afraid~|***; from now on you will be catching people.'"*

The men had fished all night without catching any fish when Jesus approached them and asked them to pull offshore to drop the empty nets. Peter knew Jesus, so he responded, *"At Your word I will let down the net"* (Luke 5:5). Though it was contrary to everything Peter had learned about fishing, suddenly, the net was so full of fish that he called for help lest his own ship sink!

They were all *"astonished"* at how Christ's word brought immediate results. Who could this person be? Jesus said, *"Stop being afraid."* Indeed, they would see greater miracles than this over the next three years. Fear kills our creativity, paralyzes our actions, and forces us to think too much about protecting ourselves. Fear should never enter into our thinking, because *"all authority in heaven and on earth has been given to [Him]"* (Matt 28:18); we can trust Him.

Peter was fearless when he responded to Christ's invitation to join Him in walking on water (Matt 14:29), but when he took his eyes off Jesus, he saw the danger he was in and began to sink. As he cried out to the Lord, *"immediately Jesus stretched out His hand and caught him, and said to him, 'O you of little faith, why did you doubt?'"* (14:31). Fear is the direct result of doubt about God's ability to intervene and control the situation for His purpose.

Jesus told Simon, *"From now on you will be continually catching men."* Their commitment, patience, and effort in professional fishing now would be applied to living persons.

Upon reaching shore, *"they forsook all and followed Him"* (Luke 5:11), and the world was never the same. They left their huge catch of fish to catch sinners, having been caught themselves by the greatest fisherman of all. They would not be perfect or always fearless, but their message was the *"power of God for the salvation of everyone who believes"* (Rom 1:16). All they had to do was to go where people had not heard and announce the message, however feebly, and then God would take over in every heart. Be fearless today!

"Lord Jesus, many of Your children are very afraid of witnessing to others of Your salvation. Give us Your perspective of their great need so we may overcome that fear and share in the wonderful experience of leading a soul to You."

NOVEMBER 23

Take the Least Important Seat

Luke 14:8–10—*"But when you are invited, **go*~ and take*~ the least important place**, so that when your host approaches he will say to you, 'Friend, move up here to a better place.' Then you will be honored in the presence of all who share the meal with you."*

It is amazing how unashamedly people will tell you how great they are. The world's wisdom is, "If no one beats your drum, beat it yourself." But Jesus's basic rule of wisdom was never to let honor be due to self-promotion.

Jesus saw how the people in the banquet clamored for the best seats, where they could be seen as important. The room was arranged in a large U shape, with the headmaster at the bottom of the U. Protocol in the ancient world was to give the most important person the seat nearest the headmaster. If one's presumption overcame his prudence, he might gamble to get closer to the more powerful or wealthier people. However, if a more distinguished person arrived, he would be embarrassed by being asked to move.

It takes a lot of arrogance to constantly exalt yourself and dominate every conversation. Such a person sincerely believes, and is quick to let you know, that he is far more intelligent than anyone else. He typically treats others as inferiors. A recent book title captures his slogan: *Enough about You, Let's Talk about Me.*

Jesus's concept of honor, given to the humble, is far from the normal way of thinking. Some attempt to give the appearance of humility, however false, to manipulate others; others misconstrue humility to mean criticizing yourself in public. True humility only compares itself to Jesus, and those who are truly humble recognize their personal sinfulness and hold a realistic view of their limitations and capabilities to serve others. A humble person is dedicated to making others successful, meeting their needs, and helping them become all they were designed to be.

The more we benefit others, the higher our probability of being recognized in due time. Waiting to be honored by others pleases the Lord and builds good relationships.

"Dear Jesus, You showed us the way to live by being born in a lowly place and living in poor surroundings, and the Father has exalted You to the highest position of all. Help me yield my aspirations of greatness to You and simply serve others."

NOVEMBER 24
Be Eager for Greater Gifts

1 Cor 12:31—*"But **you should be eager**~~ **for the greater gifts**. And now I will show you a way that is beyond comparison."*

Some of the principles established in 1 Corinthians 12 include how God chooses to distribute spiritual gifts and how every believer should be content with his gifts.

Paul exhorts the church in Corinth as a whole to *"be continually eager for the greater gifts."* We need to examine the language form to understand what Paul is saying. Because the Greek imperative is the same form as the indicative active verb, the context determines if it should be interpreted as an imperative command or a present active verb. If it is present active, it would be translated, *"But you are earnestly desiring the greater gifts."*

Secondly, if it is the command in the present active plural form, it means that it is not for individuals but for the entire congregation to "be protective of" or "deeply committed to" (Louw and Nida, *Greek-English Lexicon*) the "best" gifts. This means the "greater in status, or rank" (Louw and Nida, *Greek-English Lexicon*), or "the more useful, or profitable" (Strong) gifts. Paul's ranking or categories of spiritual gifts for those directly communicating the word of God is *"first apostles, second prophets, third teachers, after that [fourth] miracles, then [fifth] gifts of healings, helps, administrations, varieties of tongues"* (1 Cor 12:28). The gift of tongues is ranked in the least effective category, because no one can understand it, so it is last on the list.

All of 1 Corinthians 14 is dedicated to proving that the gift of tongues is totally "unprofitable" by itself. The purpose for tongues was to be *a "sign, not for believers but for unbelievers"* (1 Cor 14:22), especially for Jews who had been promised such a sign (14:21), as demonstrated on the day of Pentecost, when sixteen actual languages were spoken to the unbelieving Jews (Acts 2). Do not let phenomena distract you from your love for and study of God's word. The greater gifts that exhort and teach the congregations should be prioritized.

"Heavenly Father, the Bible is Your message for mankind. Help Your children use our speaking gifts to the greatest advantage to help prepare Your church for Your prompt return to earth."

NOVEMBER 25

Pursue Love

1 Cor 14:1—*"Pursue~~ love and be eager~~ for the spiritual gifts,* *especially that you may prophesy."*

In the New Testament, ministry is focused primarily on how believers "devoted themselves to the apostle's teaching," as well as sharing, worshipping, and praying (Acts 2:42). Paul introduced *"the most excellent way,"* as opposed to an exaggerated emphasis on one of the spiritual gifts. This *"way"* is serving each other for love's sake (*agape*-type love): not for the sake of feeling good toward each other (*eros*-type love) but for a self-sacrificing commitment to benefit each other.

The foundational concept of the spiritual gifts is described in 1 Corinthians 12:7[NIV]: *"Now to each one the manifestation of the Spirit is given for the common good,"* or a "mutual benefit" for the body of Christ. God's Spirit empowers every believer to serve other believers by complimenting each other's ministries and creating interdependence within the body of Christ.

The corporate body of Christ is to "continually or habitually be pursuing love," our highest goal. Discovering our spiritual gifts is not the most important thing. When we are committed to serving others, eventually our gifts will become evident through personal motivation and through feedback from those we have helped.

Believers are to *"be continually eager for the spiritual gifts"*: a plural corporate command, not an individual focus. The church is to seek out the gifted members and give them special functions that coincide with their spiritual giftedness for the maximum benefit to the whole body of Christ (1 Cor 12:11, 18).

Of all the spiritual gifts, Paul writes, *"especially that you may prophesy,"* which is contrasted with speaking in tongues throughout chapter 14. There are ten reasons why speaking in tongues is inferior to speaking prophecy, followed by ten rules for controlling the disruptive outbursts of tongues in the Corinthian church. Of all the gifts, Paul emphasizes that the gift of prophesy should be dominant in the church, because it allows the word of God to give insight, warning, correction, and encouragement (1 Cor 14:3), edifying the church. Believers are to follow leaders who can help them serve in their gifted areas.

"Lord, the gifts You gave the church provide avenues for each of us to serve and benefit others, not to make ourselves feel or look good. Help us understand this and live accordingly to honor and obey You."

NOVEMBER 26
Seek to Strengthen the Church

1 Cor 14:12—*"It is the same with you. Since you are eager for manifestations of the Spirit, **seek~~ to abound** in order to strengthen the church."*

Sensitive problems need to be addressed with diplomacy and tact. Paul had received a delegation from the church at Corinth about a number of problems, one of which Paul addressed in 1 Corinthians 14:12. They were *"eager ... for manifestations of the Spirit"* (Gk. *pneuma*, meaning "supernatural and non-material entity" [Louw and Nida, *Greek-English Lexicon*], not the *pneumatikon* of 14:1: "spiritual things or gifts"). This eagerness for a supernatural manifestation was a problem that blinded them to biblical values provoking three chapters of corrections (1 Cor 12–14).

The introductory phrase, *"It is the same with you,"* refers to their exaggerated focus on speaking in tongues (1 Cor 14:9–11). In pagan circles when ecstatic speaking manifested, they thought it was the language of the gods. Among believers, speaking in tongues was similar to these pagan frenzies.

Paul explained the nature of meaningful communication: it must always be understandable and intelligent. He began by illustrating the meaningful sounds of music (e.g., the flute or harp: 1 Cor 14:7). Even in the military, the bugle gives certain sounds necessary to guide the troops (14:8). Unintelligible sounds were useless.

We see in 1 Corinthians 14:9 that if you use unintelligible speech, no one will know what was said, *"for you will be speaking into the air."* Instead of speaking to God, there is really no communication! Paul defines the *tongue* as *"many different languages in the world, and none is without meaning"* (1 Cor 14:10). Tongues or languages are constructed with particular phonetic, grammatical, and linguistic structures that communicate understandable intelligence. Even real languages are unintelligible if they violate these linguistic structures (14:11).

Paul asks us to be *"continually seeking to abound in order to strengthen the church."* The command is to *"strengthen"* (*oikodome*, "build up" someone, or "increase the potential of someone" [Louw and Nida, *Greek-English Lexicon*]). As one understands the word and trusts in its truths, he is edified, which is the priority of the ministry. Are you willing to learn to communicate His word clearly to build up others? This is building fruit in others rather than ourselves.

"Dear Father, give me an eagerness to edify others in the most effective way so I may help strengthen Your church. This is Your priority, so it must be mine as well."

NOVEMBER 27

Do Not Be Children in Thinking

1 Cor 14:20—*"Brothers and sisters, **do not be children~| in your thinking.** Instead, **be infants~~ in evil, but in your thinking be mature~~."***

Becoming an adult does not necessarily bring emotional maturity, nor does being a Christian for years automatically bring spiritual maturity. Paul described the process as being *"transformed by the renewing of your mind"* (Rom 12:2). Only by being exposed to the teaching of God's word and making a conscious decision to allow His thoughts to be our thoughts will we be transformed into His likeness.

The believers at Corinth came into the church with preconceived ideas and false views. Earlier in this epistle, Paul describes them as still being *"infants in the Christian life"* (1 Cor 3:1[NLT]). Their abuse of the spiritual gifts confirmed this analysis. Wrong thinking leads to wrong beliefs and then to wrong values and convictions, generating wrong emotional responses.

Their childish thoughts and beliefs had to do with the high value they placed on the gift of tongues. Nothing else mattered. Even the Scriptures had lost their appeal, and the simple teaching of the texts was not as attractive as a miraculous tongue.

Paul was saying that their elevated view of tongues was childish because the ecstatic experiences made them feel important and spiritual. They misinterpreted the mystical feeling for reality. They had little concern for others; thus they were loveless and carnal. The Corinthians needed to be *"infants in evil"*—that is, they needed to be inexperienced, and unaware of evil.

Using the same form of the verb, Paul commands, *"In your thinking continuously be mature."* The Corinthians were not open to new teachings, nor were they interested in serving others; instead, they wanted only their emotional highs. For the immature, experience always wins over truth. To them, mystical encounters are more appealing than reason. Are you willing to imitate the Bereans (Acts 17:11), who were *"examining the scriptures carefully every day to see if these things were so"* that Paul had been teaching? One has to be committed to discovering what God's word says, not what we might want it to say.

"Dear Lord Jesus, it is childish to base my spiritual beliefs solely on my feelings and experiences. Make me wise through Your word and able to think in a mature way, opening the door for true ministry."

NOVEMBER 28

Do All Things to Edify the Church

1 Cor 14:26—*"What should you do then, brothers and sisters? When you come together, each one has a song, has a lesson, has a revelation, has a tongue, has an interpretation.* **Let all these things be done***~ *for the strengthening of the church."*

What was a typical early church like to an observer? Paul laid the foundational principles and commands (1 Cor 14:1–25) and now describes the activities of a congregational gathering. One person would sing a *"song"* with a harp as musical accompaniment. Though not a gift mentioned in 1 Corinthians 12, it was a common practice in Old Testament worship and in the New Testament to *"[speak] to one another in psalms and hymns and spiritual songs"* (Eph 5:19 and Col 3:16). Another person would teach (1 Cor 12:29; Rom 12:7; Col 3:16), another would describe a special revelation from God (possibly a practice of the gift of prophecy: 1 Cor 12:10, 29; 13:2; 14:1), and another would speak an unknown language (12:10, 28, 30) while someone else interpreted (12:30).

This is not necessarily Paul's recommendation for an order of service; rather, it is a description of the normal activities in their gatherings. His focus is not so much on what happened but on how it should happen. The priority is on orderly activities to benefit congregational needs. It seems the Corinthians were performing these activities for themselves simultaneously, causing pandemonium. Visitors thought they were crazy (1 Cor 14:23).

"From now on let all these things be done for the edification of the church." Just as one stone is added to another to build a house, so each truth, command, and piece of wisdom is to be taught. Believers must decide to be edifiers: *"Therefore encourage one another, and build up one another"* (1 Thes 5:11). *"Let each of us please his neighbor for his good, to his edification. For even Christ did not please Himself"* (Rom 15:2–3): To be like Christ is to seek the benefit of others as a priority in life. Any use of the spiritual gifts that does not fulfill this requirement is loveless.

Only one building tool builds up a believer: the word of God. Have you experienced this edification by learning new, practical truths that changed your life? This is what you now have to share. Make it your life's goal to edify others.

"Dear Father, what importance You have placed on the edification of Your church! May Your servants be ever faithful in doing everything possible to accomplish that goal in our ministries."

NOVEMBER 29
Remember, Some Should Speak and Some Should Evaluate

1 Cor 14:29—*"Two or three **prophets should speak**~~ and the **others should evaluate**~~ what is said."*

The prophets were also to make edification the priority in their teaching. The gift of prophecy and of apostleship had the task of delivering to the church the word of God, but this function ceased very early in the church age when all of God's revelation had been delivered and recorded by inspiration. These gifts were given to lay the foundation for the church (Eph 2:20). Thereafter, evangelists, pastors, and teachers would lead, exhort, clarify, and apply the content and meanings of all that the apostles and prophets gave us of the word of God: *"All Scripture is inspired by God and profitable for teaching, for reproof, for correction, for training in righteousness; that the man of God may be adequate, equipped for every good work"* (2 Tim 3:16–17). Once recorded for all time, a prophet's primary function was unnecessary since there were no more divine revelations to be given.

Revelations of God's word were given "in part" (1 Cor 13:9) and would continue "part" by "part" until the entirety of God's word was *"complete"* or *"perfect"* (*teleios*, means "finished, goal that has reached its end, wanting in nothing"). The term does not refer to an absolute perfection, but the completion of a process, in this case, the process whereby each prophet and apostle delivered another part of what God revealed to him of His word.

In the meantime, the prophets spoke for God to the churches. This was a limited group. Only two or three were allowed to speak in any one service. The rest of the church had to be familiar with all that God had revealed to make sure no one contradicted what an apostle or prophet had revealed.

Those who were not prophets were to *"be always evaluating what was said,"* to *"test the spirits to see whether they [were] from God"* (1 Jn 4:1). Nowhere does Paul suggest that preaching or "prophecy" is privileged beyond critical reflection and evaluation. By definition, someone who pretends to be speaking divine prophecy must be infallible (Deut 18:20–22). Because prophets were laying the foundation of the church, the integrity of their message was vital and unquestioned. There could be no deviations from any previous revelations. God expects us to master His word *"once for all delivered to the saints"* (Jude 3).

"Heavenly Father, Your plan for the edification of the church is perfect. May all of us be diligent by prayerfully listening and studying in order to evaluate what is taught. Give us such a high regard for Your word as to seek its true meaning always. Thank You for all You have given us to know."

NOVEMBER 30

Women, Be Silent in Church

1 Cor 14:33b–34—*"As in all the churches of the saints the women **should be silent~~ in the churches**, for they are not permitted to speak. Rather, let them be in submission, as in fact the law says."*

People are sometimes willing to put a convenient twist on Scripture to justify doing the exact opposite of what it clearly states. Paul introduces this command with the phrase *"as in all the churches"* to signify that this is not a local preference or cultural prejudice that can be ignored: *"For this reason I have sent Timothy to you . . . who will remind you of my ways in Christ, as I teach everywhere in every church"* (1 Cor 4:17).

Although the application of silence also applies to speaking in tongues, the immediate context is that of prophetic speaking: *"Let a woman quietly receive instruction with entire submissiveness. But I do not allow a woman to teach or exercise authority over a man, but to remain quiet"* (1 Tim 2:11–12).

In addition, women are not the only ones commanded to be silent. Only two, or three at most, were permitted to speak in tongues in any one service, and the same restriction was placed on the early church prophets. The remaining speakers were commanded to be silent (1 Cor 14:28,30). In this context Paul declares, *"The spirits of the prophets are subject to the prophets"* (14:32). The filling of the Spirit does not produce the loss of control; rather it empowers one's self-control (Gal 5:22). Paul inserts the reason for these restrictions—*"God is not the author of confusion"* (1 Cor 14:33)—which is followed immediately by the command for women's silence.

All three commands (1 Cor 14:28, 30, 34) use the same word *silence* (Gk. *sigao*), which means "to say nothing, [or] keep still or silent" (Strong), *"with the implication of preserving something which is secret"* (Louw and Nida, *Greek-English Lexicon*), as Romans 16:25. The fact that some women are better than men, that sometimes there is no male leadership in the church, or that a pastor authorized a woman to teach men are never justifiable excuses for disobeying a clear command in Scripture. *"If they want to learn something, let them ask their own husbands at home; for it is shameful for women to speak in church"* (1 Cor 14:35): this places a heavy responsibility on husbands. Although this is a delicate issue, our approach should be to ask, "How can I minister my gifts while obeying this command?"

"Loving Lord Jesus, You have placed men as leaders in the church. Help its women be willing to learn submission, practicing their spiritual gifts in a way that pleases You and builds the church as well."

DECEMBER 1
Acknowledge Paul's Commands

1 Cor 14:37—*"If anyone considers himself a prophet or spiritual person, he* ***should acknowledge***~~ *that what I write to you is the Lord's command."*

Under the inspiration of the Spirit, Paul's words are Christ's words and are therefore indisputable. *"The fear of the Lord is the beginning of knowledge, but fools despise wisdom and instruction"* (Prov 1:7): anyone who is unafraid to violate a command in Scripture is a fool and will reap the fool's consequences.

The reference in 1 Corinthians 14:37 to a *"spiritual person"* (i.e., "one dominated or gifted by the Spirit") refers to those who spoke in tongues. Paul established ten reasons why speaking in tongues was inferior (14:2–20), followed by ten rules for how to practice the spiritual gifts (14:21–40).

Failing to acknowledge these instructions puts a person in direct confrontation with the *"Lord's command."* A Spirit-filled person has an open, obedient heart to God's divinely inspired writings. Truly spiritual people obey the commands in Scripture.

Sadly, many placed themselves above the apostolic teaching, believing their "revelations" were superior, and voiced opposition to Paul's teachings as the opinions of a mere man.

Paul was not writing his own opinions or preferences but was communicating God's words to the church. Any person who failed to recognize the divine authority of Paul's writings was on dangerous ground.

Paul gave such people a severe warning: *"If anyone does not recognize this [is ignorant of or ignores this], he is not recognized"* (the same verb as in the passive form)—that is, God and the church will not recognize him. These are serious words to motivate us to know God's written word, understand it clearly, and obey it fully. Is this your heart's desire?

"Lord, thank You for giving us all the instructions for the church and for living through Your apostles. I declare to You from my heart that I take every word seriously as if it comes directly from Your lips."

DECEMBER 2

Do Everything Decently and in Order

1 Cor 14:40—*"And **do everything**~~ **in a decent** and orderly manner."*

Paul concludes 1 Corinthians 14 by encouraging believers to continue to grow in Christian service. The Corinthians were eager to demonstrate their gift of tongues, but Paul wanted them to give priority to the gift of prophecy (1 Cor 14:1) as the source of God's revelation, because it is more effective for edification.

Speaking in tongues edifies only indirectly, through the message conveyed by interpreting the language (14:13–14). Even though tongues were limited and only indirectly beneficial, they were not to be forbidden (14:39). Otherwise, this plural command means that it is the responsibility of the church as a whole to follow these directives to honor God in the services. Our desire should be that His word is always honored and respected.

All the other commands in this chapter define how to fulfill this command: for example, in any one service only two, or three at most, could speak in tongues (1 Cor 14:27) or in a prophecy (14:29), and they could not speak in a tongue without a known interpreter present (14:28). If they followed all the ten rules of the manifestation of gifts (14:21–40), they should not be restricted. Otherwise, pandemonium would result, violating this final command.

Decent (*euschemonos*) means "correctly, properly, [or] decorously." The phrase "in order" (*taxis*) means "a fixed succession observing a fixed time."This is just the opposite of how the Corinthians were conducting their services before receiving this epistle from Paul; visitors thought they *"were out of their minds"* (1 Cor 14:23), which uses a word describing the emotional "high" or "out-of-control" frenzy of a pagan ritual.

Worship is the core of the believer's new life in Christ and is a powerful reflection of the reality of our conversion and transformation. Having been loved by God, now we seek to love God in return with our whole being. We should never let self-glory enter into any expression of worship. God is a God of incredible order, and our public worship and life should demonstrate our likeness to Him in all things. Worship is not about us; it is all about Him. How can you demonstrate His characteristics in your thoughts, worship, and service?

"Thank You for the teachers You bring into my life. I am indebted to them for how they have taught me Your word and modeled how to live it."

DECEMBER 3

Share with Your Teacher

Gal 6:6—"*Now the one who receives instruction in the word* **must share**~~ *all good things* *with the one who teaches it.*"

In the early church, there were no buildings, only small groups of believers. The leaders met with many small groups, giving relevant instructions to be obeyed (2 Tim 2:2) while sharing in worship, intercession, and ministry. To lead multiple groups took much time and effort and limited any possibility of making a living in a regular job. To extend the kingdom of God, it was going to take dedicated, full-time ministers. Quality ministry takes quality time.

The theme of our text begins in Galatians 6:1 and is addressed to those "*who are spiritual*" ("dominated by the Spirit, or spiritually gifted")—that is, the ones God has anointed with special spiritual gifts to minister within the church body. This should not motivate someone to think "*himself to be something, when he is nothing*" (Gal 6:3): whatever effective ministry one may have is due entirely to the Holy Spirit.

Each member "*shall bear his own load*" (Gal 6:5). Some are to minister in full-time teaching, discipling, counseling, and exhorting, while others are to help support them. Jesus taught that "*the laborer is worthy of his wages*" (Luke 10:7), which Paul repeats in 1 Timothy 5:18 in the context of supporting full-time gifted leaders (1 Cor 9:11, 14).

There is an over-arching "duty" of reciprocity: "*It pleased them [i.e., the Gentiles of Macedonia and Achaia] indeed, and they are their [the Jews] debtors. For if the Gentiles have been partakers of their spiritual things, their duty is also to minister to them in material things*" (Rom 15:27).

We must express our gratitude to and partnership with those who benefit us spiritually by supporting their ministries. With whom are you partnering in the ministry through prayer, financial support, and meaningful involvement?

"*Lord, You have some godly teachers throughout Your churches who have enriched and challenged my life. Give me the opportunity to bless their lives as they have blessed mine.*"

DECEMBER 4

Sober Up and Stop Sinning

1 Cor 15:34—*"**Sober up**~~ as you should, and **stop sinning**~/! For some have no knowledge of God—I say this to your shame!"*

Why was Paul so "fanatical" about getting the gospel *"to the regions beyond"* (2 Cor 10:15)? The answer is that he personally had seen the resurrected Lord Jesus several times. Once he had been stoned to death and was *"caught up to the third heaven"* (12:2). He did not give his life for something he hoped was real or that he had to take by blind faith. A living Savior and heaven and hell were not mere doctrines but unseen realities with huge consequences.

More than half the world believes either that you cease to exist when you die (e.g., atheist Chinese), that you reincarnate into some other living creature (e.g., Hindus and Buddhists), or that your fate is an entirely arbitrary, predetermined decision made by an unfeeling, unforgiving god (e.g., Islam). How thankful we should be that Christ has shown us the reality of the resurrection, heaven, and future events!

Paul's first command in 1 Corinthians 15:34 is to *"sober up,"* meaning to "come to one's senses": literally to "come out of a drunken spell" or metaphorically to "awake from a state of stupor, ignorance, [or] delusion." We know the certainty of life beyond the grave because Jesus was there and rose to give us eternal life.

Anyone with doubts or false beliefs is commanded to "cease or stop sinning." This is not a passing thought or a Sunday reflection but an eternal reality. There is a heaven where all resurrected believers will go, but there is also a hell in which all resurrected unbelievers will spend eternity.

Today, many depend on modern media to transmit the gospel, but most of the world does not have radio, television, or computers; some do not know how to read. Someone must go! This is not God's responsibility. We were given the commission to carry the gospel to the last people group on earth. After two thousand years, you would think more people would care enough to go and tell them. Can you see why it is our *"shame"* that they have never heard? What will you do about it?

"Teach me to always live in the reality of the eternal destinies of everyone around me. My heart aches for the thousands of people groups who have never heard Your word. Give me the opportunity to make a difference for the gospel today."

DECEMBER 5

Imitate Me

Gal 4:12—*"I beg you, brothers and sisters,* **become**~~ **like me**, *because I have become like you. You have done me no wrong!"*

It can be hard to imagine the difficulties of a first-century Jew becoming like a Gentile; giving up his pride, his personal ambitions, and the respect of his people; and sacrificing his position of honor to adapt to an uncomfortable, foreign, and unpopular lifestyle, only to be rejected by those he came to love. The Galatians initially accepted the gospel, but false teachers followed Paul in every town and persuaded people to reject him and become legalistic, practicing the law in order to be saved.

In this epistle, Paul confronts the false teachers, but his tone changes as he addresses the deceived followers (Gal 4:12–20). Paul learned this approach to exhortation from the Lord Jesus Himself and sent a similar message to the Corinthians: *"I, Paul, myself urge you by the meekness and gentleness of Christ"* (2 Cor 10:1). If we are going to be effective in changing lives, we must be gentle in our approach. Paul practiced what he demanded of other servants: *"A servant of the Lord must not quarrel but be gentle to all, able to teach, patient, in humility correcting those who are in opposition"* (2 Tim 2:24–25a).

Judaizers were intimidating the readers of Galatians 4:12 to return to their former bondage of obeying Old Testament ceremonial laws. In 4:17, Paul wrote, *"They zealously court you"* (from a word meaning to "profess affection to gain someone as a follower, but for no good"). Paul accommodated his former religion, Judaism, as much as possible: *"To the Jews I became as a Jew, that I might win Jews; . . . I have become all things to all men, that I might by all means save some"* (1 Cor 9:19–21). He met the Galatians on common ground in order to win them to Christ. They accepted the gospel of a gracious forgiveness but now were wavering.

Paul commanded them to *"become free from the law as I am"* (NLT) but this did not mean freedom from morality or a license to sin. He was stressing the freedom from having to earn God's acceptance and forgiveness. Let us all live like Paul, free to focus on Christ.

"Lord, help me find people in my life who are examples to follow in their obedience to You. Give me the courage to learn from Paul's life to be like You."

DECEMBER 6
Examine Yourself

Gal 6:4—*"Let each one examine~~ his own work*. *Then he can take pride in himself and not compare himself with someone else."*

We all tend to think we are much better than we really are. We gradually become conceited, as evidenced by an increasing spirit of superiority and intolerance, leaving no room to consider the needs of others. The solution is to *"be continually examining yourself,"* which means to "[test] in battle, [be] approved, or put to the test to see if it is genuine."What are we supposed to examine? The following are a few suggestions:

- What kind of person do you love to help? *"If you love only those who love you, what reward is there for that?"* (Matt 5:46).

- What are your motives for donating to good causes? *"When you give to someone in need, don't do as the hypocrites do—blowing trumpets in the synagogues and streets to call attention to their acts of charity! I tell you the truth, they have received all the reward they will ever get"* (Matt 6:5).

- Would you fast if you could not tell anyone what you have given up? *"When you fast, do not look somber as the hypocrites do, for they disfigure their faces to show men they are fasting"* (Matt 6:16).

Everyone must answer to God for how he has lived: *"But on the judgment day, fire will reveal what kind of work each builder has done. The fire will show if a person's work has any value"* (1 Cor 3:13). If we do not know the rules for building our Christian lives, we can lose all our rewards.

By knowing what can nullify any recompense from Christ, a servant can *"take pride in himself"* ("boasting, or reporting"), but this is distinct from the *"conceit"* in Galatians 6:3. The focus is not on our own accomplishments but on what God has done through our lives. This pride exalts God, not us. We are told in Romans 12:3, *"For I say, through the grace given to me, to everyone who is among you, not to think of himself more highly than he ought to think, but to think soberly, as God has dealt to each one a measure of faith."*

The final phrase, *"not compare himself with someone else,"* means that this pride comes not from comparison but from accomplishments, especially for the benefit to others. Feel good about serving others.

"Father, Your word is my guide, but it is so brutal to my pride. With all my heart, I want to please You with a life invested in Your kingdom. May my true value to You be my sense of worth in this life."

DECEMBER 7
Test the Deacons First

1 Tim 3:10—*"And these also **must be tested**~~ first and then **let** them **serve**~~ as deacons if they are found blameless."*

Everyone who has become a follower of Christ should seek to serve Him in every way possible. The Scripture gives two official positions in the church: pastor (also called elder or bishop interchangeably) and deacon (meaning "slave, one who cares for the needs of others, [or] a helper"). Because the primary function of the pastor/elder/bishop is to *"equip the saints for the work of the ministry"* (Eph 4:12) and to dedicate himself to preparation in the word and prayer (Acts 6:4), many of the other functions of the church must be delegated to faithful men called *deacons*.

Deacon denotes not only an official position but also a style of serving ministry. Jesus identified Himself as one who *serves* in Mark 10:45. The common designation for a leader in the New Testament is "minister" or "servant": *"Who then is Paul, and who is Apollos, but ministers [or servants] through whom you believed"* (1 Cor 3:5). This term also shows an overall philosophy of ministry. Leaders must be servant-leaders.

Paul begins this section with *"likewise deacons."* Just as bishops must have qualifications, so must deacons (1 Tim 3:8–9, 11–12).

Those who serve *"well as deacons obtain for themselves a good standing and great boldness in the faith"* (1 Tim 3:13). The word *standing* means a "step or grade," from a word for an elevated footrest, which is appreciated for its relief and comfort.

The first command in 1 Timothy 3:10 is for anyone desiring to serve in a higher level of responsibility. He must "be continually tested" (meaning to "examine, or [be] proven") to determine if he is reliable and trustworthy and not seeking personal benefits. Is he a servant, or is he seeking power?

The second command is to *"let them continually serve as deacons"* (lit. to "act as go-between[s]"). Every adult should strive to qualify as a deacon or the wife of a deacon and hopefully serve His church body as such. Interested?

"No one likes to be tested, Lord, but You are testing us all the time. Keep us honest with ourselves by sending exhorters and encouragers into our lives to serve together."

DECEMBER 8
Be a Husband of One Wife

1 Tim 3:12—*"Deacons **must be**~~ **husbands** of one wife and good managers of their children and their own households."*

Culturally, marital fidelity was not as important in the first century as was maintaining family unity. Wives were necessary for continuing the family name for inheritance and procreation, but in the Greco-Roman culture, mistresses were commonplace. However, when men became believers, everything in their cultural lifestyle changed, and men had to maintain new standards.

The home became the first proving ground for a deacon's faithfulness, his commitment to principles, and his family's willingness to follow his leadership. If it did not work in the family, it would not work in the church. The same standard is set for pastors or bishops (Phil 1:1).

Monogamy did not become law for the Romans until AD 212 (through the *lex Antoniana de civitate* [Law or Edict of Antoninus of citizenship]), but Jews were exempt until AD 393, when Emperor Theodosius made a special law against polygamy among the Jews. However, 1 Timothy 3:12 refers to much more than monogamy.

This principle of fidelity is crucial because it highlights a symptom of a character weakness that affects all relationships: *"The perversity of the unfaithful will destroy them"* (Prov 11:3). Inevitably, *"the unfaithful will be caught by their lust"* (11:6). Unreliability in one area spreads into all areas: *"Confidence in an unfaithful man in time of trouble is like a bad tooth and a foot out of joint"* (25:19).

Men are expected to have learned these biblical principles (especially from Proverbs) to be *"ruling their children and their own houses well."* If they are not governed by these biblical principles at home, men will be unprincipled and impulsive in the church as well. As a man leads his family, so he will lead in a church. Since leaders have the task of maturing every man to be a biblical leader of his family and community and to serve the church, he must first be an example in his home. It is not an issue of being perfect, but being honest and transparent in gaining respect so others, especially one's family, is willing to follow your example. Become a learner from the best example you know.

"Thank You, Lord, for Your plan for marriage—if only men would listen to it. May my faithfulness to my spouse demonstrate my faithfulness to You, the lover of my soul."

DECEMBER 9

Command and Teach

1 Tim 4:11—*"Command~~ and teach~~ these things."*

In 1 Timothy 4:11, Paul is asking Timothy not to merely make some suggestions to the church but to *"command"* them to obey the principles of the word revealed by God.

The word for *"be continually commanding"* means to "give the orders, to pass on an announcement, [to] advance an order, [or to] charge or command." It is a call to obey God's authority. The second command is to *"be continually teaching these things"* ("instruct by word of mouth"), referring to everything Paul commanded that Timothy was to command others to obey.

Earlier, Paul had written a similar command: *"If you instruct the brethren in these things, you will be a good minister of Jesus Christ, nourished in the words of faith and of the good doctrine which you have carefully followed"* (1 Tim 4:6). Ministry is to be authoritative in the sense that whatever God commands, we are to obey and then to command to others. Paul told Titus, *"These things speak and exhort and reprove with all authority. Let no one disregard you"* (Titus 2:15).

To be a faithful servant, a level of boldness is required to freely confront sin, unbelief, and disobedience. Such boldness is balanced with understanding and gentleness; one should never be abusive or disrespectful. Authority is built on four pillars:

1. Commitment to the authority of God's word (i.e., the teacher practices the commands first before teaching others)

2. Grammatically and contextually correct interpretation of Scripture

3. Concern that the truth of God's word be respected and that believers be accountable to obey its precepts (1 Cor 5:1–13; 2 Thes 3:14–15)

4. Freedom from the fear of offending men

Preaching and teaching that does not lead to obedient actions is failing in its purpose to transform lives by *"renewing of the mind"* (Rom 12:2)— that is, introducing a new way of thinking and new principles to follow. Let us commit to living in conformity to the Scripture and then seek to transmit God's commands faithfully and boldly to others.

"Lord, Your word is so contrary to this world's values that most prefer to ignore it or be ignorant of it. Give me the courage to know and clarify Your commands."

DECEMBER 10

Let No One Look Down on You

1 Tim 4:12—*"**Let no one look down~/ on you** because you are young, **but set~~ an example** for the believers in your speech, conduct, love, faithfulness, and purity."*

Paul commanded the young Timothy (though probably in his thirties) to command and teach others to obey the Scripture.Timothy was to "*stop letting others look down on*" him. The verb means to "hold in contempt, or think lightly of." He was to be an "*example*," or "pattern" ("an image in metal caused by striking a die to leave an impression"). Paul repeatedly emphasized following a leader's example as the means of discipleship and mentoring: "*Brethren, join in following my example, and note those who so walk, as you have us for a pattern*" (Phil 3:17). Timothy would earn respect for his ministry in five areas.

First, he needed to be an example in "*word*," or "speech." Because "*the mouth speaks out of that which fills the heart*" (Matt 12:34), his godliness would become evident every time he opened his mouth.

Second, he was to be an example in conduct, demonstrating how he had "*put off, concerning [his] former conduct, the old man which grows corrupt*" (Eph 4:22). His daily habitual lifestyle was to purposefully demonstrate his obedience.

Third, Timothy was to be an example in love: "*Greater love has no one than this, that one lay down his life for his friends*" (Jn 15:13). He looked forward to fulfilling the daily sacrifice of his personal interests or needs to benefit believers.

Fourth, he was to be an example of faith, a demonstration of his confident prayer for God's control and intervention at critical times.

Fifth, Timothy had to be an example of purity by treating "*older women as mothers, [and] younger women as sisters, with all purity*" (1 Tim 5:2); he was to exhibit integrity and virtue in his dealings with the opposite sex.

Leadership is gained by respect in all these areas. Strive to be an example to motivate others to follow.

"If I will live in Your presence, Lord, and walk faithfully in the light of Your commands, my confidence will come from Your word, not what others might think of me."

DECEMBER 11

Give Attention to Public Reading

1 Tim 4:13—*"Until I come, **give attention to~~ the public reading** of scripture, to exhortation, to teaching."*

A mature person does the right thing when no one is looking and is able to take the initiative for God on his own. Paul trusted young Timothy to do just that and establish the church in Ephesus.

Paul told the immature congregations, *"When you come together, everyone has a hymn, or a word of instruction, a revelation, a tongue or an interpretation"* (1 Cor 14:26). They needed to correct this confusion. Then, some ten or twelve years later, he told Timothy to: *"give attention"* to three primary activities, not to the exclusion of others, but as a priority. The verb for *"give attention to"* means literally "to hold the mind or the ear toward" a speaker. As a nautical term, it means to hold a ship on a specific course.

The first focus of congregational meetings is on *"the public reading of scripture."* By this time, most of Paul's Epistles had been written, as well as the Synoptic Gospels, Acts, and all the other epistles except John's writings (his gospel, three epistles, and Revelation). These would not be written until around AD 90, or thirty years later. There were few copies of the texts, and many people were illiterate, so whatever was to be learned from God's word had to be read to them and then explained.

This was also the practice in the Old Testament. Moses wrote, *"Then he took the Book of the Covenant and read in the hearing of the people. And they said, 'All that the Lord has said we will do, and be obedient'"* (Ex 24:7). Joshua did the same: *"There was not a word of all that Moses had commanded which Joshua did not read before all the assembly of Israel"* (Josh 8:35).

Following the reading of Scripture, the congregation was to hear the *"exhortation"* from the passage. The word means to "encourage, comfort, beseech or admonish." The challenge to apply the New Testament commands and principles is the path to spiritual growth.

Finally, there must be *"doctrine"* (lit. "teaching")—that is, the explanation of the meaning of the text. The churches *"continued steadfastly in the apostles' doctrine"* (Acts 2:42), so with great care, the churches and small groups must be taught what to believe, why it is important, and how to apply it. Shouldn't we do the same now?

"Lord, the delight of my life is publicly explaining Your word. Oh, that Your word would be listened to with earnest commitment!"

Do Not Neglect Your Spiritual Gift

1 Tim 4:14—*"**Do not neglect~/ the spiritual gift** you have, given to you and confirmed by prophetic words when the elders laid hands on you."*

Recently, a major seminary surveyed its graduates, only to discover that barely 30 percent actually made it to the pastorate. The number of students and graduates often defines success for a seminary, with little regard to whether they continue into the ministry.

Timothy was already in the ministry, and Paul exhorted him to *"stop neglecting the spiritual gift within you."* This is in reference to the charisma that equipped him (and all believers) for a specific kind of ministry in the church. He may have gotten so involved in other aspects of the ministry that he was neglecting his gift. Attempting to serve in an area for which one is not gifted can result in burnout, so Timothy had to be reminded, *"Stir up the gift of God which is in you"* (2 Tim 1:6).

Paul knew there were other temptations for a young leader, so He exhorted Timothy to *"be strong in the grace that is in Christ Jesus . . . Suffer hardship with me, as a good soldier of Christ Jesus."* He warned him not to get *"entangled"* in the *"affairs of everyday life."* And finally, he was to *"flee from youthful lusts, and pursue righteousness, faith, love and peace . . . with a pure heart"* (2 Tim 2:1, 3–6, 22).

Spiritual gifts are divided into two categories: *"As each one has received a gift, minister it to one another . . . If anyone speaks, let him speak as the oracles of God. If anyone ministers [serves], let him do it as with the ability which God supplies"* (1 Pet 4:10–11). Therefore, a person has either a speaking gift (to accurately communicate God's word) or a serving gift (to reflect the serving spirit of Jesus).

Every believer receives a spiritual gift to serve others, *"but the manifestation of the Spirit is given to each one for the profit of all"* (1 Cor 12:7); *"having then gifts differing according to the grace that is given to us, let us use them"* (Rom 12:7). We are commanded to use our spiritual gifts for the benefit of others.

As you mature in ministry, others will see and confirm your gifts. Have people affirmed areas in which you are gifted? Ask them.

"Thank You, Lord, for investing in my life and enabling me to fulfill Your purpose for my life. May this satisfy my hunger to be useful to Your kingdom."

DECEMBER 13

Command the Rich to Be Humble

1 Tim 6:17—"***Command~~ those who are rich*** *in this world's goods not to be haughty or to set their hope on riches, which are uncertain, but on God who richly provides us with all things for our enjoyment.*"

Paul declared, "*The love of money is a root of all kinds of evils, for which some have strayed from the faith in their greediness, and pierced themselves through with many sorrows*" (1 Tim 6:10).

Many pray for more wealth, but God, in His mercy, withholds it so wealth does not destroy them. Jesus warned us, "*No one can serve two masters; for either he will hate the one and love the other, or else he will be loyal to the one and despise the other. You cannot serve God and mammon*" (Matt 6:24).

Paul tells the wealthy to live biblically in handling the resources God gives, adopting a kingdom priority. He uses two infinitives as warnings. First, those who are "*rich*" in material goods (i.e., "to have in abundance of earthly possessions that exceed normal experience" or needs) should "stop being haughty" (or "high-minded, proud, arrogant and conceited"). One of the perspectives to keep in mind is this: "*For we brought nothing into this world, and it is certain we can carry nothing out*" (1 Tim 6:7).

The wealthy sometimes think that money indicates their personal value and see others as inferior: "*The rich man is wise in his own eyes*" (Prov 28:11). Instead, the rich should "*be of the same mind toward one another. Do not set your mind on high things, but associate with the humble. Do not be wise in your own opinion*" (Rom 12:16).

Second, the wealthy are warned not to be secure in their riches: "*Do not toil to acquire wealth; be discerning enough to desist. When your eyes light on it, for suddenly it sprouts wings, flying like an eagle toward heaven*" (Prov 23:4–5). Enormous wealth can disappear in a moment.

If you were to lose everything, how would you feel? If you cannot handle losing everything, your identity and trust might be misplaced.

"Lord, how easy it is to find security, or lack of it, in possessions and income and then experience disillusionment when our material goods are dissolved. Teach me to enjoy the little things and to humbly serve others."

DECEMBER 14

Entrust Knowledge to the Faithful

2 Tim 2:2—*"And **entrust*** *~* ***what you heard** me say in the presence of many others as witnesses to faithful people who will be competent to teach others as well."*

Jesus said, *"By this My Father is glorified, that you bear much fruit; so you will be My disciples"* (Jn 15:8). Reproducing ourselves in other's lives perpetuates the spread of the knowledge of God and His word around the globe. *"Fruit"* is the result of the life of God flowing in the inner man made alive by the knowledge of God's word, and the catalyst for the reproducing life is the teaching of the word of God.

Timothy listened to Paul's small-group teachings and discussions over twenty years. In turn, Timothy and others were expected to take Paul's teachings and teach them to others. The glory of a teacher is not that he is inventing new ideas or revelations but that he can teach the same message that Jesus and the apostles taught. With great care, the teacher seeks to learn the word of God as it was written with the same purpose and message that can then be applied to contemporary life.

As Paul trusted Timothy to learn well, he commands Timothy to *"entrust what you heard me say"* ("to put or place near someone, or lay before," or to deposit something valuable for safekeeping). Timothy was to be careful to entrust the treasure of what he had been taught to *"faithful people who will be competent to teach others as well"* ("trustworthy, reliable or believable").

The Great Commission of making disciples is fulfilled by *"teaching them to observe [or obey] all things that [Jesus has] commanded you"* (Matt 28:20). Teaching is not just about telling the truth; it must include the practical aspect of obedience. We must teach new believers to be mutually accountable to know and to obey the commands in Scripture. Once we learn to obey these commands, we are to pass them on to others. May this daily devotional Bible study help you fulfill this commission.

"You have given me such a privilege to know Your word. Keep me faithful to it and to the commission to pass it on to my family and friends who want to know it."

DECEMBER 15
Remind People

2 Tim 2:14—*"Remind~~ people of these things and solemnly charge them before the Lord not to wrangle over words. This is of no benefit; it just brings ruin on those who listen."*

The ministry of remembering truths is emphasized eleven times in the New Testament. The present imperative to *"be constantly reminding"* with the prefix means to have a "hypermemory," or to "repeatedly be putting something in mind." Important things have to be repeated because we *"must be transformed by the [constant] renewing of the mind"* (Rom 12:2). If retention of the principles of the word of God is important for a transformed life, we must constantly remind people of these vital truths. Expecting them to remember without repetition is a foolish error.

Timothy's task was to *"remind [the church] of [Paul's] ways in Christ, as [he] [taught] everywhere in every church"* (1 Cor 4:17). Peter considered it negligence if he did not remind believers of truths until they were established (2 Pet 1:12). Jude clarified this ministry objective, saying, *"I want to remind you, though you once knew this"* (Jude 5). We cannot assume that people remember important truths.

They were *"not to wrangle over words"*; this means they were not to "contend, dispute, or debate about trifles"—that is, to have meaningless debates—just to see who could win an insignificant point. This is especially the case with false teachers, who were *"always learning and never able to come to the knowledge of the truth"* (2 Tim 3:7).

As Christians become less familiar with Scripture and are not reminded of sound teachings, they become easy prey for biblical-sounding ideas that have nothing to do with Scripture. The invasion of psychological concepts and pseudospiritual ideas (e.g., "slaying in the Spirit" and "binding Satan") in the churches tends to upstage the value of clear biblical teaching and submission to the commands to the "ruin of the hearers" ("overthrow, or overturn"). Beware when the messages are focused on phenomena and great men's views with little to do with understanding Scripture.

"Lord, we want to argue about everything except what is important. We hurt each other with accusations and self-righteous criticism just to feel as if we are right and others are wrong. Forgive us, Lord, for corrupting our hearers."

DECEMBER 16
Give a Shepherd's Care

1 Pet 5:2—*"Give a shepherd's care*~ to God's flock among you, exercising oversight not merely as a duty but willingly under God's direction, not for shameful profit but eagerly."*

Although this command is directed to the *"elders who are among you"* (1 Pet 5:1), everyone is responsible for the health and growth of *"God's flock."* In Hebrews 13:17, the author writes, *"Obey those who rule over you ... for they watch for your souls, as those who must give account. Let them do so with joy and not with grief, for that would be unprofitable for you."* Church leaders will have to give account for their leadership of God's people, but the flock can be a blessing or a cause of *"grief."*

The command to "immediately decide from now on to give a shepherd's care" means to "tend to, lead, [or] care for" God's people. This command is similar to Jesus's final recorded command to Peter: *"Shepherd my sheep"* (Jn 21:16); believers are to be led by godly leaders and fed by the teaching of God's word.

The essential focus of this command is that leaders are responsible to care for *"God's flock."* The flock is the personal property of Jesus Himself. Believers *"once were not a people, but now the people of God, who had not obtained mercy but now have obtained mercy"* (1 Pet 2:10).

To the elders at Ephesus, Paul gave his final charge: *"Therefore take heed to yourselves and to the flock, among which the Holy Spirit has made you overseers, to shepherd the church of God which He purchased with His own blood"* (Acts 20:28). The value of an object is determined by its price; the church cost the blood and life of the God-Man, Jesus Christ—an infinite price. Great care must be taken to protect His most valuable and costly possession.

If the leader is a man of God, he is characterized by selfless service and does not focus on materialism—that is, *"not for shameful profit but eagerly."* However, he should be adequately compensated (1 Cor 9:7–14; 1 Tim 5:17–18). The church is to eliminate any materialistic temptation by taking care of his material needs just as he takes care of their spiritual needs.

"Thank You, Lord, for Your church, which is Your body made up of fragile believers who need each other. Help me be an encouragement to my pastor and partner with him in caring for Your people."

DECEMBER 17

Hold to the Standard of Sound Words

2 Tim 1:13—*"**Hold to the standard**~~ **of sound words** that you heard from me and do so with the faith and love that are in Christ Jesus."*

I am continually amazed at the limited knowledge today's believers have of God's word. Any member more than five years in the Lord should be thoroughly versed in Bible doctrine, evangelism, the commands for Christian living, and discipleship. If spiritual maturity is not the church's primary internal task, then the church is negligent in her duty to the flock.

Many insist that teaching doctrine kills the spiritual life, believing that only emotional experiences can keep it alive. However, in a day when most believers were without any theological convictions, Paul told Timothy to *"be continually holding to the standard of sound words."* The imperative verb means "to have and hold as a continual possession"— that is, to be continually dealt with and applied to every situation.

Many today are more interested in feeling God than knowing Him. There are two attitudes toward Scripture to be avoided. The first focuses on dead theological systems and arguments, putting little emphasis on practical obedience and the Great Commission. The second ignores the written word, generating only a feeling-based experience.

The word of God is the only divinely inspired, Holy Spirit–revealed, infallible, perfect, and totally sufficient truth for all believers at all times. Paul wrote to Timothy, *"All Scripture is inspired by God and profitable for teaching, for reproof, for correction, for training in righteousness; that the man of God may be adequate, equipped for every good work"* (2 Tim 3:16–17).

The word is to be practiced or obeyed *"with . . . love that [is] in Christ Jesus."* Paul described the relationship as *"faith working through love"* (Gal 5:6). This is possible because the *"love of God has been poured out in our hearts by the Holy Spirit who was given to us"* (Rom 5:5). Does your knowledge of God's word motivate you to give of your time and resources for God's purposes?

"Lord, in a day of fluctuating values and worldviews, keep me true to knowing and living by every principle and command in Your word while caring for others."

DECEMBER 18

Do Not Accept an Accusation against an Elder

1 Tim 5:19—*"**Do not accept an accusation~/ against an elder** unless it can be confirmed by two or three witnesses."*

Ministers are always open to criticism, especially when they exhort people to change their habits, culture, or behavior. Unfortunately, many have the tendencies of proverbial fools, as indicated by their eagerness to accuse vulnerable leaders: *"Avoiding a fight is a mark of honor; only fools insist on quarreling"* (Prov 20:3[NLT]).

Every major leader in Scripture suffered false accusations from people seeking to discredit him. Trust is built on credibility and integrity. If a person can be discredited by an accusation, whether true or false, his integrity becomes suspect and his ministry can be destroyed. Because of this delicate trust, great care and discernment must be exercised when a leader's integrity is questioned.

The command in 1 Timothy 5:19 is to *"stop accepting an accusation,"* which means not *"to entertain or consider it in your mind."* As a present negative command, it implies that they were doing this and should stop. Other leaders and the congregation must be taught how to respond to gossip, griping, and criticism. The answer is to turn a deaf ear *"unless it can be confirmed by two or three witnesses."*

God warns His people, *"Do not touch My anointed ones, and do My prophets no harm"* (Psa 105:15). Do not treat casually the reputation of a spiritual leader unless the accusation is at least doubly confirmed. Deuteronomy 19:15 says, *"One witness shall not rise against a man concerning any iniquity or any sin that he commits; by the mouth of two or three witnesses the matter shall be established."* Jesus said, *"By the mouth of two or three witnesses every word may be established"* (Matt 18:16), and Paul quotes this passage in 2 Corinthians 13:1 when he is giving them a third warning about their sins (2 Cor 11:21).

Unsubstantiated accusations must not be tolerated; however, when confirmed by various sources, they must be seriously investigated. Without credibility, ministry to others is impossible. No one will listen to someone they do not trust. No one will listen to someone they do not trust.

"Why are we so prone to believe everything bad about a person, especially a leader? Give me the conviction to protect my leaders from gossip."

DECEMBER 19
Rebuke Elders before All

1 Tim 5:20—*"Those guilty of sin **must be rebuked**~~ **before all**, as a warning to the rest."*

Leaders, by their very nature, can be offensive, because they are called to lead us to obey God's word. No one enjoys being corrected (except the wise), so challenging people to change or conform to biblical standards can be met with resistance.

When David sinned with Bathsheba, it could not be kept secret, and the prophet Nathan publicly denounced him: *"You are the man!"* (2 Sam 12:7). David's response was, *"'I have sinned against the Lord.' And Nathan said to David, 'The Lord also has put away your sin; you shall not die"* (12:13). One has to wonder what would have happened if David had not publicly repented.

In 1 Timothy 5:20, the phrase *"those guilty of sin"* is a present participle, meaning a continuous action of persisting in sin without repenting. After being confirmed by two or three witnesses (1 Tim 5:19), the matter must be taken to the church (Matt 18:16–18).

The imperative verb *"must be rebuked"* means "to shame, disgrace, expose, [or] prove one in the wrong." Jesus stated, *"As many as I love, I rebuke and chasten. Therefore be zealous and repent"* (Rev 3:19). The objective of the rebuke is to give an opportunity to repent and be reconciled.

Timothy could not be slack in dealing with leaders who dishonored the church by their sins. Paul gave a most emphatic and authoritative command when he wrote, *"I charge you before God and the Lord Jesus Christ and the elect angels that you observe these things without prejudice, doing nothing with partiality"* (1 Tim 5:21). The standard for church leaders is higher than for other believers. James warned, *"Let not many of you become teachers, knowing that we shall receive a stricter judgment"* (James 3:1).

A healthy fear of rebuke and exposure is vital for holiness. If there are no consequences to sinning, obedience becomes optional. Can men be honored above God's word?

"It is hard to show tough love, but it is harder still to make an example of those who disobey. Lord, give me courage in my family and ministry to rebuke sin."

DECEMBER 20

Do Not Be Quick to
Lay Hands on a Pastor

1 Tim 5:22—*"**Do not lay hands on anyone hastily~/** and so identify with the sins of others. **Keep~~yourself pure.**"*

Sometimes it is hard to wait until the Lord brings the right man for ministry. Israel pushed the issue of a king prematurely and got Saul. He had all the traits of a great leader for Israel to glory in—except for a submissive will and a heart for God.

Apparently, the church at Ephesus appointed some elders who turned out to be inadequate, which provoked the discussion of discipline of disobedient elders (1 Tim 5:19–21). The command was to *"stop laying hands on anyone hastily."* In their enthusiasm to spread the ministry, Israel chose some immature, untested men to leadership roles.

The *"laying on of hands"* typically means setting apart or ordaining to a specific ministry (e.g., deacons in Acts 6:6; missionary evangelists in Acts 13:3; pastors in 1 Tim 4:14 and 2 Tim 1:6) with the full endorsement of the church body. In the early churches, men were set apart for the ministry by the apostles (Acts 14:23; Titus 1:5; 1 Tim 4:14).

This command is not to set men apart for the ministry *"hastily"* (not to be "prompt, swift, [quick,] or in a hurry"). The *"also"* in 1 Timothy 3:10 (*"let these also first be tested; then let them serve"*) implies some testing is applied for the bishop/pastor and deacon qualifications. Those responsible for the approval of leaders face the risk of *"identify[ing] with the sins of others"* (i.e., as a result of leaders being prematurely selected without testing). The word *identify* means "to be a partaker [or] participant or to share together." God's chastening may fall on a church not only for a leader's sins but also for all who participated in his selection, as it did for Israel in selecting Saul.

Saul seemed to be a great leader, so Israel disregarded wisdom and chose the wrong man! The right man would not come along for another forty years. Would you have waited?

"Lord, we want to believe the best about others but sometimes lack wisdom in waiting for spiritual maturity to be evident. Keep us free of secret sins."

DECEMBER 21

Be Ready for the Second Coming

Luke 12:40—*"You also must be ready~~, because the Son of Man will come at an hour when you do not expect him."*

In chess, it is the move that you were not expecting that kills you. Just as homeowners must take preventative measures to protect their property, so we are commanded not to be caught unaware when the King returns.

The command in Luke 12:40 is to *"be continually ready,"* or "to make ready or be prepared." His coming will be a surprise, so we must always be ready to be surprised and then prepared to stand before Him. Jesus clarified this intent when He said, *"But take heed to yourselves, lest your hearts be weighed down with carousing, drunkenness, and cares of this life, and that Day come on you unexpectedly"* (Luke 21:34). We can only imagine our embarrassment if the sudden return of Christ caught us in the act of disgraceful and secret sin.

Paul wrote similarly, *"For you yourselves know perfectly that the day of the Lord so comes as a thief in the night . . . But you, brethren, are not in darkness, so that this Day should overtake you as a thief . . . Therefore let us not sleep, as others do, but let us watch and be sober . . . putting on the breastplate of faith and love, and as a helmet the hope of salvation"* (1 Thes 5:2, 4, 6, 8).

Peter said that everything will be destroyed anyway: *"The day of the Lord will come as a thief in the night, in which the heavens will pass away with a great noise, and the elements will melt with fervent heat; both the earth and the works that are in it will be burned up. Therefore, since all these things will be dissolved, what manner of persons ought you to be in holy conduct and godliness, looking for and hastening the coming of the day of God . . . ? . . . Therefore, beloved, looking forward to these things, be diligent to be found by Him in peace, without spot and blameless"* (2 Pet 3:10–12, 14).

The sudden end of the church age and instant appearance of the Lord are themes throughout the New Testament. John concludes, *"Everyone who has this hope in Him [that His return is sudden and imminent] purifies himself, just as He is pure"* (1 Jn 3:3). Selfishness, boastfulness, pleasure seeking, and accumulation of wealth are meaningless. Stay busy for Him until He surprises you in the middle of finishing a task for Him.

"Lord, I know sin is ever at the door, seeking to motivate us to disregard Your word and act selfishly. May my heart and mind listen to Your voice always."

DECEMBER 22

Do Not Just Do Your Duty

Luke 17:10—*"So you too, when you have done everything you were commanded to do, **should say**~~, 'We are slaves undeserving of special praise; we have only done what was our duty.'"*

The statement in this verse is true: we are slaves bought with the price of the blood of our Lord and are expected to know and intentionally obey His commands. This can be done legalistically by fulfilling the letter of the law, but this is unprofitable and *"undeserving of special praise."*

There is no question that we are all unworthy of praise, but the word *undeserving* means to be "useless, of no use or profit, or worthless." Such a person is like the steward who received a talent of silver from his master (Matt 25:14–23) but was afraid to do anything with it and simply returned it to his master. There is no indication in the text that any of the three stewards were told what to do with the wealth they had been given. The one who produced nothing more than what he was given was "useless" because he was unproductive.

Employers become frustrated when they must tell their employees what to do every day. The better employee knows what needs to be done and uses his ingenuity, creativity, and skills to make the employer successful and accomplish his mission. Every employer dreams about this kind of employee.

The classic illustration of this principle is the Great Commission. Jesus told the Twelve and other listeners to make sure the gospel is preached to every tongue, tribe, people, and ethnic people group on earth (Matt 24:14; 28:19–20, etc.). He never said how it should be done or who should do it. He expects the profitable servant to figure it out so that He may reward the servant for his creative service.

The judgment seat of Christ is all about discerning who is "good" ("profitable, useful") and who is "bad" ("worthless, cowardly") for the kingdom's sake (2 Cor 5:10). It is not about who has been good or bad morally but about who has contributed to expanding the kingdom around the globe without having to be told how—just because they know it is their Savior's desire. All the rewards of heaven are promised to this kind of obedient believer. Is this you?

"Lord Jesus, You mean everything to me. I want to know whatever You want in life today, and I will do it. I will not wait for a special sign, but I will live out Your word throughout my day."

DECEMBER 23
Run to Win

1 Cor 9:24—*"Do you not know that all the runners in a stadium compete, but only one receives the prize? So* **run**~~ *to win."*

Most people cannot imagine the price an athlete pays to be a winner. The Olympic Games were already being held in Paul's time, and the Isthmian Games were held at Corinth every two years. Athletes would come from all over Greece to compete for the highest honors in the empire. They would work under a coach for ten months of self-denial, painful exercises, and unending practice.

If we knew what the promise *"great will be your reward in heaven"* (Matt 5:12) actually meant, then our lives would be completely dedicated to winning the prize for the souls of men. Jesus taught His disciples to give up their lives and ambitions to follow Him and make Him known. Have you started the journey by taking this step, or will you remain a spectator like most who heard Jesus in the first century?

The phrase *"runners in a stadium"* illustrates that every believer is on the track whether he wants to be or not. Paul is not saying that only one believer out of millions will receive the reward but that all who strive will be rewarded. He expected every believer to take his spiritual life seriously, just as an athlete takes his bodily conditioning seriously. We are commanded to *"continually or habitually be running to win"* as we serve the King. Paul said, *"By the grace of God I am and His grace toward me was not in vain; but I labored more abundantly than they all, yet not I, but the Grace of God which was with me"* (1 Cor 15:10).

What is the prize that makes it worth it all? Paul wrote, *"For what is our hope, or joy, or crown of rejoicing? Is it not even you in the presence of our Lord Jesus Christ at His coming?"* (1 Thes 2:19). His goal was not a selfish crown of glory, but all the people he had won to Christ. His relationship with his brothers in Christ meant more to him than life itself.

The race is against time. Our time on earth is brief, and opportunities to share the gospel are fleeting moments that cannot be missed. We must learn at every encounter to tell the story of Jesus's love for sinners. Will you train to run the race with your life?

"You tell me, Lord, that there is a great reward for living for Your kingdom's purposes. Whatever honor You would give Your servant is undeserved, but I thank You for the encouragement that nothing done for You is lost or in vain."

DECEMBER 24
Watch Out for the Flock

Acts 20:28—*"Watch out~~ for yourselves** and for all the flock of which the Holy Spirit has made you overseers, to shepherd the church of God that He obtained with the blood of His own Son."*

On an airline before every flight, the attendant demonstrates the oxygen mask procedure in case there is an emergency. Every time, they instruct passengers traveling with small children to place the masks over their own faces first before they help their children. If they do not, they might both could die from the sudden decompression and loss of oxygen.

Before sailing to Jerusalem, Paul instructed the elders from Ephesus to "continually be watching out for yourselves and for all the flock." If they did not learn to control their private thoughts and commitments, they would be unable to take care of the believers in the church. The command to *"be continually watching out for yourselves"* means to "care for, be in a state of alert, or [be] concerned about"; it is directed to the ministry leaders, and he later adds "the entire flock." How were the elders to do this?

One area was in teaching the word of God. Paul warns, *"Take heed to yourself and to the doctrine. Continue in them, for in doing this you will save both yourself and those who hear you"* (1 Tim 4:16). If they were going to be *"good ministers of Jesus Christ,"* they would have to be *"nourished [personally] in the words of faith and of the good doctrine which you have carefully followed"* (4:6).

Before they could be effective in ministering to others, they had to know and practice the commands and principles of Scripture. Another area was the battle with personal pride: *"Watch out! Don't do your good deeds publicly to be admired by others, for you will lose the reward from your Father in heaven"* (Matt 6:1).

The pastor and leaders of the church are to model a mutual accountability, and they must be prepared to ask and be asked the hard questions without fear. What is God teaching them in the word today? What sin are they battling? What are they praying for today? With no accountability, it is difficult to grow in our walk with Christ, and it is easy to grow cold, superficial, and defensive.

"Lord, Your church together is struggling against sin and opposition. We must watch out for each other. Give us Your love for Your church today."

DECEMBER 25

Build Carefully on the Foundation

1 Cor 3:10—*"According to the grace of God given to me, like a skilled master builder I laid a foundation, but someone else builds on it. And **each one must be careful~~ how he builds**."*

Jesus said, *"I will build my church"* (Matt 16:18), which is described as having a *"foundation."* It is a singular foundation on which all other ministries are built, *"for no one can lay any foundation other than what is being laid, which is Jesus Christ"* (1 Cor 3:11).

All believers are built up on this foundation as on a solid rock: *"You have been built on the foundation of the apostles and prophets, with Christ Jesus Himself as the cornerstone"* (Eph 2:20). Today we are not laying more foundations, but we are building upward as the church expands vertically. The quality of the foundation will support the growing church through all ages.

Each generation follows its predecessor by building the church with new believers and the careful explanation of God's word. The command in 1 Corinthians 3:10 is to *"be continually being careful"* how you build. Several other great men labored at Corinth, including Apollos (Acts 18:27–28) and "Cephas," or Peter (1 Cor 1:12; 3:22). They *"persevered in the doctrine of the apostles"* (Acts 2:42).

Paul uses the analogy of a building craftsman and expects his apprentices to perpetuate his teachings as Jesus revealed them to him. He expects skilled craftsmanship in the study and teaching of the text.

The task of Bible study is to know God as He has revealed Himself in His word. This is not a mystical encounter but a spiritual illumination of the truth recorded for all eternity to show how to know God.

As the inspired word (the foundation) is carefully used in its original sense for *"teaching, rebuking, correcting and training in righteousness, so that the man of God may be thoroughly equipped for every good work"* (2 Tim 3:16–17), the church of believers continues to be built up and matures. Is your learning of the word changing your life and others to be more Christlike?

"Lord Jesus, You have delegated to us the responsibility of caring for and building up Your church and global kingdom, which You came to establish on earth. Keep us faithful to Your purpose."

DECEMBER 26
Encourage God's Servants in the Ministry

Col 4:17—*"And tell Archippus, 'See~~ **to it that you complete the ministry** you received in the Lord.'"*

Approximately 79 percent of those who start a marathon finish it. Generally speaking, it requires six months to prepare to run a race.

Archippus was probably the son of Philemon (Philem 2) and was ministering in Colossae because the pastor, Epaphras, was in Rome caring for Paul. Paul called Philemon his *"dear friend and fellow worker"* (Philemon 1) and *"Archippus our fellow soldier"* (Philemon 2)

Paul commands the readers to *"urgently tell"* (aorist imperative) Archippus that he should *"be continually seeing to it"* (present imperative) that he *"**complete the ministry**"* ("to make full"). Many who start well encounter discouragement, isolation, failures, conflicts, disillusionments, and inadequacies, which can quench the desire for ministry.

Paul called Archippus a *"fellow-soldier,"* so there must have been many difficulties and discouragements. Similarly, Paul wrote in his final charge to Timothy, *"But you be watchful in all things, endure afflictions, do the work of an evangelists, **fulfill your ministry**"* (2 Tim 4:5). The word for *ministry* (*"diakonia"*) is the same in both verses, which refers not to the office of a deacon but to the nature of the ministry.

Likely, Archippus was a young preacher, an interim shepherd in Epaphras's absence, and was struggling to secure the church's cooperation. The apostle tactfully orders the congregation to keep on encouraging Archippus and assuring him they would help him in every way to complete his leadership responsibilities. Every leader needs this kind of encouragement.

Just as it was written of the elders of Ephesus that *"the Holy Spirit has made you overseers"* (Acts 20:28), so Paul described Archippus's ministry as one *"received in the Lord."* God engineers our desire for ministry and the opportunity to begin, but we have to depend on His grace to "keep on keeping on" until His purpose for our lives is fulfilled. Be an encouragement to someone today.

"It is so easy to become discouraged in our ministry, Lord. May I encourage all Your servants today."

DECEMBER 27

Take Pains to Know the Word

1 Tim 4:15—*"Take pains~~ with these things; be absorbed~~ in them,* so that everyone will see your progress."

Everything in life, external and internal, seems to be a deterrent to doing ministry. If we are to fulfill God's purpose for our lives, we must be prepared for an uphill battle, never believing the illusion that it will get easier someday.

Paul wrote to Timothy to *"be continually taking pains with these things"* ("take care, improve by study, practice, or cultivate" or "fix one's mind on something"). He was telling Timothy to be diligent to know and carry out all the commands and instructions in Paul's letter (and by extension, all the New Testament commands), which would take considerable effort.

Timothy was to *"be continually being absorbed in them"* (or "be immersed in or continually in something"). The NIV translates it as *"give yourself wholly to them,"* making the knowledge and application of God's commands our number one priority.

Paul later wrote Timothy to *"be ready in season and out of season"* (2 Tim 4:2): when it is convenient and when it is not. In his commentary on 2 Timothy, John MacArthur wrote, "The servant of Jesus Christ is never off duty"

Respect in the ministry never comes from a leader being perfect. It is more effective to be transparent about failures and quiet about successes. People identify with discouragements because that is where they live. The key to respect is not perfection but progress. The Apostle Paul wrote, *"Not that I have already obtained it, or have already become perfect, but I press on in order that I may lay hold of that for which also I was laid hold of by Christ Jesus. Brethren, I do not regard myself as having laid hold of it yet; but one thing I do: forgetting what lies behind and reaching forward to what lies ahead, I press on toward the goal for the prize of the upward call of God in Christ Jesus"* (Phil 3:12–14).

That *"everyone will see your progress"* is the goal. What they are witnessing is the transformation of an ordinary person into Christlikeness through the diligent study of God's word and, in particular, His commands. Respect is gained by what you are, not what you say you are. *"Take pains"* to know His word and make it your lifestyle.

"Lord, nothing is as important for me to know as Your word. Only as I learn what it means and commit to practicing its principles will others know I am Yours."

DECEMBER 28

Be Conscientious about How You Live

1 Tim 4:16—*"**Be conscientious**~~ **about how you live** and what you teach. **Persevere**~~ **in this**, because by doing so you will save both yourself and those who listen to you."*

Paul gives Timothy the keys to an effective ministry: *"Be continually being conscientious about how you live and what you teach."* Paul describes twelve characteristics of a mature servant of God (1 Tim 4:6–16): He is a good servant (4:6); he warns of error (4:6:a); he is an expert student of Scripture (4:6c); he avoids unholy teachings (4:7a); he disciplines himself in godliness (4:7b–9); he is committed to hard work (4:10); he teaches with authority (4:11); he is a model of spiritual virtue (4:12); he ministers the word (4:13); he fulfills his calling (4:14); he is totally absorbed in his work (4:15a); and he is growing spiritually (4:15b).

To accomplish the goal of being a servant of God, he must *"be conscientious about how [he] live[s]."* The word *conscientious* means "to have hold of, to fix the mind upon"; he must focus his mind and understanding on his own duties, his own gifts, his own opportunities, and his own life. He must make sure before he teaches someone else a principles in Scripture that he actually practices it first. The student will know whether this is so or not, so it is useless to fake it.

Also, he is to focus on *"what [he] teach[es]."* The servant of God does not make up teachings but clarifies and explains what God said and then adapts the application to contemporary situations without changing the original intent. Once he is certain that he understands the original historical meaning of the text, he has the confidence to teach with authority. The result is *"strengthening the souls of the disciples, exhorting them to continue in the faith, and saying, 'We must through many tribulations enter the kingdom of God'"* (Acts 14:22).

"By doing so you will save both yourself and those who listen to you": salvation is by grace through faith, not by our works (Eph 2:6–8; Titus 3:3), but holy living and sound teaching are a fruit of true faith and facilitate the same in others' lives. James said, *"Let him know that he who turns a sinner from the error of his way will save a soul from death and cover a multitude of sins"* (James 5:20). Leaders must be above reproach in order to avoid becoming a stumbling block to sinners seeking to know a genuine truth.

"Thank You, Lord, for bringing people into my life to keep me faithful to Your word. Help me today to remember Your commands and practice them in my relationships."

DECEMBER 29
Protect What You Know

1 Tim 6:20—*"O Timothy,* **protect*~ what has been entrusted to you.** *Avoid the profane chatter and absurdities of so-called 'knowledge.'"*

If there were many false notions infiltrating the church in the first century, how much more must there be after two thousand years of church history! Hundreds of thousands of believers have been brutally persecuted simply because they believed some basic doctrines of Scripture—salvation is by grace through faith and not by works; or the word of God should be translated into the common language of the people. Clear truths in Scripture must be protected, even if it costs your life.

Timothy had the privilege of handling the original copy of the texts of Scripture that would be compiled into the New Testament and become the basis of all faith and practice among believers. No higher responsibility could be placed on a mortal man than to care for and teach the word of God. The psalmist wrote, *"For You have magnified Your Word above all Your name"* (Psa 138:2). The mark of God's man is his respect for God's word: *"To this one I will look, to him who is humble and contrite of spirit, and who trembles at My Word"* (Isa 66:2).

Jude urged his readers to protect God's word, to *"contend earnestly for the faith which was once for all delivered to the saints"* (Jude 3).

The word *protect* means to "keep valuables in a safe place," and the phrase *"what has been entrusted"* means a "deposit." Paul wrote similarly to the Thessalonians, *"For our exhortation does not come from error or impurity or by way of deceit; but just as we have been approved by God to be entrusted with the gospel, so we speak, not as pleasing men but God, who examines our hearts"* (1 Thes 2:3–4). We all share this responsibility.

We must *"avoid the profane chatter and absurdities of so-called 'knowledge.'"* It is useless to spend time arguing with false teachers. *"Avoid"* means to "turn away from," and *"profane chatter"* means "fruitless speaking." The danger of these teachings is that *"their message will spread like cancer"* (2 Tim 2:17). We must explain the Scripture exhaustively so the hearer will know the whole truth. This is how to protect the text. Are you learning to teach the word?

"The riches of Your word thrill my soul and are more valuable than gold. Let nothing distract me from Your word today."

DECEMBER 30

Protect the Gospel

2 Tim 1:14—*"**Protect***~ **that good thing** entrusted to you, through the Holy Spirit who lives within us."*

Can you imagine the responsibility of the Secret Service, whose task is to protect the president of the United States? Their very lives are meaningless in this mission. The honor of being *entrusted* means to "have faith in, [or] to believe in." God believed in Timothy as much as Timothy believed in God. The *"good thing"* is in reference to the gospel: *"according to the glorious gospel of the blessed God which was committed to my trust"* (1 Tim 1:11). God trusted Timothy to communicate the truth of the gospel to others: *"But as we have been approved by God to be entrusted with the gospel, even so we speak, not as pleasing men, but God who tests our hearts"* (1 Thes 2:4).

Paul did not betray this trust but took it as the mission of his life to proclaim the gospel across the Roman Empire. All who heard, believed, and trusted in Christ's death as full payment for their sins were also entrusted with the message.

The phrase *"that ... thing entrusted to you"* is a translation of one Greek word meaning "[a] deposit, a trust, [or] something committed to one's charge." The same word is used in 2 Timothy 1:13. Paul knew he was near the end of his sojourn on earth, so he impressed on Timothy the awesome job of preserving and transmitting the sacred text to others as it was given it to him.

Timothy was to guard the text or treasure by entrusting it to other faithful men and women who could teach it to others in an endless soul-winning and disciple-making cycle. Two thousand years later, we have the same text, the same gospel, and the same teachings, and once we apply it to our lives, we are commanded to entrust it to others.

The phrase *"through the Holy Spirit who lives within us"* is in the emphatic position in the Greek and should be read with great emphasis as the key to fulfilling the mission of the *"entrusted"* word. No Christian is without the Holy Spirit: *"If anyone does not have the Spirit of Christ, he is not His"* (Rom 8:9b). How powerful is this Spirit? *"The Spirit of Him who raised Jesus from the dead dwells in you"*—it is powerful enough to resurrect Jesus from the grave, and He abides within us. He is powerful enough for us to count on for strength to communicate His word through the gospel.

"Keep my heart true to Your word and help me desire only what You desire and remember all that You have said in every circumstance."

DECEMBER 31
Compete for the Faith

1 Tim 6:12—*"Compete~~ well for the faith and lay hold*~ of that eternal life* you were called for and made your good confession in the presence of many witnesses."

A battle is raging for the minds and souls of men, even though most believers are unaware of it. The language of the text comes from an athletic competition.

This is not to suggest that one has to work extra hard to be saved; rather, it means that believers must compete against all sorts of evil and falsehoods to win the lost to eternal life. The word *compete* means to "contend for victory in the public games, fighting or wrestling." Paul said, "*I have fought the good fight, I have finished the race, I have kept the faith*" (2 Tim 4:7). It means to "take pains, straining every nerve to the uttermost towards the goal," as in Luke 13:24: "*Strive to enter through the narrow gate.*"

The word *well* in our translation, or *good* in others, is from a word meaning "beautiful, excellent, or noble." The author of Hebrews wrote, "*Therefore we also, since we are surrounded by so great a cloud of witnesses, let us lay aside every weight, and the sin which so easily ensnares us, and let us run with endurance the race that is set before us*" (Heb 12:1).

The first verb in our text is in the present tense, meaning to "*be continually competing for the faith,*"(*agonizomai*) but the second verb is an aorist imperative, meaning to once and for all time "*lay hold of that eternal life you were called for.*" Timothy did not need salvation, but he was to "get a grip" on the reality of eternal life and hell, to live his life from the perspective of eternity. The same idea is in Colossians 3:2: "*Set your mind on things above, not on things on the earth.*" Our real nationality now is in heaven: "*For our citizenship is in heaven, from which we eagerly wait for the Savior, the Lord Jesus Christ*" (Phil 3:20).

All the verbs are aorist except the first. Once and for all the reader is to "*lay hold on eternal life.*" Once and for all "*you were also called,*" and once and for all you "*made your good confession.*" These are not repeated experiences but one-time events that put every believer into the competition (2 Tim 1:6). Knowing He has a purpose for our lives, we enter the public competition against demonic enemies knowing He is with us always. Are you in the battle for the souls of men?

"Lord, it has been a good year. I recommit to living to spread the gospel and to build up Your followers. I will never turn back or abandon Your purpose for my life. May people matter to me this new year as they matter to You."

Bibliography

Akin, Daniel L. *Vol. 38, 1, 2, 3 John*. Logos Library System. Vol. 38 of *The New American Commentary*. Nashville, TN: Broadman and Holman, 2001.

Aune, David E. *Revelation 1–5*. Vol. 52A. *Word Biblical Commentary*. Nashville, TN.: Thomas Nelson, 1997. Digital version: 2002.

Baker, Warren, James Strong, and Spiros Zodhiates. *AMG's Annotated Strong's Dictionaries*. Chattanooga, TN.: AMG Publishers, 2009.

Barclay, William, ed. *The Gospel of Luke*. Daily study Bible series, Rev. ed. Philadelphia: Westminster Press, 2000.

Barton, Bruce B. *1 Peter, 2 Peter, Jude*. *Life Application Bible Commentary*. Wheaton, IL: Tyndale House, 1995.

Barton, Bruce B., and Grant R. Osborne. *1 and 2 Corinthians*. *Life Application Bible Commentary*. Wheaton, IL: Tyndale House, 1999.

———. *1, 2 and 3 John*. *Life Application Bible Commentary*. Wheaton, IL: Tyndale House, 1998.

———. *Revelation*. Bruce B. Barton . . . [et al.]; General Editor, Grant Osborne. *Life Application Bible Commentary* Wheaton, IL: Tyndale House, 2000.

Barton, Bruce B., and Philip Wesley Comfort. *Ephesians*. *Life Application Bible Commentary*. Wheaton, IL: Tyndale House, 1996.

———. *Galatians*. *Life Application Bible Commentary*. Wheaton, IL: Tyndale House, 1994.

———. *John*. *Life Application Bible Commentary*. Wheaton, IL: Tyndale House, 1993.

———. *Mark*. *Life Application Bible Commentary*. Wheaton, IL: Tyndale House, 1994.

———. *Matthew*. *Life Application Bible Commentary*. Wheaton, IL: Tyndale House, 1996.

———. *Philippians, Colossians, Philemon*. *Life Application Bible Commentary*. Wheaton, IL: Tyndale House, 1995.

Barton, Bruce B., David Veerman, and Neil S. Wilson. *James*. *Life Application Bible Commentary*. Wheaton, IL: Tyndale House, 1992.

———. *Romans*. *Life Application Bible Commentary*. Wheaton, IL: Tyndale House, 1992.

Barton, Bruce B., David Veerman, Linda Chaffee Taylor, and Grant R. Osborne. *Luke*. *Life Application Bible Commentary*. Wheaton, IL: Tyndale House, 1997.

Barton, Bruce B., David Veerman, Linda Chaffee Taylor, and Philip Wesley Comfort. *Hebrews*. *Life Application Bible Commentary*. Wheaton, IL: Tyndale House, 1997.

Bauckham, Richard J. *2 Peter, Jude*. Vol. 50 of *Word Biblical Commentary*. Dallas: Word, 2002.

Beale, G. K. *The Book of Revelation: A Commentary on the Greek Text*. Grand Rapids: W. B. Eerdmans, 1999.

Beasley-Murray, George R. *John*. Vol. 36 of *Word Biblical Commentary*. Dallas: Word, 2002.

Blomberg, Craig. *Matthew*. Logos Library System. Vol. 22 of *The New American Commentary*. Nashville, TN: Broadman and Holman. Digital version: 2001.

Borchert, Gerald L. *John 12–21*. Logos Library System. Vol. 25B of *The New American Commentary*. Nashville, TN: Broadman and Holman. Digital version:2003.

Brooks, James A. *Mark*. Logos Library System. Vol. 23 of *The New American Commentary*. Nashville, TN: Broadman and Holman. Digital version: 2001.

———. *Mark*. Logos Library System. Vol. 23 of *The New American Commentary*. Nashville, TN: Broadman and Holman. Digital version: 2001.

Bruce, F. F. *The Epistle to the Galatians: A Commentary on the Greek Text*. Grand Rapids: W. B. Eerdmans, 1982.

Carson, D. A. *New Bible Commentary: 21st Century Edition*. 4th ed. Leicester, England: Inter-Varsity Press, 1994.

Cooper, Rodney L. *Vol. 2, Mark*. *Holman New Testament Commentary*. Holman Reference. Nashville, TN: Broadman and Holman, 2000.

Bibliography

Davids, Peter H. *The Epistle of James: A Commentary on the Greek Text*. Grand Rapids: W. B. Eerdmans, 1982.

Dobson, Edward G., Charles L. Feinbert, Edward E. Hinson. *KJV Bible Commentary*. Nashville, TN: Thomas Nelson, 1997.

Dunn, James D. G. *The Epistles to the Colossians and to Philemon: A Commentary on the Greek Text*. Grand Rapids: W. B. Eerdmans, 1996.

————. *Romans 1–8*. Vol. 38A of *Word Biblical Commentary*. Dallas: Word, 2002.

————. *Romans 9–16*. Vol. 38B of *Word Biblical Commentary*. Dallas: Word, 2002.

Edwards, James R. *The Gospel According to Mark. The Pillar New Testament Commentary*. Grand Rapids: W. B. Eerdmans, 2002.

Ellingworth, Paul, and Howard Hatton. *A Handbook on Paul's First Letter to the Corinthians*. UBS Handbook Series; Helps for Translators. New York: United Bible Societies, 1995.

————. *The Epistle to the Hebrews: A Commentary on the Greek Text*. Grand Rapids: W. B. Eerdmans, 1993.

Elliot, Elisabeth. *A Lamp unto My Feet*. Grand Rapids: Regal Books, 2004.

Maier, Paul L. *Eusebius: The Ecclesiastical History*. Grand Rapids: Kregel Publications, 1999.

France, R. T. *The Gospel of Mark: A Commentary on the Greek Text*. Grand Rapids: W. B. Eerdmans, 2002.

Freeman, James M., and Harold J. Chadwick. *Manners and Customs of the Bible*. Rev. ed. North Brunswick, NJ: Bridge-Logos, 1998.

Friberg, Timothy, Barbara Friberg, and Neva F. Miller. *Analytical Lexicon of the Greek New Testament*. Vol. 4 of *Baker's Greek New Testament Library*. Grand Rapids: Baker Books, 2000.

Garland, David E. *1 Corinthians. Baker Exegetical Commentary on the New Testament*. Grand Rapids: Baker Academic, 2003.

George, Timothy. *Galatians*. Logos Library System. Vol. 30 of *The New American Commentary*. Nashville, TN: Broadman and Holman, 1994, Digital version: 2001.

Hagner, Donald A. *Matthew 1–13*. Vol. 33A of *Word Biblical Commentary*. Dallas: Word, 2002.

Harris, Murray J. *The Second Epistle to the Corinthians: A Commentary on the Greek Text*. Grand Rapids: W. B. Eerdmans, 2005.

Harris III, W. Hall. Director and Managing Editor. *The Bible First Edition with Notes*. Dallas: Biblical Studies Press, 2006.

Hawthorne, Gerald F. *Philippians*. Vol. 43 of *Word Biblical Commentary*. Dallas: Word, 2004.

Hendriksen, William, and Simon J. Kistemaker. *Exposition of the Gospel According to Luke*. Vol. 11 of *New Testament Commentary*. Grand Rapids: Baker Book House, 1953, Digital version, 2001.

————. *Exposition of the Gospel According to Matthew*. Vol. 9 of *New Testament Commentary*. Grand Rapids: Baker Book House, 1953, Digital version: 2001.

Jamieson, Robert, A. R. Fausset, and David Brown. *Commentary Critical and Explanatory on the Whole Bible*. Oak Harbor, WA: Logos Research Systems, 1997.

Jobes, Karen H. *1 Peter. Baker Exegetical Commentary on the New Testament*. Grand Rapids: Baker Academic, 2005.

Keenan, Thomas, and Subhadra Evans. *An Introduction to Child Development*. Thousand Oaks, CA.: Sage Publications, Inc., 2009.

Kistemaker, Simon J., and William Hendriksen. *Exposition of James and the Epistles of John*. Vol. 14 of *New Testament Commentary*. Grand Rapids: Baker Book House, 1953, Digital version: 2001.

————. *Exposition of the Acts of the Apostles*. Vol. 17 of *New Testament Commentary*. Grand Rapids: Baker Book House, 1953. Digital version: 2001.

Köstenberger, Andreas J. *John. Baker Exegetical Commentary on the New Testament*. Grand Rapids: Baker Academic, 2004.

Lane, William L. *Hebrews 9–13*. Vol. 47B of *Word Biblical Commentary*. Dallas: Word, 2002.

Bibliography

Lincoln, Andrew T. *Ephesians*. Vol. 42 of *Word Biblical Commentary*. Dallas: Word, 2002.

Longenecker, Richard N. *Galatians*. Vol. 41 of *Word Biblical Commentary*. Dallas: Word, 2002.

Louw, Johannes P., and Eugene Albert Nida. *Greek-English Lexicon of the New Testament: Based on Semantic Domains*. Electronic ed. of the 2nd ed. New York: United Bible Societies, 1996.

Lukaszewski, Albert L., Mark Dubis, and J. Ted Blakley. *The Lexham Syntactic Greek New Testament: Expansions and Annotations*. Bellingham, WA.: Logos Research Systems, 2010.

Keenan, Thomas, and Subhadra Evans. *An Introduction to Child Development*. Thousand Oaks, CA.: Sage Publications, Inc., 2009.

MacArthur Jr., John F. *1 Corinthians. MacArthur New Testament Commentary*. Chicago: Moody, 1984.

————. *1 Peter. MacArthur New Testament Commentary*. Chicago: Moody, 2004.

————. *2 Corinthians. MacArthur New Testament Commentary*. Chicago: Moody, 2003.

————. *2 Peter and Jude. MacArthur New Testament Commentary*. Chicago: Moody, 2005.

————. *2 Timothy. MacArthur New Testament Commentary*. Chicago: Moody, 1995.

————. *Acts. MacArthur New Testament Commentary*. Chicago: Moody, 1994.

————. *Colossians. MacArthur New Testament Commentary*. Chicago: Moody, 1992.

————. *Ephesians. MacArthur New Testament Commentary*. Chicago: Moody, 1986.

————. *Galatians. MacArthur New Testament Commentary*. Chicago: Moody, 1983.

————. *Hebrews. MacArthur New Testament Commentary*. Chicago: Moody, 1983.

————. *James. MacArthur New Testament Commentary*. Chicago: Moody, 1998.

————. *Luke 1–5. MacArthur New Testament Commentary*. Chicago: Moody, 2009.

————. *Matthew. MacArthur New Testament Commentary*. Chicago: Moody, 1985.

————. *Philippians. MacArthur New Testament Commentary*. Chicago: Moody, 2001.

————. *Revelation 1–11. MacArthur New Testament Commentary*. Chicago: Moody, 1999.

————. *Romans 9–16. MacArthur New Testament Commentary*. Chicago: Moody, 1994.

————. *Romans. MacArthur New Testament Commentary*. Chicago: Moody, 1991.

Marshall, I. Howard. *The Gospel of Luke: A Commentary on the Greek Text*. The New International Greek Testament Commentary. Exeter, England: Paternoster Press, 1978.

Martin, Ralph P. *2 Corinthians*. Vol. 40 of *Word Biblical Commentary*. Dallas: Word, 2002.

————. *James*. Vol. 48 of *Word Biblical Commentary*. Dallas: Word, 2002.

McGaw, Francis. *Praying Hyde*. Philadelphia: The Sunday School Times Company, 1923.

Melick, Richard R. *Philippians, Colossians, Philemon*. Logos Library System. Vol. 32 of *The New American Commentary*. Nashville, TN: Broadman and Holman. Digital version: 2001.

Metzger, Bruce Manning, and United Bible Societies. *A Textual Commentary on the Greek New Testament*. 2nd ed. Companion Volume to the United Bible Societies' Greek New Testament (4th rev. ed.). London: United Bible Societies, 1994.

Michaels, J. Ramsey. *1 Peter*. Vol. 49 of *Word Biblical Commentary*. Dallas: Word, 2002.

Nolland, John. *The Gospel of Matthew: A Commentary on the Greek Text*. Grand Rapids: W. B. Eerdmans, 2005.

————. *Luke 1:1–9:20*. Vol. 35A of *Word Biblical Commentary*. Dallas: Word, 2002.

————. *Luke 9:21–18:34*. Vol. 35B of *Word Biblical Commentary*. Dallas: Word, 2002.

O'Brien, Peter T. *Colossians-Philemon*. Vol. 44 of *Word Biblical Commentary*. Dallas: Word, 2002.

————. *The Epistle to the Philippians: A Commentary on the Greek Text*. Grand Rapids: W. B. Eerdmans, 1991.

Pannenberg, Wolfhart. *Systematic Theology*. Grand Rapids: W. B. Eerdmans, 1991.

Bibliography

Phillips, J. B. *The New Testament in Modern English*. New York: HarperCollins Publishers, 1962.

Polhill, John B. *Acts*. Logos Library System. Vol. 26 of *The New American Commentary*. Nashville, TN: Broadman and Holman. Digital version: 2001.

Richardson, Kurt A. *James*. Logos Library System. Vol. 36 of *The New American Commentary*. Nashville, TN: Broadman and Holman. Digital version: 2001.

Schreiner, Thomas R. *1, 2 Peter, Jude*. Logos Library System. Vol. 37 of *The New American Commentary*. Nashville, TN: Broadman and Holman. Digital version: 2007.

————. *Vol. 6, Romans. Baker Exegetical Commentary on the New Testament*. Grand Rapids: Baker Books, 1998.

Smalley, Stephen S. *1, 2, 3 John*. Vol. 51 of *Word Biblical Commentary*. Dallas: Word, 2002.

Thiselton, Anthony C. *The First Epistle to the Corinthians: A Commentary on the Greek Text*. Grand Rapids: W. B. Eerdmans, 2000.

Vincent, Marvin Richardson. *Word Studies in the New Testament*. New York: Charles Scribner's Sons, 1887.

Walls, David, and Max Anders. *I and II Peter, I, II and III John, Jude*. Vol. 11 of *Holman New Testament Commentary*. Holman Reference. Nashville, TN: Broadman and Holman, 1999.

Walvoord, John F., Roy B. Zuck, and Dallas Theological Seminary. *The Bible Knowledge Commentary: An Exposition of the Scriptures*. Wheaton, IL: Victor Books, 1983.

Weber, Stuart K. *Matthew*. Vol. 1 of *Holman New Testament Commentary*. Holman Reference. Nashville, TN: Broadman and Holman, 2000.

Wiersbe, Warren W. *With the Word Bible Commentary*. Nashville, TN: Thomas Nelson, 1997.

Wuest, Kenneth S. *Wuest's Word Studies from the Greek New Testament: For the English Reader*. Grand Rapids: W. B. Eerdmans, 1997.

Wychopen, Forest. *Abide in Christ*. Maitland, FL.: Xulon Press.

Zodhiates, Spiros. *The Complete Word Study Dictionary: New Testament*. Electronic ed. Chattanooga, TN: AMG, 2000.

Zuck, Roy. "Romans." *The Bible Knowledge Commentary: An Exposition of the Scriptures*. Holman Reference. Nashville, TN: Broadman and Holman, 2000.

Index

by Scripture Reference

Index

Luke

Index

John

Acts

Romans

1 Corinthians

Index

Index

Philippians

Index

2 Thessalonians

1 Timothy

2 Timothy

Index

Index